Alternative Library Literature, 2000/2001
A Biennial Anthology

Edited by
Sanford Berman
and
James P. Danky

McFarland & Company, Inc., Publishers
Jefferson, North Carolina, and London

Cover from a concept by Christine Schelshorn and Paul Hass; neon by Denis Eckstein, Neon Lab, Madison, WI; photos by Andy Krauschaar.

The Library of Congress has catalogued this serial publication as follows:

Alternative library literature: a biennial anthology.—1982/1983—

    v. : ill. ; 28 cm.

    Biennial.
    Includes index.
    Edited by Sanford Berman and James P. Danky, 1982/1983—
    ISSN 0749-6885=Alternative library literature.

    1. Libraries and society—Addresses, essays, lectures. 2. Underground press—Addresses, essays, lectures. 3. Anti-nuclear movement—Addresses, essays, lectures. 4. Women in library science—Addresses, essays, lectures. 5. Library science—Addresses, essays, lectures. I. Berman, Sanford, 1933– . II. Danky, James Philip, 1947–

    Z716.4.A47   020'.5—dc19   84-646841
                           AACR2   MARC-S

Alternative Cataloguing-in-Publication Data

Alternative library literature: a biennial anthology.
    1982/83–2000/01. Jefferson, NC : McFarland & Company, Inc., Publishers.
    Ceased publication with 2000/2001 edition.

    Editors: 1982/83–2000/01, Sanford Berman and James P. Danky
    Illustrators: 1984/85–1986/87, Jackie Urbanovic; 1988/89, Bert Dodson, Luna Ticks, bulbul, Joe Grant, Jim Buckett, Paul Haas.
    1982/83 edition published by Oryx Press.
    "Special Features": 1984/85, The South African connection; 1986/87, The Central American/Nicaraguan connection; 1988/89, The Arab connection; 1990/91, The Columbus Quincentenary; 1992/93, Sex, censorship, and H. W. Wilson; 1994/95, The Zine connection; 1996/97, The Hawaii outsourcing scandal.
    PARTIAL CONTENTS: People/work.—Women.—Nukes/peace.—Censorship/human rights.—Alternatives.—Service/advocacy/empowerment.—Kids.—A/V.—Multiculturalism/Third World.—Cyberspace/virtual libraries.—Books and reading.—Just for fun.

    1. Library science. 2. Libraries. 3. Censorship. 4. Librarians—Social responsibility. 5. Alternative press. 6. Women librarians. 7. Children's library services. 8. Audiovisual library service. 9. Women's library services. 10. Disabled persons' library services. 11. Minority library services. 12. Libraries and nuclear warfare. 13. Teenagers' library services. 14. Library humor. 15. Apartheid. 16. Anti-Apartheid movement. 17. Libraries—Nicaragua. 18. Central America—Bibliography. 19. Anti-Arabism. 20. Columbus Quincentenary, 1992–1993. 21. Zines—History and criticism. 22. Information policy. 23. Information superhighway. 24. Multiculturalism in libraries. 25. Wilson Library Bulletin—Censorship. 26. Children's literature—History and criticism. 27. Erotica in libraries. 28. Mass media bias. 29. Libraries—Technical services—Outsourcing—Hawaii. 30. Materials selection (Libraries)—Outsourcing—Hawaii. 31. Hawaii State Public Library System—Outsourcing. 32. Internet—Social aspects. 33. Internet—Political aspects.
I. Berman, Sanford, 1933–   editor. II. Danky, James P., 1947–   editor.

ISBN 0-7864-1313-1 (softcover; 50# acid-free natural paper)

©2002 Sanford Berman and James P. Danky. All rights reserved

No part of this book may be reproduced or transmitted in any form or by any means, electronic or mechanical, including photocopying or recording, or by any information storage and retrieval system, without permission in writing from the publisher.

Interior illustrations with articles copyrighted by individual illustrators.

Cover © 2002 James P. Danky

Manufactured in the United States of America

McFarland & Company, Inc., Publishers
    Box 611, Jefferson, North Carolina 28640

Contents

Dear Library People / *James P. Danky and Sanford Berman*   1

People/Work
Library Viewing / *Lucy Fairchild*   5
The Commons / *Sue Halpern*   7
Ricardo Mestre (1906–1997): A Man Who Devoted His Life to Disseminating "The Idea" / *Alison Lewis*   9
What Makes Librarianship Exciting to You? / *Chris Dodge*   13
Bad Libraries / *Carol Reid*   14
The Real Thing: Democracy as a Contact Sport / *Russell Mokhiber and Robert Weissman*   16

Women
Smarty Girl: Three Librarians on Film / *Abigail Leah Plumb*   21
Person of the Year: Debra Davis / *Ellen Lansky*   25
New Waves in Lesbian Publishing / *Suzanne Corson*   29

Censorship/Intellectual Freedom
Intellectual Freedom Within the Profession / *Toni Samek*   35
Discourse and Censorship: Librarians and the Ideology of Freedom / *Steven R. Harris*   43
Berman's Bag: The Top Censored Library Stories of 1998/2000 / *Sanford Berman*   49
Where Have All the "Berman Books" Gone? A Series of Memoranda and Letters / *Sanford Berman*   54
Almost Banned Books, 1998 and 1999 / *Earl Lee*   58
Free Press for Sale: How Corporations Have Bought the First Amendment; an Interview with Robert McChesney / *Derrick Jensen*   64
Down by Law / *Carrie Bickner*   73
Targets of Repression   77
Three Decades of Film Censorship … Right Before Your Eyes / *Chris Roth*   82

Alternatives
Libraries as Media: The Struggle Against Corporate and Government Indoctrination in American Schools and Universities, and in Daily Life / *Charles Willett*   95
A Question of Balance: The Role of Libraries in Providing Alternatives to the Mainstream Media / *Nancy Kranich*   108
The Other 90 Percent: What Your MLS Didn't Teach You / *Byron Anderson*   112
Taking the Good (News) with the Bad: Alternative Publications Build a Movement on the Margins / *Abby Scher*   115
The Alternative Media: Open Sources on What's Real / *Daniel C. Tsang*   119
Independent Publishing Matters / *Beth Schulman*   122
Pursuing Small, Independent Book Publishers / *Byron Anderson*   124
Minneapolis Community and Technical College Alternative Press Collection / *Tom Eland*   128
Continuing a Legacy: Collecting for a Special Collections Library / *Julie Herrada*   129
"They Sure Got to Prove It On Me": Millennial Thoughts on Gay Archives, Gay Biography, and Gay Library History / *James V. Carmichael, Jr.*   132
Becoming a Gay, Lesbian, Bisexual, or Transgender Collector / *Steven J. Schochet Center for GLBT Studies*   141
Interview with David Barsamian of Alternative Radio / *Scott Long*   143

Service/Advocacy/Empowerment
Where Stories Aren't Important: An Alternative Perspective on Library and Information Science Education / *Wayne A. Wiegand*   153
Against National Poetry Month as Such / *Charles Bernstein*   157
Library of Congress Service Erosion / *Maureen Moore*   159

Tending to the City's Needs, Serving Newcomer Immigrants: The Value of Community Information / *Chryss Mylopoulos* 162

Berman's Bag: Must "The Poor" Always Be Among Us? / *Sanford Berman* 169

Express This—The Road to Ruin / *Jenna Freedman* 177

James Chaffee's Fight Against the Bond Issue for the San Francisco Public Library 181

Free Money, Just Sign Here; Or the Bill Gates Road Show Comes to SF / *James Chaffee* 187

Cyberspace/Virtual Libraries

Digital Libraries for All / *Donny Smith* 191

Blind-Sided by Amazon.com / *Barry Hoffman* 197

On Electronic Civil Disobedience / *Stefan Wray* 199

The Ethics of Hacktivism / *Abby Goodrum and Mark Manion* 206

Local Cyber-Activism in the Age of Globalization / *Martin Eder* 211

A Model of Cyber Volunteerism 214

Look What Activist San Diego Has Done in Two Years! 215

Index 217

Dear Library People

After 20 years of scouring the wide world of print (and now cyberspace) for gems fit to reprint in *Alternative Library Literature*, it seems right to ask what it all means. The answers to such a question are varied and many no doubt personal, but since we're the editors, we'd like to venture an opinion, too. The items in this, our 10th and last, volume are intended to stimulate the tentative and provoke the satisfied, like newspaper mottoes of days past. In this biennial process, the editors hoped to build a humane, equitable, and critical politics of libraries where the exceptional people, programs, and perspectives highlighted in these pages could become standard. For those seeking "balance," we suggest they look elsewhere, since the vast majority of library lit expresses the dominant corporate and conservative views of what librarianship is all about—and hardly needs (or deserves) our help in purveying those messages.

We honor a representative sample of library union activists on our dedication page. Many critics of the pervasive "'inside' censorship" that belies the profession's loudly-proclaimed devotion to intellectual freedom note the comparative dearth of labor-related materials in most library collections. To somewhat offset the preponderance of business and financial resources, we warmly suggest that selectors consider the fine wares either produced or distributed by:

- Union Communication Services (165 Conduit Street, Annapolis, MD 21401-2512; www.unionist.com; 1-800-321-2545; FAX: 410-626-1353; email: ucsbooks@unionist.com). UCS not only offers a rich variety of tools for labor leaders and activists—on topics ranging from grievances and arbitration to contracts and rights—but also markets children's books, labor histories and dictionaries, and inspirational biographies, for instance of Mother Jones, Gene Debs, and Cesar Chavez. It additionally publishes a bimonthly *Steward Update Newsletter* and sends subscribers two monthly packets: one composed of labor news, features and cartoons, the other a collection of 30 to 40 humorous graphics, "message" spots, and filler art.

- Labor Heritage Foundation (888—16th Street, NW, Suite 680, Washington, DC 20006; 202-974-8041; www.laborheritage.org; FAX: 202-974-8043). LHF stocks a cornucopia of items reflecting working class culture and the union experience: tapes and CDs (e.g., *Coal mining women, Don't mourn—organize!: songs of labor organizer Joe Hill, In love and struggle: the musical legacy of the Jewish Labor Bund, Si se puede*, and *This line is singin'*); song, photo, cartoon, and story books; buttons (like "Bosses beware—when we're screwed we multiply!," "Support your local steward," "I'm not for sale—don't privatize me," and "Friends don't let friends cross picket lines"); posters, some by Ricardo Levins Morales, Mike Alewitz, Carlos Cortez, and Ralph Fasanella; and videos, including the under-shown *Cradle will rock, Germinal* (the film version of Zola's classic strike novel), Michael Moore's *Roger and Me*, and *Silkwood*, starring Cher and Meryl Streep.

Although they *should* be a truly neutral, proactive source for facts, ideas, and options concerning public issues and policies, it appears that most American libraries—at least in early November 2001, nearly two months after the unspeakable events of September 11th—have *not* met the challenge to underpin and promote a national discourse and understanding related to why those vile acts happened and how best to respond. Instead, much like a decade ago—before, during, and after the Persian Gulf War—the library attitude (with honorable exceptions) seems to be either denial that anything important enough is happening to command their special attention and involvement, or outright cheerleading with respect to military action, jingoist conformity, and constriction of civil liberties. Here, however, is an example of a user-originated effort to get libraries to actually contribute to wide-ranging dialogue and learning in this period of crisis. It's a letter sent to 60 public library directors on October 20, 2001 by the Minnesota Alliance of Peacemakers (511 Groveland, Minneapolis, MN 55403-3240):

Dear Director,

Public libraries rightly regard themselves as "bulwarks of democracy" and sources of truly diverse viewpoints and perspectives, as mandated by the Library Bill of Rights. In this time of national and global crisis, we urge your library to genuinely become a "bulwark," contributing directly to greater knowledge and more informed opinions among your users by:

- mounting displays of relevant books, pamphlets, videos, and other materials dealing with Islam, the Middle East, terrorism, racism, anti–Americanism, civil liberties, Arabs, and U.S. foreign policy
- arranging in-house programs on these topics, featuring speakers, panelists, films and open forums
- preparing and distributing both online and hard copy pathfinders and resource guides, embracing wide-ranging print, AV, and Web resources
- expanding collections to ensure ample information and analysis from a variety of political and religious standpoints, including voices of nonviolence, social justice, and multiculturalism.

We will be delighted to cooperate and consult on such projects. Kindly indicate what your library has already done, or plans to do, to further educate and inform the public about these serious issues of war, peace, justice and human rights.

With warmest regards,

Mary White

Mary White, President
Minnesota Alliance of Peacemakers

Yours for peace, justice, and joy,

    James P. Danky
    Newspaper and Periodicals Librarian
    State Historical Society of Wisconsin
    816 State Street
    Madison, WI 53706
    608-264-6598
    jpdanky@mail.shsw.wisc.ed

    Sanford Berman
    4400 Morningside Road
    Edina, MN 55416
    952-925-5738

PEOPLE/ WORK

Library Viewing

Lucy Fairchild

Many years ago I read an article on Japanese cherry blossom viewing. Every year in the spring people travel, sometimes hundreds of miles, to see the newly opened buds. Sometimes they picnic in family groups in the orchards themselves and sometimes they simply stand at a distance and look. This idea seemed so wonderful to me that I attempted to stage my own re-creation of cherry-blossom viewing by walking up to the Capitol and walking by the spindly little saplings planted in a semi-circle around the building. The trees were so skinny and the blossoms so few that I don't think I quite got the right effect. It did get me thinking about what I do observe.

I watch libraries. The actual physical buildings, the interior space, the people who work there and patronize them, the displays and art on the walls, the smell of books and furnishings and now the faint hum of computers in use. Everything. In a way I can measure out my life according to library stories.

The old Salt Lake City Main Library (located in what is now Hansen Planetarium) remains my favorite library of all, perhaps because it is associated with childhood and my initiation into literature. Not just the books themselves, but the momentous event of receiving my own library card and the privilege to choose my own books.

I was raised Catholic and at the time I received my first card I was also involved in receiving the first sacraments given to young Catholics. These deep and rich rituals were inexplicable to me at the time, as few little children are capable of understanding the mysteries of Holy Communion.

But the other gift of grace I received at this age, one bestowed by the secular world, was my own library card, a white piece of cardboard with a metal plate inserted somehow. This metal had embossed numbers, my numbers, and I used that card so much that both cardboard and metal wore out. I didn't understand about first amendment rights at that time any more than I understood the mysteries of Catholicism. What I did understand, down deep in every cell and bone, was what it felt like to choose a book because I wanted to read it. Thus began my self-education, which left my formal schooling far behind, all because of the library and the freedom to range where I wished.

The children's room in the old library was in the basement. I still remember the light, the just-the-right-size furniture, the gentle librarian craning over the wooden check-out table at me. When I had acquired my books I would go upstairs to the adult part and wait for my mother. I could see into stacks and stacks of books, books piled high and chaotic, books for which there was no room. I knew that one day I, too, would choose my books from this new land and I believe there was something about this knowledge that was tinged with erotic feelings. Sex and the grown-up part of the library were both things I would have to wait to grow into.

I worked at the old library almost every Saturday with my mother and sister. As I was on the brink of adolescence, the new library opened. It was almost everything the old library was not: brightly lit, spacious and modern, the children's section was even on the second floor connected by escalators which made it a quasi adventure to rise up to the area and then return down to check-out with a teetering stack of books.

My mother treated this new library like it was the promised land delivered at last. I never found myself at peace with this new building. However, there was a great deal I liked about it—real art on the walls, the listening stations in the art department, elevators lit like a cocktail lounge, the inspired placement of the library just across the street from Junior's Tavern.

The biennial book sales are always a moment of triumph for me whenever I can carry home a treasure for a dollar or so. But I still feel something missing, a lack of warmth, some missing human scale.

Reprinted with permission from *Catalyst*, March 2000, p. 40.

Last night my husband and I looked down at the model for the new library. All I could say was, "My." How can I tell what this building will feel like? Will I be able to find my way around? It looks clean and modern, intriguing in its lines. It has a level of sophistication in design that I don't usually associate with Salt Lake. How will it settle into its urban landscape?

After a few minutes of model library viewing we took the elevator down to periodicals. This is my favorite place in our current library, the one that most approximates my childhood memories of early book life. Snug, underground, quiet, the giant folio of Audubon birds always encased in glass—I stopped for a moment, took it in once again and felt deeply grateful.

Lucy Fairchild is an artist living in Salt Lake City. Check out the model for the new building at the current Main library, Fifth South at State St. (just north of Junior's).

NEIGHBORS & PLACES by Stell Halpern

Speaking Volumes

When a small town set out to create a library, it took the first step toward building something far more elusive—a community.

It is a typical Wednesday at the Town of Johnsburg Library. John, a chimney sweep who sometimes sells cutlery door to door, is studying the classifieds. Joyce, who is retired, is shelving returns. Mitch, a pastor, is talking about fly-fishing with one of his parishioners, a 14-year-old who is also a library volunteer. Voices rise and fall like breathing. Children's voices, adult voices, and rarely a "shhh" among them. Somewhere in the minutes there is a policy about this: Johnsburg is not to be a quiet library. Other towns have other places—a coffee shop, say, or a park, or even a 7-Eleven—where people come together and do the unconscious work of being neighbors. In Johnsburg, the remote and isolated township in the Adirondack Mountains of New York state where I live, that place is the library.

As if to prove my point, in walks Bill Thomas, taking a break from his job as town supervisor. Maybe he meant to look for a book, but he stops short of the stacks to console a man whose relatives have just lost their house to a fire.

"Got to go back to work," Bill says after visiting with the man. But he is savvy enough to know that he has been working the whole time.

A woman who cleans houses for seasonal residents comes in with her two children, who disappear into the children's area and flop down on a beanbag panda. She trails behind, pausing in front of the videos. Over by the videos, too, another mother is trying to get a rise out of her disaffected teenage daughter, who has a tattooed leg and a pierced nose. "It's really good. It has Dustin Hoffman." The girl looks skeptical, says nothing. The mom tries again. "I really liked it when I was your age," she says. She holds out *The Graduate* as if it were an exotic vegetable, a rare wine. And in a way it is. Videos and books and magazines for free are still a novelty in Johnsburg: The library is just three years old.

Most of the time, we take our civic institutions for granted. They were there before us, they'll be there after us. In the geologic time of our democracy, they are the mountains and we are the dirt—actually, we are the topsoil, and sooner or later we blow away. Something like that. What I mean is that the institutions we inherit have lives of their own. As individuals, we are consequential only to a point.

But not in Johnsburg. Four years ago, after a quietly insistent one-man campaign, Arnold Stevens convinced the town board to put up money for a library. A friend of mine from New York City guessed that Arnold was a college professor when she heard him speak in church one Sunday. In fact, he's a carpenter in the local lumberyard. He is also an avid reader, and he was tired of having to drive 45 miles to get to the nearest sizable library. Reluctantly, the board, of which he is a longstanding member, set aside $15,000 and asked three residents—two retired schoolteachers and me—to find six others with whom we could figure out how to do the bunny-from-the-hat trick of turning that amount of money into books and equipment and a librarian.

A year later, when the Town of Johnsburg Library opened in a small room in the back of the town hall, we had 600 books of our own, a librarian who really did materialize from nowhere, and modest expectations. We had ordered 500 library cards, calculating that they would take us through the first year. They took us through the first month. There are now more than 1,700 card-carrying patrons in a township of just over 2,000 people, and 8,000 books on the shelves, and a brand new addition, filled with brand new shelves, because the little room got too crowded and it became necessary to knock down the south wall and push out into the parking lot.

Back in the children's room, the librarian, Russell Puschak, is introducing a new patron, who is 7, to the shelf of *I Can Read* books. "You mean I can take as many books as I want?" she asks Russell, and is incredulous when he nods his head. She starts clearing off the shelf, like someone who has won one of those

---

Reprinted with permission from *Mother Jones* (731 Market St., Suite 600, San Francisco, CA 94103), July/August 1999, pp. 33–35. © 1999 Foundation for National Progress.

contests where you have 15 minutes to fill a supermarket cart with all the groceries you can grab.

"Take your time," Russell tells her, but she's not listening. Or she is listening, but to something else, to the voice of abandon.

This sense of abandon, of freedom, is the unspoken perk of getting a library card. Wander through fiction, picking novels like ripe apples. Huddle over the atlas. In the Johnsburg library, the atlases are right by the window that looks out onto North Creek. The creek joins the Hudson a few hundred yards later, and the river runs to the ocean some 200 miles south, and who knows where that goes. I would like to say that the library trustees put the window over the creek because it was a perfect visual metaphor for the connections and expansiveness that flow when books are shared, but that would be untrue. It just happened to fit there. But it's an apt metaphor nonetheless.

Which is why, when one of the libraries in our regional system, a library that happens to serve a population that is richer and more numerous than ours, decided to charge nonresidents an annual fee of $128 to borrow materials, people in Johnsburg felt betrayed more than they felt angry. It was as if the library system were one great circuit, and this fee-imposing library were flipping a breaker.

"What do we do," the Johnsburg library trustees asked each other, "if someone over there requests a book from us through interlibrary loan?" The conversation was heated. Some thought we should refuse, on principle. Others thought we should comply, on principle. But in the end we consoled ourselves with this thought: What could patrons of a big library want from the nominal collection of a small rural library?

Plenty, it turns out. So we send what they request. But we also send a letter. It says: "Hello. Just a little note to let you know that your excellent and huge and well-funded library would not extend the same privilege to us that we are extending to you. [We] believe this to be a rather ungenerous attitude that your town has adopted. We believe in sharing what we have and you are welcome to borrow from our very small and meager resources."

OK—it's not very subtle. But neither is charging $128 a year. (Happily, New York State Librarian Janet Welch agrees. She has convened a panel to try to figure out how to keep free libraries free.)

Not long after the Johnsburg library's board of trustees met to discuss our lending policy, we went back to the town board to ask for more money. We were armed with all sorts of statistics: circulation data that showed that more and more things were going out the door each month, and that Johnsburg residents used the library more than patrons of most other rural libraries. Bill Thomas, whose office is adjacent to the library, listened politely, but was not interested in the numbers. "Everyone knows that the library is the best thing that has happened to this town in a long time," he said.

The other members of the town board agreed. And this was before we had Internet access or a preschool story hour or a classic movie series followed by a group discussion that routinely packs the house—all for free. And before the book club and the theater group and the Friends of the Library and the army of volunteers, young and old. The budget was doubled, and offered with thanks. It's gone up since then.

LATE ONE NIGHT, I WAS DRIVING HOME from a board of trustees meeting. The mountains that ring the town were backlit by a yellow moon. The Hudson ran fast— the ice was out. Most of the houses I passed were dark, and as I went by them I realized I knew almost everyone inside. But more than that: In many cases, I knew what the occupants were reading. It is intimate knowledge, and one more way books bind us. The radio was on, tuned to the only station we can get here in the mountains, an NPR affiliate that was playing Sibelius.

The theme in my head, though, was local and vernacular. It was a rebroadcast of what I'd heard when I took a break from the meeting and stepped out into the corridor. The discussion was about public events—why we shouldn't charge for them. Earlier we had talked about computers and censorship, adding books to the young adult section, expanding the hours of operation. Those were the particulars, but it was the sound they made together that caught my ear.

In the library, there are books about this sound, some of them very old. *The Republic. The Politics. Leviathan.* How are we going to live together? That is always the question. In the back of town hall that night, I was hearing the answer. ∎

Ricardo Mestre (1906-1997)– A Man Who Devoted His Life to Disseminating "The Idea"

Translated by Alison Lewis

One day in April, 1997 I was hanging around the Multiforo Alicia in Mexico City, an alternative space where young people gather for rock concerts, meetings, and discussions. This particular day the event was to honor an anarchist who had founded a library in the center of town. The honoree was Ricardo Mestre, who died two months later at the age of 91, and those honoring him were his young anarchist friends. That is to say, an elderly anarchist was being honored by his young colleagues in one of the few places that could be called "alternative" in Mexico. Why? Who was this Mestre?

Ricardo Mestre was born in 1906 in Vilanova i la Geltrú, an industrial town on the Catalan coast, near Barcelona, which even then had a long-standing liberal tradition. At that time, Vilanova had some 17,000 inhabitants, and there were factories for making textiles, electrical and telephone cables, small foundries, and a cement factory.

Like most of his contemporaries, Mestre did not attend school very long; in fact, he did not complete his primary education. At the age of twelve, he began an apprenticeship in a weaver's shop, and later he was apprenticed in a cabinetmaker's shop. Everything moved quickly in Mestre's life. At thirteen he was arrested at an underground meeting and at sixteen he organized an anarchist group in Vilanova in which comrades such as Juan Peiró participated. He was a construction worker for the Barcelona subway system and a chauffeur, and at age twenty-one he married a girl of seventeen. Selling newspapers in the Minerva kiosk in Vilanova, Mestre was for years an underground CNT member during the dictatorship of Primo de Rivera. In 1932, he took part as a delegate in the formation of the Federación Ibérica de Juventudes Libertarias, and two years later he became a member of the FAI (Federación Anarquista Ibérica).

There were also the years in which Ricardo Mestre (under another name, José Riera, which accompanied him throughout his life) initiated himself into the task which he would never abandon: disseminating ideas through the press. He was involved in the Catalán anarchist periodical *Terra Lliure*; editor of the periodical *Catalunya* (written in Catalán), which had certain similarities to the periodical *Solidaridad Obrera*, the official organ of the CNT; and at the same time he was the editor of the *Boletin Oficial* de Vilanova i la Geltrú. At the height of the revolution, Mestre was designated a judge in his town.

In the early hours of January 26, 1929, before Franco's troops arrived, he left for Barcelona. After six months in the Argelès concentration camp on the French Mediterranean, he and his companion succeeded in boarding the ship *Ipanema* bound for Veracruz. Arriving there with sixteen pesos in his pocket and a lost war, Mestre at once began his disseminating of ideas. Within a few months he had published his first Minerva Editions book, the story *Exodus: Diary of a Spanish Refugee* (with a prologue by León Felipe), by his companion Sylvia Mistral. He worked on commission, selling books for

Editorial América and established the Unión Distribuidora de Ediciones.

Failed businesses and changes of jobs all happened during the fifty-six years Mestre lived in México. But, in spite of everything, he continued spreading anarchist ideas, no matter what happened. Before he died, he had published more than two hundred books (the first Spanish edition of *The Treasure of the Sierra Madre* by B. Traven, the first edition of *Songs of the Spanish Civil War* by Pedro Garfias and, especially, the books of the greatly admired anarchist theoretician Rudolph Rocker, including his *Nationalism and Culture*), he was the driving force behind the magazines *Social Studies, Chaos*, and the collective *Testimonies*. Most importantly, he founded, in his own office, the Library for Social Reconstruction. It is because of this institution that his death does not end evidence of his labor. Gabriel Zaid, the Mexican intellectual whom Mestre greatly respected for his honesty, wrote an article after Mestre's death which did a good job of describing the intellectual position of this man who, without the benefit of education, dedicated his entire life, under whatever circumstances and no matter where he was ("my country is the world and my tribe is humanity"), to spreading the Idea: "His faith in discussion, books, and the press as means of liberation impressed me, especially because he had only a minimum of formal education. I was able to see the contrast between two institutions that both had an affinity and were opposed: free reading and the university. Formal education is of a tradition in which knowledge is hierarchical, vertical, transmitted from above, and accredited by an authority that hands out credentials. Free reading is a discussion among equals that is extended and on-going: it is knowledge that is critical, horizontal, open, and without credentials, where the only authority that matters is moral authority."

From the Mouth of Mestre, the Anarchist Librarian

(The following paragraphs are extracts from sixteen interviews which Enrique Sandoval conducted with Ricardo Mestre between March and May of 1988 in México City. This extensive document, 712 pages in length, has not yet been published.)

"My parents were very modest people; my mother was a servant, my father had two jobs but never earned very much... He was a man who was basically liberal and he worked in the Pirelli factory. He was employed there and became the head of the cable section. But from a political point of view, he was a liberal admirer of the Modern School.

At first they sent me to various elementary schools, later to a secondary teacher, but I was very, very rebellious and I was expelled from school. Finally my mother placed me in the parochial school, where they had two sections, one for the rich kids and one for the poor kids. I had a tendency to play truant, to cut classes, although I had an ulterior motive for these truancies. I had heard my parents say that it was bad to hit children at night. Because I was being a truant, I didn't return home until night and sometimes they found me—and I believe this is so because I learned to read as soon as I left my mother's womb—reading a book underneath a streetlight.

When I was a little older, but not much older, I began to devour books in the Library-Museum Balaguer in Vilanova, and in spite of the fact that some of the books weren't for children, I was still able to check them out because when I was 14 years old I already weighed 80 kilos. It was there that I swallowed up the works of Emile Zola, who had a great deal of influence on the development of my thoughts. I also devoured the adventure stories of Rocambole, *Le Miserables* by Victor Hugo, *Toilers of the Sea, The Man Who Laughs*, that is to say, most of this type of literature."

"My father belonged to the Pirelli worker's union and on Sundays the workers would go to pay their dues and sometimes they would pick up copies of the magazine *Solidarida Obera*. And I began to take a look at *Solidarida Obera* as well. At this stage I already owned fourteen or fifteen books, and had begun my own small library."

"I'm not sure what the reason is, perhaps it was the fault of Tolstoy and his bit about the Yasnaia Poliana school, but I had a pedagogical and intellectual passion to be a critic of the educational methods of my time, which were punitive, involving slapping, standing in the corner, simply a series of punishments you'd have to endure. This desire I had to teach, to be a teacher, I had since my childhood, but to teach in a way that was different from the way I was being taught. In my opinion, one of the best things about school was reading. At that time, the schoolteacher priests put me in a circle of children and had me read to them. Since there was a certain amount of independence in this activity, I started telling them racy stories in which the principle protagonists were priests. And one day I was telling one of these racy stories and I didn't realize that Father Piera was standing behind me. Anyway, I've always had this passion for teaching. But I didn't even finish primary school, I read like a madman, but I didn't get into the discipline of education."

"At this stage, when I was sixteen years old, I had already read an enormous amount of anarchist literature as well as everything else, because of course I was reading everything. But at that time I was reading more about anarchism than any other thing."

(In the twenties, when the CNT was underground, the anarchists had a factory in Igualada where they were manufacturing bombs. One day, the mainstream press discovered the factory. But most of the bomb-making materials were salvaged. Mestre kept several boxes of these materials in his house in Vilanova.)

"Here in my house some peasants gathered, small landowners of the district. All of them, each one, had his own library. And in a village called Lleger, a very small village near a larger one called Sant Jaume dels Domenys, there, under absolute monarchy, no one was married in the church, nor baptized their children, and the priest who came on Sundays was so bored that he stopped coming. And the peasants went to Sant Jaume, to the church there, and when the priest gave his talks they challenged him to a debate and created controversy. And they were just small landowners, but all of them read a lot, all of them had their libraries. When a relative died, and it came time to bury the person, they called on me, and I would give the eulogy."

"What we had there was very good because the Federation of Local Unions had a library in my town, where a thousand workers would always read. And in all the regions, in the unions that were influenced by anarchists, culture was held above all else. Even more importantly, in the Posito society they successfully started a circulating library, and they also read a lot. It was a semi-official organization, but the sympathetic fishermen, the few who were sympathetic to us—later there were more—also started a circulating library and so the fishermen also began to read a lot. When the revolution of '36 came, without any committee organizing it, they collectivized the fishing industry very well and did so with a great sense of responsibility. The sympathetic fishermen proposed to the board of directors of Posito that they create a library and they agreed to it. At that time, they acquired books from cultural institutions—books that included our own ideas—and then the directors were very proud of having done something cultural, even though they were some real blockheads.

At a social club called Union Villanovense we also inspired a circulating library. Later, at the Athenaeum, we sponsored a series of sociological studies in order to camouflage ourselves and take direct action even while we were underground, and we were once again pushing to provide cultural opportunities. For example, there was the library, which was a very rich library with all kinds of literature and, naturally, a lot of literature about ideas. More than a thousand readers of one type or another were always there. The unions associated with the CNT had at the maximum four or five thousand people. The UGT, the socialist union, had two or three hundred; they were more moderate and…, but they were people who read."

"Before, including the time when we were beginning the CNT in 1910, the workers' unions which were influenced by libertarian thought always gave importance to starting rationalist schools and lending libraries. That is to say, they gave importance to the intellectual formation of the worker, who wasn't like the worker who, in the past century, would often go to the tavern on Sundays and not go to work on Mondays. The intention was to contribute to creating conscious individuals, including the workers.

The libertarian cultural associations were organized much later, about at the same time as the formation of the official CNT in 1910."

"And this got me thinking a lot about why as anarchists in the workers' movement we sometimes collaborated in actions that didn't correspond to our ideas. Because to murder, for some economic grievance, for money, a scab who has come to work because of his hunger and misery … that is to say, that's really something… We had fallen into the trap of class struggle. We also believed that the classes were each homogeneous and that the proletariat had a collective consciousness that… It's wrong, like it's wrong to have capitalism. The capitalists fight among themselves and even provoke international wars for business reasons; they don't have any humanism. And, in spite of everything, in the anarchosyndicalist movement there is indeed humanism. In spite of numerous faults, there is humanism. What we had to insist upon was that the workers were not sheep, that the workingman had a consciousness. It was because of this that we wanted them to read, in order to form their personalities."

"With my children, I never thought to indoctrinate them, but to provide them with a completely free education. Here in Mexico, they attended the Madrid school. One day my eleven-year old daughter came to me and said, "There is a boy at school who doesn't believe in God, either." I asked her why she wanted to say "either," and she told me "Because you don't believe and I don't either." "That's fine, but, when he was alive, my father smoked; my father smoked but I don't smoke. You don't understand that if children always did what their parents do, we'd still not have come down from the trees. Here in the library you have access to the Koran, the Bible, the Laws of Manu, all the Greek myths, etc. etc. Read them, study them, and if you want it and it's necessary for you to have a religion, chose one willingly." "Yes, papa," she said, in a humorous mood, "and when I'm older, I'll become a tobacconist."

"No, no, no. I don't have any regrets. My wife and

my daughter returned to Vilanova and many people there remembered me. Also, a strange thing happened to my son in Vilanova. He went to visit the Balaguer Library. They had no idea who he was, because a great number of years had passed and my son had been born in Mexico. But they asked him if he was my son. The library director had recognized him as my son. I believe that in spite of my radical anarchism, in spite of my radical anti-clericalism, in spite of my not giving any concessions to the church, many people remembered that I was very humane, and that is what is most important.

But I'm not sad. It's because the things that have shaped my sensibilities have been very different. Since I almost never went to school, I haven't been intellectually poisoned by the school system. Here in Mexico when, for example, I saw the civics textbooks that they gave my children, I was outraged. That's because I educated myself. Because I have hardly any historical influences, the part about the history of Catalonia I found ridiculous. They were talking about heroes, etc., but instead of heroes there were people who fought, not for Catalonia, but because of dynastic disputes between the Austrians and the Bourbons. This wasn't right. The only thing in the history of Catalonia that had any social content was Els Segadors.

When I thought about returning [to Spain], I had already started plenty of activities for disseminating ideas in Mexico, I had already become very involved with the problems in Mexico, but with an eye for universal application like I had back there. The aspect of Spain that interested me was the human contact with friends. But, there were too few survivors and too much tragedy that instead of enjoying myself, I would have gone there and opened all the old emotional wounds again. So no.... I never had this thing about putting roots down somewhere, and also I never felt that because I was from Catalonia I had a certain status or prestige; it was merely a fact of circumstance. At times, when I'm being vulgar, I'll merely say that this is where my parents once had sex.

The people feel sad, though. But this is possibly influenced by the fact that they don't have close enough ties to others who share their same ideas. That is to say, the family that is most important to me is the family of friends who share my same ideas, and this family has practically been eliminated. I hold on to my natural family, who I have contact with, some of whom are here as well. But I don't feel sad now…. To the contrary, I'm indignant when people exalt the Catalonian historical figures. But I'm also indignant when they exalt the historical figure of El Cid and the Castilians."

"On certain occasions, such as at social gatherings I was attending, Léon Felipe and Moreno Villa would come up and greet me. Léon almost always signed on to the things the communists were doing. But, he was a very intelligent communist, a good poet, very sectarian but easy to get along with. Juan Rejano, an Andalusian and a member of the Central Committee of the Communist Party of Spain in exile would come up and say "sign this" and Léon Felipe would sign.

One day my wife, my young daughter, and I were hanging out in the Paris café with Léon Felipe. My daughter was only six or seven years old and Léon Felipe asked her: "What are you reading?" "Tolstoy," she responded. This was because we had some editions of the classics that Vasconcelos had put out, and one of them was Tolstoy. Being in our home library, she grabbed this book because she liked the title and started reading it. Then Léon said to me: "Christ! You are already poisoning your daughter!"

"Authentic anarchist periodicals can't be the least bit closed. All of the periodicals that I have worked on were authentically anarchistic, though they were collaborations by very different people. This is anarchistic. Because if something is purely dogmatic, if we only have our own causes in mind, we are being selfish."

"When I was eighty years old, I had an attack of an ulcer that I didn't even know I had. It was so bad that they had to operate on me the same night in the hospital. They told my wife that it was quite possible that I wouldn't come out alive. It was very serious to be having this operation at the age of eighty. But, I tricked them and managed to get out of there. While I was recuperating from this, I remembered various friends of mine who had developed their concerns for freedom by disseminating publications, books and pamphlets. When they died, their work stopped and was unable to continue. I had edited many books and I told myself that when I died I wanted to make sure my work continued, and this is the reason why I founded the Library of Social Reconstruction."

What Makes Librarianship Exciting to You?

Chris Dodge

Sharing books and magazines and videos and zines and CDs and information that people want (and need) to know about, if only they had a clue.

Making connections fortuitously in the cause of a happier, more joyful world.

Imparting passion about poetry, truth, beauty, freedom, ornithology.

Teaching people to do it themselves.

Linking those who quest for knowledge, those who love learning, with the tools and resources necessary to learn and to grow.

Promoting alternatives to mass media which offer a respite from cynicism and foster the idea that committed individuals and groups can make a difference.

Saving the past from being forgotten. (Viva Voltairine de Cleyre!)

Keeping hope alive for the future.

Ensuring real diversity in library materials.

Imparting curiosity.

Working to make public libraries free for all.

Countering consumerism and commercialism in publishing.

Educating library users to stand up for their rights, how to ask for what they want, even though their stereotypes of what sort of things are generally not in libraries (but OUGHT to be) are often accurate (say, adult comics, punk music, erotica, small circulation magazines, zines, and street newspapers, to name a few).

Modeling appropriate technology, from the grassroots: pen and paper and phone calls, sometimes.

Showing that a library is not so much about a collection of books on shelves so much as an attitude that can move wherever the librarian goes.

To continue to dream and invent the role of activist librarian.

Reprinted with permission from *NewBreed Librarian* (www.newbreedlibrarian.org), v. 1, no. 1 (February 2001).

Bad Libraries

Carol Reid

Bad libraries, like bad marriages, used to be a matter of relative privacy. But, as with everything else, we've learned some things. For some, the problem is an autocratic patriarch (or matriarch). Others quarrel over the children. Many fight about money. Quite a few form questionable alliances. But, as long as the lines of communication are kept open, such sticking points can often be convincingly resolved. Perhaps the most alarming trend then, or at least one we seem to be hearing a lot more about lately, is the attempt by library administrators to quell communication and quiet their critics, especially those from within the "family."

Take the case of Sanford Berman, the up till now irrepressible Minneapolis gadfly, who has gained the admiration, bordering on hero worship, of librarians worldwide. He is the author and editor of numerous books and articles about cataloging, social responsibilities, and intellectual freedom in libraries. Through persistent petitioning he has persuaded the Library of Congress to drop or amend hundreds of outdated, inaccurate, and politically incorrect subject headings (most famously, "Jewish Question" and "Yellow Peril") and to add countless others. Berman has given many inspiring addresses and won several major awards. Though still alive (thankfully, after a serious surgery last spring), a Festschrift has already been published in his name.

It is because of him that the Hennepin County Library has acquired the outstanding reputation among catalogers that it currently enjoys. HCL's records, especially its fiction records, are of the highest quality, surpassing those of LC itself. Where LC subject headings prove inadequate, catalogers now borrow Hennepin headings instead. As head of Cataloging there, he had also elected to depart from Anglo-American Cataloguing Rules, by writing out or translating obscure abbreviations and Latinisms, and avoiding unnecessary punctuation. All in the noble aim of increased "accessibility and intelligibility," as one bemoaning admirer wrote to *American Libraries*, in the wake of Berman's sudden and unimaginable retirement.

Hennepin, you see, had recently been asked to become a major contributor to OCLC, an outline database of bibliographic records. In the press release announcing this fact, Berman's part was warmly acknowledged. However, back at work, he was being rebuked for having stated his opinion to staff that HCL should insist on OCLC paying royalties for some of their records, for having failed to be in lockstep with AACR2, and for objecting to a PR-skewed misquoting of his views. While unsure of the business aspect, I suspect he had a point, and, as the man of the hour, was in a good position to push it. When his boss refused to withdraw the reprimand and continued to harass Berman privately, while "praising Caesar" publicly, ultimately "kicking him upstairs" to produce a manual on the type of cataloging for which he had put them on the map, Berman had finally had enough and disgustedly decided to resign.

He had also been upbraided a couple of years ago for the "insubordination" of speaking out against his library's bizarre proposal to double the overdue fines on children's books as a means of increasing revenues. Jane Rustin, director of the Allegheny County Library System, in Maryland, who also believed that the kids in her library were being ill-served, felt similarly at pains to relinquish her post in November 1998 when the library board cobbled together a filtering policy in too-ready response to the admonishments of three area ministers about the ensnarements of the Net. Presumably, like Berman, she felt that political concerns had overridden professional ones.

Another library director who was unable to withstand the force of facile change-mongers was West Virginia's Fred Glazer, described by John Berry, the editor of *Library Journal*, as "arguably, one of the greatest state librarians in the history of our nation." During 24 years of dedicated (or, as *American Libraries*' Will Manley sadly put it, "joyous") service, Glazer managed to increase the number of public libraries in that often benighted state from 25 to 179. He also raised the amount of money allocated them from five cents per capita in 1972 to $3.81 in 1996, which put them in the top five nationwide. Glazer died from kidney failure a year and a half after his "nasty shove out the door." The cause of death did not, but perhaps should have listed a broken heart, and the stress of being assailed by yuppie downsizers.

Although the Leroy C. Merritt Humanitarian Fund of the American Library Association gave funds to help Glazer fight his unjust firing, which, according to Berry, "reek[ed] of political and professional vendetta, personal disloyalty and jealousy, and incredible misuse of the power of the state," it was tragically a case of too little, too late. Although the ridiculously low salary advertised for his replacement attracted very few applicants, the state commission eventually gave the job to David Price, who, amid controversy over his management abilities, had left two different California libraries—most egregiously the San Francisco Public Library, where he supervised the contentious opening of their new facility.

Sometimes the ethical catalyst that leads to such upsets has to do with a perception of the way employees in general are being treated. This is what happened here at the Albany Public Library, long a site of physical disrepair and staff disaffection. One fateful day in 1993, the director decided to dock the pay of managers who had chosen to close the library and send people home during a blizzard. This penurious act proceeded to snowball as it attracted the detritus of those workers' wintry discontent, along with some local and national media attention. Subsequently, the library's employees joined a union and the director eventually stepped down.

Most librarians possess a fundamental belief, intuitive or practiced, in intellectual freedom, or freedom of speech. So it tends to rankle when they're told not to talk, or even, as is their celebrated wont, to whisper amongst themselves. In Hawaii, it was an interoffice "gag order" that galvanized the mobilization culminating in the cancellation of the outsourcing contract with Baker & Taylor, the firing of the State Librarian, and a legislative edict against further such outsourcing in Hawaii libraries. Again, as I always say, nothing backfires quite so satisfyingly as censorship does.

As in Hawaii, bad publicity has forced the main players to move on, yet fallout from the San Francisco Public Library "book dumping" debacle continues to cast a pall over its long-suffering staff, notably one distinguished children's librarian, who "just happened" to have been the primary signatory on a petition protesting the ill-conceived plans for the New Main Library, and was then falsely accused of child molestation and hitting on female colleagues (despite his being openly gay) and summarily fired from his job three years ago. Fortunately, SFPL is a union shop and the local is at long last taking up his cause.

One of the rarest qualities, and therefore most prized in my estimation, is the ability of those in authority to concede an error, or confess that a wrong has been done. Most such people, perhaps out of a nagging need to justify how it is they merit so much more money than their coworkers, invest tremendous amounts of energy rationalizing these things, because to allow their own fallibility might be to suggest that they do not deserve their exalted status. It is for this reason that I was so gratified, after slogging grimly through all the plausibly deniable accounts recounted here, to have come across one about a librarian in Victoria, British Columbia—a lovely place where I am lucky to have an uncle now living, once again due to the inability of those in high places to admit the colossal mistake that was the Vietnam War—fired during the fifties for at one time having edited a left-wing publication.

Half a century later, the Greater Victoria Public Library has publicly apologized to this former employee, and acknowledged the grave insult to both him and our wonderful, freedom-loving profession that such craven and conformist conduct implied. Canada is often characterized as a more censorious place than America, with our vaunted Bill of Rights, but in this humble and belated act of contrition, they evinced a greater regard for the rights of the individual and intellectual freedom than some wielders of library power I this country have recently shown themselves to possess.

The Real Thing: Democracy as a Contact Sport

Russell Mokhiber and Robert Weissman

A couple weeks ago, we received an invitation to attend an event at the Library of Congress.

Coca-Cola was about to make an "historic contribution" to the Library of Congress, and the Library, and Coca-Cola, were inviting reporters to cover the event. We accepted the invitation.

We learned from the morning papers that the "historic contribution" was a complete set of 20,000 television commercials pushing Coca-Cola into the American digestive system.

Remember the one where the kid hands Pittsburgh Steeler Mean Joe Greene his bottle of Coke, and in return, Mean Joe tosses the kid his football jersey? Or what about on a hilltop in Italy where the folks start sing "I'd like to buy the world a Coke and keep it company"?

The event was at the Great Hall of the Thomas Jefferson Building—named after the Thomas Jefferson who, in 1816, wrote: "I hope we shall crush in its birth the aristocracy of our monied corporations which dare already to challenge our government to a trial of strength, and bid defiance to the laws our country."

Anyway, we pull up at the appointed hour (7:15 P.M. on November 29, 2000) at the Thomas Jefferson building, and there's a traffic jam created by stretch limousines blocking the entrance.

In addition to lowly reporters, the 400 or so guests included ambassadors, members of Congress, corporate chieftains and other dignitaries. Good thing we dressed up.

The Main Hall is this absolutely stunning room, with marble staircases. A string quartet is playing. Waiters are serving Coke in classic bottles. The food is fabulous—lamb chops, trout, Peking duck. We rub shoulders with the Ambassador from Burma.

The "aristocracy of our monied corporations," as Jefferson put it, had taken over the place, and Coca-Cola wanted to make sure that everybody knew it.

After all, Coke could have just donated the ads to the Library and left it at that. But this wasn't about Coke's largesse. It was about public relations—whether the public would view the company as a racist company (Coke had just agreed to pay $192.5 million to settle allegations that it routinely discriminated against black employees in pay, promotions and performance evaluations) or a junk food pusher (consuming large quantities of sugared Coca-Cola has led to ours being one of the most overweight generations in history)—or instead, a generous contributor to the Library of Congress.

James Billington, the Librarian of Congress, was called on to deliver good things to Coke, and he did. He turned over the keys of the Main Hall to Coke, and Coke decked the place out with its logo, stitched in red beside the logo of the Library of Congress. Television sets were placed throughout the hall, the better for the Ambassadors and members of the Democratic Leadership Council to check out the commercials.

Billington was selling the soul of the library to one of the world's most powerful corporations. In addition to the ads, Coke was establishing a fellowship at the Library for the study of "culture and communication"—one fellow will receive $20,000 a year for the next five years.

Gary Ruskin, director of Commercial Alert, was outside the event, protesting. "It is not the proper role of the taxpayer-financed Library of Congress to help promote

---

Reprinted with permission from Focus on the Corporation Internet Column (http://www.corporatepredators.org) in *Library juice*, 4:1 (January 3, 2001), pp. 6–8.

junk food like Coca-Cola to a nation that is suffering skyrocketing levels of obesity," Ruskin said. "It is crass commercialism for James Billington to degrade Jefferson's library and founding ideals into a huckster's backdrop."

But without shame, Billington introduced Doug Daft, the president of Coca-Cola, who said that "Coca-Cola has become an integral part of people's lives by helping to tell these stories." Nothing about profits. Nothing about overweight kids. Nothing about racism.

After Daft spoke, the room went dark, and the ads ran on the television screens. Nostalgia swept the room. When the ads were finished, the lights went back on and the crowd cheered.

About 80 high school students, dressed in Coca-Cola red sweaters, filled the marble staircases and sang—"I want to buy the world a Coke." Again, the crowd cheered. Doug Daft, standing downstairs, came back to the microphone to continue his statement. We were upstairs at this point, and we looked down at him and asked, in a loud voice—"Why are you using a public library to promote a junk food product?"

The room went quiet. Library of Congress police charged up the marble staircase. Doug Daft put his hand to his ear and shouted back to us: "What did you say?"

In a louder voice, we shouted back: "Why are you using a public institution to promote a junk food product?"

The next thing we know, we are on the ground. The Library of Congress police had tackled us. Again, the crowd cheered—not for our question, but for the tackle.

We were dragged downstairs, past the Ambassador from Burma, and hauled outside, where police officers from the District of Columbia were waiting for us.

Out of the Thomas Jefferson building came running a man from Coke. "This is a private event," the man from Coke told the police. "I'm from Coca-Cola."

At first, the police wanted nothing to do with the man from Coke. But the man from Coke insisted. They huddled.

Apparently, the man from Coke didn't want us arrested for asking an obvious question. Apparently, the man from Coke didn't want a public trial. The man from Coke was standing up for our First Amendment rights to ask his boss a question.

The police said we were to leave the grounds. And we weren't to come back. Ever.

Russell Mokhiber is editor of the Washington, D.C.-based Corporate Crime Reporter. Robert Weissman is editor of the Washington, D.C.-based Multinational Monitor. They are co-authors of Corporate Predators: The Hunt for MegaProfits and the Attack on Democracy (Monroe, Maine: Common Courage Press, 1999). (c) Russell Mokhiber and Robert Weissman.

WOMEN

Smarty Girl: Three Librarians on Film

Abigail Leah Plumb

We all know what a librarian looks like: She keeps her hair in a bun, wears glasses, favors tweed. She is not widely considered to be attractive. She doesn't go to parties—parties are loud; librarians are slaves to silence.[1] Librarians have a lot of cats to replace their sadly lacking social lives. They are nearsighted from staring at all those books. They are known for their love of cardigans, comfortable shoes, and enormous dangly earrings. They are not known for their love of people who need help navigating the library. (Did I mention that librarians exist to keep these people from touching the books?)

How do we know all this? From books, television, and movies. The Music Man's famed Marian the librarian is feared by her family to be relegated to a life of spinsterhood due to the mere fact of her braininess. In Betty Smith's 1943 novel A Tree Grows in Brooklyn, the neighborhood librarian is removed by virtue of her traditional intellectual life from the poverty around her, but as a result she is closed off, incapable of empathy with the young protagonist. In It's a Wonderful Life's alternate George Bailey–less universe, Mary Hatch becomes a cold, haughty librarian, doomed to loneliness.

Furthermore, pop culture's librarian—a woman,[2] bespectacled, surrounded by books—can be read as a stand-in for smart women in general. The image of the librarian illustrates the idea that, in the popular imagination, a woman can be smart or fun, smart or sociable, smart or desirable. A brainy woman is a bluestocking, too bookish for sex, boring, and stifled by her own intellect. The only way these filmic librarians have been able to become sexy is to literally cast off the trappings of their profession: They remove their glasses, release their hair, reveal their previously obscured bodies. With this physical transformation their intellect is drained away, replaced—not accompanied—by sexuality.

But every so often, a movie or other media event will go against the grain of the usual pop cultural assumptions about women and intelligence. For this essay, I've picked three very different movies—*Desk Set* (1957), *The Gun in Betty Lou's Handbag* (1992), and *Party Girl* (1995)—all of which depict smart, complex women behind the reference desk, and present libraries as locations in which women's intellectual curiosity has inherent positive value. In a triumph over the brains-or-body, smarts-or-conviviality binary, each protagonist comes into her own, intellectually, in the course of the plot—but not at the cost of her sexuality or individuality.

In *Desk Set*, intelligence is central to the attractiveness of the main character. Bunny Watson (Katharine Hepburn) is the vivacious head of reference for a major broadcasting company—a job that showcases, rather than hides, her brilliant wit. She's a sharp dresser (and an ardent shopper), an avid social drinker, a party girl. Bunny's confidence and competence as a librarian make her more, rather than less, interesting. She has a green thumb, as evidenced by the enormous philodendron vine decorating her office. She has a variety of functional relationships with other people: She is an understanding boss, and she's demonstrably friendly with workers in other areas of the building. She finds her romantic life disappointing, but not because it's nonexistent—rather, her longtime boyfriend doesn't seem to take her intelligence or her job seriously enough. Perhaps most important, she is a very, very good librarian; her demonstrations of reference

---

Reprinted with permission from *Bitch: Feminist Response to Pop Culture* (2765-16th Street, San Francisco, CA 94103), no. 14 (2001), pp. 30–33, 88.

brawn bring the romantic lead—computer guru Richard Sumner (Spencer Tracy)—to his knees. As Bunny's romance with Richard develops, the viewer sees her intelligence and grace through his eyes: She is profoundly desirable. But desirability does not define Bunny; it is a by-product of the richness of her character—a richness to which her very librarian-ness is integral. Her vast knowledge (gleaned, one supposes, on the job) coupled with her razor-sharp tongue make her a formidable heroine, but also an approachable one—she does not, it is clear, have all she wants in the world, despite her considerable charms.

Desk Set ultimately uses the image of the librarian to endorse intellectual ambition for women, and to suggest that women need not abandon intellectual curiosity for love. The crux of the film is the obsolescence of the human librarian; the folks in the reference department are convinced that they are slated for replacement by a gigantic computer called EMERAC.[3] There is a clear conflict between Richard's feelings for Bunny and his supposed plans for her job. Does he want to preserve her or wipe her out entirely? It turns out that EMERAC is meant to supplement the librarians, not replace them; the movie's denouement demonstrates not only Bunny's intelligence, but also her professional competence.[4] The viewer leaves *Desk Set* with the image of Bunny and Richard, pursuing their complementary intellectual goals in tandem, rather than existing in conflict. It's a triumph for the smart ladies: a saucy, sharp librarian who finds love without giving up her identity.

When we meet Betty Lou (played by Penelope Ann Miller, as yet sans gun and handbag), we quickly learn that she is second-in-command at her small town's public library, taking her orders from a librarian in the old-biddy mode. The supervisor is gray-haired and dowdy; she refuses to allow Betty Lou to display books at the library fundraiser because they'll be too close to the hors d'oeuvres and forces her to end children's story hour because it involves rambunctious kids and speaking out loud—after all, "This is a library."

Betty Lou is astonishingly meek and quiet, a doormat for both her boss and her policeman husband.[5] The film's plot turns on her desire to be seen differently, to be listened to: When the mousy Betty Lou tries to tell her husband about finding a gun while walking their dog—a gun that turns out to be the only piece of evidence in a high-profile murder case—he hangs up on her, not believing she could possibly have something important to say. Through the ensuing comedy of errors, Betty Lou herself becomes the prime suspect in said murder, gets a sassy haircut and sexy new clothes with the help of the women she meets in jail, begins speaking up for herself, and helps solve the crime. Though her sartorial makeover recalls the more common librarian-gets-gorgeous scenario, her transformation is not largely physical. By the movie's end, she has reinvented herself as assertive, sensual, and confident.

The Gun in Betty Lou's Handbag is a screwball comedy; as the protagonist of such, Betty Lou must scramble to invent a wholly implausible tale that explains how she supposedly came to commit a crime of passion. (She pretends that she had taken a lover and shot him to death in a cheap motel.) But what's revealed along the way is instructive in spite of its wackiness. Betty Lou embodies many of the traditional librarian qualities, and the film positions her quiet, bookwormish nature as diametrically opposed to her constructed suspect-ness. She's described by the town newspaper as "a model librarian," code for "the last person you'd expect to have done something so interesting" (the townspeople's shock is largely focused on the passion rather than the crime).[6]

But once her brush with felony coaxes Betty Lou from her shell, she uses her newfound qualities in service of the library, displaying her confidence at the fundraiser and using her notoriety to draw people to the books. The library has become both a site for intellectual curiosity, and an area—perhaps the area—of expertise for Betty Lou. Nowhere is this more evident than during the scene set at the library fundraiser. "I'm going to give you what you want," she announces to the group of gossip-seeking community members. "Sex. Crime." The townspeople gasp. "And mystery. And romance," she continues, listing other abstract pleasures to be found among the stacks. Although her transformation has been brought about, at least in part, by scandal and the community's disapproval, Betty Lou comes into her own as she demonstrates the passionate love of books that brought her into the library field to begin with. Betty Lou becomes both more of a librarian (more competent at her job) and less of one (having cast off the stereotypical librarian traits)—and in the process plays some interesting pop cultural tricks on the viewer: The film both endorses notions of librarians as elderly and dried-out (and more interested in preserving the books than in appreciating their content) and gives these images the lie.

As the titular party girl, Parker Posey is Mary, a pretty, spoiled pouter who initially spurns work as a library clerk but is forced to take the job in order to pay back bail money loaned by Judy (Sasha von Scherler), her librarian godmother. At the movie's outset, Judy appears as dry and unappealing as the library itself (her generosity notwithstanding). But the film's presentation of librarianship changes along with Mary's experience of the library. Unlike Betty Lou, who discovers hitherto unseen parts of herself, Mary comes to see the library as an outlet for qualities she already possesses.

The library, once forbidding (it's presided over by a terrifying poster of Melvil Dewey), becomes a place in which Mary can shine as something other than an Ecstasy-popping party fixture. In one notable scene, she provides offhand snappy answers to patrons' questions and throws a characteristic Posey hissy fit at an errant misshelver. One of *Party Girl*'s most effective tricks is its transformation of Mary's worst quirks—her bossiness, her insistence on the careful and absolute order of her designer wardrobe—into managerial acumen and a previously untapped affinity for the Dewey Decimal System. It's not an easy transition—at its rockiest, we find Mary arranging her dj roommate's records according to Dewey ("It's perfect for a small collection like yours!")—but by the movie's end, Mary has enlisted the help of Judy and the other library denizens in applying to graduate programs around the country.[7] She's finally found a job she actually likes; she has a goal she can attain. She was always capable, the film demonstrates, and the library becomes the site for the full integration of her desire for organization, her sharp tongue, and her fierce intelligence.

So what's the significance of all this?[8] when we're interested in what pop culture thinks of smart women, we would do well to study what they give us of librarians. And when culture producers frequently present women's intelligence, or individual intelligent women (as I would assert is the case now), as unimportant or unattractive, these three films stand as exceptions. The library in each of these movies provides a structure and a symbol—it's the physical and psychic location of a sea change for each heroine. In a world, cinematic or otherwise, in which tradition holds that we undervalue women's intelligence, these movies can serve as a potent refutation. Instead of portraying the intellectual woman as neurotic, lonely, or trapped between her desire for love and her need for intellectual fulfillment, each film shows its protagonist changing and flourishing in the space the library provides, and reshaping that space to better accommodate her own intellect.

Abigail Leah Plumb is a candidate for a master's degree in library and information services at the University of Michigan at Ann Arbor. She has a cat, glasses, and a lot of cardigans, but—at press time—no bun.

Five Librarians on Librarians

A variety of hip young librarian types are producing websites that play with—or outright defy—librarian stereotypes. Sometimes poetic, sometimes whiny, these five sites display a far broader range of librarian behaviors, beliefs, and obsessions than we typically see depicted in the mass media.

Anarchist Librarians Web
burn.ucsd.edu/~mai/librarians.html

"The revolution will be catalogued!" Although it's not updated very frequently, this home of often tongue-in-cheek anarchist and left-libertarian thought on librarianship, among other things—certainly not the staid conservatism frequently associated with libraries—is articulate, informative, and refreshing, even for those who don't agree with all the beliefs or positions expressed. And if the term "anarchist librarian" seems like a contradiction in terms, there's a faq to set you straight.

Librarian Avengers
www.librarianavengers.com

Erica Olsen (who—full disclosure—happens to be my library school classmate) has one of the snappiest, Flash-iest websites going, at least on the topic of cranky librarianship. Includes stupid research tricks and an admonishment that "librarians are all-knowing and all-seeing. They bring order to chaos." Favorite feature: a section on librarians with cool and unusual jobs, such as the Citadel's librarian and a Masonic librarian.

Lipstick Librarian
www.teleport.com/~petlin/liplib/

"She's Bold! She's Sassy! She's Helpful!" This site is dedicated to the librarian with a hankering for Mizrahi and M.A.C. as well as marc records. "Lipstick Librarianship is a state of mind," so diagnose your LL tendencies with the handy-dandy quiz, and then treat yourself to a t-shirt.

The Modified Librarian
www.bmeworld.com/gailcat/

"Welcome to the web page of the Modified Librarian. Here we will discuss the concept and practice of body modification as it relates to librarians as persons and professionals." Multipierced and tattooed librarians, with pictures—'nuff said.

NewBreed Librarian
www.newbreedlibrarian.org

This "one-stop shop for new or soon-to-be librarians" offers "communication, collaboration, and developing a professional presence on the web that librarians can identify with." Includes saucy interviews, profiles of information professionals, features, and a frequently updated weblog.—A.L.P.

Notes

1. More than once, standing with a cigarette and a drink at a party, I have had someone tell me, "Whoa, you don't seem like a librarian"—because, of course, librarians don't wear low-cut shirts and bum Parliaments off tipsy strangers.

2. Movies have generally hit the mark in portraying librarians as predominantly female. Since the professionalization of librarianship in the late 1800s, librarians have traditionally been women. You may not be surprised to learn that since that period, the largely female profession has been typically underpaid, overworked, and underappreciated (not that that ever makes it onto celluloid).

3. It's worth noting here that even 50 years ago, technology was a professional bull with which librarians wrestled. *Desk Set* came out at a time in between Vannevar Bush's invention of Memex—the first electronic database—and Herbert Simon's "thinking machine."

4. It's also worth noting that emerac is referred to as "Emma" and as female, associating the female with technological adeptness as well as competence. (Emma proves in the end to be a very helpful library component.)

5. I wondered how she got through graduate school, but, unlike *Desk Set* and *Party Girl*, Betty Lou doesn't treat librarianship as a profession with prerequisites.

6. A further exchange on this topic also bears comment: "She's perfectly normal," insists Betty Lou's husband in her defense. "Well, maybe she reads too much," he adds, implying both that she is far too boring to have a life that would include a lover and also that, in fact, her intellectual pursuits may not be quite normal after all.

7. With gratifying accuracy, this film, unlike most others, demonstrates the difference between librarians and library paraprofessionals such as clerks and assistants. "A librarian," Judy announces dramatically, if didactically, "is a professional, with a degree in library science." However, one problematic aspect (among several) of *Party Girl* is its presentation of all paraprofessionals as up-and-coming young librarians-to-be, when the truth is far more complicated and the value of a professional degree in librarianship frequently comes into question.

8. As a library chick, I feel (dare I say it?) validated by these movies, and a little more convinced that libraries might be an integral part of my getting my shit together. But that's a pretty specific and limited reading.

Person of the Year–Debra Davis: Lessons about Acceptance, Respect, and Love from Minnesota's Most Fabulous Transgender Librarian

Ellen Lansky

Let's begin with the bathroom, a contested site in discussions about gender expression and human rights. When I was in high school, the Equal Rights Amendment had been sent to the states for ratification. One of the big debates in my sociology class concerned the possible effects of the ERA. The language of the ERA was simple, and most of the effects seemed simply positive to me and to most other people in my class.

However, there was a general panic when an ERA opponent trotted out the standard anti–ERA rhetoric, one aspect of which was that women would be drafted into the army and put into combat units. The argument was that women toting weapons on the front lines of wars was an inhumane and unthinkable notion, though nobody seemed to have any trouble thinking about putting young men on the front lines and instructing them to kill or be killed.

The other anti–ERA threat was even more discomfiting—nay, horrifying: the specter of "unisex" restrooms. This was the late 1970s, and by that time, most people—even the people who lived where I did in Overland Park, KS—a conservative, upwardly mobile suburb of Kansas City—had accustomed themselves to unisex hairstyles and unisex clothes. People of all genders wore Levis and had shag haircuts. But unisex bathrooms? It was just too much. The ERA was defeated by a landslide in Kansas, and it ultimately vanished from the nation's classroom discussions and political scene.

Now, as the Human Rights Act has been enacted in Minnesota and the millennium approaches, a person can find and use unisex bathrooms all over the map: in coffee shops, in gas stations, in public libraries. I bet there're even a few back in Overland Park. Here's a typical scenario: A person who expresses masculinity goes in the door marked "Restroom" and does his business. Next in line is a person who expresses femininity. When the guy comes out, she goes in the same door and does her business. No problem.

Maybe not. At Southwest High School in Minneapolis, the "bathroom issue" is a big, big problem for one particular teacher, Carla Cruzan. Recently, Cruzan filed a complaint with the Minnesota Human Rights Department because she felt that Debra Davis, transgender activist, executive director of the Gender Education Center at Maple Grove, and long-time librarian and Media Center teacher at Southwest, should not use the women's restroom. Ostensibly, Cruzan's problem was that Debra Davis uses the women's restroom. Her complaint,

---

Reprinted with permission from *Lavender Magazine* (2344 Nicollet Ave. S., Minneapolis, MN 55404), issue 120 (December 31, 1999), pp. 9–13.

according to Constance Hope, Debra Davis's lawyer and partner, was dismissed as having "no probable cause."

Even so, the teacher would not relent; she took her complaint to the EEOC. Hope explains that the complaint is now directed at the school, and that the plaintiff aims to sue.

"Tom Pritchard from the Minnesota Family Council wrote to the Minneapolis Police Department and asked them to arrest Debbie for using the 'wrong' bathroom,'" Hope says. "In their various complaints, they are misstating the law in two ways. They are alluding to a Minneapolis City ordinance about window-peeping, which makes it unlawful to enter the opposite-gender bathroom to peep at people. And while there is a narrow bathroom exemption in the Human Rights Act, it doesn't apply to Debbie. But somehow, this woman [Cruzan] and these folks from the extreme right think it's all right for a transgender person to be asked to use a different bathroom." The complaint is so specious that it is almost laughable, particularly the "peeping" charge. Furthermore, Cruzan's real problem really has nothing at all to do with the bathroom and who uses it; her problem is her own fear and loathing of differently gendered people.

The Real Peeper

Cruzan is pursuing Debra with such venomous vigor that the real peeper in the case seems to be Cruzan herself. She's the one who can't stop watching the traffic in and out of the women's room. Still, ridiculous as it is, attention must be paid to this complaint and to the threats that accompany it. When somebody threatens to arrest Debra Davis, she has to take that threat seriously.

"This person is spreading fear about transgendered or differently gendered people," Davis observes. "She's trying to make people think that we are people who will come into the bathroom and do terrible things. It affects the whole atmosphere of the building. For me, the threat of arrest was scary. You don't know what the cops are going to do."

"Yes," Connie Hope adds. "We didn't know what would happen. If the police arrested Debbie, would they let her get her purse? And where would they put her? Would they put her in a holding cell with men, which would be completely inappropriate, or with women?"

"Luckily," Davis says, "the cops laughed."

She gives a nervous laugh herself as she tells this story. When she talks and laughs about her ongoing dilemma, two scenes from *Boys Don't Cry* come to mind. If you've seen the film or you know the story, then you know the fear you feel for Brandon Teena when he is pulled over by the cops and has to produce a driver's license. Second, you know the shame you feel for/with Brandon when he is arrested and has to explain to his girlfriend Lana why he is incarcerated with women.

Unlike Brandon Teena, however, Debra Davis has excellent community support as well as the protection of the law, the police, and her school.

Librarian—and Lightning Rod

"I've become a focal point for the extreme right and their attack on the Human Rights Act," Davis says. "But there are so many gender-transition stories that don't even make the news. The difference, I suppose, is that I'm successfully living my life as a differently gendered person, and I work with young people. I was surprised by the acceptance at my school. When I came out, it was not a big hullabaloo. A student came up to me, and she looked at me, and she said, 'You know, you're the same person. You go, girl.' Now, I usually don't allow students to speak to me in that way, but that time it was OK because she was respectful.

"I'm the only out transgender librarian in the country in public education, and the school district has never wavered. My principal is great; my colleagues and the students, too. On the day I came out, there were three hundred phone calls to the Minnesota School Board's voice mail. Three hundred. And all of them were positive. My transition was a success because of allies—the GLBT community and all those other friends who are out there.

"It's true that I'm the only out transgender librarian in the country in public education, but I don't want to be in the media. I made a commitment to the district to keep a low profile with the mainstream media. But the school district has never wavered."

Davis's transition and coming out in a public school are a milestone, a victory for human rights in this state. Her emergence as a transgender activist also makes her a major force for education on transgender issues. Although she's maintained her commitment to keep a low profile with the mainstream media, Davis has provided ongoing educational services to media members and operations that have been, in the past, insensitive and/or hostile to transgender people and transgender issues. "I'm the executive director of the Gender Education Center," Davis explains. "It's a nonprofit organization, and since 1991, I have done probably 40 to 60 training and speaking engagements per year. I've gone in as a consultant in workplaces, trained management, and answered questions about transgender people and the transition and coming out process.

"I've visited organizations all over the Midwest, and

I've been a featured speaker at Morris Pride, at Pride in Minneapolis, and in dozens of workshops. I've also been on KFAI radio, 'T Time with Debra Davis.'

"The GEC has a fabulous board of directors, and we operate on a shoestring—basically next to nothing. But it keeps me going. This work has been a big part of my survival, even when I wasn't out as Debra."

Last spring, Davis participated in *Cross Fire: A Journey Through Gender Mayhem*, a project that Eleanor Savage coordinated at IntermediaArts to foster, encourage, and stimulate discussions, and to get people to think critically about gender. On a panel about gender issues in the media, Davis appeared with, among others, Rosalind Bentley of the *Star Tribune*. Bentley and Davis discussed their alliance, which had come about because Bentley was willing to learn and Davis was willing to teach. Bentley has written key feature articles about Debra Davis, and she has also been able to make some inroads in the newsroom. She has taught her colleagues—or at least presented them with information—about the differences between transvestites, transsexuals, and transgender people, and she has emphasized and modeled in her writing the necessity to respect a differently gendered person's pronouns of choice.

Much work remains to be done with the mainstream media. Davis notes that she established the first television studio in a Minnesota high school, and she has worked professionally in television herself.

"I worked for the North Stars, the Twins, the Vikings, and I used to produce all the Gophers games. I've worked for ESPN, ABC, and NBC as an associate director. I was called to work when the Timberwolves were in the basketball playoffs the weekend I came out, but I haven't been called since. It's freelance work, so I can't claim that they're discriminating. Still, I haven't worked in sports TV since I came out."

A Need for Consciousness-Raising

It may not come as much of a surprise that people in sports television and publications are rather in need of education, general enlightenment, and consciousness-raising where transgender issues are concerned. Last summer, for example, in a *Sports Illustrated* column called "The Life of Reilly," Rick Reilly wrote a positively befuddled and ultimately telling piece about Nong Toom, a transgender Thai kickboxer. Reilly called his column "He'd Rather Fight and Switch," and he incorrectly tagged Nong Toom as "a transvestite." He used masculine pronouns and a sneering tone. Reilly's article was mostly a string of ill-conceived and badly expressed comments about Toom's breasts and her personal style. He did not even attempt to hazard a guess why Toom began to cry when officials asked her to weigh in naked, in a room filled with cameramen and photographers. Granted, Rick Reilly does not expect his readership to ask him to exhibit much ability to think critically about, well, anything, and certainly not about gender. Still, one can take it as a sign of incipient intellectual activity when a guy like Reilly can make an attempt to articulate his fascination, however sophomoric and prurient, with a kickboxer whose body "is broad-shouldered, slim-waisted and ripped like an Olympic swimmer's, only with B cups." The writing is bad, but at least he's writing. If he can write, he can probably read as well. It's possible to educate him.

Certainly, the job of educating the masses of Reillys out there cannot and should not fall upon Debra Davis alone. It is at this point where alliance with the GLBT community comes in, especially with OutFront Minnesota, whose mission is "advocating for the gay, lesbian, bisexual, transgender, and allied communities." Davis is extremely enthusiastic about OutFront's work forging and maintaining alliances and educating. "OutFront really gave a lot of time to building relationships with the transgender community. OutFront gathers members of the transgender community and keeps people informed. The transgender community is large and diverse, and OutFront helps us feel included as a community. "Last spring, there were more people than ever at OutFront's annual lobby day at the Capitol. It was awesome to see all those differently gendered people."

Here, Davis pauses and seizes an educational moment. "I use the term 'differently gendered' because it includes people who might be trans or who might not. The law states that a person can't be discriminated against for 'having a self-image or identity not traditionally associated with one's biological maleness or femaleness.' The law provides for people who are differently gendered. You don't even have to be queer!" Finally, Davis attributes much of her success in living her life as an out transgender person who works with young people to family support, community alliances, and the power of acceptance, respect, and love.

"I graduated from Southwest High School myself, and after that I was the president of my college fraternity. That tells you how hard I tried to be the other person. I just wanted to be like everybody else, but I knew that wasn't going to happen. But I knew I was going to be OK. My parents gave me lots of self-esteem, and I have such wonderful friends and allies.

"It's not how I'd planned my life. I knew I'd be comfortable, but I had no idea this would happen. I really am a reluctant activist. I'm an activist because of who I am.

As Davis sums up, "I just want to live my life as

who I am. If I were at a company, my coming out would be no big deal. But for now, it's hard being the center of attention. I have to maintain this constant vigilance and wonder what those people from the extreme Right are going to do to make me feel bad. Those people look for reasons why they should hate people rather than why they should love and respect and accept them."

New Waves in Lesbian Publishing

By Suzanne Corson

When we opened Boadecia's Books in the San Francisco Bay Area, in 1992, one of the first book orders we placed was with Naiad Press. "Send us two of everything," we said, knowing that would give us the start of a solid lesbian fiction section. Naiad was then publishing two books per month, every month. Other lesbian, feminist, and gay presses were publishing then as well, but Naiad had the volume to fill our lesbian fiction wall in one order.

For the next seven years, Naiad published two, sometimes three, books every month like clockwork. Many customers had the timing down and knew which week we received our new Naiad books each month. Others were on a revolving list—"call me when the new Naiads are in." Some called them "candy," others called them "escape," but whatever the label, many, many people enjoyed them. In October 1999, we heard that Naiad was going through some transitions.

While rumors flew and all the details weren't known at first, we did know that we would not be receiving any new Naiad Press books for the first few months of 2000. Those monthly doses of lesbian life in book form that many women looked forward to would not be there.

Then a few months later, we received a heartfelt letter from Nancy Bereano of Firebrand Books announcing her decision to leave publishing. While her company did not publish the volume of books that Naiad did, Firebrand's books were some of the best quality and most loved books on our shelves. Dorothy Allison's *Trash*, Jewelle Gomez' *The Gilda Stories*, Leslie Feinberg's *Stone Butch Blues*, and Alison Bechdel's *Dykes to Watch Out For* series were just a few of the gems that Firebrand has brought readers. The thought that we would no longer have Nancy Bereano's hand guiding books like these to print was very scary.

Papier Mache Press (best known for its anthologies on aging, such as *When I am an Old Woman, I Shall Wear Purple*), Kitchen Table: Women of Color Press (original publisher of the classic *This Bridge Called My Back*, which will be republished by Third Woman Press in 2001), Madwomen Press, Laugh Lines Press, and too many others have all ceased publication in the last few years. Feminist and lesbian publishers are being battered by a number of factors.

Megastores, both those with actual storefronts and the ones in cyberspace, place large book orders and subsequently return large numbers of unsold copies, often in poor condition. These same conglomerates demand more favorable discount schedules and more time to pay bills than usual. Some authors are more inclined to submit their work to larger, mainstream presses that are now publishing "lesbian" work, rather than smaller, more specialized publishers. These publishers also face the burnout factor of working many years with low pay, long hours, and unlevel playing fields.

There's Some Exciting News

In spite of these startling and depressing developments, all the news is not bad, and some of it is downright exciting. The biggest news is that many of the authors who published books with Naiad now have contracts with newcomer Bella Books. Bella publisher Kelly Smith served as an intern with Naiad Press for a year to learn the publishing business, and became the de facto protégé that Naiad owners Barbara Grier and Donna McBride had wished for when they began to think about slowing down their schedules. Through a decidedly feminist arrangement, the authors were transferred from Naiad's house to Bella's, and Bella began publishing this fall with new books by Peggy Herring (*Calm Before the Storm*), Jackie Calhoun (*Off Season*), Therese Szymanski (*When Evil Changes Face*), and Diana Tremain Braund (*Bold Coast Love*). Kelly Smith is also a bookseller, and her experience at A Woman's Prerogative will provide additional input for her publishing and marketing decisions. Improvements already in place include the printing of four-color covers and publishing longer books. Bella has also contracted with additional authors besides those previously with Naiad. Naiad has not, repeat not, gone out of business. Besides handling its extensive backlist of lesbian favorites like Katherine V. Forrest's *Curious Wine* and Jane Rule's *Desert of the Heart*, Naiad will continue to publish new titles by three of their authors: Linda Hill, Karin Kallmaker, and Claire McNab. New books by Kallmaker and McNab were released in May 2000, and readers were especially pleased by the 250-plus pages of Kallmaker's new book, *Unforgettable*. This fall Naiad released *Treasured Past* by Linda Hill and *Death Understood* by Claire McNab.

In addition to the transition with Naiad Press and Bella Books, Rising Tide Press has experienced a significant change. Owners Alice Frier and Lee Boojamra sold their press to Debra Tobin and Brenda Kazen. The first six books put out by the new owners were recently released, including *Storm Rising*, the long-awaited new book in the Delta "Storm" Stevens mystery series by Linda Kay Silva, and new books by Joan Albarella, Gerri Hill, Katherine Kreuter, Sandra Morris, and Nancy Sanra.

Several brand new outlets for lesbian and feminist literature have sprouted up in the past year. Some of these are making use of new technology, such as Print-on-Demand, which allows them to print books on an as-needed basis. This helps with several challenges found in traditional publishing, like how to warehouse hundreds or thousands of books waiting to be sold and the significant expense of having those books printed all in one print run. A few of these companies are also finding authors in less traditional ways, such as utilizing the World Wide Web.

Robin Paterson-Reed, who founded Justice House Publishing, had spent some time on line in what is known as the Xenaverse, a collection of websites which host fiction written by fans of the *Xena: Warrior Princess* series. Many of these stories feature a romantic coupling of the series' stars, Xena and Gabrielle. Ms. Paterson-Reed began to hear that readers were printing out these stories and in some cases, even bringing them to copy centers to have them bound. She asked in a survey if these stories were available in conventional book form, would women buy them? The answer was a resounding "yes," and Justice House was born. They have already brought out six books. Though they are of several genres (mystery, western, contemporary romance), they share several traits: they are much longer and have more complex plots than typical lesbian novels, and many have the tall, powerful, brunette/short, spunky, blonde couple reminiscent of the Xena and Gabrielle pairings in the fan fiction published on the net. *Tropical Storm*, Justice House's first title, is still one of its most popular. Though it is a conventional lesbian romance in some ways, author Melissa Good does an incredible job of portraying the romantic and sexual tension that can exist as women get to know one another. There's not so much as a kiss for the first 200 pages! Renaissance Alliance Publishers has also found authors from the pool of those who publish work on line. It is also a press imbued with feminist principles, such as the "alliance" in the name, a tribute, says publisher Cathy LeNoir, to the many friends who supported her through the "dyke drama" that helped compel her to start the business. Many of these same friends are now colleagues in this new company. Renaissance has a broad vision, with several imprints established to publish books in particular genres. Already they have published poetry (yes, a new outlet for poets), and a few romances, including *True Colours* by Karen King and Nann Dunne, which

features a rarity in any fiction, let alone lesbian-themed—a woman in a wheelchair as the romantic lead. This publisher has been the most prolific this year, with over a dozen new titles available. Due in forthcoming months are some mysteries and sci-fi/fantasy titles.

LONGER BOOKS, MULTI-LAYERED PLOTS

Readers have noticed that the books that both Justice House and Renaissance Alliance publish are more expensive than those two-to-three per month books that Naiad used to put out. But most feel they are getting good value for their money, since these new books are considerably longer and have multi-layered plots, not just another variation on the familiar girl-meets-girl standby. Justice House's *Lucifer Rising* by Sharon Bowers and Renaissance Alliance's *True Colours* are both over 300 pages long; *Tropical Storm* is over 400 pages, and all of these books feature multiple story threads and complex characters.

Though the most prolific so far, Renaissance Alliance and Justice House are not the only new homes for lesbian writing. Margaret Gillon of Odd Girls Press started out by creating and publishing the ambitious bibliography *Lesbians in Print*. In recent years, she has helped keep alive some voices first published by presses that are no longer in business. She republished Linda Kay Silva's wonderful WWII-era romance *Tory's Tuesday*, which was first published by Paradigm Publishing, and brought out a new title, *First Resort*, by Nanci Little, whose first two books were released by Madwoman Press.

Hadra Books is the name of the publishing company set up by author Diana Rivers to republish her fantasy series of the same name. Her backlist titles, like *Daughters of the Great Star*, had been unavailable for several years, and it is wonderful that they will be on the shelves again for new readers to discover. Fans will be pleased to know that a new Hadra adventure, *Clouds of War*, is scheduled for publication soon. And yet another new lesbian press has opened: Ruth Colbourne started Shady Ladies early this year to publish lesbian romances. She wants to publish well-written and entertaining stories about women falling in love. Shady Ladies' first title will be *Surne in Gold* by Nene Adams.

Even the raunchier lesbian novels have a new home, albeit with a mainstream press. Masquerade Books used to have a lesbian imprint named Rosebud that published erotic novels and collections of stories, but this imprint, as well as its gay male counterpart, Badboy, are no longer in existence. A division of Virgin Publishing, called Sapphire, is publishing erotic novels for lesbians. They have put out nine novels already, such as *Millennium Fever* by Julia Wood and *All That Glitters* by Franca Nera, and another four are scheduled for the remainder of this year. Editor Kathleen Bryson wants to publish books that depict a positive sexuality. As she puts it, "There are many different types of sexual pleasure, and Sapphire aims to be a wide church."

For independent booksellers these new publishers are largely a welcome addition to the scene—readers want new books to read that are entertaining and reflect a bit of their own lives, and these publishers are helping provide them. The catch comes from one of the new tools previously mentioned, the World Wide Web. Many of these new publishers have become either associates of online giant amazon.com or provide links to that conglomerate for their customers to use. If independent publishers give their nods to chains and online-only companies by providing these links, it cuts out a core part of the feminist and lesbian ecosystem—feminist bookstores. And as has been written in these pages many times, feminist bookstores need feminist publishers need feminist customers need feminist bookstores. It is promising that when contacted about this topic, several of the publishers made changes accordingly, by including links to feminist bookstores that are on line, or by including lines like "Support your local independent bookstore" in their marketing emails to customers.

For readers, these new publishers, and established favorites like Cleis, New Victoria, Onlywomen, Press Gang, Seal (which is publishing fiction again!), and Spinsters, among others, will give us books that contain portraits of women like us and those we know, will continue to affirm our lives and lifestyles, and will continue to inspire, entertain, and enrich us. With both our purchasing and moral support, may they long flourish and publish books like those we have been privileged to enjoy from Naiad and Firebrand these many years.

Suzanne Corson lives in the San Francisco Bay Area and is one of the owners of Boadecia's Books. She has been published in Feminist Bookstore News *and* Girlfriends.

CENSORSHIP / INTELLECTUAL FREEDOM

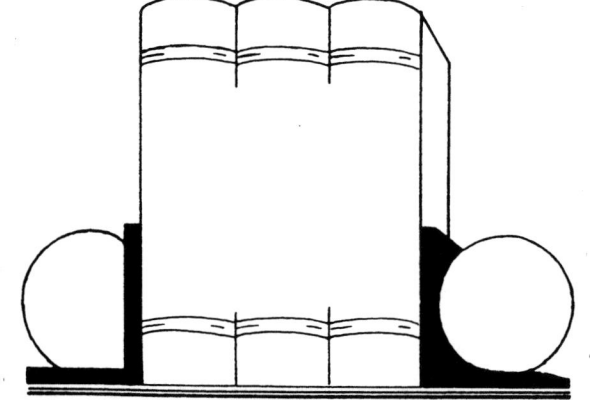

Intellectual Freedom Within the Profession: A Look Back at Freedom of Expression and the Alternative Library Press

Toni Samek

School of Library and Information Studies, University of Alberta
Toni.Samek@ualberta.ca

Momentum for an alternative library press was slow to build. But by the 1960s, social protest movements in larger society were mirrored in American librarianship. Activist librarians became more socially aware through involvement in the causes and issues espoused by the era's alternative press. Some librarians were intrigued by the novelty of the messages in the alternative press, others by the freshness of the medium itself. When, for example, publications like *The Oracle* (San Francisco), *The East Village Other* (New York), *The Fifth Estate* (Detroit), *The Paper* (East Lansing), *The Los Angeles Free Press* (Los Angeles), and *The Berkeley Barb* (Berkeley) began attracting national recognition because they questioned the objectivity of the establishment press in the mid-1960s, a subset of American librarians took note. They began to publish their own alternative library press. This new wave of library titles created a fresh forum for activities on behalf of *freedom of expression* within the library profession. The new publications printed viewpoints not treated by mainstream library periodicals such as *Library Journal*, *Wilson Library Bulletin*, and *American Libraries* and challenged the conformity of the professional discourse.

For context, this article begins with a Selected Alternative Library Press Chronology that traces key contributions to the alternative library press in the United States from its origins in the late 1960s to recent times. While all but two of the alternative library titles included in the Chronology are American, *Emergency Librarian* (Canadian) and *Librarians for Social Change* (U.K.) are included to illustrate that the alternative library press is not restricted to the U.S. And while the Chronology reflects print publication, the article's closing comments highlight key electronic forums that evolved out of the alternative library print publication base.

Revised version of article published in *Counterpoise* (1716 SW Williston Road, Gainesville, FL 32608), v. 4, nos. 1/2 (January/April 2000), pp. 10–16. Reprinted with permission.

Selected Alternative Library Press Chronology

1967–1973	*Synergy*
1969–1975	*Liberated Librarian's Newsletter*
1969–1979	*Women Library Workers*—continued as *WLW Journal* until 1994
1970–1995	*Sipapu*
1970	*Women in Libraries*
1971	*Prejudices and Antipathies: A Tract on the LC Subject Heads Concerning People*
1971–1980	*Alternatives in Print*
1971–1999	*Unabashed Librarian*
1972	*Revolting Librarians*
1972–1984	*Librarians for Social Change*—continued as *Social Change and Information Systems* (1985–)
1972–1980	*Current Awareness-Library Literature*
1973–1976	*Booklegger Magazine*
1973–1979	*Young Adult Alternative Newsletter*
1973–1998	*Emergency Librarian*—continued as *Teacher Librarian* (1998–)
1975	*The Living Z: A Guide to the Literature of the Counter-culture, the Alternative Press, and Little Magazines*
1977–	*On Equal Terms: A Thesaurus for Nonsexist Indexing and Cataloging*
1978–	*VOYA, Voice of Youth Advocates*
1979–	*New Pages*
1980–	*Feminist Collections*
1982	*Alternative Materials in Libraries*
1984–	*Alternative Library Literature*
1985–	*Social Change and Information Systems*
1990–	*Progressive Librarian*
1993–	*Librarians at Liberty*
1994–	*Information for Social Change*
1994–	*Alternative Publishers of Books in North America*
1995	*Zoia! Memoirs of Zoia Horn, Battler for the People's Right to Know*
1996–	*Alternative Literature: A Practical Guide for Librarians*
1997–	*Counterpoise: For Social Responsibilities, Liberty and Dissent*
1998	*Poor People and Library Services*

Each of the alternative library publications listed in the Chronology has a unique history. Because this article cannot accommodate each history, the author has chosen to profile three early alternative library titles in order to explore limitations to the *freedom of expression* that took place within library and information publishing in the formative years of the alternative library press's development. The three profiled titles are vanguard alternative library publications. They are also those titles for which the author has gathered the most primary research material.[1]

The first title profiled is *Synergy*—a periodical that *Library Journal* called "a vital acquisition for … feminist views … and a superb … example of lively, liberated library journalism."[2] *Synergy* paved the way for *Revolting Librarians, Booklegger Magazine, Emergency Librarian, Alternatives in Print, Prejudices & Antipathies*, and all of the other alternative library publications listed in the Chronology. But *Synergy*'s staff did more than spur interest in the alternative press. These librarians also urged library professionals to address social issues and to recognize the political context of their work. Ultimately, this threatened a profession that prided itself on its "neutral stance" by raising the important question—was librarianship "neutral" when it came to the provision of access to *any* form of information?

SYNERGY

In the late 1960s, the San Francisco Public Library's experimental Bay Area Reference Center (BARC) provided support reference services to 17 North Bay Cooperative Library System libraries scattered across six counties. BARC looked to non-commercial book publishers to find information on new areas of interest and in 1967 began to publish a monthly newsletter titled *Synergy* to serve as a reference tool and disseminate news of the project. *Synergy*'s "Update" section listed outstanding new additions to the San Francisco Public Library reference collection, while another section included a bibliography of topical importance "not obtainable through usual channels."[3]

San Francisco was a hotbed of social activity in 1967. From the city's 65,000 person anti-war demonstration held concomitantly with the Spring Mobilization Committee's New York City protest, to the influx of thousands of people for the "Summer of Love" activities, the Bay community manifested social change.[4] Celeste West, *Synergy*'s first editor commented on the relationship between San Francisco's transformation and the local library scene. She described the city as "a trend-mecca—whether it be communal living, campus riots, gay liberation, independent film making … you name it and we've got it." But what San Francisco had, she argued, was not reflected in library collections unless somebody took the time to pull together "the elusive printed material."[5] Thus, *Synergy* began examining the nature of library card catalogs, indexes, and selecting tools because its staff believed that such tools were mostly "rear-view mirrors" that provided little or no bibliographic access to the public's current information needs.

Synergy's staff believed that because librarians were not sufficiently trained to create access to and/or learn about where to find many forms of information, they were unable to fulfil their professional mandate to present balanced/multiple points of view. The passive nature of library practice grounded on a myth of "neutral" service understated this information access problem. Because librarians were followers and not leaders in the information marketplace, alternative press related topics received attention only when big publishers sensed profit. *Synergy* consistently included information about neglected topics. The April-May, 1968 issue, for example, criticized conventional library literature's lack of attention to subjects like astrology, Native Americans, the women's liberation movement, ecology, the drug revolution, library service to prisoners, the occult, the family, the underground press, and the criticisms of the establishment. In subsequent issues, *Synergy* provided coverage of these and other topics. But *Synergy* stood for more than just information access. Under West's direction, it called on librarians to become "pivotal agents to enforce" the Library Bill of Rights (see Closing Comments), to support a free press, and to develop a new professional attitude by shifting from "conserving and organizing" information to "generating or promoting it."[6] *Synergy* defined an alternative library culture that worried less about the library as a keeper of the cultural record, and more about the library as an active agent for change.

For a number of years, as part of its effort to provide information about the alternative press and alternative library activity, *Synergy*'s staff lobbied for the "Great Unreviewed," which constituted "60%+ of all books published."[7] Because standard reviewing journals like *Kirkus Reviews*, *Publishers Weekly* and *Choice* did not cover the alternative press, *Synergy* tried to fill the void. It encouraged subscribers to read intensively in their areas of specialty and to get involved in self-publication. But by the summer of 1973, problems arose.

In August, 1973, the *SRRT Newsletter* announced that California State librarian Ethel Crockett was terminating federal funding for *Synergy*—the journal that jump-started the library social responsibility movement in 1967. Crockett maintained that Title I of the Library Services and Construction Act funded demonstration projects for not more than two years and because *Synergy* had already received five, she told it to seek financial assistance elsewhere.[8] But while Crockett initially claimed she notified BARC of the funding cut on April 26 and followed it up with a May 4 memorandum to "Persons Interested in the Future of *Synergy*," she later admitted that somehow the "information was not given to the *Synergy* staff, so that the announcement that funds would, indeed, be cut off after this June 30 came as a shock." Celeste West maintained that the abrupt notice left little time to save *Synergy* and, disgusted with the funding flap and tired of hassles, she resigned. In her resignation letter, West asked "WHAT DOES THE STATE LIBRARY HAVE IN ITS CROCK O'RELEVANCE?" She believed *Synergy*'s many bibliographies/reviews on topics such as feminism, native Americans, unions, children's liberation, occultism, head comix, radicals in the professions, free schools, and independent publishing were very "relevant" to the contemporary library world.[9]

The San Francisco Public Library talked publicly of taking over the magazine, but BARC feared censorship. BARC members recognized the library press was not free. In general, it was monopolized by a blend of associations and institutions and was controlled by particular publishing interests. Even the vanguard alternative library title *Synergy*, for example, was not only financially dependent on a federal grant, but each issue required San Francisco Public Library's approval before publication. The library had previously "bollixed five different reprint offers which might have brought in money," West argued, "choked creativity on the bone of prior censorship," and suppressed "protesting editorials." West maintained she had to kidnap the final *Synergy* issue from the printer just to get it published. Other staff members complained of "odd military-school-like reprimands" and threats that they would be denied legal salary increases.[10]

Ironically, in its last year of existence *Synergy* received its second H.W. Wilson Periodical Award and sold 2,000 copies per month. In hindsight, West argued (without providing evidence) that Crockett's real objection to the high-impact periodical was not a question of money. Instead, she asserted, California governor Ronald Reagan had appointed Crockett state librarian, and in West's view, directed Crockett "to kill" *Synergy*—the flagship alternative library publication that fostered an attitude for change in the profession, gave rise to a wave of alternative library literature, provided a ground for library activists to express their opinions and make connections, and "upped the ante on library periodicals" at a time when most librarians remained the "purveyors of Reader's Digested Status Quo print."[11]

ALTERNATIVES IN PRINT

At the American Library Association's (ALA) annual 1970 conference in Detroit, the Round Table on the Social Responsibilities of Libraries elected Patricia Schuman (New York City Community College) as Action Council Coordinator. She immediately welcomed volunteers for a new Task Force on Alternative Books in

Print. The Task Force evolved out of the Round Table on the Social Responsibilities of Libraries's interest in the Radical Research Center's efforts (most notably its *Alternative Press Index*, 1970–) and the lack of information about small groups working for social change and what they were publishing.[12] Brooklyn College activist librarian Jackie Eubanks spoke about her embarrassment that the *Alternative Press Index* began outside ALA and urged those in Detroit not to allow the same end to come to other materials produced by groups in struggle for change.[13] As an active Round Table on the Social Responsibilities of Libraries member, a volunteer indexer for the Radical Research Center, and a veteran in the alternative press movement, Eubanks took a leadership role in the new task force.

Almost immediately, the Task Force on Alternative Books In Print began work on a strategy to make libraries and their collections relevant for their publics.[14] First, the Task Force proposed to compile a list of non-serial publications available from underground movement presses and allied organizations left out of *Books in Print*. Second, it planned to revise ALA exhibit policies which reinforced the concept that "the biggest are best" and which charged "too much for the small publisher to afford to exhibit at ALA meetings."[15] Initially the Task Force planned to create an adjunct to regular reference tools that would enhance library and bookstore access to media produced by nonprofit, anti-profit, counterculture, third world, and other activist groups.

When *Synergy*'s October, 1970 issue went into distribution, Eubanks and fellow New Yorker Mimi Penchansky of Queens College had just completed a letter campaign to over 1,500 organizations, many of which had been listed in the *Directory of the American Left*. They had identified 250 non-serial materials for the Task Force on Alternative Books In Print's proposed publication project—*Alternatives in Print*. Next, they adopted the *Alternative Press Index* subject headings and persuaded Ohio State University Library Director Hugh Atkinson to get the university press to publish it.[16]

The Task Force opted for an academic publisher for several reasons. First, commercial publishers judged the proposed publication unprofitable and not sufficiently market tested. Second, alternative press publishers did not have enough start-up capital to get the project off the ground. Third, ALA's publishing procedures were too arduous for a project intended to move quickly. Round Table on the Social Responsibilities of Libraries member Joan Marshall (Brooklyn College) was especially angry with ALA and library leaders for not picking up projects rejected by commercial publishers. She believed ALA needed to support the alternative press.[17]

Round Table on the Social Responsibilities of Libraries members like Marshall, Eubanks, and Penchansky were deeply committed to providing access to the alternative press because they recognized librarians' traditional inability to balance collections by ignoring relatively inaccessible materials. They had no illusions about the profession's "neutrality" and believed that ALA-accredited library schools trained students to build collections using mainstream selection tools and venues. In their view, the Task Force on Alternative Books In Print offered an opportunity to counter the effect of conventional training. Eubanks cited her own experience at library school as an example.

Throughout her University of Chicago library education, she noted, she had passively accepted many traditional views. Only on the job did she learn to "hear and respect the real questions" put to her as a reference librarian at Brooklyn College Library. This experience persuaded Eubanks that many librarians made purchases "in a fog" and needed to pay more attention both to the types of information to which patrons needed access and to the political economy of publishing. She believed the prevailing mode of education to be insufficient because the models on which the purchasing policies were based were commercial. Eubanks was disheartened, for example, that library schools lacked courses in publishing and the book trade, and that the collections and acquisitions courses were too often "concentrated entirely on the freedom to read issue" and seen "entirely from a civil libertarian standpoint." In her opinion, librarianship's commitment to the dissemination of information, as expressed in the Library Bill of Rights (see Closing Comments), was largely ineffective. If librarians really wanted to convey information to the public, she believed, they needed to get involved in publishing.[18]

With Eubanks at the helm, the Task Force on Alternative Books In Print lobbied to get small and alternative presses into the standard library indexes, catalogs and bibliographic references. It also launched a campaign to change ALA's policies on the leasing of exhibit-hall space so that ability to pay would replace set fees. Because small presses had less money to spend on booth space they were often excluded from library conferences. Large commercial publishers were a regular presence.[19] Initially the Task Force used the Round Table on the Social Responsibilities of Libraries as a vehicle for setting up small press displays at ALA conferences. On varying occasions, displays at the Round Table on the Social Responsibilities of Libraries exhibit-hall booth were regarded as a part of the Round Table's programs. Eventually the Task Force succeeded in getting ALA's approval for a special section of less expensive exhibit space where small presses could afford to exhibit.[20] The Task Force also set up exhibits at smaller regional library conferences, at meetings of the American Booksellers Association, and at the National Women's Studies Association. Furthermore, when Eubanks and other Task Force members attended national and international book fairs, they took Round Table on the Social Responsibilities of Libraries materials with them.

While the Task Force on Alternative Books In Print stood out as the Round Table on the Social Responsibilities of Libraries group most involved with the alternative press, the Round Table's general goal—to make libraries more relevant to the public—provided the impetus for other task forces to address issues of access. The Ethnic Materials Task Force (later an ALA round table), for example, sought to make ethnic materials by and for Blacks, Puerto Ricans, American Indians, Asian Americans, and Chicanos more accessible to patrons and to make the materials better known to other librarians. The Task Force produced lists of publishers who were producing ethnic materials as well as descriptions of the kinds of information that was being published—short stories, poetry, fiction, informational guides, and so on. Task Force members spoke with publishers to develop better working relationships and invited them to participate in ALA programs. Other task forces focused on literature for women, gays and lesbians, labour workers, political prisoners, migrant workers, etc. And all benefited from the efforts of the Task Force on Alternative Books in Print, which functioned as a central part of both the Round Table on the Social Responsibilities of Libraries's structure and mission.

Prejudices and Antipathies: A Tract on the LC Subject Heads Concerning People

Sanford Berman earned his library degree from the Catholic University of America in 1961. By 1970, he had worked in libraries in the United States, Germany, Zambia, and Uganda. Berman had an avid interest in radical literature and a talent for library acquisitions as well as cataloguing and classification. His involvement in the library movement largely developed through his interest in the alternative press. For example, he read *Synergy* regularly, he corresponded with the Radical Research Center's Mary McKenney, he published his own alternative bibliographies, and he drew attention to and criticized undemocratic library practices. In early 1969, for example, Berman sent a letter to *Library Journal* from Zambia arguing that the Library of Congress' subject heading list enshrined and perpetuated "a racist/colonial bias." He further requested the Round Table on the Social Responsibilities of Libraries to undertake a study "of the extent to which our major cataloguing and classification schemes are white, imperialist and Christian-oriented," and to make suggestions for improvement.[21]

On May 12, 1970, ALA's Publishing Services Senior Editor Richard A. Gray asked Berman about his "provocative" letter. Gray agreed that subject headings were "saturated with Western chauvinism," argued that such research was "urgently needed," encouraged Berman to undertake a comprehensive study of the ethnic prejudices, and indicated that ALA Publishing was "seriously interested" in such a work. Gray warned Berman, however, that the study would be controversial, but that in his view "a good lively controversy" was just what ALA needed "to counteract the prevailing tone of dullness in professional literature."[22] Berman accepted Gray's challenge. Because he conceived the project as part of a Round Table on the Social Responsibilities of Libraries study, he enlisted the aid of several Round Table members. Together they intended to harness the concept of social responsibility for the proposed publication, and while Berman recognized the study would not only "jolt" the profession to reconsider "one of its most basic tools in a more discriminating analytic manner," he also suspected it would infuriate many people.[23]

Berman's tract was not designed as "an attack" on the Library of Congress editors, but as a means to increase librarians' awareness that "inherited assumptions and underlying values" influence their work. He argued, for example, that the entry of works in library catalogues under the term "NIGGER" was "obviously biased." Thus, he asserted, "if librarians defend their right as educators to present all points of view in their collections, they must accept their obligation to provide an approach to their collections that is equally without bias, and which does not reinforce the psychological, sociological, economic, political, etc. assumptions and prejudices of their readers." Ultimately, his manuscript focused on the "realm" of subject headings "that deal with people and cultures—in short, with humanity," and included revised headings for subjects such as race, nationalities, faiths, ethnic groups, politics, peace, Labor, law enforcement, man, woman, sex, children, and youth.[24]

In August, 1970, Gray wrote Eubanks that the association intended to publish Berman's manuscript after "suitable revisions," but that because of her involvement with the alternative press and being under "current pressures for new directions" within ALA, he sought her counsel and advice.[25] Eubanks agreed to read the manuscript. Meanwhile, however, Gray began expressing reservations about publishing the work. In an August 18 letter he asked Berman to "tone down the emotionally charged phrases and locutions."[26] Berman refused, arguing that he would rather see the book go unpublished than for it to become a "mish-mash of compromises."

"Will ALA print *what* I write the *way* I write it?" he asked brashly on August 30. "And is ALA *ready* to issue a radical, muckracking tract even though it may not wholly accord in form or philosophy with your usual editorial policy and predilections, nor perhaps with the current sentiments and sensibilities of a majority of the profession?"[27]

Gray responded on October 6. It was normal procedure that highly argumentative works proceed slowly through the publishing process, he said, and because ALA was an academic publisher, it required "thorough scholarly documentation," especially because Berman's work was "severely critical of an old and venerable institution." ALA could publish a "temperately reasoned critique" of Library of Congress subject headings," he said, but it could not, "by its imprint, endorse a book which often partakes of the nature of a diatribe." Gray ended by saying Berman was free to confer with other publishers and that the Memorandum of Agreement between them was terminated.[28]

On January 4, 1971, Berman asked Eric Moon (who had become President of Scarecrow Press in 1968) if he was interested in publishing *Prejudices and Antipathies*.[29] Moon did not hesitate. After reading only part, he wrote Berman that it was a landmark book and enclosed a publishing contract. Berman quickly signed it, and Moon turned the manuscript into what Berman called "an honest-to-God book within nine months, static-free."[30]

Jackie Eubanks, who watched all this from the sidelines, was pleased that Scarecrow had picked up *Prejudices and Antipathies* and furious that ALA had rejected it. She recognized in the Berman-ALA brouhaha a common association practice, i.e., ALA said it supported the idea of collecting material on all sides of issues, but it did not practice what it preached. She later asked ALA Editorial Committee Chairman Donald E. Wright if he had seen the correspondence between ALA and Berman, and informed him that the Task Force on Alternatives in Print would not submit *Alternatives in Print* to ALA for publishing—first because it was so slow, but more importantly because of the kind of "pre-censorship" efforts Berman experienced with his manuscript. Did not ALA Publishing Services, she asked, support intellectual freedom?[31]

Closing Comments

Because this article profiles only three select alternative library titles, it is difficult to draw broad conclusions about the whole of the alternative library press. However, even the brief histories provided supply some evidence that there have been limitations to the *freedom of expression* within library and information publishing. On one hand, ALA's 1967 version of its Library Bill of Rights (see Appendix)—instituted the same year that *Synergy* began publication—instructed librarians to combat censorship and to protect *freedom of expression*. On the other hand, some of the alternative voices in library publishing were outright censored, others were simply ignored.

Regarding the latter, in May, 1970, James O. Lehman published a survey of what 101 American colleges used as selection tools. He found that librarians favoured *Choice, Library Journal, New York Times, Saturday Review, Publishers Weekly, Booklist,* and *Wilson Library Bulletin* as selection aids. Survey respondents seemed unaware of the alternative press review media as a tool for the library selection process.[32] Lehman's conclusions came as a reminder to alternative library publishers that despite the directive in the Library Bill of Rights to represent all points of view, some librarians failed to stretch their imaginations beyond the mainstream horizons. The same can be said for some mainstream library publishers. For example, editors of *Library Literature*—the conventional indexing tool published by H.W. Wilson Co.—delayed coverage of many alternative library titles. The award-winning *Synergy* was not indexed until 1972, one year before its demise. Other titles were never covered by the periodical index. In practice then, American librarianship disseminated a subtext that offset the formal message of the Library Bill of Rights. The subtext reinforced the preservation of the status quo.

Today, library association groups such as the Alternatives in Print Task Force of the Social Responsibilities Round Table (formerly the Round Table on the Social Responsibilities of Libraries) of ALA (publisher of *Counterpoise: For Social Responsibilities, Liberty and Dissent*), independent library groups such as the Progressive Librarian's Guild (self-described as "left-wing" of the Social Responsibilities Round Table of ALA and publisher of the *Progressive Librarian*), independent library publishers such as CRISES Press (publisher of *Librarians at Liberty* and *Alternative Publishers of Books in North America)*, and a broad range of electronically-based forums such as *Anarchist Librarians Web, Street Librarian, Library Juice,* and *librarian.net* carry on the work started by *Synergy* more than thirty years ago.[33] They continue to examine the library in its social context. They extend the reach of the professional discourse beyond the status quo. Perhaps most importantly, they provide forums for *freedom of expression* within the library and information studies press. This is as it should be. As professionals, librarians have the responsibility for "the development and maintenance of intellectual freedom."[34] As citizens, librarians have the fundamental right to *freedom of expression*.

Author's Notes

Much of the material included in this paper is taken from my dissertation. See Toni Samek. (1998) *Intellectual Freedom and Social Responsibility: An Ethos of American Librarianship, 1967–1973*. Madison, Wisconsin: University of Wisconsin-Madison. [Dissertation]

A longer version of this paper appeared as "Library and Information Studies Press and Freedom of Expression" in *Information science: Where has it been, where is it going? Proceedings of the 27th Annual Conference of the Canadian Association for Information Science*, 267–301.

Thanks to the Faculty of Education, University of Alberta for a grant to fund post-doctoral research related to this paper. Thanks to Kate MacInnes for her research assistance on the University of Alberta grant project. And thanks to Taralee Alcock for her comments.

Appendix—ALA's Library Bill of Rights, 1967

The Council of the American Library Association reaffirms its belief in the following basic policies which should govern the services of all libraries.

1. As a responsibility of library service, books and other library materials selected should be chosen for values of interest, information and enlightenment of all the people of the community. In no case should any library materials be excluded because of the race or nationality or the social, political, or religious views of the authors.
2. Libraries should provide books and other materials presenting all points of view concerning the problems and issues of our times; no library materials should be proscribed or removed from libraries because of partisan or doctrinal disapproval.
3. Censorship should be challenged by libraries in the maintenance of their responsibility to provide public information and enlightenment.
4. Libraries should cooperate with all persons and groups concerned with resisting abridgement of free expression and free access to ideas.
5. The rights of an individual to the use of a library should not be denied or abridged because of his age, race, religion, national origins or social or political views.
6. As an institution of education for democratic living, the library should welcome the use of its meeting rooms for socially useful and cultural activities and discussion of current public questions. Such meeting places should be available on equal terms to all groups in the community regardless of the beliefs and affiliations of their members, provided that the meetings be open to the public.[35]

References

1. Unpublished manuscripts, archival papers, and published primary and secondary literature constitute the formal research base. Three manuscript collections were particularly important: (1) the American Library Association's Social Responsibility Round Table Papers and (2) the Sanford Berman Papers, both housed at the University Archives, University of Illinois, Urbana-Champaign, and (3) the Radical Research Center Papers housed at the State Historical Society of Wisconsin. Published primary literature consists of newsletters, journals, monographs, and conference proceedings. The secondary published literature for this paper consists of research studies, dissertations, journal articles, and monographs from a variety of disciplines including mass communications, cultural studies, women's studies, and anticanonical studies.
2. "SYNERGY," *Library Journal* 96, no. 15 (1 September 1971): 2593.
3. Richard Cronenberg, "SYNERGIZING Reference Service in the San Francisco Bay Region," *ALA Bulletin* 62, no. 11 (December 1968): 1379, 1384.
4. Edward P. Morgan, *The Sixties Experience: Hard Lessons About Modern America* (Philadelphia: Temple University Press, 1991), xix–xx.
5. Celeste West, "Stop! The Print Is Killing Me," *Synergy* 33 (1971): 3.
6. Celeste West, "Congloms: Stalking the Literary-Industrial Complex," *American Libraries* 13, no. 5 (1982): 299; "A Conversation with Celeste West," 3–6.
7. West, "Stop!," 3.
8. *Synergy* (1973), ALA's Sanford Berman Papers, University of Illinois at Urbana-Champaign, University Archives. See also Edward Swanson, "*Synergy* Protest" *American Libraries* 4, no. 7 (July/August 1973): 408; Noel Peattie, "The Fortunes of *Synergy*," *Sipapu* 4, no. 2 (July 1973): 8–10.
9. "*Synergy* Editor Resigns," *American Libraries* 7, no. 4 (July/August 1973): 412.
10. "Celeste West on Synergy," *Sipapu* 4, no. 2 (July 1973): 71.
11. "A Conversation with Celeste West," *Technicalities* 2, no. 4 (April 1982): 3–6.
12. Add a note about RRC.
13. ALA Meetings, 1969-70, SRRT-ALA General Meeting Proposal for an Alternative "BIP" National Task Force, ALA's SRRT Papers, Box 8, University of Illinois at Urbana-Champaign, University Archives.
14. Noel Peattie, *A Passage for Dissent: The Best of Sipapu, 1970–1988* (Jefferson, NC: McFarland, 1989), 138.
15. Jackie Eubanks to Martha Ann Kollmorgan, 25 March 1974, ALA's SRRT Papers, Box 7.
16. "Librarians in Action," *Workforce* (March-April 1973): 20–23.
17. "SRRT-ified Action—A Task Force Report for SLJ," 734–735.

18. *Sipapu* 7, no. 2 (July 1976): 1–5.

19. Jackie Eubanks to Martha Ann Kollmorgan, 25 March 1974, ALA's SRRT Papers, Box 7.

20. Betty-Carol Sellen (1970–87), Getting Library Attention, ALA's SRRT Papers, Box 11.

21. Sanford Berman, "Chauvinistic Headings," *Library Journal* 94, no. 4 (February 15 1969): 695.

22. Richard A. Gray, Senior Editor (ALA) to Sanford Berman, 12 May 1970, SRRT Correspondence, 1969–75, ALA's Sanford Berman Papers.

23. Sanford Berman to Patricia Schuman, Joan Marshall, and Sandy Goin, 17 June 1970, SRRT Correspondence, 1969–75, ALA's Sanford Berman Papers.

24. Sanford Berman, *Prejudices and Antipathies: A Tract on the LC Subject Heads Concerning People* (Metuchen, N.J.: Scarecrow Press, 1971), ix–xiv.

25. Richard A. Gray to Jackie Eubanks, 13 August 1970, SRRT Correspondence, 1969–75, ALA's SRRT Papers, Box 11.

26. Richard A. Gray to Sanford Berman, 18 August 1970, ALA's SRRT Papers, Box 11.

27. Sanford Berman to Richard A. Gray, 30 August 1970, ALA's SRRT Papers, Box 11.

28. Richard A. Gray to Sanford Berman, 6 October 1970, ALA's SRRT Papers, Box 11.

29. Sanford Berman to Eric Moon, 4 January 1971, ALA's SRRT Papers, Box 11.

30. Sanford Berman to Gerald R. Shields, 18 February 1972, ALA's SRRT Papers, Box 11.

31. Jackie Eubanks to Donald E. Wright, 22 February 1971, ALA's SRRT Papers, Box 11.

32. James O. Lehman, "*Choice* as a Selection Tool," *Wilson Library Bulletin* 44, no. 9 (May 1970): 960.

33. *Alternative Publishers of Books in North America* 4 was produced by the Alternatives in Print Task Force of the Social Responsibilities Round Table of ALA, but published by CRISES Press.

34. Canadian Library Association Statement on Intellectual Freedom (1974).

35. *Intellectual Freedom Manual*, 5th ed. (Chicago: American Library Association, Office for Intellectual Freedom, 1996), 13–14.

"Discourse and Censorship: Librarians and the Ideology of Freedom"

Steven R. Harris
University of Tennessee

By way of introduction, I would like to give a few warnings about my point of view, just so there will be no confusion about my political orientation or the impression that I have a hidden agenda:

First, while I believe strongly in the rights of individuals regarding intellectual freedom, there are certain of these rights that I think should *not* be applied to corporations.

Secondly, my goal today is to alienate you from the perceived principles and foundations of librarianship. I do this, however, not because I enjoy antagonizing people, but because there are areas that I think we could make valuable changes in the profession.

Third, I must say that I'm an unrepentant post-structuralist. You can go ahead and blame me now, as seems popular in the media these days, for all the problems of academia.

And since I will be talking about post-structuralism, I might as well also warn you that I will undoubtedly be using the "F" word today: "*Foucault*!" A quotation from Michel Foucault (1984) may serve to explain my intent. He says:

> The critique of what we are is at one and the same time the historical analysis of the limits that are imposed on us and an experiment with the possibility of going beyond them.

To begin then, it is a widely held belief that intellectual freedom is at the very foundation of what librarianship is all about. Gordon Conable states in the "Intellectual Freedom Manual" that:

> Libraries embody the firm belief that information must not be the exclusive province of a privileged few and that it should be widely and freely available to all.

Yet, it seems the rhetoric of this statement does not coincide with library practice. This may appear, on the face of it, to be completely absurd. Any casual examination of our literature will reveal an abundance of books and articles touting the importance of these values to the profession of librarianship. I would argue, however, that a "close" examination of the literature reveals uncertainty and vagueness on these issues.

Wayne Wiegand makes a similar charge in a recent issue of *Library Trends*, and furthermore, remarks that we are blind to ideas outside our own discipline:

> [T]he library profession has, for several generations now, been content not to engage in debate with outside experts, not to leave its insulated world ... nowhere are the unquestioned absolutes more evident than in the discourse surrounding the Library Bill of Rights ... by the last decade of the twentieth century, this discourse seems

---

Reprinted with permission from *Counterpoise* (1716 SW Williston Road, Gainesville, FL 32608), v. 3, nos. 3/4 (July/October 1999), pp. 14–18.

to have evolved a reality of its own that declines to engage the powerful ideas being debated in a broader intellectual world.

The ideas of the broader intellectual world that Wiegand refers to are mainly those of "cultural critique" and "post-structuralism." Although many of these methods have been applied in other social and humanistic fields for over 30 years, librarianship has remained fairly impervious to them—excepting the occasional incursion by Michael Harris, Wayne Wiegand, and a few other scholars.

Discourse theory is one of the recent critical ideas that can, I think, shed light on how librarians have come to adopt certain ideologies and how those ideologies operate, through discourse, within the profession. It explores how our discourse reproduces, over and over, the values of the ruling ideology. It is also a method we can use to examine how our current beliefs came to hold their current configuration. This is not actually "history" per se, but what Nietzsche called a "Genealogy of Morals":

> [T]here is a world of difference between the reason for something coming into existence in the first place and the ultimate use to which it is put, its actual application and integration into a system of goals...

Louise Robbins observed this phenomenon at work in the library profession through the "sometimes contradictory dual purposes" of our intellectual freedom stance, which is divided in its goals, as I shall explain later, between a desire to protect individual rights, and a need to establish professional autonomy.

Discourse, as Foucault repeatedly noted, is a system of meaning formation that is grounded in social and material institutions. But is not a system that is taught and learned in the traditional sense of those words. It arises only through initiation and experience. The truth that a particular discourse reveals, however, always masks the very process that produced it. Edward Said describes this process more extensively:

> One does not really make discourse at will, or statements in it, without first belonging—in some cases unconsciously, but at any rate involuntarily—to the ideology and institutions that guarantee its existence.

Louis Althusser extends this idea to say that ideologies are always expressed in material existence; that ideologies regenerate themselves through the material institutions that they create; that ideology becomes (or is *always*) identical to the "lived experience." Thus, in librarianship for example, there is no difference between "*being*" librarian and "*believing*" in the ideology of librarianship.

Foucault has discussed this model a great deal, particularly as it applies to the development of "disciplines" within the social sciences. He has identified the gatekeeper function that all disciplines perform, and how the gatekeepers of a discipline maintain and confer status within the field. Educational programs, such as library schools, perform the initial indoctrination, but many other institutions continue the function of delimiting the field of study. Institutions such as professional, peer-reviewed journals maintain a unity of voice within the subject. The process of promotion and tenure insures that an acceptable approach to the subject is employed. All these mechanisms provide the discipline with a means of maintaining its chosen ground. There is a sort of play on words throughout Foucault's work that all disciplines (noun) involve the discipline (verb) of its subjects. That the disciplining of knowledge involves the literal physical disciplining of bodies. Ultimately, this means that all disciplines practice a rather severe form of censorship on their practitioners.

Another focus of post-structuralist critical theory has been an interrogation of the principles of Enlightenment liberal humanism—principles which librarianship takes as sacrosanct. Some have called this vein of post-modern discussion "anti-humanism." Others have said that this approach demonstrates a lack of belief in individual freedoms on the part of the post-structuralist practitioners. The recent so-called "Culture Wars" is an attack on the supposed "undemocratic" impulse behind current theory. But I think this is a misreading of the post-structuralist approach. Theorists like Foucault and Althusser along with Adorno, Horkheimer, and Marcuse have noted repeatedly that many of the ideas of "enlightenment" are in fact used as instruments of oppression.

Not surprisingly, much of this critique proceeds from a belief in Marxist principles and a rejection of capitalism. Sue Curry Jansen says, for example, that "libertarian ideals arose under conditions of colonial repression and matured in consonance with the maturation of industrial capitalism." Adorno, Horkheimer, and Herbert Schiller further assert that the development of a "culture industry" has enabled certain "elites" to monopolize and manipulate the "culture" and "media"—and present an outward belief in freedom while at the same time actually rejecting any true freedom of expression. This establishes, in the words of Horkheimer and Adorno, an "Enlightenment of Mass Deception."

Herbert Marcuse expands on this idea in an article entitled: "Repressive Tolerance":

> [T]olerance is an end in itself only when it is truly universal, practiced by the rulers as well as by the ruled, by the lords as well as by the peasants, by the sheriffs as well as by their victims."

Lest we think Marcuse refers only to a feudal past, rather than our own modern times, Robert McChesney observes that "In our society, corporations and the wealthy enjoy a power every bit as immense as that enjoyed by the lords and royalty of feudal times."

McChesney also recognizes the hypocrisy of a corporate media establishment that goes to great lengths to tell us that any challenge to their power is a challenge to democracy itself. Thus, the recent Telecommunications Act, which gave away great amounts of public bandwidth to a very few media conglomerates, is touted as a "Great Day for America." Or, to give another example, any discussion of limiting campaign spending by the very wealthy is called an infringement of First Amendment principles.

Librarianship functions pretty much in ignorance of this kind of cultural discussion. As Michael Harris noted almost 15 years ago, librarianship is founded on a firm belief in the pluralism of our society—that we are all free agents with equal access to ideas and that ideas circulate freely within a system of production that controls only the "quality."

The notion of intellectual freedom in librarianship rests largely on Enlightenment ideals, such as the concept of a free press. Journalism, itself, reveres revolution-era America as the birthplace of a fully free and autonomous press. Part of this belief is a mythology that arises, as Sue Jansen notes, in the need to establish journalism as a discipline, to elevate it to a Profession.

"Journalistic professionalism," she says, "succeeded in reducing the visibility of abuses of the free press. But it also disenfranchised lay criticism by fostering the impression that members of the public lack the "expert technical and managerial knowledge necessary to comprehend and debate, competently, issues involving editorial decision-making." Today, however, as press ownership has become more and more obscured by corporate bureaucracy, the notion of who, precisely, is responsible for the editorial content becomes more and more obscured also. As Jansen notes, this renders the true censor "invisible and thereby permit[s them] ... to operate outside of the rules of participatory democracy."

As in the journalistic professions, a reverence of librarianship for the ideas of liberal Enlightenment will not allow for a questioning of those writings. This is not unusual, in view of that fact that the profession's own immediate past is infused with anything but liberal enlightenment. It is as though we would skip backward over our own history and adopt something nobler. Therefore, we frequently see appeals to John Stuart Mill, John Locke and John Milton in the library literature. Milton's "Areopagitica" is particularly popular.

Fred Stielow, for example, who is an otherwise insightful historian I might add, quotes extensively from Milton ("As good almost kill a Man as kill a good Book.") and then asserts that this view "prefigures the opinions of many librarians today." That may literally be true, but it is a view of Milton that fails to look behind the rhetoric of "Areopagitica," which was, after all, an impassioned and partisan plea delivered before Parliament. Jansen says it is better "read as personal and sectarian pleading: as a lobby for special privileges for authors who belong to certain Puritan churches..." and that "this apostle of Liberalism served as a Censor to Cromwell's government."

What then is the history that we skip over when me embrace the Enlightenment? A number of historians, including Stielow, Harris, Wiegand, Louis Robbins, Evelyn Geller, and Dennis Thomison have noted that it is a history of continually striving to attain professional respect and autonomy, and that censorship figured prominently in that history from start to finish.

The America of the late 1800s was a decidedly different place than what we now occupy. The society of the time clearly favored "high" over "low" culture, aristocratic over proletarian values. Librarianship in American developed squarely within this milieu. Harris argues that it arose *because* of this sentiment. the desire not only to "uplift" the masses, but perhaps more so, to "control" them. It was probably not that clear-cut; many librarians truly wanted to do both. When married with the idea, firmly held by librarians, of the inherent pluralism of our society, the desire to uplift can then be seen as a simple technical problem—"The Best Books to the Most People" in Dewian terms—and requires no thought as to ideology or social ramifications.

In the nineteenth century, the desire to procure the "best books" meant censorship was viewed as a vital part of what a librarian did. In an article entitled "The Librarian as Censor," written at the beginning of the 20th century, Arthur Bostwick makes a humorous reference to Shakespeare in saying that librarians had censorship "thrust upon them." This is a rather inaccurate or at least misguided view of library history. If anything, librarians seized upon censorship as their own personal bailiwick. As Evelyn Geller notes, the value of censorship was that it allowed for professional autonomy for librarians, autonomy from the clientele and superiority to the clientele. The values of the librarian rather than the interests of the public drove book collecting. This attitude developed, in Geller's view, largely because the public was the most easily confronted constituency. At a time when their professional values depended to a degree on community acceptance, "the notion of censorship or freedom required a community mandate, " and "acceptance of the librarian's authority." Rather than seek autonomy from government of public agents, librarians sought autonomy from public opinion. They curried favor, however, with their boards and government superiors by adopting a class view of freedom. Censorship could be attacked, if you were talking about restricting the rights of the upper crust, but since the lower classes could be adversely affected by "coarse" literature, they had best be protected from such materials.

Geller and Stielow note how the professional attitudes toward censorship gradually began to change as the 20th century progressed, but ironically, that this change was still motivated by the desire to maintain professional autonomy. By the 1920s, Geller says:

> The freedom invoked was the institutional defense of freedom, in which trustees and librarians united against community censors—a defense consistent with ALA's courtship of trustees.

The opposition to censorship lay in protecting the librarian's discretion in developing the collection. Self-censorship, after all, could achieve the same end as legislated or legalistic measures.

It was only in the wake of McCarthyism that librarianship began to develop a different notion of freedom, one that insisted on the librarian's autonomy from direct government control. But Red Baiting inspired the profession to adopt a different tactic in defending their prerogative—Patriotism! We began to wrap ourselves in the flag to fend off attacks by McCarthy's goons. And we had a new weapon in this defense: The Library Bill of Rights. The LBR is an interesting document from a discourse point of view. Its references to the U.S. constitution are of course clear. It implies that librarians were, after all, defending the freedoms handed down to us by the Founding Fathers. ALA adopted its first LBR in 1948, but it was a several years before the values it espoused were widely held by librarians.

In 1953, the "Freedom to Read" statement was drafted, as an augmentation of the LBR. In the FTR, librarians enlisted the support of publishers and booksellers. FTR stated that "Freedom to read is ESSENTIAL to our democracy." Much like the LBR, it said that the library was "an institution to educate for democratic living." As though "democratic living" was impossible without libraries. Librarians began to trot out the LBR and FTR as a demonstration of their unbiased defense of intellectual freedom, despite the fact that, as Robbins observes, "their boards were composed almost exclusively of white middle- to upper-class individuals." And males at that, I might add.

Both these documents, however, are full of equivocation about intellectual freedom. In the freedoms that it outlined, the FTR made concessions to the great fear of obscenity, stating that the laws against it should be vigorously enforced. The LBR in its various revisions went to great pains to deny protection to "untrue" publications, leaving to the librarian the determination of what was and was not true. It was only in the late 1960 that these equivocal elements were edited away.

Even after many revisions the LBR continues to be a problematic document. It calls itself a "bill of rights," but its points don't address whose rights are being protected, in fact, most of the statements don't sound like rights at all, but more like professional obligations. Use of the passive voice is pervasive: "Materials should not be excluded," it says. Excluded by whom, we are not told. Libraries should provide materials on a variety of issues, it says. As though libraries were themselves autonomous. "Libraries should challenge censorship." Can a library challenge censorship, or isn't that the task of the librarian? "Libraries should cooperate" with those who oppose censorship. Again, can libraries act in this manner?

The absence of any librarians in the LBR, much less an active verb, is unusual and very telling. Clearly, the document is intended to educate us about our professional responsibilities, but is also seems addressed to the general public, stating in a very passive aggressive way that "this is the way libraries are—get used to it."

Only in the late 1960s and early 1970s did some notion that perhaps librarians were not doing such a great job of protecting democracy begin to penetrate the profession. In 1968 the Social Responsibilities Round Table was born, riding on the belief that many kinds of publications were *not* finding their way onto the library shelf—that librarians were guilty of holding the same biases and prejudices as the population at large. In 1972 this view came into full conflict with the status quo, when the old guard made a frontal assault on the new socially responsible upstarts. David Berninghausen, a former chair of ALAs Intellectual Freedom Committee, in an article published in *Library Journal*, attacked the notion of Social Responsibility within librarianship: "Antithesis in Librarianship: Social Responsibility vs. the Library Bill of Rights." The language of the title itself clearly delineated Berninghausen's view. There is no gray area: librarians cannot be socially responsible and uphold the LBR at the same time. Since, as he goes on to state, intellectual freedom is the very foundation of librarianship, then those who practice social responsibility are doing something other than librarianship. A collection of essays

Berninghausen published a few years later takes the same moral high ground. In *The Flight from Reason* he implies that maintaining an unbiased attitude toward the library and its collections is a direct philosophical descendant of rational Enlightenment humanism. He takes great pleasure in casting his own point of view as "rational" and the opinion of his opposition as based only on "gut reaction," as he calls it.

While the whole conflict probably cemented SRRT's place within ALA, as Toni Samek has pointed out, Berninghausen really won out in the end

> [Berninghausen scared] librarians away from the topic of social responsibility by playing to ALA's deep concern for legality and ... "action-crippling fear" about its "extremely favorable tax-status."

Such fears "paralyzed the library community" from further involvement in social responsibility.

I want to turn for a moment to a discussion of the term "marketplace of ideas," because it is often recognized as an important element of Enlightenment thinking. I believe it is a damaging metaphor when used to describe how ideas should circulate and how libraries should operate.

The notion that ideas can and should function much like products in a market is often attributed to J.S. Mill, but it is a phrase, much like "Survival of the Fittest," that is associated with a thinker who never actually used it. The idea of the marketplace probably owes more to Supreme Court Justice Holmes than to Mill. Holmes stated in one opinion the "the best test of truth is the power of the thought to get itself accepted in the competition of the market." Mill however went to great lengths to say that power of the most popular ideas should never be absolute over minority opinions. He held such a power to be as dangerous as any direct government control:

> [Society] practices a social tyranny more formidable than many kinds of political oppression, since, though not usually upheld by such extreme penalties, it leaves few means of escape, penetrating much more deeply into the details of life, and enslaving the soul itself... There needs protections also against the tyranny of the prevailing opinion and feeling."

This view is nearly identical with the post-structuralist notions of cultural hegemony. The idea that the market will produce truth is the most dangerous aspect of such thinking. As social theorist Jill Gordon states, the market responds most to those with the most money or those who are most numerous. Or as Robert McChesney says, "a commercial marketplace of ideas may generate the maximum returns for investors, but that does not mean it will generate the highest caliber of political exchange."

It is apparent that an ever-increasing amount of the cultural output of our society is control by an every fewer number of corporate entities, and that our continued belief in the pluralism of our information pathways is untenable. A growing body of library literature makes this point. Pat Schuman, for example, pointed out nearly 20 years ago that the library community was neglecting the alternative press and thus presenting a biased view of the world. Judith Serebnick has shown how libraries depend on a limited number or review sources when making selections, and how reviews themselves are not equitably available. A large corporate press, for example, can afford to distribute review copies in numbers that a small publisher could never do. Therefore, many titles are never reviewed at all.

In another study, Anna Perrault has shown that many academic libraries are becoming more and more homogeneous, as they depend for their collections on the same few vendors and the same few approval plans. Rita Marinko and Kristin Gerhard have also shown that although many academic libraries subscribe to the *Alternative Press Index*, very few of them hold subscriptions to more than a few of the periodicals indexed there.

I have sketched here a general problem with our worldview, but what should librarians do to change the effects of this ideological stance?

1. Librarians should start recognizing that there are inequities in both the production and consumption of information, and that libraries themselves can reinforce those inequalities. The ALA statement "Libraries: An American Value" says that libraries are the "cornerstones of the communities they serve." But since only about 20 percent of the people in any community ever enter a library, we must admit that either we are not as important as we think, or we are only getting about 20 percent of the democracy that we could.
2. Library research should concentrate on the effects on libraries of media conglomeration and homogenization.
3. We should start taking the LBR at its word and begin partnering with organizations that promote the small press and oppose publishing conglomeration—since to do so would be to oppose censorship. Groups such as the Project on Media Ownership, Small Press Distribution, Alternative Press Center should be welcome partners in any ALA effort.
4. When we see conglomeration happening, like when Bertlesman is buying half the publishing

world, that should be an intellectual freedom issue. When the Congress gives away large chunks of public bandwidth to an elite few, that should be an intellectual freedom issue. When telecommunications monopolies say they can not afford to grant the e-rate discount to schools and libraries, that should be an intellectual freedom issue.

5. Finally, we should stop congratulating ourselves on how important we are to democracy and start behaving as though democracy really matters.

References

American Library Association. (1999). *Libraries: An American Value*. Online: <http://www.ala.org/alaorg/oif/lib_val.html>.

Althusser, Louis. (1971). *Lenin and Philosophy and Other Essays*. New York: Monthly Review Press.

Berninghausen, David. (1972). Social responsibility vs. the Library Bill of Rights. *Library Journal*, 97 (20), 3675–3681.

Berninghausen, David. (1975). *The Flight from Reason: Essays on Intellectual Freedom in the Academy, the Press, and the Library*. Chicago: American Library Association.

Bostwick, Arthur Elmore. (1969). The librarian as censor. In *Library Essays: Papers Related to the Work of Public Libraries*. Freeport, NY: Books for Libraries Press, 121–139.

Conable, Gordon M. (1996). Public libraries and intellectual freedom. In *Intellectual Freedom Manual*, Fifth Edition (pp. 259–267). Chicago: American Library Association.

Foucault, Michel. (1972). *Archaeology of Knowledge*. New York: Pantheon.

Foucault, Michel. (1984). What is Enlightenment? In Paul Rabinow (ed.), *The Foucault Reader*. New York: Pantheon.

Geller, Evelyn. (1984). *Forbidden Books in American Public Libraries, 1876–1939: A Study in Cultural Change*. Westport, CT: Greenwood Press.

Gordon, Jill. (1997). John Stuart Mill and the "marketplace of ideas." *Social Theory and Practice*, 23 (2), 235–249.

Harris, Michael H. (1986). State, class, and cultural reproduction: Toward a theory of library service in the United States. *Advances in Librarianship*, 14, 211–252.

Holmes, Oliver Wendell, Jr. (1919). *Abrams v. United States*, 250 U.S. 630 (dissenting).

Horkheimer, Max, and Adorno, Theodor. (1994). *Dialectic of Enlightenment*. New York: Continuum.

Jansen, Sue Curry. (1991). *Censorship: The Knot that Binds Power and Knowledge*. Oxford: Oxford University Press.

Marcuse, Herbert. (1965). Repressive tolerance. In Robert Paul Wolff, Barrington Moore, Jr., and Herbert Marcuse, *Critique of Pure Tolerance* (pp. 81–117). New York: Beacon Press.

Marinko, Rita A, and Gerhard, Kristin Heidi. (1998). Representations of the alternative press in academic library collections. *College and Research Libraries*, 59 (4), 363–377.

McChesney, Robert W. (1998). The new theology of the First Amendment: Class privilege over democracy. *Monthly Review*, 49 (10), 17–34.

Mill, John Stuart. (1991). *On Liberty, and Other Essays*. Oxford: Oxford University Press.

Milton, John. (1927). *Areopagitica and Other Prose Writings*. New York: Macmillan.

Nietzsche, Friedrich. (1996). *On the Genealogy of Morals*. Oxford: Oxford University Press.

Perrault, Anna H. (1995). The changing print resource base of academic libraries in the United States. *Journal of Education for Library and Information Science*, 36, 295–308.

Robbins, Louise S. (1996). Champions of a cause: American librarians and the Library Bill of Rights in the 1950s. *Library Trends*, 45 (1), 28–49.

Said, Edward. (1978). *Orientalism*. New York: Vintage Books.

Samek, Toni. (1996). Library Bill of Rights in the 1960s: One profession, one ethic. *Library Trends*, 45 (1), 50–60.

Schiller, Herbert. (1989). *Culture, Inc.: The Corporate Takeover of Public Expression*. Oxford: Oxford University Press.

Schuman, Patricia Glass. (1982). Libraries and alternatives. In *Alternative Materials in Libraries*. Metuchen, NJ: Scarecrow Press.

Serebnick, Judith. (1992). Selection and holdings of small publishers' books in OCLC libraries: a study of the influence of reviews, publishers, and vendors. *Library Quarterly*, 62, 259–294.

Stielow, Frederick J. (1983). Censorship in the early professionalization of American libraries, 1876 to 1929. *Journal of Library History*, 18 (1), 37–54.

Thomison, Dennis. (1978) *A History of the American Library Association, 1876–1972*. Chicago: American Library Association.

Wiegand, Wayne. (1996). Introduction. *Library Trends*, 45 (1), 1–6.

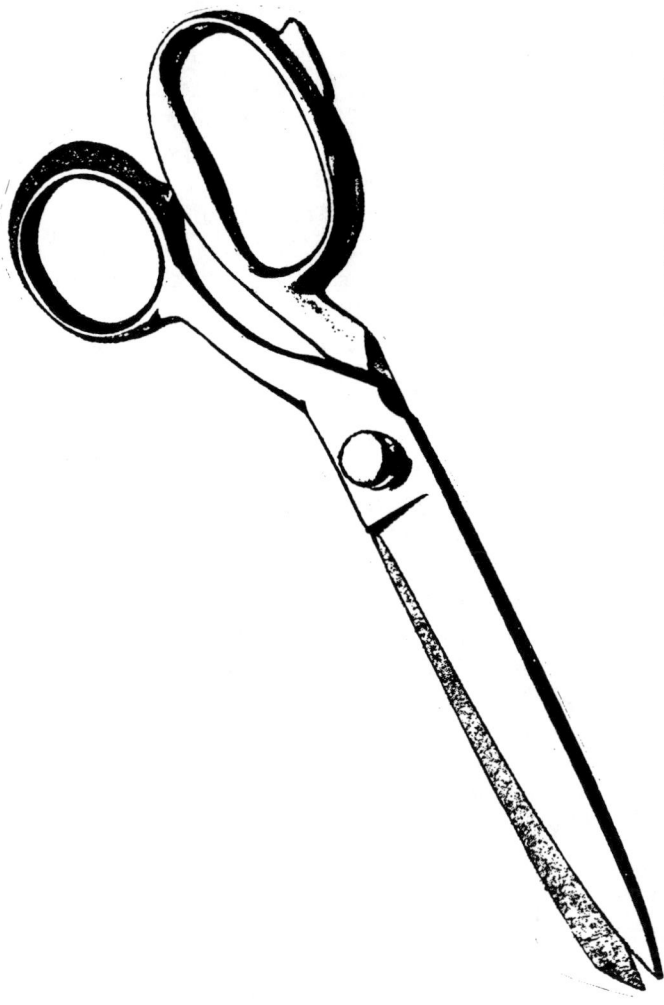

BERMAN'S BAG: THE TOP CENSORED LIBRARY STORIES OF 1998/2000, by Sanford Berman, U*L Contributing Editor

Since 1976, Project Censored, founded by Carl Jensen at Sonoma State University in Rohnert Park, California, has diligently (and appallingly) identified critical public issues and events that mainstream media either underreported or failed to report at all. In that same spirit and format, these are stories that the orthodox library press--most notably *American Libraries* and *Library Journal*--altogether ignored or minimized, even though they dealt with clearly significant professional matters. And it's not that AL and LJ didn't know about these things. They did. Fortunately, other sources recognized the importance of these challenges and developments, but their reports and analyses hardly reached the substantial readership commanded by the two leading journals.

1. HEIGHT-SHELVING PROPOSED BY LIBRARIAN OF CONGRESS

Synopsis: James Billington, the Librarian of Congress, hoping to save space in LC's Capitol Hill collections, announced a plan to shelve books there *by height*, which would effectively eliminate useful browsing by reference librarians and scholars, and might well be disastrously copycatted throughout the library community. Billington apparently believes that everything will ultimately be digitized and available on the tube so why bother about shelving the physical volumes in any classified order? And he also seems to suffer from the delusion that standard, LC-type cataloging is so adequate, so functional, that relevant, wanted materials can be easily and confidently discerned through the catalog. Every LC professional organization openly opposed this potentially precedent setting, wrong-headed idea. And critiques appeared in several "alternative" media, resulting in the proposal being put "on hold."

Sources: Thomas Mann, *Height Shelving Threat to the Nation's Libraries* (Washington, DC: Library of Congress Professional Guild, AFSCME 2910, 1999), reprinted in *Counterpoise*, v. 3, nos. 3/4 (July/Oct. 1999), p. 19-38, and *Alternative Library Literature*, 1998/1999 (Jefferson, NC: McFarland, 2000), p. 338-56; Sanford Berman, "Keep It Classed!," *ibid.*, p. 337; Grace Palladino, "Out of Sight, Out of Mind: Shelving by Height at the Library of Congress," *Chronicle of Higher Education*, v. 45, no. 40 (June 11, 1999), p. B6-7; "Good Reasons To Oppose Height-Shelving at LC," *Bulle-

---

Reprinted with permission from *Unabashed Librarian* (P.O. Box 325, Mt. Kisco, NY 10549), no. 118 (2001), pp. 16–19, no. 119 (2001), p. 24. © U*N*A*B*A*S*H*E*D Librarian™: The "How I Run My Library Good" Letter℠.

tin Board: the Voice of the Library of Congress Professional Guild, AFSCME 2910*, December 6, 1999, p. 3, reprinted in *The U*N*A*B*A*S*H*E*D Librarian™*, no. 114 (2000), p. 13; Robert Anderson, "Research Collection Shelved by Subject--an Endangered Species?," *LG Communicator*, v. 33, nos. 4/5 (July/October 1999), p. 16-17.

2. THE WEEDING EPIDEMIC IN AMERICAN LIBRARIES

Synopsis: Discarding damaged or truly obsolete library materials is a practical necessity, but lately--in part flowing from a reigning mentality that deemphasizes print and AV, in favor of purely digital resources--there's been a virtual epidemic of trashing, hiding, or selling arguably historic and valuable items without proper review or consultation. At San Francisco Public Library, for example, an expensive new downtown building was constructed with ample accommodation for computer terminals but hugely insufficient shelf space for books, resulting in thousands of volumes (some estimates suggest half-a-million!) being unceremoniously and often secretly pulped or remotely stored. Variations of this frequently appearance- or circulation-driven practice are now so common that a Midwest library user was even prompted to write a scorching poem in California's *Anderson Valley Advertiser*.

Sources: Fred Whitehead, "'To Thine Own Shelves Be True': a Call for a Working Group in Defense of Library Collections," *People's Culture*, no. 37 (1997), p. 1-2, reprinted in *Alternative Library Literature, 1996/1997* (Jefferson, NC: McFarland, 1998), p. 180-81; Fred Woodworth, "Report from Arizona," *People's Culture*, no. 37 (1997), p. 3-5, reprinted in *Alternative Library Literature*, 1996/1997, p. 182-83; Clark Dissmeyer, "Public Library, R.I.P.," *Anderson Valley Advertiser*, v. 47, no. 26 (June 30, 1999), reprinted in *Alternative Library Literature, 1998/1999* (Jefferson, NC: McFarland, 2000), p. 86; Fred Whitehead, "Update on Library Collections," *People's Culture*, new series no. 42 (1997), reprinted in *Alternative Library Literature, 1998/1999*, p. 87-89; Bill Witherup, "The Burning of the Books: 2000 A.D.," *People's Culture*, new series no. 42 (1997), reprinted in *Alternative Library Literature, 1998 1999*, p. 90; Fred Woodworth, "One of the Strange Features of Life and Civilization," *Mystery & Adventure Review*, no. 34 (Summer 1998), p. 4-7, reprinted in *Alternative Library Literature, 1998/1999*, p. 91-94; Mark Campos, "The Wishing Ring" (comic strip), *Exapno Mapcase*, no. 2 (1998), reprinted in *Alternative Library Literature, 1998/1999*, p. 95-99.

3. FREE SPEECH FOR LIBRARIANS

Synopsis: Early in March 1999, hoping to prevent other colleagues from undergoing the same denial of on-the-job intellectual freedom that I was experiencing at Hennepin County Library, I proposed this resolution to the American Library Association Council:

WHEREAS the American Library Association is firmly committed to human rights and freedom of expression (Policies 53 and 58.4.1); and

WHEREAS candid, robust debate is essential to the making of sound policy; and

WHEREAS library staff do not universally enjoy the right to openly discuss library and professional issues without fear of reprisal;

THEREFORE BE IT RESOLVED that ALA Council amends the Library Bill of

Rights (53.1) by adding:

> 7) Libraries should permit and encourage a full and free expression of views by staff on professional and policy matters.

On Tuesday, June 29th, in New Orleans, ALA Council overwhelmingly voted to refer the amendment to its Committee on Professional Ethics. As I feared, that referral effectively killed any possibility of amending the Library Bill of Rights. Indeed, the Ethics Committee subsequently determined that workplace free speech was already addressed by ALA's Code of Ethics, opting simply to draft a clarifying document, "Questions and Answers on Librarian Speech in the Workplace;" presumably to be presented to Council for approval. In a "brief reply" (12-18-00), I remarked that "while it may be a reasonable statement (with certain noted reservations) on how things are, it does not ringingly declare--as only an amendment to the Library Bill of Rights could--how things should be, unequivocally establishing as professional philosophy and principle that library staff ought to enjoy the right to full and free expression of views on professional and policy matters." I concluded that "despite the admonition to library administrators (pages 3-4) to encourage staff input and discussion, the document frankly appears to be a manifesto supporting 'managerial prerogatives,' not free speech." Neither *AL* nor *LJ* traced or commented upon the tortured history of the original resolution and its abject fate, even though the issue is central to librarianship itself.

Sources: Sanford Berman, "Rights or Ethics?" (letter), *American Libraries*, September 1999, p. 40, reprinted as "An Open Letter to ALA Members," *Alternative Library Literature, 1998/ 1999*, p. 85; letter from Sanford Berman to Charles Harmon, 5-3-00; "Draft ALA Committee on Professional Ethics Minutes, 2000 Midwinter Conference, San Antonio, TX," p. 7-11; letter from Charles Harmon to Sanford Berman, 12-14-00, with 5-page "Draft Questions & Answers on Librarian Speech in the Workplace"; letter from Sanford Berman to Charles Harmon, 12-18-00; John Buschman/Mark Rosenzweig, "Intellectual Freedom Within the Library Workplace: an Exploratory Study in the U.S.," *Journal of Information Ethics*, v. 8, no. 2 (Fall 1999), p. 36-45.

4. BIBLIOPHILES AND LIBRARY LOVERS OPPOSE SFPL BOND ISSUE.
Synopsis: A committed band of citizen activists and watchdogs, led by James Chaffee and Peter Warfield, unsuccessfully--albeit energetically--tried to sink the San Francisco Public Library's Fall 2000 quest for over $105,000,000 to ostensibly "improve" library branches. Save Our Libraries--No On Prop. A argued, in effect, that the SFPL management and Foundation had badly mismanaged earlier bond issues, made fraudulent claims regarding such matters as earthquake risks, seemed to be promoting the privatization and corporatization of library service, and just couldn't be trusted to responsively and efficiently handle the wanted funds.

Sources: Gray Brechin, "SF Hoodwinked on Library" (letter), *Bay Area Reporter*, v. 30, no. 42 (19 October 2000); James Chaffee, "Library Privatization Concerns" (letter), *Independent*, October 21, 2000); various press releases and manifestoes, some reprinted as "San Francisco Public Library: the Fight Against the Bond Issue in the 2000 Election," *Librarians at Liberty*, v. 8, nos. 1/2 (December 2000), p. 1, 3-7.

5. LC DOES COKE

Synopsis: As another troubling instance of a now-"normal" trend--the commercialization of libraries--the Library of Congress in late December 2000 not merely accepted a gift of some 20,000 Coca-Cola TV commercials (which would have been unexceptional), but shamelessly conducted a PR extravaganza for the pop-maker within LC's hallowed halls. Police ejected protesters who questioned the propriety of a public institution shilling for a "junk food pusher" which incidentally had just agreed to pay millions to settle a suit contending it had discriminated against Black employees. While AL noted the donation, neither major library periodical reported on the protest or editorialized on the menace of commercialism and the cascading erosion of library "neutrality."

Source: Russell Mokhiber/Robert Weissman, "The Real Thing: Democracy As a Contact Sport," reprinted from the Focus on the Corporation Internet Column (http://www.corporatepredators.org) in *Library Juice*, 4:1 (January 3, 2001), p. 6-8.

Sanford Berman, U*L Contributing Editor

6. SELF-CENSORSHIP: LIBRARIANSHIP'S "DIRTY LITTLE SECRET"

Synopsis: The mainstream library press and Intellectual Freedom Establishment seldom acknowledge the rampant failure to select whole categories or genres of material, despite public interest and demand on the one hand or the mandate to reflect a broad spectrum of human belief and activity on the other. Instead, ALA officialdom proclaims an annual "Banned Books Week," largely based on individual "challenges" reported by mainly school and small-town libraries, that effectively masks the far more pervasive self-censorship practiced by librarians themselves. For example, most libraries don't collect comics or many graphic novels. Few get any zines whatever, even though that's arguably the hottest current publishing scene. Recent surveys—resolutely ignored by *American Libraries* and *Library Journal*—demonstrate that small press fiction and poetry, as well as numerous other well-reviewed freethought, labor, and alternative press titles, are woefully underrepresented in public and academic libraries alike. And then there's sex, particularly if it's in the form of photos or film or deals with beyond-the-pale topics like anal intercourse or S&M. Such books and videos—like the excellent products from Down There Press (San Francisco) and Factor Press (Mobile, Alabama)—top most lists of virtually banned material. By contrast, the ongoing trend, particularly in public libraries, is to buy large quantities of circulation-boosting "popular" materials, especially conglomerate-produced, heavily-hyped "blockbusters" that typically end up being sold for 25¢ a piece within 6 to 8 months.

Sources: Rory Litwin, "Issues of Inside Censorship and the ALA," *Counterpoise*, January 1998, p. 11-13, reprinted in *Alternative Literature, 1998/1999* (Jefferson, NC: McFarland, 2000), p. 78-80; Charles Willett, "The Almost Banned Book Awards," *Counterpoise*, January 1999, p. 20, reprinted in *ALL, 1998/1999*, p. 111; Earl Lee, "Really Banned Books," Counterpoise, April 1998, p. 7-10, reprinted in *ALL, 1998/1999*, p. 112-115; "Almost Banned Book Awards of 1998," *Counterpoise*, January 1999, p. 21, reprinted in *ALL, 1998/1999*, p. 116; Scott Walter, "RLIN Holdings of Books Reviewed in *Counterpoise*, Volume 2 (1998)," *Counterpoise*, April 1999" p. 15-19, reprinted in *ALL, 1998/1999*, p. 117-123; Rita A. Marinko/Kristin H. Gerhard, "Representations of the Alternative Press in Academic Library Collections," *College & Research Libraries*, July 1998, p. 363-376, reprinted in *ALL, 1998/1999*, p. 219-229; Sanford Berman, "Foreword," in Toni Samek, *Intellectual Freedom and Social Responsibility in American Librarianship, 1967-1974* (McFarland, 2000), p. xi-xviii; Charles Willett, "Alternative Libraries and Infoshops: the Struggle Against Corporate and Government Indoctrination in American Schools and Universities...," *Librarians at Liberty*, December 2000, p. 11-25; Earl Lee, "Almost Banned Books, 1998 and 1999," *Counterpoise*, January/April 2000, p. 32-37; Daniel C. Tsang, "The Alternative Media: Open Sources On What's Real," *International Journal on Grey Literature*, v. 1, no.2 (2000), p. 61-63; Stephen Harris, "Discourse and Censorship: Librarians and the Ideology of Freedom," *Counterpoise*, July/October 1999, p. 14-18; Nancy Kranich, "A Question of Balance: the Role of Libraries in Providing Alternatives to the Mainstream Media," *Counterpoise*, July/October 1999, p. 7-10; Jason

Kucsma, "Preserving Zines in the Library: Countering Marginalization & Extinction," *Zine Guide*, no.3, p. 11-19.

7. BIBLIO-STALINISM AT HENNEPIN COUNTY LIBRARY

Synopsis: In a scenario uncannily reminiscent of the kind of Soviet (and other totalitarian) excess that George Orwell fictionalized as the "memory hole"—that is, removing inconvenient or undesirable people, events, and ideas from public awareness or consciousness by destroying all references to them and, in the case of persons and groups, also wholly erasing their words and images—all five works in the Hennepin County Library collection *by* me, together with another *about* me, in late January 2000 no longer appeared in the HCL online catalog and likewise seemed to have vanished from the shelves. A December 6, 1999 *Library Journal Digital* article ("Hennepin County Drops Cataloging Bulletin") speculated that the late-1999 termination of the 26-year-old, award-winning *HCL Cataloging Bulletin* "may be an attempt by HCL to purge itself completely of former Head Cataloger Sandy Berman, founder of the *Bulletin*, who resigned earlier this year after a clash with the library's director." In a February 1, 2000 press release, I wondered aloud:

Is that also why the books have disappeared? Am I being morphed into a non-person, flushed down an Orwellian "memory hole"?

Library Journal Digital (2-21-00), *American Libraries* (April 2000), *Library Hotline* (2-21-00), and *American Libraries Online* (2-14-00) reported the initial discovery, most noting my charge of "bibliocide" and quoting HCL's Spinmeisterin, who declared that no formal recall had been issued, that a few physical volumes had since been found, and that the wipeout may have been "inadvertent." That concluded coverage of this genuinely unique and extraordinary episode by the orthodox library press. Except that the "episode" was far from over. Developments during the next 8 months included brazen stonewalling by HCL management and the Library Board, failure to notify law enforcement agencies about the indisputable database-tampering and book thefts, rigid denial that any "censorship" had taken place, refusal to share essential details of the event with system staff, no indication of what (if any) measures had been instituted to prevent recurrence of such an intellectual freedom travesty, and—finally—engagement of an outside investigator, who in October produced a lengthy study confirming "that it is unlikely that the deletions...were anything other than deliberate," but that no "smoking gun" could be identified. No *American Libraries* or *Library Journal* readers knew anything about the post-February saga, even though both publications had been fully informed through press releases, clippings, and documents, among them the 27-page "redacted" investigative report.

Sources: "Books by Sanford Berman Removed From Hennepin County Library Catalog," *LG Communicator* (LAPL Librarians' Guild), January/April 2000, p. 20-21; Robert Franklin, "Publisher's Comments," *Journal of Information Ethics*, Spring 2000; Robert Halfhill, "Forced Resignation Sparks Protest" (letter), *Lavender: Biweekly Magazine for the Midwest Gay-Lesbian-Bisexual-Transgender Community*, June 2, 2000; R. Halfhill, "Shelving Sandy Berman" (letter), *Siren*, June 1, 2000, p. 3; S. Berman, "Where Have All the 'Berman Books' Gone? A Series of Memoranda and Letters," *Librarians at Liberty*," December 2000, p. 29-32; "Biblio-Stalinism," *City Pages*, January 24, 2001, p. 6; "Sanford Berman Censorship/Intellectual Freedom Issue," *LG Communicator*, November/December 2000, p. 7; "Where Have All the 'Berman Books' Gone?" (press releases): 2-1-00, 2-23-00 (reprinted in *Library Juice*, March 8, 2000, p. 3-4); 4-27-00, 5-23-00; 6 "Request for reconsideration of materials" forms, submitted 2-8-00 by S. Berman; Charles Brown letter (in response to reconsideration requests), 3-2-00; S. Berman letter to Charles Brown, 3-4-00; Thomas O'Neill (HCL Sr. Human Resources Representative) letters to S. Berman: 7-28-00, 10-13-00, 11-9-00 (with "redacted" report), 12-12-00; S. Berman letters to T. O'Neill: 8-1-00, 10-2-00, 10-25-00, 11-23-00, 11-30-00, 1-16-01.

WHERE HAVE ALL THE "BERMAN BOOKS" GONE?
A Series of Memoranda and Letters. Part 1

THE INITIAL BERMAN STATEMENT
February 1, 2000
TO: Local/library press
FROM: Sanford Berman
  Former Head Cataloger
  Hennepin County Library
SUBJECT: WHERE HAVE ALL THE "BERMAN BOOKS" GONE?

The *HCL Catalog* currently shows 9 entries under the author, "Berman, Sanford, 1933– ." In each case, I am listed because of being associated with the individual title as a contributor, coeditor, or interviewer. The following five works, either written or compiled solely by me, *have* been in the HCL collection, but no longer appear in the catalog:

- *Joy of cataloging* (Oryx Press, 1981)
- *Cataloging special materials: critiques and innovations* (Oryx Press, 1986)
- *Subject cataloging: critiques and innovations* (Haworth Press, 1984)
- *Worth noting: editorial, letters, essays, and interview and bibliography* (McFarland, 1988)
- *Prejudices and antipathies: a tract on the LC subject heads concerning people* (McFarland, 1993)

Further, *Everything you always wanted to know about Sandy Berman but were afraid to ask*, edited by Chris Dodge and JanDeSirey (McFarland, 1995), has similarly vanished, although initially there were at least three copies in the system.

A December 6, 1999 *Library Journal Digital* news report ("Hennepin County Drops Cataloging Bulletin") speculated that termination of the 26-year-old *HCL Cataloging Bulletin*, which once garnered the prestigious H. W. Wilson Library Periodical Award, "may . . . be an attempt by HCL to purge itself completely of former Head Cataloger Sandy Berman, founder of the *Bulletin*, who resigned earlier this year after a clash with the library's director." Is that also why the books have disappeared? Am I being morphed into a non-person, flushed down an Orwellian "memory hole"? For answers to these tantalizing questions, contact HCL's Collection Management Service (CMS) at 612-847-8588. Ask for the Lead Senior Librarian.

# # #

THE FOLLOW-UP STATEMENT
February 23, 2000
TO: Local/library press
  Hennepin County Board of Commissioners
  Hennepin County Library Board
  Hennepin County Administrator
FROM: Sanford Berman
  Former Head Cataloger
  Hennepin County Library
SUBJECT: WHERE HAVE ALL THE "BERMAN BOOKS" GONE: UPDATE

In late January, I inadvertently discovered that six books either by or about me, all of which *had* been in the Hennepin County Library (HCL) collection, no longer appeared in the HCL online catalog. They had totally vanished, the records almost certainly having been deleted deliberately and systematically.

On February 1st, I issued a one-page statement detailing what had apparently happened, citing the six missing books and speculation that the catalog-record obliteration may have been an attempt by HCL management to further–in *Library Journal Digital*'s words–"purge itself completely of former Head cataloger Sandy Berman . . .who resigned [in Spring 1997] after a clash with the library's director."

Seven days later, I submitted formal Requests for Reconsideration for each of the disappeared volumes.

To date, there had been no official communication from HCL management to me regarding this matter, although the Community Relations Manager has been quoted in the press as saying that anyone at any HCL branch could have deleted the records, that the materials do not seem to have been formally recalled or weeded, and that "some of the titles were still physically on the library shelves" (*American Libraries Online*, 2-14-00).

My understanding is that copies of at least one title (*Prejudices and Antipathies*) have been located and a catalog record recreated for that work. Additionally, I'm told that all the wayward books have been reordered, although several are now out-of-print and thus unlikely to be replaced.

What more do I want? These things:

1. An accounting of exactly which books have been found in the system and which remain physically missing.

2. An unequivocal declaration by the HCL management that this calculated removal of books and catalog records constitutes a despicable act of censorship and clearly violates the Library Bill of Rights. (Even more serious than the physical withdrawal of some works is the indisputable destruction of the catalog records for all six titles, which in effect rendered them inaccessible and unavailable. This is flagrant bibliocide.)

3. An explicit and sincere commitment by HCL management to identify and discipline the perpetrators.

(To simply claim that "anyone could have done it" is not enough. To be blunt, anyone *could* have done it, but I personally know of *no one* at HCL–outside of several members of top management–who had a possible or plausible motive for doing it. It seems like logical next step for the very persons who had last year expelled *me* from the system to now expel my words and ideas from the shelves and catalog, especially since I have been unremitting in the many months since my forced retirement in attempting to secure personal justice: the cancellation of an unjust reprimand and an apology for the mistreatment and abuse inflicted upon me. I have also sought redress for the outright censorship of corrections and additions I submitted–at their request–to the *OCLC Newsletter*. And I have repeatedly asked HCL management to explain how their ostensible guarantee to preserve high cataloging standards and quality squares with the demonstrable deterioration of cataloging at Hennepin County. Finally, I have inquired about the apparently lessened "urgency" to fashion a Cataloging Practices Manual, which had been the stated reason for my sudden and involuntary reassignment last Spring. There has been no response to any of these requests and queries.)

4. Institution of measures at HCL to prevent the recurrence of such an intellectual freedom travesty.

# # #

REPLY TO THE HCL DIRECTOR

March 4, 2000

Charles M. Brown
Hennepin County Library
12601 Ridgedale Drive
Minnetonka, MN 55305-1909

Charles M. Brown:

While I appreciate the uncommonly prompt response to the six Requests for Reconsideration I submitted on February 8th, I am distinctly *not* satisfied with the content.

1. It is much too coy and evasive to assert that "Hennepin County Library did not formally recall these titles from the HCL Collection" and that "the bibliographic records were removed from the on-line catalog by some mechanism as yet to be determined." Even if not "formally" recalled, some person or persons at HCL apparently removed copies of several titles from the circulating shelves. That this may have been done covertly does not make the Library itself any less accountable. Similarly, there is no mystery about the "mechanism" for deleting online catalog records. Most agency and technical services staff know how to do it. And it had to have been done deliberately to all six records, one by one. There's no single "magic button" to push. So the record-demolition was hardly accidental. Whoever did it knew what they were doing. The question, then, is: WHO committed this unmistakable act of bibliocide and censorship? Will HCL accept responsibility for the sabotage of its own collection and catalog since this was almost certainly an "inside job"? Will HCL management publicly condemn what happened, immediately and energetically seek to identifiy and discipline the perpetrators, and institute measures to prevent the recurrence of such an intellectual freedom travesty?

2. It's nice that titles that you "have not been able to locate" have been reordered. Several of the six works, however, are now out-of-print. Hence the likelihood of replacing them is remote. They have probably been purged permanently. I beleive that I, HCL staff, the profession, and the public deserve a detailed accounting of how many copies of which titles were found, and wherre and when they were located.

3. During two-and-a-half decades at HCL, I witnessed or experienced a number of "internal censorship" cases. None, however, approaches the gravity of this one: the conscious, wholesale obliteration of six catalog records for works by or about a single person: me. And the probable, willful withdrawal of some physical copies from the open shelves. I frankly do not detect in communications from either you or Nancy LeReau Perron any suitable outrage at the callous expulsion of a whole canon of work—mine—from the catalog nor any readiness to accept accountability. Perhaps there would be somewhat more passion and determination in your response if my name were "Judy Blume" or "R. L. Stine."

Expectantly,
Sanford Berman

# # #

THE HENNEPIN COUNTY LIBRARY BOARD MEETING OF APRIL 26, 2000

April 27, 2000
TO: Local/library press
Hennepin County Board of Commissioners
Hennepin County Library Board
Hennepin County Administrator
FROM: Sanford Berman
Former Head Cataloger
Hennepin County Library
SUBJECT: WHERE HAVE ALL THE "BERMAN BOOKS" GONE: UPDATE

Yesterday I attended a Hennepin County Library Board meeting. Under "New business," Director Charles Brown was slated to present a five-minute "information-only" item: "Missing Bibliographic Records/Books."

He noted that several works by "Sanford Bierman" (that's how he managed to mispronounce my surname) did seem to be physically missing from the HCL collection and their bibliographic records purged from the online catalog. A Board Member asked how many titles. He thought perhaps 7 or 8. Elizabeth Feinberg suggested 10 to 15. No one seemed sure. He said an "investigation" had been conducted, involving "consultation" with the County Attorney's Office. "Did we also consult with the Sheriff?," he asked aloud. No one knew, although all of HCL's top management was present. What was the nature of the consultation with the County Attorney? He divulged no details. Nor was any other evidence offered to suggest that any genuinely substantial "investigation" had been undertaken.

It was claimed that such an event might be prevented in future by introducing more stringent "protocols" and reducing the number of staff able to perform catalog deletions. Without amplification, these did not appear to be truly tangible, convincing means to offset later intellectual freedom travesties.

I requested permission to address the Board, then posing these questions:

• Does the Administration intend to reply to inquiries made by the Minnesota Library Association and Minnesota Coalition Against Censorship in mid-March?

No answer. Stony silence.

• Does the Administration intend to inform HCL staff about what happened? (To date there has been no mention of the incident either in the *Staff Newsletter* or by e-memo, with the result that the matter is effectively unknown and invisible for the majority of HCL employees.)

No answer. Deathly silence.

• Is there any intention to pursue the four, eminently reasonable recommendations I made to Charles Brown and Community Relation Manager (Spin Doctor) Nancy Perron in letters dated March 4th and March 1st, respectively? [The suggestions: 1) a public accounting of exactly which and how many books have been found in the system (and where) and which remain physically missing; 2) an unequivocal, public condemnation of this act of censorship, making it unmistakably clear that such behavior is unacceptable; 3) an explicit and sincere effort to identify and discipline the perpetrators; and 4) institution of measures to make such bibliocide less likely to recur.]

No answers from HCL management. One (relatively new) Board member, after I had formally requested the Board to direct the HCL Administration to address the four recommendations, assured me that it would be considered. But not at *that* meeting.

Following adjournment, one Division Manger–incidentally, one of the three or more who successfully conspired to force my retirement last year–approached me with two of her own questions:

> How could I possibly think that anyone in the Administration was involved in the book-and-record purge?
>
> Why did I insist on calling the act "censorship"?

Unnecessary (yet inescapable) conclusion: HCL management does *not* regard the elimination of my words and ideas from the shelves and catalog as a particularly grave matter. (Indeed, it appears to win their reluctant attention only because of potentially damaging press coverage. Otherwise, they manifestly find the event no more than a trivial annoyance. None of them even knew how many titles had been expunged. Six. And no one could say for sure that HCL had contacted the County Sheriff regarding these palpably criminal acts of database tampering and book theft.)

Not that it matters any longer, but I remain deeply disappointed. And thoroughly disgusted. Hennepin deserves better leadership than this. And the library profession deserves that its basic canons regarding free speech and intellectual freedom be respected in practice.

# # #

THE HENNEPIN COUNTY LIBRARY BOARD MEETING OF MAY 24, 2000

Date: May 24, 2000
TO: Local/library press
 Hennepin County Board of
  Commissioners
 Hennepin County Library Board
 Hennepin County Administrator
FROM: Sanford Berman
 Former Head Cataloger
 Hennepin County Library
SUBJECT: WHERE HAVE ALL THE "BERMAN BOOKS" GONE: UPDATE 3

My last "Update," following a Hennepin County Library Board meeting on April 26th, glumly concluded that "HCL management does not regard the elimination of my words and ideas from the shelves and catalog as a grave matter." After this morning's Board meeting, I sadly conclude that–with one honorable exception–the HCL board doesn't much care, either.

Although I had asked the Board in April to direct the Administration to answer questions I posed relating to MLA and MCAC inquiries, as well as their failure to inform staff of the book/record wipeout, and to pursue four specific recommendations, the subject did NOT EVEN APPEAR ON THE MEETING AGENDA. One Board member asked why there was no slotted opportunity for discussing the matter, but got no comprehensible explanation. During "public comment," I echoed that concern, stating that I was disturbed and disappointed that the episode was being treated so casually, perhaps being dragged out, ignored, and postponed in the hope that eventually everyone would forget about it.

It is now four months since the bibliocidical scandal erupted, and in that time I've detected absolutely no sense of outrage or urgency on the part of HCL management or board, only a vaguely-expressed worry about the "corruption and integrity" of online resources like the catalog. NO ONE SEEMS MORALLY OR INTELLECTUALLY ABLE TO SAY THAT THE RECORD-DELETION AND BOOK REMOVAL WAS A DELIBERATE, DAMNABLE ACT OF CENSORSHIP. NOR DOES ANYONE INSIST THAT THE LIBRARY BE ACCOUNTABLE: PROVIDING DETAILS ON MISSING AND FOUND VOLUMES AND SERIOUSLY INVESTIGATING WHO DID IT (IDEALLY, THROUGH THE AUSPICES OF THE COUNTY ATTORNEY OR SHERIFF).

The Board, at least, is supposed to represent the public. Well, as a member of that public, I don't feel at all well represented.

# # #

The next installment of "WHERE HAVE ALL THE 'BERMAN BOOKS' GONE?" and other reports by Sandy Berman will appear in L@L volume 9, number 1.
Contact Sandy Berman at:
 4400 Morningside Drive
 Edina, MN 55416
 612/925-5738

Almost Banned Books, 1998 and 1999
by Earl Lee
Earl Lee is Coordinator of Technical Services and Collection Development Librarian,
Leonard H. Axe Library, Pittsburg (Kan.) State University
<ewayne@mail.pittstate.edu>

Almost Banned Books, 1998

Following up on our survey ("Really Banned Books," *Counterpoise* vol. 2, no.2, pp. 7–10) of books reviewed in *Counterpoise* in Volume 1 (1997), I recently searched the OCLC database and counted the number of libraries showing holdings for books reviewed in Volume 2 (1998). The results were pretty depressing, as evidently the continuing merger mania among publishers, distributors, book stores and book venders continues to take its toll on the small presses. First of all, there were more books bunched into the lower numbers—three books showing 2 holdings, five books showing 5 holdings, etc., suggesting that there appears to be a slippage in the number of small press books finding their way into libraries. And, unfortunately, there were fewer books in the top range. For example, the most popular book last year, ***Betrayal of Science and Reason***, had 1,279 holdings. This year the most popular book was ***Sex Side of Life*** with 828 holdings.

Some of the observations I made last year continue to hold true to form. Some of the least "popular" titles were books that dealt with sex. For example, ***I Am My Lover*** shows 2 holdings, as does ***Full-Frontal***. Books published in other countries continue to show low numbers, and these include ***Flights from the Iron Moon*** (3 holdings), ***So Far*** (5 holdings), and ***Summer Was a Fast Train without Terminals*** (5 holdings). Similarly, reference books that have a politically progressive and/or multicultural focus had problems finding their way into libraries, particularly the three ***Cross-Border Links*** directories published by Resource Center Press which barely made it into the double digits. These low numbers may also reflect a bias on the part of libraries against reference materials that are seen as too "political" in their cultural focus. This may account for low numbers for ***Connecting Children to the Future*** and ***Children Are Dying***. Certainly self-censorship is a major force in keeping books out of libraries.

Finally, it is clear from the numbers that more has to be done in promoting small press books to libraries and bookstores.

Reprinted with permission from *Counterpoise* (1716 SW Williston Road, Gainesville, FL 32608), v. 4, nos. 1/2 (January/April 2000), pp. 32–37.

OCLC Holdings of Books Reviewed in *Counterpoise*, Volume 2 (1998)

Based on an OCLC Search in May 1999 by Earl Lee, Pittsburg State University
(Sequence: OCLC holdings; brief title; place of publication; publisher; Counterpoise *entry number)*

1-10 libraries
2 *I am my lover*. San Francisco, CA: Down There Press. #26
2 *Gardening the arid land*. La Mesa, NM: Brooker Pub. #259
2 *Full-frontal*. Companion Press. #280
3 *Flights from the iron moon*. Huddersfield, ENGLAND: Hilltop Press. #94
3 *Cross-border links fair trade directory*. Albuquerque, NM: Resource Center Press. #245
5 *Torn shapes of desire*. Philadelphia, PA: Intangible Assets Manufacturing. #45
5 *Children are dying*. New York, NY: International Action Center. #285
5 *So far*. Ontario, CANADA: Fitzhenry & Whiteside. #306
5 *Summer was a fast train without terminals*. Melbourne, AUSTRALIA: Spinifex. #307
5 *Connecting children to the future*. Washington, DC: Center for Media Education. #80
6 *Low-hanging fruit*. Los Angeles, CA: GrapeVine Press. #297
7 *Best of* Temp Slave! Madison, WI: Garrett County Press. #115
8 *Cross-border links environmental directory*. Albuquerque, NM: Resource Center Press. #244
9 *Pain on their faces*. New York: Apex Press. #265
10 *Cross-border links labor directory*. Albuquerque, NM: Resource Center Press. #243
10 *Roots of justice*. Berkeley, CA: Chardon Press. #268

11-20 libraries
11 *Animal ingredients a to z*. Dayton, OH: EG Smith. #78
12 *Keep simple ceremonies*. Portland, ME: Astarte Shell Press. #29
13 *Snake that lived in the Santa Cruz Mountains*. Berkeley, CA: Oyate. #305
14 *Language crisis in Tanzania*. Dar es Salaam, TANZANIA: Mkuki Na Nyota Pub. #103
15 *Putting out*. San Francisco, CA: Cleis Press. #82
17 *Suicide machine*. Detroit, MI: Detroit Free Press Books. #113
17 *Raw deal*. Cooper Station, NY: Blast Books. #302
19 *Beyond Bookchin*. Detroit, MI: Black and Red. #17
19 *Crisis and hope in Africa*. Washington, DC: Inter-Agency Group/Center of Concern. #20
19 *Uncovering the right on campus*. Boston, MA: Center for Campus Organizing. #119

21-30 libraries
22 *I am a Martinican woman*. Pueblo, CO: Passeggiata Press. #290
22 *Keep on knocking*. ZIMBABWE: Baobab Books. #293
23 *Manufacturing African studies and crises*. Dakar, SENEGAL: CODESRIA. #106
23 *Politics of liberation in South Sudan*. KAMPALA: Fountain Pub. #301
26 *Over our heads*. Seattle, WA: Northwest Environmental Watch. #264
28 *World guide*. Oxford, ENGLAND: New Internationalist Pub. #282
29 *Awakening to disability*. CA: Volcano Press. #283

31-50 libraries
31 *Metal of dishonor*. New York: International Action Center. #298
32 *Access to the airwaves*. Port Townsend, WA: Loompanics Unlimited. #14
32 *Chira*. Nairobi, KENYA: East African Ed. Pub. #89
33 *Endogenous knowledge*. Dakar, AFRICA: CODESRIA. #33
35 *Jobs you can live with*. Washington, DC: Student Pugwash USA. #81
36 *Women's circus*. North Melbourne, AUSTRALIA: Spinifex Press. #50
38 *Zelda*. North Melbourne, AUSTRALIA: Spinifex Press. #51
38 *Green guide to cars and trucks*. Washington, DC: American Council for an Energy-Efficient Economy. #252
40 *Tales from the clit*. San Francisco, CA: AK Press. #43
40 *I never read Thoreau*. Norwich, VT: New Victoria Pub. #99
41 *Like there's no tomorrow*. Monroe, ME: Common Courage. #296
42 *Indelible Alison Bechdel*. Ithaca, NY: Firebrand Books. #102
42 *23 shades of black*. East Satuket, NY: Imaginary Press. #308
47 *Pirate radio operations*. Port Townsend, WA: Loompanics Unlimited. #109

51-75 libraries
51 *Beyond heroes*. Washington, DC: Network of Educators of the Americas. #79
53 *Queer view mirror 2*. Vancouver, BC CANADA: Arsenal Pulp Press. #39
56 *Arcade*. Berkeley, CA: Kelsey St. Press. #15
60 *Outlaws, renegades and saints*. Greenfield Center, NY. #108
61 *Reinventing anarchy, again*. San Francisco, CA: AK Press. #40
61 *Seizing the airwaves*. San Francisco, CA: AK Press. #304
66 *I'll sing 'till the day I die*. Toronto, CANADA: McGilligan Books. #101

69 *Change of plans.* Toronto, CANADA: Garmond Press. #19

69 *Endangered African social sciences.* Dakar, AFRICA: CODESRIA. #24

76-100 libraries

80 *From our eyes.* Toronto, CANADA: Garamond Press. #96

89 *Heartbeat of the earth.* East Haven, CT: New Society Pub. #98

93 *Collected stories of Maria Cristina Mena.* Houston, TX: Arte Público Press. #90

96 *Power and counterpower.* London, ENGLAND: Pluto Press. #37

100 *Keepers of the story.* Maryknoll, NY: Orbis Books. #294

101-150 libraries

106 *Africa: Africa world press guide.* Trenton, NJ: Africa World Press. #77

109 *Ecoforestry.* Stony Creek, CT: New Society Pub. #22

109 *Social services for senior gay men and lesbians.* New York: Harrington Park Press. #42

109 *Global focus.* Albuquerque, NM: Resource Center Press. #248

109 *Political parties and democracy.* London, ENGLAND: Pluto Press. #110

116 *Censored 1997.* New York: Seven Stories Press. #88

120 *Bear book.* New York: Harrington Park Press. #16

124 *Reworking success.* Gabriola Islands, BC, CANADA: New Society Pub. #267

126 *Mammoth book of gay short stories.* New York: Carroll & Graf. #32

134 *Read my lips.* Ithaca, NY: Firebrand Books. #303

136 *Pioneering.* Ithaca, NY: ILR Press Sage House. #300

140 *Reclaiming the vision past, present and future.* Greenfield Center, NY: Greenfield Review Press. #111

150 *North enough.* Saint Paul, MN: Graywolf Press. #36

151-200 libraries

152 *Liberating minds.* Jefferson, NC: McFarland. #295

158 *Juarez.* New York: Apeture Foundation. #263

167 *Tibet.* Berkeley, CA: Pacific View Press #117

175 *Images of American radicalism.* Hanover, MA: Christopher Pub. #291

184 *If you had a family.* Seattle, WA: Seal Press. #100

192 *Limits of tolerance.* Lanham, MD: Scarecrow Press. #104

200 *Trouble with Dilbert.* Monroe, ME: Common Courage Press. #46

201-300 libraries

204 *Project death.* Houston, TX: Arte Público Press. #38

213 *"We called each other comrade."* Champaign, IL: Univ. of Ill. Press. #47

217 *American Indians.* Halifax, NS, CANADA: Clarity Press. #85

221 *Love canal.* Gabriola Island, BC, CANADA: New Society. #182

224 *Woman between two worlds.* Champaign, IL: Univ. of Ill. Press. #49

227 *Capitalism and the information age.* New York: Monthly Review Press. #258

227 *Turning away from technology.* San Francisco: Sierra Club Books. #270

228 *Multicultural literature for children and young adults.* Madison, WI: Cooperative Children's Book Center. #281

228 *Escape artist.* Ithaca, NY: Firebrand. #25

228 *Kashmir in the crossfire.* London, ENGLAND: I.B. Tauris. #28

236 *Bloomsbury Review booklover's guide.* Denver, CO: Bloomsbury Review. #284

236 *Daniel.* Farmington, PA: Plough Pub. House. #286

239 *Women's periodicals in the United States.* Westport, CT: Greenwood. #13

251 *From a native son.* Boston, MA: South End Press. #95

268 *Women's guide to the Internet.* New York: Feminist Press. #254

281 *Beautiful flowers of the maquiladora.* Austin: Univ. of Texas Press. #87

286 *Gender blending.* Amherst, NY: Prometheus Books. #97

295 *Late great Mexican border.* El Paso, TX: Cinco Puntos Press. #30

301-400 libraries

301 *James Baldwin.* New York: Chelsea House Pub. #105

306 *Natural eloquence.* Madison, WI: Univ. of Wisconsin Press. #34

308 *History of the black press.* Washington, DC: Howard Univ. Press. #289

326 *Living inside our hope.* Ithaca, NY: Cornell Univ. Press. #31

351 *Tree huggers.* Seattle, WA: Mountaineers. #269

357 *Earth for sale.* Boston, MA: South End Press. #21

360 *Atomic audit.* Washington, DC: Brookings Inst. Press. #256

371 *African studies companion.* West Sussex, ENGLAND: Hans Zell. #9

371 *Appalachian tragedy.* San Francisco: Sierra Club Books. #255

378 *Zinn reader.* New York: Seven Stories Press. #52

395 *Global spin.* White River Junction, VT: Chelsea Green Pub. #261

398 *What is secret.* Fredonia, NY: White Pine Press. #121

401-500 libraries

404 *First person, first peoples.* Ithaca, NY: Cornell Univ. Press. #93

424 *Conglomerates and the media.* New York: New Press. #91

427 *New lesbian studies.* New York: Feminist Press. #35

432 *Skull measurer's mistake.* New York: New Press. #112

467 *We'll call you if we need you.* Ithaca, NY: ILR Press. #310

483 *Recycling organic waste.* Washington, DC: Worldwatch Inst. #266

501-1,000 libraries
515 *Exterminate all the brutes*. New York: WW. Norton. #92
524 *Nazis*. New York: New Press. #299
532 *Grand Central winter*. New York, NY: Seven Stories Press. #288
582 *Minutes of the lead pencil club*. Wainscott, NY: Pushcart Press. #33
598 *20 years of censored news*. New York: Seven Stories Press. #118
633 *Who owns the sun*. White River Junction, VT: Chelsea Green Pub. #48
690 *Greening the college curriculum*. Washington, DC: Island Press. #262
743 *Boards that make a difference*. San Francisco: Jossey-Bass Pub. #257
751 *Glass ceilings and bottomless pits*. Boston: South End Press. #260
823 *Talking about people*. Phoenix, AZ: Oryx Press. #83
828 *Sex side of life*. New York: New Press. #41

Almost Banned Books 1999

The current list of Almost Banned Books contains a number of surprises, especially of titles that showed *no* holdings on OCLC. Of the enormous number of libraries using OCLC, none had a copy of these titles. For example, **The Black Book** (#12) is now in its 5th edition, yet no libraries appear to own the current edition, and only two libraries own the 4th edition. This book is a directory of "sex-positive services and organizations" located all over the U.S. and Canada.

Similarly, there are several very good reference sources that show very few holdings. **Cross-Border Links** (#182) has only three holdings on OCLC libraries. Even more surprising, Russ Kick's **Psychotropedia** (#89) shows only 11 holdings; but this book should, like his earlier book **Outposts**, be in every reference collection in the United States. Larger libraries need this book as a selection guide to what is available on all sorts of obscure and strange topics. Smaller libraries need this book as a resource for inter-library loan requests. Another sadly overlooked source are the two **Good Vibrations guides** (#4 and #5), which have, respectively, six and eight holdings each.

There were many non-reference books that, surprisingly enough, have found their way into very few libraries. Craig O'Hara's **The Philosophy of Punk** (#208) and Ken Ragge's **The Real AA: Behind the Myth of 12-Step Recovery** (#56) are excellent books that should find a wider audience. Not surprising was the fact that many of the books on this list are important books that happen to be published abroad, and therefore escape the notice of the big review journals that most librarians rely on in making purchases. Clearly, acquisitions librarians, myself included, can do a much better job of locating and selecting alternative sources, particularly Canadian and African publications. —*Earl Lee*

OCLC Holdings of Books Reviewed in *Counterpoise*, Volume 3, (1999)

Based on an OCLC Search on 8 September 2000 by Earl Lee, Pittsburg State University (Sequence: OCLC holdings; brief title; place of publication; publisher, date, Counterpoise *entry number)*

0 libraries
0 *The Black book*. 5th ed. San Francisco: Black Books, 1998. #12
0 *Diggers and dreamers: the guide to communal living, 1998/99*. London: D&D Publications. #22
0 *Managing the democratic process in a co-operative*. Sillery, QUE, Canada: Orion, 1999. #204

1-5 libraries

1 *La Cocina cubana sencilla=simple Cuban cooking*. Paul L. Adams. Louisville, KY: Butler Books, 1998. #196

1 *History of the world according to Jack T Chick*. Robert B. Fowler. San Leandro, CA: R.B.Fowler, 1997. #104

3 *Cross-border links*. Albuquerque, NM: Interhemispheric Resource Center, 1998. #182

5 *Engaging the public on biodiversity*. Madison, WI: Biodiversity Project, 1998. #100

5 *Sex toy tales*. Anne Semans & Cathy Winks. San Francisco: Down There Press, 1998. #6

6 - 10 libraries

6 *Assume nothing: evolution of a bi-dyke* (comic). Leanne Franson. Hove, UK: Slab-O-Concrete. #93

6 *Objectivity and liberal scholarship*. Noam Chomsky. Detroit: Black & Red, 1997. #207

6 *The Good vibrations guide: adult videos*. Cathy Winks. San Francisco: Down There Press, 1998. #5

8 *The Good vibrations guide: the g-spot*. Cathy Winks. San Francisco: Down There Press, 1998. #4

8 *Real education: varieties of freedom*. David Gribble. Bristol: Libertarian Education, Phoenix House. #210

9 *Against civilization*. John Zerzan. Eugene, OR: Uncivilized Books, 1999. #91

11 - 29 libraries

11 *House on Armus Square* (novel). Samar Attar. Pueblo, CO: Passeggiata Press, 1998. #105

11 *Psychotropedia: a guide to publications on the periphery*. Russ Kick. Cookville, TN: Headpress, 1998. #89

11 *Tales of a punk rock nothing* (novel). Abram S. Himelstein. New Orleans: New Mouth from the Dirty South, 1998. #215

14 *Confronting the cuts: a sourcebook....* Luciana Rucciutelli. Toronto: Inanna Publications and Education, 1998. #197

17 *Appreciating the difference*. Donald E. Herdeck. Pueblo, CO: Passeggiata Press, 1998. #18

19 *Roberts' rules of lesbian break-ups*. Shelly Roberts. Duluth, MN: Spinsters Ink, 1997. #36

20 *Roberts' rules of lesbian dating*. Shelly Roberts. Duluth, MN: Spinsters Ink, 1998. #35

20 *Women in Malawi* (*Beyond Inequalities* series). Peter Mvula. Harare, Zimabawe: Southern African Research and Documentation Centre, 1997.

22 *Farm folk, city folk*. Herb Barbolet. Vancouver: Douglas & McIntyre. #200

25 *Anal pleasure and health*. Jack Morin. San Francisco: Down There Press, 1998. #17

30 - 49 libraries

30 *Changing gender relations in Southern Africa*. Anita Larsson. Roma, Lesotho: National University of Lesotho, 1998. #98

30 *Raw deal: horrible & ironic stories of forgotten Americans*. Ken Smith. New York: Blast Books, 1998. #209

34 *Terrorism & the constitution: sacrificing civil liberties in the name of national security*. James X. Dempsey. Los Angeles: First Amendment Foundation, 1999. #216

35 *Slumming it at the rodeo: the cultural roots of Canada's right-wing revolution*. Gordon Laird. Vancouver: Douglas & McIntyre, 1998. #212

37 *Child's life and other stories*. Phoebe Gloeckner. Berkeley: Frog Ltd, 1998. #195

40 *Chiapas: el fin del silencio*. New York: Aperture, 1998. #21

41 *Barbie unbound: a parody....* Sarah Strohmey. Norwich, VT: New Victoria, 1997. #20

41 *Call me crazy: stories from the mad movement*. Irit Shimrat. Vancouver:Press Gang, 1997. #96

45 *Looking east leftwards*. David Mandel. Montreal: Black Rose Books, 1998. #15

47 *Philosophy of punk*. Craig O'Hara. Edinburgh: AK Press, 1999. #208

47 *Women in Tanzania* (*Beyond Inequalities* series). Fenella Mukangara. Harare, Zimbabwe: Southern African Research and Documentation Centre, 1997. #193

50 - 99 libraries

50 *Selected speeches of Kwame Nkrumah*. Accra, Ghana: Afram, 1997. #90 (v.1)

51 *Women in South Africa* (*Beyond Inequalities* series). Tania Flood. Harare, Zimabawe: Southern African Research and Documentation Centre, 1997. #192

52 *International Directory of Little Magazines and Small Presses 1998-99*. Len Fulton. Paradise, CA: Dustbooks. #14

54 *Hans-Georg Gadamer: a bibliography*. Joan Nordquist. Santa Cruz, CA: Reference and Research Services, 1998. #184

56 *The Real AA: behind the myth of 12-step recovery*. Ken Ragge. Tucson: See Sharp Press, 1998. #86

62 *Orlando's sleep: an autobiography of gender*. Jennifer Spry. Norwich, VT: New Victoria. #32

63 *Merchants of Venus: inside Harlequin....* Paul Grescoe. Vancouver: Raincoast Books, 1996. #107

89 *Split-level dykes to watch out for* (comic). Alison Bechdel. Ithaca, NY: Firebrand, 1998 #113

92 *Mamie's children*. Judy Schultz. Red Deer, Alberta, Canada: Red Deer College Press. #29

98 *Beyond bedlam: contemporary women psychiatric survivors speak out*. Jeanine Grobe. Chicago: Third Side Press, 1995. #94

100 - 199 libraries

103 *A National crime: the Canadian government & the residential school system, 1879-1986*. John S. Milloy. Winnipeg:Univ. of Manitoba Press, 1999. #205

104 *Nobody's children: Jamaican children in police detention & government institutions*. New York: Human Rights Watch, 1999. #206

106 *Simple annals* (poetry). Robert H. Allen. New York: Four Walls Eight Windows, 1997. #37

119 *Alcoholics anonymous: cult or cure?*. Charles Bufe. Tucson, AZ: See Sharp, 1998. #85

122 *Woman determined* (novel). Jean Swallow. Duluth, MN: Spinsters Ink, 1998. #117

124 *Travels in the skin trade: tourism & the sex industry.* Chicago: Pluto Press, 1996. #39

131 *The Idea of prostitution.* Sheila Jeffreys. N. Melbourne, Australia.:Spinifex. #25

139 *Rethinking Columbus.* Bill Bigelow. Milwaukee: Rethinking Schools, 1998. #110

141 *Annotations: a guide to the independent critical press.* Marie Jones. Baltimore: Alternative Press Center, 1999. #178

141 *New good vibrations guide to sex....* Cathy Winks. Pittsburgh: Cleis Press, 1997. #31

144 *Living at night* (novel). Mariana Romo-Carmona. Duluth, MN: Spinsters Ink, 1997.

150 *Hip mama survival guide.* Ariel Gore. New York: Hyperion, 1998. #13

151 *Detroit, I do mind dying.* Dan Georgakas. Cambridge, MA: South End, 1998. #99

153 *The Mediator's handbook.* Jennifer E. Beer. Gabriola Isl., BC: New Society Publishers. #82

155 *For mortal stakes: solutions for schools & society.* Paul F. Cummins. New York: Peter Lang, 1998. #101

186 *Gift of the emperor* (novel). Therese Park. Duluth, MN: Spinsters Ink, 1997. #24

194 *Reasons for success:... rural development.* Norman T. Uphoff. West Hartford, CT: Kumarian Press, 1998. #8

200 - 299 libraries

207 *Giusseppe Rocco* (novel). Ronald L. Ruiz. Houston: Arte Público, 1998. #102

209 *Don't explain: short fiction.* Jewelle Gomez. Ithaca, NY: Firebrand Books, 1998. #23

212 *Facilitator's guide to participatory decision-making.* Sam Kaner. Philadelphia: New Society, 1996. #83

212 *Toward sustainable communities.* Mark Roseland. Stony Creek, CT: New Society, 1998. #84

218 *Talking about a revolution: interviews....* Cambridge: South End Press, 1998. #115

220 *Libraries in the age of mediocrity.* Earl Lee. Jefferson, NC: McFarland, 1998. #27

221 *NASA/Trek: popular science and sex in America.* Constance Penley. New York: Verso, 1997. #30

223 *Poor people and library services.* Karen M. Venturella. Jefferson, NC: McFarland. #33

228 *The Shadow* (novel). Americo Paredes. Houston: Arte Público Press, 1998. #112

236 *The Sex sector: ... prostitution in Southeast Asia.* Lin Lean Lim. Geneva: International. Labour Office, 1998. #26

265 *All-American anarchist: Joseph A Labadie....* Carlotta R. Anderson. Detroit, MI: Wayne State Univ. Press, 1998. #191

269 *Trips: how hallucinogens work in your brain.* Cheryl Pellerin. New York: Seven Stories Press, 1998. #217

270 *Wise choices beyond mid-life.* Lucy Scott. Watsonville, CA: Papier-Mache Press, 1997. #41

272 *Zine scene.* Francesca L. Block. Los Angeles: Girl Press, 1998 #42

288 *Two-fold thought of Deleuze and Guattari.* Charles V. Stivale. New York: Guilford, 1998. #219

293 *Zapata's disciple.* Marin Espada. Cambridge: South End Press, 1998. #220

295 *Knocking at our own door: ... the struggle to integrate New York City schools.* Clarence Taylor. New York: Columbia University Press, 1997. #106

299 *Portrait of the walrus by a young artist: a novel....* Laurie Foos. Minneapolis: Coffee House, 1997. #108

300- libraries

309 *Players and issues in international aid.* Paula Hoy. West Hartford, CT: Kumarian Press, 1998. #7

344 *Cannibals with forks: the triple bottom line of 21st century business.* Stony Creek, CT: New Society, 1998. #97

355 *Baby help* (novel). Marilyn Reynolds. Buena Park, CA: Morning Glory Press, 1997. #19

355 *Real girl/real world.* Heather M. Gray. Seattle: Seal Press, 1998. #211

383 *Against the grain: biotechnology and the corporate take over of your food.* Marc Lappe. Monroe, ME: Common Courage Press, 1998. #92

388 *The Activist's daughter* (novel). Ellyn Bache. Duluth, MN: Spinsters Ink, 1997. #16

392 *Sugar land: a novel.* Joni Rodgers. Duluth: Spinsters Ink, 1999. #114

403 *Turnip blues* (novel). Helen Campbell. Duluth, MN: Spinsters Ink, 1998. #40

424 *Living on the edge: fiction....* John Coyne. Willimantic, CT: Curbstone Press, 1999. #203

425 *Tropic of orange: a novel.* Karen T. Yamashita. Minneapolis, MN: Coffee House Press, 1997. #116

434 *Bounded people, boundless lands.* Eric T. Freyfogle. Washington, DC: Island Press, 1998. #95

444 *Pornography: private right or public menace?.* Robert M. Baird. Amherst, NY: Prometheus, 1998. #34

453 *Zinn reader.* Howard Zinn. New York: Seven Stories Press, 1997. #44

470 *Strike!* Jeremy Brecher. Boston: South End Press, 1997. #214

502 *Alternative Library Literature: a biennial anthology.* Sanford Berman & James Danky. Jefferson, NC: McFarland, 1984– #88

510 *Fat! so?* Marilyn Wann. Berkeley: Ten Speed Press, 1998. #201

517 *Rights of the poor.* Helen Hershkoff. Carbondale: S. Illinois University Press, 1997. #111

552 *Dark alliance: the CIA, the Contras, and the crack cocaine explosion.* Gary Webb. New York: Seven Stories Press, 1998. #199

567 *Guide to graduate environmental programs.* Student Conservation Association. Washington, DC: Island Press, 1997. #103

847 *Crossing borders.* Rigoberta Menchu. London: Verso, 1998. #198

924 *African American quotations.* Richard Newman. Phoenix, AZ: Oryx Press, 1998. #87

983 *Talking about people: a guide to fair & accurate language.* Rosalie Maggio. Phoenix, AZ: Oryx Press, 1997. #38

Free Press for Sale: How Corporations Have Bought the First Amendment; an Interview with Robert McChesney

Derrick Jensen

For nearly two decades, Robert McChesney has been a modern Paul Revere raising an alarm about the growing domination of the media by giant firms and special interests. There are many sharp academic critics of our corporate media system, but McChesney stands out because of his straightforward writing style and populist commitment to democracy and social change.

What does it mean for democracy, McChesney asks, when a small elite determines the information the rest of us receive about the world? Though every new technology—from radio to television to the Internet—has held out the promise of increased democratization, in the end it's those in control of the medium who have determined what stories get told. In other words: freedom of the press belongs to the person who owns one.

Before earning his Ph.D. in communications from the University of Washington, McChesney worked as a sportswriter, published a weekly newspaper, and cofounded the Seattle rock magazine the Rocket. *He now teaches at the University of Illinois at Urbana-Champaign, where he is a professor in the Institute of Communications Research. His work is primarily concerned with what he calls "the contradiction between a for-profit, highly concentrated, advertising-saturated, corporate media system and the communications requirements of a democratic society."*

McChesney is the author or editor of seven books. His recent tour de force Rich Media, Poor Democracy: Communication Politics in Dubious Times *(University of Illinois Press) has earned accolades from, among others, Ralph Nader, Barbara Ehrenreich, and Bill Moyers, who said, "If Thomas Paine were around, he would have written this book." McChesney's other books include* Corporate Media and the Threat to Democracy *(Seven Stories Press);* Global Media: The Missionaries of Corporate Capitalism *(Cassell Academic), with Edward S. Herman; and, most recently,* Free the Media: Unleash the Democracy *(Seven Stories Press), with John Nichols. McChesney is also co-editor of the* Monthly Review, *an independent socialist magazine founded in 1949.*

I first met Robert McChesney through John Stauber, critic of the public-relations industry and editor of the journal PR Watch, *who invited me to a party at McChesney's home in Madison, Wisconsin. A longtime fan of McChesney's work, I eagerly accepted.*

Radicals of every stripe were in attendance. Walking from room to room, I overheard conversations about everything from the role of the media in maintaining current social structures to a really good recipe for banana bread. When I met McChesney, I discovered him to be a big man, warm and self-effacing. I also got to talk to his wife, Inger Stole, an intelligent woman with a strong Norwegian accent.

Reprinted with permission and corrections from *The Sun*, September 2000, pp. 4–13.

At the end of the evening, I mentioned to McChesney that I would like to interview him someday. His response was easy and accommodating, and we quickly set a date. I later returned to Madison, and we talked through the hot afternoon in his living room, moving upstairs when one of his daughters needed the space to do her homework.

Jensen: We hear over and over that the United States has the freest press in the world.

McChesney: Yes, we're told that a private, commercial press system is innately American and democratic, and that, in fact, it's the only true free-press system. We internalize this notion early on. It's not a debatable point in our society. The problem, however, is that the type of media system we have today bears almost no resemblance to the type glorified in that mythology, where anyone who wants to can start a newspaper; where if you've got something to say, you can stand up and say it, and you can't be censored. It's true, you can stand on a street corner and state your opinion more or less without fear, but it's also true that, unless you're a billionaire, you won't be able to reach any sort of mass audience, because that's what kind of money it takes to run a major media outlet, like a television network or a film studio.

The way the media giants—the handful of companies that own and operate our media system—present the case to us, you'd think our current media monopoly is divinely ordained, as if Moses handed a tablet to Thomas Jefferson, who handed it to Abe Lincoln, who handed it to Rupert Murdoch. But the media system we have today is purely a twentieth-century phenomenon, quite unlike the one that existed in the first hundred-plus years of the republic. And, in most respects, it's diametrically opposed to the type of media system we had at the time the First Amendment to the Constitution was adopted in 1791.

For the first couple of American generations, our media were largely partisan, closely linked to the political process, not especially profitable, and mostly noncommercial. Newspapers in those days were *always* connected to political parties and factions. You needed your own newspaper in order to be a political force. The whole reason you published one was to convince people to share your political ideas—a completely different purpose from the commercial logic that rules today's media.

Thomas Jefferson and like-minded individuals included freedom of the press in the First Amendment because they knew that if the party in power were able to outlaw dissident newspapers, it could essentially abolish any dissent whatsoever. And, just as Jefferson had foreseen, in the late 1790s, President John Adams and the significantly antidemocratic Federalists who supported him tried to purge many of the radical newspaper editors in the country by means of the Alien and Sedition Acts. So the First Amendment wasn't something the Founders dreamed up in order to protect Philip Morris investors two hundred years later. They had a very real, immediate political cause: the survival of democracy.

Another difference between the press at the time of the nation's founding and the press today is that, prior to the twentieth century, the person who owned the newspaper or magazine was always the editor. And the owner-editors usually didn't start the paper to make money, but to spread ideas. The business aspect was just to put food on the table and to allow the press to continue. Our mythology of the "bulldog press" is built on this notion of crusading owner-editors who print the news as they see it, special interests be damned. But by the twentieth century, that standard of owner-editor had pretty much disappeared, and the real power had passed over to the shareholders and corporate managers. These people have the First Amendment rights to hire and fire editors and do as they please, but they have no more interest in politics or democracy than people in the shoe business. They're just out to make money. So in today's media, the power is purely in the hands of commercial interests. Reporters and editors have no power except that which they're granted by the owners.

Jensen: It seems to me that investors and managers in the newspaper business—or the shoe business, or any other business—have a distinct interest in politics insofar as it affects their bottom line.

McChesney: What I mean is that the owners of the media today don't have an intrinsic political affiliation. If you started a newspaper in 1803, you were a Federalist or a Democrat or had some other partisan political agenda driving you. The idea of making huge profits from a newspaper would have been unlikely. But today the primary goal is to make as much money as possible.

Jensen: Yet, around the start of the twentieth century, historian and writer Henry Adams said: "The press is the hired agent of a monied system, set up for no other reason than to tell lies where the interests are concerned."

McChesney: Exactly. By then, the purpose of the newspaper had already changed. The years between the Civil War and World War I saw the transition from political to commercial newspapers, which was part of a larger transition toward commercialization of the culture. Around the 1880s, people began to see that you could make real money running a newspaper.

But despite increasing commercialization, the press in the late nineteenth century was still largely a competitive arena. In 1870, in any major city in the U.S., you'd have a number of newspapers to choose from, representing a wide range of political opinions. And if you didn't like any of them, you could always start your own; it didn't cost that much.

But over time — especially as advertising became an important source of revenue — the number of newspapers began to diminish, and it became more difficult to start one. By the turn of the century, most smaller American cities had become one-newspaper towns. Even the larger cities had only three or four dailies. The very largest cities, like New York, still had eight or nine dailies until the 1940s and 1950s, when the number was cut down to three, where it remains today.

So what happens to journalism if you've got only one newspaper in town, and that newspaper gets most of its money from advertisers? For one thing, the newspaper can't be highly partisan, because it would antagonize a significant percentage of its readership, and that would be bad for business. Advertisers, of course, want as large a market share as possible, so owners must try to sell as many copies as possible. Also, as papers got bigger, the owners got wealthier, and it became less likely that their opinions would go against the interests of the rich.

This is the spawning ground for the modern notion of professional, "objective" journalism. In order to maximize market share, newspapers had to avoid pissing people off, so they created the essentially fictional idea that their editorial content wasn't controlled by the owners and advertisers but by journalists with professional standards of neutrality. The idea was to make capitalist, advertising-supported media seem — at least superficially — to be an objective source of news. But that's a myth based on the notion that journalists can act independently of owners and advertisers.

The reality is that reporters knew from the start not to trash advertisers and always to take care of the owners' interests. But, more important, the values of commercialism were smuggled in and internalized, and they have increasingly permeated professional journalism ever since. For example, why are crime stories always considered news, even when there's no specific public issue raised by them? The primary reason is that crime sells newspapers. Because such scare stories are commercially viable, they have become, almost by default, good journalism. But there is nothing inherent in stories about crime and violence that makes them newsworthy outside of the communities where the crimes occur.

Another problem is that professional journalism relies heavily on official sources. Reporters have to talk to the White House press secretary, the cop on the beat, the army general. What those people say is news. Their perspectives are automatically legitimate. But if you talk to prisoners, strikers, the homeless, or protesters, you have to paint their perspectives as unreliable, or else you've become an advocate and are no longer a "neutral" professional journalist. This reliance on official sources gives the news an inherently conservative cast and gives those in power tremendous influence over defining what is or isn't news. This is precisely the opposite of what a functioning democracy needs, which is a ruthless accounting of the powers that be.

Jensen: I can't tell you how many environmental reporters I've seen get canned or sent to cover "community activities" because they've become "too close to the issues."

McChesney: You'll notice that doesn't happen on the business beat. There, getting close to your subject is simply "cultivating your sources."

The state of journalism today is woeful, and exactly what you'd expect in a media system owned by a handful of huge firms controlled by some of the wealthiest individuals in the world. They make billions providing a product that serves the needs of the two hundred largest advertisers — essentially, the largest corporations in the world. And whom do these advertisers want to reach? The richest segment of the population. So the news media are pitched almost exclusively to this demographic group. Thus, it's considered normal for a paper to print eight pages of business news and zero on labor. Imagine what an anomaly it would be if you had a newspaper that contained eight pages on labor issues and none on business and gave lots of sympathetic coverage to strikes and rallies. People would say, "What the hell's going on here? Who's running this newspaper?"

Yet, as recently as the 1940s, it was standard for every midsize or larger U.S. daily to have a full-time labor-beat reporter. In a city like Detroit or Chicago or Milwaukee, there would be several. It's been estimated that there were more than a thousand full-time labor reporters and editors at daily newspapers in the forties. So labor issues were covered. When a strike took place, a reporter would talk to union members and find out what they were thinking and doing. The 1937 sit-down strike in Flint, Michigan, which led to the creation of the United Auto Workers union, was front-page news in every paper in the country. Even the *Chicago Tribune*, which was semifascist under Colonel McCormick, covered the Flint strike on its front page; it trashed the strikers, but at least its readers knew there was a strike going on.

Do you know how many full-time labor-beat reporters there are in U.S. daily newspapers today? Four, at most. The position has been all but eliminated. Even in Detroit — the center of the American labor movement in the twentieth century — the last full-time labor-beat reporter was laid off shortly after owners broke the union at the city's two newspapers. In the same year, those papers added fifteen new reporters to cover mall expansions and other "crucial" stories in the suburbs.

This means we have no coverage of labor news in our press, except in those rare cases where the papers absolutely can't avoid paying attention. So if you're a working-class person who's interested in working-class issues—which describes the bulk of the population—our media's news coverage is irrelevant to you. Proof of this came in 1989, when the largest sit-down strike in fifty years took place. Do you know where?

Jensen: I've got no clue.

McChesney: How would you? It wasn't covered. It was a mineworkers' strike in Pittstown, Virginia. And the strikers won, too. But average Americans probably know less about it than they do about Greek philosophy—and certainly less than they do about the Dow Jones index. The only significant national coverage of the Pittstown strike came when some striking Soviet coal miners traveled from Siberia to show solidarity with their brothers and sisters in western Virginia. Finally, the *New York Times* decided to cover that.

Jensen: What little coverage I have seen of strikes is universally negative.

McChesney: That's because strikers are a thorn in the side of society's rightful rulers: the investing class. Our media system is a firm believer in the idea that big business should run society and everyone else should do what's best for big business.

Jensen: To what degree do you think most journalists and journalism professors are aware that they're servants to power?

McChesney: Part of the function of professional standards in journalism (and I suspect it works similarly in other professions) is to make journalists oblivious to the sort of compromises they must constantly make. The point is to make journalists think they're just being responsible and following ethical codes. And journalists have bought into this ideology to such a degree that, especially in the last thirty years, they have been fiercely resistant to any criticism of our media system.

In the last five years, however, I've noticed a major shift in this regard. I used to be a freelance journalist, reporter, and magazine publisher, until I went back to graduate school in 1983. I still periodically see my journalist friends, and I give them my radical critique of the news media and how they serve the interests of the rich and powerful. Throughout the 1980s, my friends would respond: "Bob, you don't know what you're talking about anymore. It's not as bad as all that. You've completely lost touch." Now, when I offer the same critique, my friends say, "Bob, you don't know what you're talking about. You're completely out of touch. It's much *worse* than you think."

There's been a demoralizing crisis of confidence among thoughtful journalists. You can see it in all the books by ex-journalists lamenting the collapse of their profession under commercial and corporate pressure. The upside of this is that it's made people listen to criticism of our media system.

Jensen: But do you actually think some editors and reporters consciously ignore stories and lie to serve the ruling class?

McChesney: I would compare how our system works to the old Soviet press before glasnost. If you'd gone into a newsroom of *Pravda* in 1975, you wouldn't have seen KGB guards with guns aimed at the editors' heads, forcing them to stick to the party line. By the time those journalists got to the top of their profession—the equivalent of working for the *New York Times* or the *Washington Post*—they'd already internalized the values of their society, meaning they believed that what was good for the Communist Party was good for their society. If a story came along that challenged that presumption, they'd instantly dismiss it. No one had to instruct them to do that, because any journalists who had a problem with the Soviet system had been weeded out long before then. If you published an article or two that was critical of the Communist Party, you were likely sent to sell classified ads in Uzbekistan.

And the same thing happens in our media system. By the time you get to the *New York Times* newsroom, you've internalized the values of the ruling class. So when a war comes along in, say, Kosovo, you don't ask such rational questions as "What gives the U.S. the right to invade any country it wants, for any reason it chooses?" or "Why do no other countries have this right?" Instead, you simply assume that the U.S. can do whatever it wants.

Now if, say, Iraq had invaded Yugoslavia, you would have been highly critical of Iraq. And if Iraq had responded, "Well, we've got our own military alliance, just like your NATO. It's called IRAQO, and the invasion is justified because IRAQO voted to do it," our reporters and editors would have laughed and called it a fraud. Yet when Clinton does the same thing, it's perfectly reasonable.

Jensen: Whenever I write for big, commercial magazines, I become discouraged. They go through what I've written and extract the teeth, then go through again to make sure they didn't miss any the first time around. The final result says nothing, offends no one, and has neither substance nor style.

McChesney: That's exactly how the process works. Let's say a journalist at the *New York Times* who isn't completely brainwashed gets the crazy idea that she'll study the relationship between the CIA and illegal drugs. Her editors won't come right out and say, "That's nonsense." Rather, they'll say, "OK, Sally, work on that for a while." But then she'll find she's not getting any support, and that the piece is being harshly edited. Still, she'll put all her time, energy, and heart into this piece and call in all her favors with sources, editors, and other writers in the hopes that she can uncover this important story. She'll go way out on a limb personally, emotionally, professionally, politically. And then the story won't run. Or if it does run, the newspaper won't stand behind her, the way the *San Jose Mercury News* didn't stand behind Gary Webb after he reported just such a story. After that, Sally will have to win back favor by doing puff pieces about how great our system is, how stupid protesters are, how greedy strikers are. Over time, she's likely to say, "Why should I beat my head against the wall doing hard work that gets me nowhere, when everyone kisses my behind for quoting politicians and reciting government policies?"

Jensen: A line I hear all the time to defend corporate journalism or sensationalistic stories is "We're just giving people what they want."

McChesney: That's a flawed argument on a number of levels. First, journalists who say they're "giving people what they want" are essentially acknowledging that they're no longer journalists, even by their own standards. The ostensible principle behind journalism is that you give people what they need, not what they want. They need information to help them understand the world and public life. Giving people what they want is the job of the entertainment industry.

Second, it's not even true that they're giving us what we want. Yes, if you're constantly exposed to something, it's easy to develop a taste for it. After a year and a half of the O.J. Simpson trial, I was sort of interested in what Kato Kaelin was doing, but that doesn't mean it was what I wanted. I would bet that if people were exposed on a regular basis to really good, hard-hitting journalism, they'd develop a taste for it, too.

The real reason we get so much coverage of O.J. Simpson, Joey Buttafuoco, and JonBenét Ramsey is that they're extremely inexpensive stories to cover and require no journalistic skill, so media corporations save a ton of money. Also, these stories never cause trouble with anyone in power, which means the newspapers don't have to worry about losing sources or being sued.

Here's a classic example of journalism by the bottom line: Iowa used to have one of the great American newspapers, the *Des Moines Register*. One reason it was such a great paper is that it had a full-time reporter in each of the state's ninety or so counties. Then, in the mid-1980s, the Register was purchased by the media giant Gannett. The first thing Gannett did to fatten up the bottom line was fire almost all those county reporters. Next, the new owners looked at the Washington, D.C., bureau, where the Register had a staff of knowledgeable reporters covering agricultural policies full time. The bureau wasn't bringing in any advertising dollars, however, so they fired just about everyone.

Was Gannett giving the people what they wanted? No, but it's easy for them to make that claim, because after fifteen years without coverage of Iowa counties, if you did a survey of twenty-five-year-old Iowans today, they almost certainly wouldn't say, "I want good coverage of local issues around the state," because they don't even know that's an option.

Media giants don't give people what they want; they give people what's most profitable to produce. Then, because you consume it, they claim that it's what you wanted in the first place. It's an insult to democracy.

Jensen: When the Soviet Union collapsed, I kept reading in newspapers that Russia was moving "from communism to democracy." It seemed to me that journalists were routinely substituting the word *democracy* for *capitalism*.

McChesney: To use those two words interchangeably is an ideologically loaded construct, because equating them makes it impossible to discuss the antidemocratic implications of our capitalist society. And if you can't discuss those implications, you can't proceed to the next logical step: taking action to preserve democracy.

Jensen: Can capitalism and democracy coexist?

McChesney: Obviously, societies can be both capitalist and democratic, but there will always be a tremendous tension between the two and limits on one or the other, or both. The greater the power of capitalist forces, the weaker the democratic values.

To have a viable, working democracy, you need three things. First, people have to be informed on the issues. This means they must be given a range of high-quality information and opinions, along with a ruthless accounting of the powers that be—and the powers that *want* to be. These are the tools that allow people to engage in debate, make informed decisions, and govern themselves. If you don't have access to those tools—that is, if your media system doesn't make them readily available—your ability to have a genuine, functioning democracy is reduced.

Second, you need to have some measure of political equality. You've got to believe, no matter how poor you are, that you have as much decision-making power in this society as everyone else—even Bill Gates. If you don't believe that, then you don't live in a democracy.

The third thing necessary for democracy to work—really, for any society to work—is a belief that your happiness, your fate, your lot in the world is dependent on your neighbors'. You can't believe that you can have a great life while everyone around you is unhappy or dying. You've got to have faith in community, or else the whole social fabric unravels. Democracy is predicated on such communal beliefs, while capitalism promotes economic inequality and the individual fight for survival. Its motto is "Take care of number one. You're competing with everyone else for scarce resources, and if you turn your back, they'll screw you, so you'd better screw them first." Everyone knows this is what capitalism is about, but journalists can't admit it, because that wouldn't be in the interests of their employers.

Jensen: I've heard about studies suggesting that the more you watch television news, the less you know. How does that work?

McChesney: Danny Schechter wrote a book called *The More You Watch, the Less You Know* (Seven Stories Press). The book's title refers to a number of surveys showing that the people who consume the most commercial-TV news know the least about the subjects covered in those newscasts. The most famous study was done during the Gulf War, in 1991. Three University of Massachusetts social scientists found that people who watched the most CNN coverage of the war knew the least about who the participants were, what the different political positions were, and so on. Also—and this is very frightening—they were the most likely to support U.S. government policy.

One reason these findings are troubling is that they match the plan laid out by Joseph Goebbels in Nazi Germany during the 1930s. His goal for the Nazi media was that the more people consumed of it, the less they would understand the issues, and the more they would support Nazi policies. So our so-called free press produces the same type of results that Goebbels—a man with profound contempt for both democracy and public discourse—was trying to produce in Germany.

Another of Goebbels's theories was that, rather than inundate the media with heavy-handed political messages, it was better to give people lots of light entertainment, which he felt made much more effective propaganda. And in our own media today, there is little serious drama to be found. A good mystery is about as close as you can get.

There's more. Another of Goebbels's instructions for the German media was that they should give the illusion of diversity, but that every single program should contain the same underlying message. That's an accurate description of our cable television and magazine racks today: seemingly diverse, until you look below the surface.

In effect, our propaganda system is much better than anything Goebbels dreamed up, because it has the illusion of freedom. If you disagreed with the government in Nazi Germany, you got locked up and maybe even executed, so it was apparent that you were living in a repressive society. Here in the U.S., you can blow off steam with a rant on some community radio station or by writing for some fanzine that eight people read, and then you're supposed to shut up and be happy because it proves we have a "free" press. But the dominant system remains highly repressive and undemocratic.

In many respects, we have the greatest propaganda system in human history, much superior to the Soviet or Nazi systems, because our system delivers the message that, if you don't like it, it's your own fault. That's the primary message in our society: If you're not a success, it's your fault. If you're in prison, it's your fault. If you're not happy, it's your fault. It's never the fault of our flawed system. The preservers of the status quo do not want that idea to enter our minds.

Jensen: Let's get back to "the more you watch, the less you know." I still don't understand how that works.

McChesney: Basically, it means that the coverage is so skewed toward the official version that you never learn anything of critical importance. So the more you consume—the more you're spoon-fed the party line—the less you're able to engage the difficult questions.

Take Kosovo, for example: If you watch a lot of mainstream news, instead of being able to provide a rudimentary explanation of why the different factions acted the way they did, you're more likely to know only that "They're bad guys. They broke the law, so now we have to punish them." The basic lesson we learn over and over from TV newscasts is that we're the good guys who must deal with all the bad people around the world—people our leaders fortunately identify for us before taking them out.

Jensen: All of this goes hand in hand with the near-total silence in the press concerning our appalling military spending.

McChesney: Even when reporters still had some autonomy from owners and advertisers, certain issues were completely off-limits. And those tended to be issues of critical importance to the ruling class, the one-half of 1 percent who own much of the stock. If the members of the ruling class are in agreement on an issue, debate on it is off-limits for the rest of us. Only if they disagree—or, more often, if an issue is irrelevant to their control of society—is it fair game for journalists and the public. So whether the U.S. has an innate right to invade other countries is off-limits, because maintaining that "right" is crucial to protecting our business interests overseas. It's not in the *popular* interest, but it's imperative to big business that the U.S. have the ability to overthrow any government it chooses. Even those members of the ruling class who have been opposed to various wars—and there are some—never oppose our innate right to invade whenever we want; they oppose only specific military actions.

The elite is divided on some issues, and those are the ones we get to talk about. And then there are the issues that are irrelevant to the elite's control of society: abortion, gay rights, and so on. This doesn't mean these aren't important issues—just that they aren't important to the ruling class.

Now, you were asking about military spending. That's the one form of government spending that offends no one at the top. Any other form of government spending is subject to at least some skewed form of debate: "Do we really need to spend all that money on healthcare and education? And surely we shouldn't be spending all that money on poor people." But military spending is basically massive corporate welfare for the industrial sector. Many people in that top one-half of 1 percent benefit from it directly by owning stock in Lockheed Martin, Boeing, or some other military contractor. The rest would rather see the money go to the military than elsewhere. If it went toward mass transportation, for example, it would hurt the car companies and the oil companies. The products of military spending don't compete with any other products in the market. What's more, if the planes and bombs are used, it will likely be to toss out a government that's unfriendly to U.S. business interests. And even if there's a major war, none of the richest kids will have to fight, because in this country, rich people are, for all intents and purposes, excused from military service.

Jensen: There's a quote dating from the Civil War that sums this up perfectly. Judge Thomas Mellon, an extremely wealthy man, wrote to his son, who was feeling guilty for buying his way out of the army: "In time you will understand and believe that a man may be a patriot without risking his own life or sacrificing his health. There are plenty of other lives less valuable."

McChesney: Some extraordinary studies have been done documenting the degree to which the poor alone fought the Vietnam War. If you look at the graduating classes of all the Ivy League universities and other elite private universities during the Vietnam War era—from 1960 to 1975—you find that out of that couple of hundred thousand people, something like five or ten were killed in Vietnam. But in South Boston, an Irish working-class neighborhood, there were maybe a hundred kids within a twenty-square-block area who died. That's another subject we can't talk about in the media: that poor kids fought that war. And black kids. And, of course, Vietnamese kids. But upper-middle-class white kids by and large didn't fight.

One reason Bill Clinton didn't get trashed for avoiding the draft is because he was just doing the same thing almost every other middle-class kid did. If you had money, there were ways to get out of serving. I'm sure you've heard that Al Gore served in Vietnam, but that was only because his father was running for reelection in Tennessee and was being called a liberal. Gore went to prove his dad was a patriot, but of course he got a cushy desk job. His life was never in danger. You know the song "Fortunate Son," by Creedence Clearwater Revival? Remember the line "I ain't no senator's son"? They were protesting the fact that Gore was over there serving cocktails to officers while poor kids were dying.

This may seem to be off the subject of the media, but it's crucial, because the idea of a "classless" society is the single biggest lie of our time. We're not allowed to talk about the fact that we live in a class-based society.

Jensen: We've been discussing newspapers so far, but the conglomerates that control the media extend far beyond print media.

McChesney: In all the companies that dominate the news media, journalism is rarely more than half of their activities, and often—as in the case of the News Corporation, Disney, or Time Warner—news represents less than 10 percent of their activities and revenues.

If you look back at the U.S. media industry in the 1940s and 1950s, you'll see seven major media sectors: newspapers, radio, movies, books, magazines, music, and the brand-new medium of television. Each of those sectors was dominated by anywhere from a handful to a couple of dozen companies. With newspapers, it was maybe twenty-five large companies. And these sectors tended to be distinct. In other words, big newspaper companies didn't also own film studios or TV networks.

Two things have happened in the last fifty years. First, there has been a tremendous consolidation within each sector, so instead of twenty-five or thirty newspaper chains, we've now got five or six huge newspaper companies. And instead of fifteen or twenty big music companies, today only four companies sell 87 percent of the music in the U.S.

More significant, however, has been the rise of the media conglomerate, a media company that owns businesses in not just one sector, but several. If you look at the holdings of the three largest media companies in the U.S. today—Time Warner, Disney, and Viacom—you find that each is among the biggest players in six or seven different media sectors.

Time Warner, for example, is the second-largest cable-TV provider and owns by far the most channels, including CNN, TNT, TBS, Court TV, HBO, and Cinemax. It has two big film studios—Warner Brothers and New Line—and is the largest magazine publisher in the U.S., producing *Time, People, Sports Illustrated, Fortune*, and many others. Warner is also a big book publisher and one of the three or four largest music companies. Let's not forget 150 retail stores and several amusement parks.

Jensen: Why is this consolidation taking place now?
McChesney: If you believe another myth of our

media system, domination by giant corporations is inevitable, some sort of natural selection. Of course, that's nonsense. The reason this overwhelming consolidation is taking place now is that our antitrust regulations have been gutted. Until fairly recently, regulations prevented linkage of broadcast companies with newspapers and other types of media. Moreover, there were strict regulations that prevented those who owned TV stations and networks from producing the shows that appeared on them. All those regulations have now been tossed out or weakened, making these media giants possible. And the profit from these interlinked parts is much greater than from the sum of each part working separately, because they all work together instead of competing with each other.

For example, in 1994, Disney made a children's movie called *The Lion King*. Since I have a young daughter, I saw it more than a dozen times. It grossed about $700 million at the box office worldwide. Disney got to keep about half of that, while theater owners got the other half. That's $350 million in revenues. But look at all the other things Disney can do with *The Lion King* besides theatrical distribution. They can put it on their Disney Channel, and on ABC, too. They can make *Lion King* spinoffs and sequels. They've produced all sorts of *Lion King* merchandise to sell in their 660 Disney stores around the world, not to mention other retail outlets. They can make amusement-park rides, CD-ROMS, books, and soundtracks from the movie. The possibilities are endless. By the time it's all counted, Disney has made probably more than a billion dollars in profit on *The Lion King*. In fact, Disney can make a movie that flops at the box office and still make a profit. This means that if you're trying to enter the animated-film business, you'd better have the same merchandising arsenal, or you won't be able to compete.

The possibility of in-house promotion actually makes the market even *more* slanted toward the big conglomerates. When Viacom-owned Paramount Pictures made a movie from the children's show *Rugrats*, it could advertise the movie incessantly on Nickelodeon, MTV, and all the other media outlets Viacom owns, whereas an independent filmmaker who made the same movie would have had to pay a fortune for that advertising. So Viacom spent $10 million on that movie and cleared something like $80 or $90 million just in box-office revenues; and that's before they even started counting all the other profits.

Jensen: I think it's pretty clear what's wrong with having just a half dozen companies deliver almost all the news, but what's wrong with having a half dozen companies make all the movies? Aren't movies just entertainment?

McChesney: First of all, these few companies have tremendous control over what movies can be made. The movies that get produced are the ones that will make the most money and don't rock the ideological boat. Hollywood history is replete with stories of talented people who've fought hard and gotten good movies made, but for every good movie that's released, dozens more are cranked out purely to make a profit.

Second, and probably more important, is that the films themselves have in some ways become almost incidental to the industry. Many films are now just part of a broader marketing scheme to sell "brands." A good example is the movie *Space Jam*, which came out several years ago, starring Michael Jordan and Bugs Bunny. Basically, Time Warner didn't even care whether anyone went to see the movie in the theater, because they'd already figured out how to make millions from selling cups, mugs, t-shirts, sweat pants, and other merchandise with images of Michael Jordan and Bugs Bunny affixed to it. They've turned our entire media system into a commercial. Any notion of integrity, of separating the creative product from the commercial, is collapsing under the weight of these money-hungry giants.

These days, the only way a piece with a powerful political message can get made is if a big star is willing to use all of her or his influence to force it through. This takes enormous determination and sacrifice, and afterward the star will have to go back and do more insipid moneymakers to build up her or his stock again. Take *Bulworth*, a great movie with a great message. If it hadn't been for Warren Beatty, the script wouldn't have gotten past the intern at the front door. And now, because that movie didn't make as much money as the studio wanted, Beatty will probably have a harder time making another political movie. As with journalists, it doesn't take long for an actor or director with a strong egalitarian vision to get beaten down.

Jensen: But even with all the rewards out there for going with the flow, there are still a lot of people who are fighting against it.

McChesney: That's right. We don't have to accept this system as a given. It exists simply because our laws created it—with no public participation in the process—and we have a right and a duty to change those laws, to go back and create a media system that serves democracy. Why should we allow Wall Street and Madison Avenue to turn us upside down, shake the money out of our pants, and then drop us and move on to the next target audience?

Even in today's depoliticized society, there's an increasing interest in these issues. Fifteen years ago, I'd say these things, and people would look at me as if I were anti–American, but nowadays people understand that the situation has gotten out of hand. We're talking about the commercial carpet-bombing of our brains in a way that was unthinkable twenty-five or thirty years ago. Our society talks about how much it loves kids, yet we subject our children to twenty-four-hour cable channels that bombard them with advertisements. The average American kid today sees maybe thirty thousand commercials a year. And now these Madison Avenue hotshots are marketing to two-year-olds. They've got scientific plans on how to get into preschoolers' heads. We have no idea what this will do to the next generation, but the hotshots don't care. They're just out to make money.

Some exciting organizing has already begun to battle this. Communities around the country are pressuring their local TV news shows to stop depending on violence and racist crime reporting and actually practice journalism that will help their communities. Some working-class and minority neighborhoods are fighting to get billboards taken down. It's startling for a middle-class person to go into a poor neighborhood and see the booze and cigarette ads everywhere.

On the national level, there are movements to establish nonprofit, noncommercial public broadcasting with enough money to develop great programming without corporate support. Another important effort is to try to require commercial broadcasters to perform real public service in exchange for their licenses. Probably the largest sector of corporate welfare—arguably even greater than the military budget—has been the government's gift of the public airwaves to corporations. They don't pay a penny for the broadcast rights that have allowed them to build these massive companies. Why not make it a condition of having a broadcast license that they accept no political advertising during electoral campaigns? Expensive television ads have turned our electoral politics into a sick joke. Getting rid of them would eliminate more than half the money spent on campaigns and make it easier for someone who's neither a billionaire nor beholden to billionaires to get involved in politics. And why not make it illegal for broadcasters to advertise to kids under twelve? That's already the case in Sweden, and may soon be throughout Europe.

Finally, we need viable antitrust regulations in this country. We have to work to break up these huge media giants. We can't allow this much cultural power to rest with such a small number of institutions.

The first step is to say, "We don't have to accept this. We can change it." We should refuse to be defined as consumers. We are citizens, active participants in our own communities. The biggest fear the media giants have is that the public will find out what's going on and get involved. That's why they bend over backward to sneak laws through in Washington with no public discussion. And when news accidentally does get out, they put their top PR people on it to drown out any reasoned debate and discussion. They're afraid that, once the public really understands how our media system works, we will demand change. They don't want us involved in politics, so they do everything in their power to keep us on the couch in front of the TV. But they can't hide forever the fact that the power really is ours, if we choose to use it.

Down by Law

Carrie Bickner

A LIBRARY'S CORE MISSION is to provide free and full access to a world of ideas. The most exciting thing to happen in libraries in the last decade has been to see that mission extended to include access to the Internet. New library services, funded by generous federal support, have made more Internet access available to more and more people. Now, those same sources may force public libraries to censor Internet access.

Censorship and Poverty

A new law sponsored by Senator John McCain is scheduled to go into effect this month. This law is paved with good intentions but its consequences will be dire. By constricting the intellectual freedom and access to information guaranteed by the U.S. Constitution, this legislation will punish the poorest of the poor.

Public institutions like libraries offer the only point of Internet access for many poor and minority Americans. The new law will force public libraries to censor the web via filtering software or lose their funding. If libraries reject the law, their budgets will shrink, seriously curtailing their ability to provide any Internet access whatsoever. If they accept the law, they will be embracing censorship that is antithetical to a public library's core mission. It's a Sophie's Choice.

A LOSE-LOSE PROPOSITION

The legislation is designed to protect children from pornography. No one can argue with the decency of that intention. But while this clumsy attempt may or may not succeed in protecting children, it is certain to undermine adult readers' intellectual freedom.

This choice between censoring web access or losing funding is made even more painful by the fact that filtering software is widely acknowledged to be seriously flawed, often blacklisting useful, intelligent sites instead of simply blocking access to pornography.

But regardless of the flaws of existing filtering software programs, the real problem is that filters censor. When censorship software is in place, those who depend entirely upon libraries for Internet access will be stuck in a constricted world of ideas and discourse.

The Law Is an Ass

On December 20th, 2000, President Bill Clinton signed the Children's Internet Protection Act (CIPA) and the Neighborhood Internet Protection Act (NCIPA) into law. This new federal law was cobbled together hastily and attached to a larger spending bill (H.R. 4577). If it takes effect on April 20th, as it is scheduled to, libraries and schools that receive certain forms of federal funding must begin to implement "Internet safety policies." Implementation of these policies will be gradual, and will culminate with Internet filtering.

Two federal funding sources will send libraries down the censorship path. The first is the Library Services in Technology Act Grant Program (LSTA), an initiative that funds some of the most progressive work taking place in the field of librarianship.

The second funding source is the Universal Service Fund for Schools and Libraries, or E-rate Discounts Program, that has connected thousands of schools and libraries to the Internet by providing lower-priced telecommunications and Internet access services.

These two sources of funding, designed to open a larger world of reading to a new audience, may now be the mechanism used to make that world smaller.

Reprinted with permission from *A List Apart* (www.alistapart.com), no. 104 (April 6, 2001), pp. 1–5.

No one wants children to be exposed to harmful content, but this law has implications for all people who access the web from libraries and schools, and those implications are harmful.

How the Law Sidesteps Freedom of Speech

In an attempt to avoid the free speech problems that previous legislation has faced, the language in the new law is carefully worded. Filters, as such, are not named but "technological protection measures" are. The law does not elaborate on what these measures are.

In another piece of linguistic maneuvering, the law requires that these protection measures block "**visual depictions,**" not words. This way, the law does not *technically* limit speech.

How Filters Fail

It is easy to focus on how flawed Internet filters are; anyone can generate a list of good sites that are blocked by filters. One shining example is Jeffrey Pollock's Congressional Campaign site. Pollock, an Oregonian Republican who supported filtering legislation and wrote about that topic on his congressional campaign site, found that Cyber Patrol blocked his site because it shared a server with a pornography site. Besides being deliciously ironic, this is a clear example of how *random* filtering can be.

Then we have more targeted blocking that results from *keyword filtering*. This very site, for example, was blocked for using the phrase "topless dancing" metaphorically.

These stories are important, compelling and scary. They also make great copy. They are the *least* threatening portion of a two-part problem, and they are being addressed by software producers.

Why Even "Good" Filters Are Bad News

When Crystal Roberts, a Legal Policy Analyst At the Family Research Council, gives an interview on CIPA, she can sell the idea that the software is getting better. SurfControl, the maker of Cyber Patrol, has promised that the next release of the software will correct the particular problem that caused Pollock's site to be blocked.

Since the new law requires that filtering software be installed eventually but not immediately, it is reasonable to hope that by the time libraries and schools are actually required to install the stuff, the software will have improved. Let's assume that when the time comes, libraries will have access to a product that will:

- Be sophisticated and far more accurate.
- Disclose its list of blocked sites and keywords.
- Be open so that libraries will be able to create customized lists of blocked sites.
- Be free of cultural and political biases.

As libraries become a big new market, we will demand a better product and we will get it.

Would that make filtering okay? Uh-uh. We still face the second and more threatening problem: if libraries are forced to filter, some agent will still be responsible for a list of blocked sites, words or images. *That agent, whether human or machine, will be a censor.* Library users will be subject to censorship.

For the many librarians who entered the profession because they are driven by a commitment to intellectual freedom, the idea that this law will impose censorship is enough to raise grave concerns about the future of public library service.

Confessions of an Intellectual Freedom Fighter

My first public library job was at The New York Public Library in the famous beaux arts building at 42nd Street and 5th Avenue. The place was grand, but what made me want to work there was the collection. A copy of *The Gutenberg Bible*, a first edition of *The Little Engine that Could* and an almost complete run of *Screw* magazine—an entire world of reading—awaited any visitor.

I worked in the Rose Main Reading Room, helping readers use our twenty-four Internet PCs. This was 1998, and a new generation of easy-to-use GUI interfaces was making more information easier to access.

A Class Menagerie

Mine was not an easy job. *Let's Go: The Budget Guide to New York City* had announced that anyone could check email for free in the very room where I worked. While some days I got to teach senior citizens how to use a mouse, or to show new Americans how to search for job listings on the web, a good deal of my time was spent preventing fistfights between email-deprived tourists and urban teens wanting to chat or play games.

Sometimes I dismissed the work as unprofessional,

unrewarding and potentially dangerous. Other times I felt a chill run up my spine over the fact that anyone could use our Internet connection and that we were there not only to help, but also to protect privacy. Like the reader's activities or not, they were there to exercise their intellectual freedom.

Changing Lives

After a little more than a year in the Reading Room, I moved into web development. One of the first projects I worked on was <u>Writer's Voices</u>, an online journal of writings of adult literacy students at The New York Public Library.

My colleagues in community outreach had designed the project and written a good grant proposal. They secured funds from the Library Services in Technology Act (LSTA) Grant Program, the very funding source that now subjects us to the new filtering law.

Where my previous job had given me chills, this one was making me misty. *People who once could not even read were now authoring stories and publishing them on the web.*

Closing the Digital Divide

My personal anecdotes are instances of a more general phenomenon. There are studies that suggest that libraries are often the primary or sole means of Internet access for certain populations and therefore key players in any effort to close the digital divide.

The phrase "digital divide" initially referred to PC ownership. It was a term used to point out the fact that while computer ownership was generally increasing, this increase was limited to certain ethnic groups with particular economic means in limited geographic areas. As the use of the term evolves, a better definition begins to include those who are more generally cut off from information. A more up-to-date definition would include the idea that lack of access and lack of training are barriers to information wealth.

A National Telecommunications and Information Administration <u>study</u> found that:

> ...schools, libraries, and other public access points continue to serve those groups that do not have access at home. For example, certain groups, such as the unemployed, Blacks, and Asian Americans and Pacific Islanders, are more likely to use public libraries to access the Internet. (NTIA. Falling Through the Net, Toward Digital Inclusion. (October 2000: Accessed: April 1, 2001. http://search.ntia.doc.gov/pdf/fttn00.pdf)

In fact, in my city, libraries are the primary place where one can find free access to the Internet.

Professor David Birdsell, Executive Director of Academic Programs School of Public Affairs, Baruch College, found in his 1999 study that libraries accounted for 98% of New York City computers accessible to the public without fee, course registration, institutional membership, or other restriction. In that year, only 54 open-access computers were situated outside of public libraries. The report of his study, funded by the Pricewaterhouse Coopers Endowment for the Business of Government, is forthcoming.

Libraries are closing the information gap. That is why we started *Writers Voices*. That is why programs like the Library Services in Technology Act Grant Program and the E-rate discount program exist. *Now the very tools created to close the digital divide will be used to widen the gap between the information-rich and the information-poor.*

Exceptions Dumber Than the Rules

Perhaps the most troubling aspect of this legislation is the discretion that libraries will have to temporarily disable Internet filters. While all Internet workstations will need to be filtered, schools and libraries held to CIPA *will* have the option to turn filtering off "to enable access for bona fide research or other lawful purposes." What are these purposes? The law does not say.

"Hey, lady! You doing bona fide research, or looking for smut?"

The idea of probing a reader to determine if her research is bona fide or lawful is as abhorrent to me as eating anything but fish on Friday would have been to my great-grandmother.

When I think about a member of the public brave enough to approach a librarian to request unfiltered access, I have to make two educated assumptions about that person. The first assumption is that she knows the law; this knowledge indicates a certain amount of information wealth. The second assumption is that she knows libraries and is comfortable in them; this too would indicate possession of information wealth. I fear that the information-poor will be the *least* likely people to ask librarians to turn off Internet filters, and will therefore suffer the most from this legislation.

What Happens Next?

April 20th will be an important day in the evolution of this story. That is the date on which the FCC is required to publish a list of criteria for compliance.

Earlier this month, the American Library Association filed suit to overturn CIPA. Some state library associations have adopted resolutions supporting the American Library Association challenge.

The American Civil Liberties Union has also filed suit, and some content providers have joined this effort. Remember our Oregonian friend, Mr. Pollock? He is among those content providers.

The contention behind these suits is that the law violates the First Amendment's guarantee of freedom of speech.

The flow of information is necessary to any free society, and libraries are a key mechanism in that flow. It's important to protect children from harmful subject matter, but clumsy, half-baked measures will not achieve that goal—they will only succeed in sacrificing the First Amendment. If libraries are forced to filter Internet access, the cost will be intellectual freedom.—**CARRIE BICKNER**

Carrie Bickner is the web coordinator for The Branch Libraries of The New York Public Library. In her free time, she is the Rogue Librarian and the guide to JavaScript at About.com.

Targets of Repression

Documented by IMC Contributors Ryan Baghdad, Mark Burdett, Otto Nomous, Becky Perrine, Jeff Perlstein and Michelle Steinberg

A reporter from a mainstream Canadian newspaper recently asked for an interview on the upcoming protests against the Free Trade Area of the Americas (FTAA). He specifically sought the perspective of "a woman involved with the alternative media" who intended to be in Quebec City during the April 2001 Summit. Apparently my affiliation with the SF/Bay Area Independent Media Center (IMC) fit the profile and he enthusiastically encouraged me to go on record. Though an ideal opportunity to articulate the issues surrounding the demonstrations, I found myself balking at his offer. "Would my name have to be included," was my immediate response. "Yes, absolutely," he replied, vetoing any possibility of anonymity. Attempting to explain my reluctance, I described the numerous activists (including other IMCers) who had already been denied entry into Canada. He assured me that the issue would not hit the streets until the day after my scheduled arrival. I politely declined, further deterred by the potentially incriminating nature of a public statement, should I face any unexpected legal troubles following the events.

Turning the tables, I began questioning him on the political climate facing the media in Quebec City. He informed me that the government was planning to issue only one press and photo pass per mainstream publication. Then, pausing to confirm with his boss, he noted that officials had instituted an unspoken ban on the presence of independent press within the metal-fenced security perimeter. Though not surprising, considering the trend of criminalization and censorship of alternative media at previous mass protests, it was disconcerting to hear a corporate reporter confirm this fact.

As mainstream media has become increasingly consolidated into the hands of the wealthy few, ensuring distorted coverage and diminished content, the independent media movement has gained momentum. However, in an age when even the illusion of transparent government has ceased to exist, the unauthorized wielding of pens, microphones, cameras, and computers poses a serious threat to the powers that be. Not surprisingly, the state has responded through increased criminalization of the alternative press. The defeat of low-power FM radio exemplifies this crack-down. Early this year, congress caved in to the corporate broadcast lobby by passing legislation that crippled the FCC's fledgling micro-radio program, which was designed to allocate a fraction of the airwaves to community groups. During recent demonstrations, including those against the World Trade Organization, World Bank/ International Monetary Fund, and the various charades that constitute the U.S. electoral process (from conventions to inauguration), authorities have taken unprecedented steps to silence both voices of dissent and the vehicles that relay them to the public.

The Independent Media Center (IMC) has been a repeated target in the campaign against the alternative media. A collective of independent journalists and media organizations, the IMC is dedicated to providing democratic, grassroots coverage of issues ignored or distorted by the corporate media. The IMC is run with an infrastructure maintained by dedicated volunteers and supported through the content of an open publishing model that accepts all contributions, as published directly by the authors themselves. Established in Seattle during the November 1999 World Trade Organization protests, the IMC served as a clearinghouse of information throughout that momentous week, acting as both a content

---

Reprinted with permission from *Clamor*, July/August 2001, pp. 39–43.

provider and a direct media outlet. The center generated up-to-the-minute articles, photos, and audio/video footage that reached thousands through its web site at www.indymedia.org. As the corporate media refused to offer fair and accurate reporting of the critical events, the IMC also spread the word through its own newspaper, video documentaries, and radio broadcasts. A decentralized and autonomous network of over forty IMCs has since sprung up internationally, offering continuous coverage of local concerns and grassroots perspectives on global issues.

The following accounts by IMC participants reflect some of the ways in which the authorities have attacked the indy-media centers or threatened the distribution of dissenting media during mass protests. Jeff Perlstein begins by examining the circumstances that greeted the IMC's inception in Seattle. Mark Burdett recounts the police shut-down of both public printing facilities and the IMC's micro-radio affiliate during the April 2000 World Bank/IMF demonstration in D.C. Ryan Baghdad discusses the implications of the Philadelphia Police affidavit that enabled a raid on a convergence space used by the IMC. Lastly, Otto Nomous describes how the authorities' COINTELPRO-style use of an alleged bomb-threat prevented an IMC broadcast during the LA Democratic Convention.

Seattle

November 30, 1999

"No. You're one of them."

"I'm a journalist. Here's my WTO host committee press pass. Now, please, May I cross the street?"

"What's that? [points to IMC pass] I saw you talking with them. You're not real media."

"It's my job to talk with people out here. I'm a journalist and…"

Blasting pepper spray into Craig Hymson's face at point blank range, the officer abruptly ended the conversation. When listening to an audio recording, one hears the awful sound of the liquid hitting Craig's skin, his pained cry, and then the impact of the spray splashing onto the cold Seattle sidewalk.

Hymson was one of more than 500 journalists and community members who participated in a bold new experiment in media democracy during the week of the anti-WTO mobilizations in Seattle—the Independent Media Center (IMC). While he was one in a small minority of those involved with the IMC who also held an official WTO host committee press pass, he was part of a significantly larger group of IMC participants who experienced all-too-close contact with members of the city, state, and federal government's police forces.

As soon as Craig and the others wearing IMC passes ventured into the public sphere—practically anywhere outside the carefully controlled and cordoned, corporate/government banquet—they were all equally fair game for the pumped-up and over-worked officers who'd pledged to "serve and protect." According to the Seattle National Lawyers' Guild report entitled "Waging War on Dissent," IMC reporters repeatedly "found themselves having to explain what the IMC was when they tried to get through the demonstrators' lines." (http://seattle.indymedia.org/local/images/NLG-REPORT.pdf). Meanwhile corporate network reporters with big cameras and logo-splashed vans moved about freely (or with as much ease as possible amidst the gloriously massive demonstrations and the not so glorious imposition of the "no protest" zone).

In Seattle, the indy-media movement had in its favor a vast number of material, social, and historical conditions converging in a unique and powerful way. The ever-present camcorders, the magnitude of increase in audience and distribution venues available via the internet, the establishment of a large-scale, low-cost work and media training facility, and dozens of dedicated activists and coalition supporters—all of these contributed to the heightened presence and impact of independent news. Despite the tear gas and rubber bullet touting authorities' efforts to intimidate and trivialize dissenting press coverage, alternative media makers proved that resistance is (truly) fertile, as they helped lay the groundwork for a thriving international IMC network.

Washington DC

In April 2000, activists gathered at the IMF and World Bank meetings in Washington, DC to protest global monetary policies that have contributed to worldwide social and economic injustice. Throughout the demonstrations, the DC IMC published a daily newspaper, *Blind Spot*, for distribution to protesters and local residents on the streets of the city. IMC radio volunteers set up Mobilization Radio, an unlicensed low-power radio station at 97.5 FM, to disseminate similar information to the community. The station worked closely with the IMC, carrying on-the-spot interviews with participants and detailed reports on the World Bank blockade and police activities, as well as commentary, speeches and music.

On Saturday, April 15, police and federal agents attempted to ban publication of *Blind Spot* by closing local copy shops on the pretext of "riot activity." Troy Skeels, an IMC print collective volunteer, learned about the shut-downs as he was trading literature at a Kinko's near the White House. An employee asked the group to leave, stating that their presence put his shop in danger of closure. The manager then explained that police had already shut three other downtown Kinko's. Meanwhile, at the 24th and K Street branch, another IMCer was only able to print one box of pamphlets before he was forced to leave. Police entered the shop, harassed anyone printing what they termed "pro-demonstration" or "anti–IMF" literature, and asked the manager to close the shop until further notice, citing "riot activity." Needless to say, there was no "riot activity" in sight. In asserting that independent media would promote illegal activities, the police employed "prior restraint" to curb journalists' freedom of speech.

A few days later, on April 17th, the FCC, FBI, and DC Metropolitan Police raided the Mobilization Radio transmitter site. The enforcement squad arrived at 3:30 P.M. without a warrant. They attempted to knock down the door of the building and ordered the station closed. During the ensuing standoff, the authorities refused to comment, offering no legal explanation for their presence. The radio operators placed calls to both the IMC and demonstration organizers, and a small number of media representatives and activists rushed to the scene to investigate the situation. More police soon showed up, blocking traffic on the entire street and restricting access to the alleged broadcast center and adjacent buildings.

Shortly before 4 P.M., a crowd of over three hundred demonstrators deviated from their march to a jail solidarity action to support activities at the transmitter site. At that point the police donned riot gear and formed a line in front of the building. The protesters, carrying puppets, signs, and drums, demanded that the police leave the area "in 5 minutes." What happened next was unprecedented in the history of micro-radio: the police, FBI, and FCC agents left the scene within 30 seconds. The crowd immediately took over the street in celebration. For a half-hour they basked in the glow of a decisive victory, before relinquishing the street to neighborhood traffic and continuing on their path toward jail solidarity.

After a week of broadcasting, Mobilization Radio was already in the process of closing down when law enforcement arrived. After the police departure, participants disassembled the station and cleared out the building, before regaining anonymity amidst the crowd of protesters.

Philadelphia

During the massive demonstrations at Philadelphia's Republican National Convention in July–August 2000, police arrested over 400 people, attacking crowds of nonviolent, unarmed protesters, and detaining them on false charges. The legal battles continue well into 2001, as those held on outrageous bails and trumped-up felony counts slowly avenge themselves in the court system. The Philadelphia police crackdown alerted Independent Media Centers everywhere that they were under intense scrutiny when a police affidavit named the IMC as a communications and organizing vehicle for protest activities.

The sworn testimony of the authorities was released in the "Affidavit of Probable Cause in Support, Search and Seizure Warrant, #97832, which stated: "Independent Media Centers were established in Seattle during the WTO protests and in Washington, D.C. during the IMF protests. They focus on the protest marches, rallies and what they perceived as police misconduct and brutality. Information indicated that members of the IMC conducted counter surveillance of law enforcement. They also monitored broadcasts of police radio communications and provided real time broadcasts of them over the Internet. The IMC provided communications between groups of demonstrators and orchestrated their movements."

An examination of how this document was produced and subsequently used to shut down protest organizing in Philly offers insight into the workings of the U.S. police state. The Philly PD needed the affidavit to arouse fear in the judges who could grant probable cause for invading the media center and convergence space. Using 50-year-old red-baiting techniques, the authorities declared that, "[protest] funds allegedly originate with Communist and leftist parties and from sympathetic trade unions. Other funds reportedly come from the former Soviet-allied World Federation of Trade Unions." Such statements capture the sympathies of the many judges who still believe that Communists fund a significant amount of dissent in the U.S.

In addition, Philly PD used "evidence" from a report released by The Maldon Institute, a right-wing think tank. John H. Rees, a frequent contributor to the ultranationalist and racist John Birch Society, is the Institute's head. Over the years, the organization has kept anti-red hysteria alive by voluntarily infiltrating left-leaning groups and providing free intelligence work to police departments. Perhaps too nutty to be on the official payroll of COINTELPRO-style government programs, Rees nonetheless contributes to a culture of fear and political repression that seems to resonate with some members of the Philly PD. Their affidavit specifically cites the Maldon report as corroborating evidence. According to Jack Lewis, a Philly state police spokesperson, the government will not release the Maldon report to the public.

Kris Hermes, who works with the R2K Legal Collective, believes that the authorities' distortion of the truth has several objectives. First, the affidavit granted probable cause to physically harass activists and enter their workspace. Second, the document contributes to a campaign of defamation against the protesters by associating them with Cold War–era Soviet political front groups. In addition, attacking the organizations as "Radical" and funded by foreign governments can help destroy the fragile broad coalitions that have been the hallmark of recent mass organizing.

Los Angeles

5 PM
"The police are shutting us down!"
"What?"
I couldn't believe what had just hit my ear through the electronic air waves.
"They've shut down our broadcast!"
Approximately 7 PM
"They said there was a bomb threat," explained the IMC dispatcher as I grasped the walkie-talkie with one hand and the camcorder with the other. Crouched behind an abandoned protest sign that leaned against a thirteen foot-high fence, I was trying to dodge the hail of pepper spray and rubber bullets, while documenting the whole thing on video. Inside the "protest cage" next to the Staples Center, the site of the 2000 Demublican National Convention, Rage Against The Machine was finishing their set—which kicked off with "Kick Out the Jams," re-enacting the MC5's performance at the Chicago '68 DNC protest. In the police riot that followed, scores of people were clubbed, shot, and trampled by cops on horseback. A terrified crowd running for cover knocked the walkie-talkie out of my sight, eliminating my immediate contact with the dispatch. I eventually returned to the IMC headquarters to get the dirt behind the alleged bomb scare.

In a war, an aggressor or occupying force begins by disabling its enemy's communication systems. For example, during the 1991 Gulf War, prior to bombing Baghdad, the allied forces first knocked out Iraq's communication networks. On August 14, 2000, the police prevented the LA IMC from presenting its first live satellite television broadcast by blocking access to the satellite truck, under the pretext of a bomb threat. It later became obvious that they weren't looking for any bombs.

Apparently, at around 4:30 PM, the police advised people in the building that a van in the parking lot contained a possible bomb. At 5 PM, the police detained three activists who were taking a break from IMC to enjoy tofu sandwiches in their van. They were told to put the sandwiches down and step back from the vehicle. I can only guess how deadly that tofu must have been. Strangely, the police "searched" the van without protective gear or special equipment. For a time, the bomb squad even refused to visit the scene, citing insufficient evidence.

In a picture of the incident posted on the IMC web site, you see four cops standing within ten feet of the van which housed the "bomb" that had shut-down a non-approved political broadcast. On finishing, the police said there was no bomb and that they obviously had the wrong van. The police action began just as the IMC satellite show was preparing to go on-air and ended ten minutes after the program was scheduled to conclude. How convenient that they got to shut down the satellite broadcast to protect us (so we can't watch the cops firing concussion grenades at protestors.)

These were clearly COINTELPRO-style tactics if I ever heard of them. And it's a sure indication that activist/independent media has become a serious threat to the current establishment's corporate-owned propaganda machine.

Conclusion

As recognition of the IMC as an important source for independent news increases, the authorities correspondingly escalate their attempts to interfere with the center's activities. In general, police combine preemptive measures designed to block the IMC's dissemination of information during actions with a campaign of slander in the aftermath, seeking to earmark the media-makers as instigators. During the September 2000 World Bank/IMF protests in Prague, the Czech government issued a report suggesting that an unnamed media group had sought to deliberately "denounce the Czech Republic and Czech Police." According to a Czech newspaper article, "Prime Minister Milos Zeman stated … that it was an international media institution which organized something similar in Seattle."

The line between demonstrators and independent reporters has become increasingly blurred, as activists, facing the impenetrable wall of the corporate media, regularly cover their own actions. The corporate press, choosing to ignore or failing to recognize the importance of an event in advance, may often resort to using alternative media footage after the fact. In the current climate, any security that a press pass (including those officially sanctioned) once afforded has vanished. The act of possessing a camera or a recording device frequently designates one as a target. Fortunately, as the state's repression becomes more egregious, the tactics of dissent become more refined—and our decentralized global network of IMC's continues to grow...

Postscript

On April 21st, during the FTAA protests in Quebec City, the Independent Media Center in Seattle was served with a sealed court order by FBI and Secret Service agents. The order stated that it was part of an ongoing criminal investigation into acts that could constitute violations of Canadian law, specifically theft and mischief. In addition, a gag order was imposed, barring the IMC from disclosing any details of the visit or order. The gag order was lifted on April 27th, and now the IMC is in an escalating battle to protect free speech. See http://seattle.indymedia.org for further details and updates.

On May 8, the owner of the Ohio Valley IMC domain (ovimc.org) was served with a subpoena directing him to appear before an Ohio grand jury this Friday, and to hand over server log information related to a particular article posted to their open-publishing newswire. Unlike the court order served to the Seattle IMC, the Ohio Valley subpoena was not issued under seal, and the server log request applied to a single post rather than to two days of website traffic.

The posting in question at the Ohio Valley IMC includes what might be interpreted as an implied threat to Cincinnati Police Officer Steve Roach. On May 7, Officer Roach was indicted by a Hamilton County, Ohio grand jury on misdemeanor counts of Negligent Homicide and Obstructing Official Business for his role in the April 7 shooting of Timothy Thomas. If convicted on both counts, Roach faces a maximum of nine months in jail.

The owner of the ovimc.org is currently in consultation with lawyers and activists who have been dealing with the recent federal request for logs from the Seattle IMC site. According to a post at the Ohio Valley IMC, the request is for naught, as the 'custom written software [for the site] doesn't keep IP logs, or ANY tracking information for that matter."

Three Decades of Film Censorship ... Right Before Your Eyes

Chris Roth

In the United States, a powerful, private film-rating system has the effect of limiting what material can be presented to willing adults, even though the system is not law. Because it is based in the entertainment industry, and media outlets frequently treat entertainment stories less critically than other news stories, the system is seldom seen as a problem.

Making change even more difficult to bring about are the misconceptions about the rating system and its outcome that have been repeated so often that large segments of the population accept them as fact. However, censorship—in whatever form—is a basic First Amendment issue, deserving serious debate and action. Therefore a candid exposé of today's film-censorship-by-ratings machine is long overdue.

The Big Picture

Those films that circulate freely throughout society must pass muster at two stages. First, they must pass through the filter of the motion picture industry, centered in southern California. This industry is dominated by seven majors—huge studios that arrange for the production and distribution of films. The largest studios are members of the Motion Picture Association of America (MPAA), a private organization that assigns one of five ratings to incoming content.

In the booklet *Everything You Always Wanted to Know About the Movie Rating System* the MPAA states: "The rating system is strictly voluntary and carries no force of law." It also indicates that the system is not based on adult standards of content:

> The movie rating system is ... to provide *parents* with advance information on films, enabling the parent to make judgments on movies they want or don't want their *children* to see... While the decision to enforce the rating system is purely voluntary, the overwhelming majority of theaters follow ... and diligently enforce [it] [emphasis added].

However, MPAA member companies and their subsidiaries are obligated to submit their films to the association's Classification and Rating Administration (CARA); nonmembers, including independent filmmakers, also may submit feature films. And usually top directors aligned with the big studios are contractually obligated to deliver films with ratings other than NC-17, the most restrictive class. In 1997 *The Los Angeles Times* bluntly reported, "Sony and most other studios will not release NC-17 movies."

The rating system has been in place since November 1, 1968, in response to circumstances over the previous four decades. Before 1945, the MPAA was known as the Motion Picture Producers and Distributors of America (MPPDA). Formed in 1922 by major Hollywood

---

Expanded and corrected version of an article published in *The Humanist* (7 Harwood Drive, P.O. Box 1188, Amherst, NY 14226), v. 60, no. 1 (January/February 2000), pp. 9–13. Reprinted with permission © 1999, 2000 by Chris Roth. All rights reserved.

studios, the MPPDA defended and advanced the studios' varied interests. The trade association organized industry practices and policies. It functioned as a centralized representative to interact with governmental and private organizations. A title registry was established. According to Ira Konigsberg's *The Complete Film Dictionary*, the MPPDA "at first fought outside censorship and sought to improve the industry's image." In 1930, the MPPDA adopted a voluntary production code, drawn up by two Roman Catholics. For example, no "ridicule on any religious faith" was permitted and "Ministers of religion in their character as ministers of religion should not be used as comic characters or as villains." No "excessive and lustful kissing" and no "suggestive postures." Expressly prohibited were the words *gawd*, *pansy*, and *slut*. Entire social problems were forbidden.

In 1934, in response to condemnations by the Catholic Church and others, the MPPDA added enforcement. Although the system was one of self-regulation, the vertically integrated structure of the film industry made enforcement possible. Studios owned many theaters, so the code's dictates were obeyed for decades. A $25,000 fine could be imposed on a production company for release of a film without a Production Code Administration (PCA) seal of approval. Even as late as 1966, Warner Brothers removed dialogue from the award-winning *Who's Afraid of Virginia Woolf?* to obtain a seal.

In the May 1999 *Federal Communications Law Journal*, Professor Angela Campbell of the Georgetown University Law Center identified five circumstances that eroded the production code:

- the public's reaction to World War II may have caused a demand for realism
- the new medium of television created competition
- an antitrust decision weakened code enforcement because studios had less control of exhibition
- more films were being produced independently and some of them presented serious topics or were mildly risqué
- in 1952 the U.S. Supreme Court ruled that movies are protected by the First Amendment

Add to Campbell's list the cultural revolution of the 1960s—an era that saw the rise of movements that challenged assumptions about sex, art, war, and institutions—as well as the fact that theaters, disproportionately based in urban centers, were negatively affected by suburbanization, putting pressure on movie executives to do something about sagging attendance. All of these factors loosened the code's chokehold on creativity. Moviegoers were demanding unrestrained themes, while some wanted to shield youngsters from such fare.

Then in March 1968 the U.S. Supreme Court released its *Ginsberg* and *Dallas* rulings, suggesting that cities and states could constitutionally eliminate minors' access to some films if age-classification laws were concocted and passed. The MPAA, in consultation with representatives of the theater and international film distribution industries, moved remarkably fast to establish a private regulatory system—so fast that not one locality passed a law targeting kids.

Since then the original 1968 four-category design of G, M, R, and X has evolved into today's G, PG, PG-13, R, and NC-17 scheme. Moreover, according to the MPAA's website (www.mpaa.org), "The ratin (sic) symbols are federally-registered certification marks of the MPAA and may not be self-applied." The MPAA never trademarked the X rating and no longer uses it for films. However, filmmakers are free to self-apply the X.

So, who applies the MPAA ratings? A small group of anonymous parents gathered in Encino, California. Between eight and thirteen of these individuals, whose views are supposed to reflect those of the average American parent (whatever that means), constitute the film-rating board CARA and have signed confidentiality agreements. They screen films sometimes weeks or months before the premieres. The MPAA has not disclosed how much rating board members are paid.

After viewing a film, these board members have a group discussion and then vote on a rating. Outsiders know that if a majority of them vote for NC-17 then NC-17 is assigned. The MPAA says CARA members make "an educated estimate as to which rating most American parents will consider the most appropriate." However, there is no requirement that guarantees board members are credentialed experts in the process and effects of mass communication. Art degrees and artistic skill are not required, and nonparents are not represented at all. Still, MPAA President and Chief Executive Officer Jack Valenti defended this lopsided system to *USA TODAY* in 1999 as the only thing protecting the country from government censorship.

The second stage of the rating game is spread out across the United States. This "back end" of the film industry—multimall operators, cineplex chains, retail giants, and home-video chains—is the means by which Americans can or cannot watch films. Although a true democracy allows access to different ideas and images, many back-end film outlets deny adults this access because of the presence of the MPAA's centralized rating system.

When was the last time you saw an advertisement for the showing of an unrated film? Probably not recently. According to Marjorie Heins' 1993 book *Sex, Sin, and Blasphemy: A Guide to America's Censorship Wars*, "Most theaters adhere to the National Association of Theatre Owners [NATO], a cosponsor of the rating system, and thus will not show unrated films." How about an advertisement for an NC-17 film? According to Frank Miller's 1994 book *Censored Hollywood: Sex, Sin, and Violence on Screen*, "Hundreds of movie theaters routinely refuse to book films rated NC-17. In fact, many malls, which house a significant percentage of U.S. movie screens, contractually bar their theaters from presenting [them]."

Home video markets are also dominated by pinched polices. *USA TODAY* reviewer Mike Clark wrote in the March 10, 2000 issue that "Warner Home Video has a policy of not releasing NC-17 movies on video." According to a 1992 report by William Grimes in *The New York Times*, "Blockbuster Video, Kmart, and Wal-Mart, which account for more than half of all video sales in the United States, will not handle NC-17 titles." Add to this private censorship an overlay of pressure groups targeting every part of the pipeline from production to distribution to exhibition to sales. Indeed, the current rating system provides organized agitators with easy-to-identify targets and, since businesses tend to avoid risk and controversy, the pipeline is increasingly obedient to these agitators, many of which are conservative religious groups.

As a practical matter, this grand mess has created an autocratic bottleneck that films must squeeze through, being careful not to get derailed along the way. Since there is only one monolithic rating organization, a studio whose work is assigned an undesirable rating cannot shop around for a comparable service. Similarly, if several theater chains refuse to book NC-17 films, distributors cannot respond by quickly constructing hundreds of auditoriums.

Where does all this leave directors and screenwriters? It means an NC-17 rating is to be dreaded, as the film will likely be unmarketable. So sometimes a contemplated film is never made. Or it is made but without the high production values that a major studio can provide. Or it is made but adults have little or no access to it. Often a film that receives an NC-17 warning is simply dumbed down to earn an R.

Behind Closed Doors

For over three decades, MPAA rating board members have done more than assign ratings or warnings of probable ratings. Sometimes ratings are changed. Indirect negotiations can materialize, with the director receiving clues through an intermediary about which sequences are controversial. The film might be edited, resubmitted, and re-rated. Or the original rating might be assigned again. Combine this time-consuming process with pressure from financial backers, and directors have an added incentive to create only those films that will avoid an unwanted rating later.

If the appeal process is undertaken, however, films are then considered by the MPAA's rating appeals board. This board is made up of fourteen to eighteen "men and women from the industry organizations that govern the rating system." It can therefore be argued that these members are predisposed in favor of the system. And like the MPAA's film rating board, its rating appeals board is not made up of aesthetes, critics, and consumer advocates. After viewing a film, appeals board members take a secret ballot. A two-thirds majority is required to re-rate a film.

An MPAA summary of the procedures of its twin boards repeatedly refers to the entity submitting films as "producer/distributor." The auteur (or director) is not described as present during the fateful gatherings. The resulting insulated obstacle-course-cum-roulette-wheel is therefore quite unlike a legal court, where a citizen can see who is making judgments and may speak on her or his own behalf.

Of the thousands of films rated in the three decades since the rating system was implemented—662 films in 1998 alone—the most disturbing cases involve those which were initially assigned—or warned about being assigned—the most restrictive rating available and were subsequently edited and later granted R status. This scenario is unsettling because legal, adult-to-adult communication was eliminated.

By contrast, in the parallel world of First Amendment law, precedents say that government regulations intended to block minors' access to controversial content are constitutional only if adult access is unimpeded. In other words, efforts to shield children must be narrowly tailored to do that—and nothing more. This guarantee currently does not exist in the private sphere, even though one of the stated objectives presented when the rating system was unveiled in 1968 was "to encourage artistic expression by expanding creative freedom." Another objective was to "assure that the freedom which encourages the artist remains responsible and sensitive to the standards of the larger society."

Popular Beliefs About Cinema Ratings

After two decades of attending public forums and listening to people express their views about censorship and related topics, it has become apparent to me that a number of myths exist about the film rating system. Let me state and respond to the eleven most common:

Myth #1: The rating system creates no incentive to

add sex-related and violence-related content to any film. Robert B. Radnitz, producer of the critically-acclaimed *Sounder*, spoke to the Congressional subcommittee on small business problems on April 14, 1977:

> If the violence and sex is gratuitous, they, the audience, do reject it; however, if it is indigenous, endemic to the story, the objection generally ceases. Most parents truly do not want their children protected from the truth, but the rating system has so structured people's thinking that a G has become synonymous with the sort of pap and suet concoction even youngsters don't wish to view.
>
> Nobody wants to be talked down to, young or old, and that has become by and large the stigma attached to the G.
>
> Picture, if you will, this: A scene, a sneak preview, a theater in Westwood, Phoenix, Denver, San Jose, or anywhere.
>
> Action, the theater darkens, the sneak begins. The pretitle card, 'Rated G.'
>
> Generally, gentlemen, you will get an audible moan from the audience.
>
> In fact, those of us who make films have now become the Kafkaesque victims of an absurd situation.
>
> Example: You wish to make a serious film which just happens to have no sex or violence; after all, not all stories of a serious nature contain these ingredients. At any rate, you make the film and end up with a G, but that rating will, by its nature, initially put off a good part of the audience that might otherwise want to see the film.
>
> It is true, of course, that the negative aspects of a G film can be circumvented in the long run. Our *Sounder* was a good example of this. I submit that it is tough enough to sell a film on its own merits without having to spend an equal amount of time convincing the audience that your product is not a taffy pull.
>
> And though some G's have made it big, I also submit that lately these successes have diminished. In 1968, according to the code, 38.7 percent of the pictures produced were G rated, and 20.2 were R rated. In 1976, 12.8 were G rated, and 44 percent were R rated.
>
> That the G-rated film is an endangered species does not really concern me. What does concern me is this: Because of the public's antipathy to the G, we filmmakers are eschewing certain fine film subjects, and the treatment of same.

Producer Radnitz said that "a G has become a stigma, meaning good to an audience" and added:

> The tendency that I have seen on the part of young people, college people, high school youngsters, what I call the first phalanx of people who go to the movies today—that's an important point, who goes to the movies today—the first phalanx of people who go to the movies today are young people. The G is off-putting to them, because they think what they're going to see is, as I said earlier, sort of a gooey concoction, and because of that, one might well think of putting something in the film— I'm quite literal about this—that might move it to a PG or an R.
>
> I have heard discussion since I have been in the industry between distributors of films where they do not— were not particularly happy about having a G-rated film, in spite of everything that I have read to the contrary— this has been my experience—because of the fact that they feel—they themselves have a pretty good finger on the pulse of what happens at the box office, have been able to track this situation insofar as the G-rated film is concerned.

Two months later, Kenneth H. Davidson, a Congressional staff assistant, told the committee "PG is considered the optimal rating by most producers. It avoids the 'goody two shoes' image of a Disney-type film and does not have the limiting restraints of an R."

Myth #2: The purpose of the rating system is to provide information to adult moviegoers. Universal rating systems are so pervasive that they are thought to be part of the natural order of things, like rain or sunsets. Many adults use film ratings to decide if they will attend a showing. This misconception that all adults need or potentially need film ratings acts to strengthen requests for government-coerced and other repressive rating systems. However, the MPAA clearly states that the purpose of its film-rating system is to provide information for parental decision making only: "If you are 18 or over, or if you have no children, the rating system has no meaning for you. Ratings are meant for parents, no one else."

Myth #3: Edits to secure an R rating don't significantly change a film. Often they do. For example, films with an anti-violence message—such as *Soldier Blue* or *Scarface*—are less able to communicate that message once edited. Reducing simulated violence in the early part of a film can eliminate a character's motivation, making a later scene—such as revenge behavior or a courtroom confrontation—gratuitous or meaningless. Cutting sensual shots can similarly affect subsequent plot developments. If a finished film is edited, then information can become less connected and random, like confetti.

"Sometimes deletion affects the plot. Sometimes it only changes the tone," said Leonard Levine, board member of the Milwaukee Area Chapter of the American Civil Liberties Union (ACLU). "The 'look and feel' of the film can be changed when a sequence is cut or shortened. It is very difficult to put limits and bounds on things and pretend that the film is not being significantly altered." As director James McNaughton explained to *The Hollywood Reporter* in 1992, "Often a film is like a house of cards." Remove one and something collapses.

Myth #4: Edits to secure an R rating are not burdensome. Producer Jonathan M. Dana shared this with the aforementioned subcommittee on May 12, 1977:

> MR. LYNCH: Mr. Dana, we have been told that you can reedit a film as many times as you want to resubmit it. But the impression we got is that there was not a cost.

You just resubmit it. Have you run into that? Is there a cost for doing that?

MR. DANA: There is a fee of $800 to resubmit a picture for a new rating. In other words, there is a fee to rate the picture. Then there is an appeal fee. Then, to rerate the picture, there is another $800 fee, which is what we will be carrying into the MPAA next Thursday when we bring *Sandstone* back to them.

MR. RUSSO: For the second appeal?

MR. DANA: No, for a rerating. We are at a point where we must cut the film. We need to have a picture that will play in more theaters than an X film can play in. So we are going to cut the film, and we are going to give them the $800 to get them to look at the film again.

MR. RUSSO: Does it cost money to cut a film?

MR. DANA: Yes. It makes all the prints in existence obsolete. Depending on the way you choose to alter those particular prints, you either throw them out or cut them. Then you end up with a picture either of high quality or not so high quality.

If you literally cut the prints you are going to have rough transitions, particularly in music scenes where those cut scenes are butted up against each other. To redo that entire section would involve remixing the film. In other words, this means splitting all the soundtracks again and basically building the film again.

MR. RUSSO: Do you do that after you get the rerating?

MR. DANA: I do not know what most people do. We are just going to cut the film. We do not have the $10,000 or $20,000 to remix that section of the film in terms of labor and rescoring and remixing and that sort of thing.

That same day, producer Earl Owensby spoke about the calendar factor:

> But we could not release our motion picture into the prime playing time after Labor Day, and I do not think anyone would argue with that. From Labor Day to Thanksgiving you might as well put the film on the shelf and leave it. School starts back, football games start, and what have you. Your primary movie-going public is 25 and under, so they have things to do. They start back at Thanksgiving. By begin delayed in that area you go into August, and then you cannot go out and get play dates that are good.

Myths #5, #6, #7, and #8: Big Hollywood studios are to blame for producing and distributing X-rated and NC-17 fare. Those films have big budgets. There are many of them. They drain funding away from films with less restrictive ratings because of Gresham's Law. In the 1977 hearings, producer Jonathan M. Dana testified: "Now, it so happens that most X-rated films are made by independent producers. Why, because by and large there is not enough money in it for the big guys." Substitute *NC-17- rated* for *X-rated* and Dana's description remains true. Compile a list of the number of NC-17 films exhibited in your area or just produced during the last year. Or any 12-month period after the NC-17 trademark was unveiled on September 27, 1990. Then compare those short lists to the total number of films produced or distributed by the major studios. Also hunt for the names of the majors in capsule descriptions of NC-17 films.

Myth #9: The rating system is necessary because otherwise filmgoers would have no way of knowing in advance if a film might be inappropriate. Posters, advertising, news reports, interviews, and reviews in print and electronic outlets provide information about films.

Myth #10: It is possible to create a clear line between R and NC-17 material. This is another way of saying that it's possible, without vagueness and overbreadth, to create a written definition of what is disallowed in one category and allowed in another. However, the task is impossible. Guidelines cannot always indicate in advance if an explicit sequence will or won't trigger an NC-17.

Myth #11: The elimination of some adult-to-adult communication is not a significant effect of the rating system. A variation on this myth is the notion that film ratings are better than censorship, that categories exist in place of limits.

In the February 20, 1996 *Milwaukee Journal Sentinel*, television columnist Joanne Weintraub wrote: "Movie ratings aren't perfect, but, as a filmgoer, I'm glad that a brilliant but brutally explicit movie like last year's *Crumb* was stamped with an R, not cut down or cleaned up for the sake of 'values.'" However, this reinforces the notion that ratings are not a form of censorship—and that could not be further from the truth. The belief that the current system preserves adult-to-adult communication is blown out of the water with just a glance at the list of films edited for "the system" (see sidebar).

The negative effects of the current rating system elude perception because they are so pervasive and gradual. And they are difficult to articulate in a six-second sound bite, so even if negative effects are perceived they are less likely to be reported. Similarly, it is difficult for people in the United States to accept that the rich and famous who make films have been hand-tied by a small group who are told to represent "average American parents." People also confuse *intent* with *effects*. Although MPAA employees may not intend to extinguish adult-to-adult communication, confining words, images, and sounds to cutting-room floors nevertheless sometimes is an outcome.

Fighting the System

There is little chance the current rating system will change unless the level of serious debate about it is raised.

However, raising the level of debate means also raising a number of important questions about the system and society that have yet to be broached:

- Who is to blame for the belief that words and books are more deserving of First Amendment protection as compared to moving images or images?
- The word *sex* is frequently misused. What can be done to encourage use of accurate terms like *simulated sex* and *sex-related content*?
- Why did George Roy Hill's *The Great Waldo Pepper* and Sam Peckinpah's *The Killer Elite* both receive the same rating?
- Stephen Farber was a rating board member during 1970. His insightful 1972 hardcover, *The Movie Rating Game*, describes an era when a psychologist and psychoanalyst were raters. According to Farber's book, both of those individuals allegedly made questionable statements. Years later, on March 24, 1977, Jack Valenti described what kind of people were then being selected as raters: "[I] don't want psychologists, psychiatrists, Ph.D.'s, novelists. I don't want people out of the mainstream or the main stratum of American society. I want people who can relate to others." The MPAA's current *How It Works* website document mentions "intellectual maturity" as one of three qualifications. Has psychobabble been the deciding factor in any recent rating outcomes?
- Is there a double standard insofar as simulated sex and simulated violence?
- Sometimes raters decide if a film is R or NC-17. Should those decisions be linked to changes in the overall political climate?
- In the 1999 release *American Pie*, a sequence suggests that a teenager inserts his penis into a pie. What is the rational basis for the apparent board decision that five thrusts were unacceptable for R status while two or three were acceptable?
- Consider writers and speakers who have their own newspaper columns, television talk shows, and radio "call in" programs, opinion forums, and news-and-interview platforms. Why does it seem that so many professional communicators rarely use negative words like *grandiose, authoritarian, repressed, alienated, jealous, envy, leveling impulse, sex-negative conditioning, erotica, bully, neurotic, meddling, bossy, control freak,* and *player hater* when the topic is a demand for censorship? Why are positive words like *erotica, fun,* and *enjoyable* so rarely associated with sex-related content?
- Which is the most accurate way to describe the rating system: government-coerced or voluntary? Or both?
- If a director shows a white person getting shot in the face, is that more likely to trigger the most restrictive rating as compared to a black person being shot? (The creators of *To Live and Die in L.A.*, a film about Secret Service functions, may have faced that question.)
- Suppose only the final minutes of a story has violence-related content. Does the rating system take something vital away from the artist who wants to create a surprise ending?
- Does the rating system create an incentive for acquisition directors at libraries to refrain from purchasing unrated films or films with the most restrictive rating?
- Alexander Meikeljohn (1872–1964) was an influential censorship theorist. He devised a two-level approach to interpreting the First Amendment. Under Meikeljohn's system, only content that is about public policy would receive "absolute" protection. Alexander Meikeljohn's idea might form the basis for a persuasive argument:

Many films are in part "about" one or more controversial issues of public importance, even though the advertising has no obvious political component. Sometimes one sequence of a film inadvertently explores a significant issue, at the personal or societal level. Sometimes the component is overt; other times it requires thinking to detect. (Some feminists insist that "the personal is political." Under that mantra, *every* film is political.) Political content assists in self-governance. Should anticensorship activists point out that many motion pictures have at least one scene that arguably touches on a public policy question? And that such films, for some viewers, can have the effect of stimulating thoughts, feelings, discussion, and debate about public policy?

On the other hand, a Meikeljohn-inspired two-level approach might have the long-term effect of weakening First Amendment protection for some films or even the medium itself. That is because a second-class status is an inherent part of the model. High Court Justices construct precedents. In the long term, weakened protection for one purported class of content can be followed by outright censorship.

Is the political component argument useful? Is the distinction between political and nonpolitical expression fuzzy?

- An unrelated two-level argument involves venues. Films are viewed in theaters and private households. Courts have generally ruled that citizens have the highest levels of autonomy at home. In the 1969 Stanley decision, Justice Thurgood Marshall, on behalf of the High Court, wrote "If the First Amendment means anything, it means that a state has no business, telling a man, sitting alone in his own house, what books he may read or what films he may watch. Our whole constitutional heritage rebels at the thought of giving government the power to control men's minds." Should critics of the system point out that one effect of some rating decisions is to prevent adults from watching unedited films in the privacy of their homes? Or does a home venue argument weaken protection for art in theaters, as happened beginning with the High Court's unfortunate 1991 Barnes ruling?

- The MPAA says its raters evaluate by considering "the film in its entirety." How can that be reconciled with reratings that have been based on editing brief sequences?
- Since some ratings have been challenged and changed with no editing, why wasn't the second rating assigned in the first place?
- In 2001, *The Chicago Sun-Times* film critic Roger Ebert criticized retailers: "Some chains want to protect you from yourself. They ban unrated and NC-17 films, but don't put their money where their mouths are by refusing to carry such films altogether. Instead they offer edited versions, which distort the director's original vision. The chains should be honest enough to ban the films outright, instead of taking business from stores that respect the original versions." Shouldn't home-video stores and cineplex chains that currently refuse all NC-17 and unrated content begin to offer some NC-17 films, perhaps in their least conservative markets, or request two versions of the same film so adults can choose which one to see?
- Opposition to content dictates can be described as probusiness. As a practical matter, identifiable products (sales of NC-17 films) and a service (screenings and rentals of those same films) are both being suppressed. Should opponents of arts censorship use language from the world of law and regulation such as *capitalism, competition, free enterprise system, profits, business, antitrust, fair trade, access, level playing field, restraint of trade,* and *structural regulation*? Or is a freedom-of-expression argument more effective than a business culture argument, given that opponents can respond to a business-oriented argument by asserting that distributors, exhibitors, retailers, and telecommunications giants have a right to not offer targeted content? Is the approach weak because products and services—which can be regulated or banned without damaging civil liberties—and artistic expression are simply not the same thing?
- The rating system was originally approved by the MPAA's member studios, NATO, and the International Film Importers and Distributors of America (IFIDA). In some ways, the MPAA is the most visible part of the rating mess. Yet needlessly restrictive policies at the exhibition and retail end are also part of the problem. Should more blame be assigned to NATO, some of the largest NATO members, chain retailers, and real estate companies?
- Should advocates point out to the business sector that procensorship organizations and leaders who directly pressure companies want to eliminate a lot more content than whatever happens to be targeted at the moment? And that procensorship organizations are predisposed to also lobby the government for more content-based censorship?
- Should specific churches be described as procensorship organizations?
- In academe, who spreads the notion that words are inherently more sophisticated as compared to images? Are English departments magnets for that kind of distorted thinking?
- The Federal Communications Commission (FCC) requires that all television receivers with screens 33 centimeters or larger must have a V-chip. (Many public figures assume that the V stands for violence. The Canadian inventor says it stands for viewer control.) The microprocessor can be programmed, intentionally or inadvertently, to automatically eliminate display of any rated content. According to *A Parent's Guide to the TV Ratings and V-Chip*, a booklet from The V-Chip Education Project, the microchip can be used to "block" movies "shown on premium cable channels." So the V-chip blackout function is triggered by both the television rating scheme (TV-Y, TV-Y7FV, TV-14LD, TV-MAVSLD, and other busy symbols that look like Snellen eye charts) and the MPAA rating categories (G, PG, PG-13, R, and NC-17). Does penetration of those five categories into television circuitry make the film rating system more entrenched?
- Editing can transform a well-crafted sequence with visual unity into a jumble of discontinuities.

- Should activists make aesthetic arguments against disruption of continuity? Should meddling with the pace and rhythm of a sequence be a separate argument?
- How can "most parents" guidelines make sense given the diverse nature of U.S. citizens?
- Why should adults who have grown children or no children be prevented from seeing legal content?
- The laboratory experiment is one of five main ways of attempting to research the process and effects of mass communication. (Others include the field study, the field experiment, the correlational study, and the longitudinal study.) In the laboratory experiment, subjects are positioned in front of a screen and their responses are quantified. The laboratory experiment has three unintentional flaws. One is that the laboratory setting is unnatural. Another is that subjects can receive subtle incentives to respond within an expected range of behaviors or provide a single "right" answer. Yet another persistent flaw is that a unit of analysis has to be decided on in advance. This means that something as complicated as a work of art with hyperbole, surrealism, speech, color, motion, sounds, music, well-crafted imagery, and multiple meanings is transformed into one of a very small number of simple, inflexible *this* or *that* categories. Do the deficiencies that plague experimenters exist when the setting is not the laboratory but the Encino projection room where a few employees hold lighted clipboards? Or is this a forced analogy?
- Screenings are followed by a discussion. In Sharon Waxman's report in the April 8, 2001 *The Washington Post*, former rater Jay Landers offered his opinions on the post-screening discussion process: "It's very intimidating. You sit there with someone who hired you, who has the ability to fire you at any minute, since you are an at-will employee … casting a particular vote and critiquing your judgment or someone else's judgment. It's tatamount to a judge telling a jury how to think when they're trying to deliberate in a case. It's not appropriate." Mr. Landers began in 1995. He reportedly sought to change the system from the inside and failed. The rater exited in 2000.

Outsiders with dissimilar agendas have offered their proposals for changing the system. Still more reform packages can be imagined. Virtually all proposals have the effect of either increasing or preserving the elimination of content. Should it be assumed that anything described as reform is worth implementing? Is the very existence of any universal film rating system the problem?

- Why can't the universal rating system be dissolved to facilitate the rise of hundreds of film-rating systems, each from a different subculture?
- Should psychology and psychiatry associations be encouraged to formally proclaim that the impulse to censor art is undesirable? If censorship demands are not associated with distorted thinking and antisocial behavior, then will those demands multiply and become recognized as a norm by more subcultures?
- Film, television, the compact disc (CD), the videogame, and the comic book are modes of expression burdened by universal rating systems. Do people approve of universal rating systems because they intuitively sense that they tend to limit what creative people can communicate? Is it effective to complain that the establishment of any universal rating system tends to legitimize preexisting and proposed universal rating systems for other media? Or is the best strategy for any given volunteer to specialize and challenge one rating system?
- Are there arenas where is difficult to determine where studios end and the theater industry begins? If yes, then is the level of coordination and crossownership enough to make it difficult for directors and other creative people to ignore the rating system?
- The word *violence* is frequently misused. What can be done to encourage use of accurate terms like *simulated violence, onscreen violence, two-dimensional violence*, and *violence-related content*?
- Procensorship groups and politicians are most persuasive when they use words like *movie industry, Hollywood* and *executives*. Generally, they are less persuasive when they mention specific film titles. And they are even less persuasive when they name the director. So the savvy agitators omit both kinds of information. What can be done to put a human face on films?
- Definition-stretching occurs when a writer or speaker proceeds from the unstated premise that violence and violence-related content are the same thing. Is the blurring of *conduct* and *communication* inadvertent or deliberate? If deliberate, then dishonest? What problems does definition-stretching create for survivors of actual violence? How should survivors respond when someone says that the horrendous experiences they survived are just like flat images?

- If a director with a completed motion picture hopes for an R and instead receives an NC-17, then the MPAA rules allow for editing and resubmission. The process can be repeated, although an R is not guaranteed. A new MPAA rule requires a one month interval after three screenings. Is the delay too long? Given the realities of motion picture financing and fixed marketplace conditions like the calendar factor, does the one-month rule have the effect of eliminating even more speech, sounds, images, and ideas as compared to a shorter delay?
- Suppose a film suggests that a couple has sex. Later in the plot, no negative consequences arise. Is that more likely to trigger the most restrictive rating as compared to a film where a comparable sexual encounter is followed by a violent or merely negative consequence? (Compare the NC-17-rated *Henry and June* to *Fatal Attraction* and *Dressed to Kill*, both R-rated.)
- Suppose a director wants to make a film about the design of unsafe vehicles. Or persecution of atheists. Or genocide. Or Third World factories. Or nuclear contamination. The film may be purported to be historically accurate. Or fiction. Or both. If the simulated violence is "sanitized" to avoid an NC-17, then is the result disrespectful to the deceased? Does the dumbed down film give legitimacy and credibility to history revisionists?
- In 1999, *The New York Times* published a letter from a registered nurse. She wrote that efforts to shield minors from simulated onscreen violence divert attention away from real-life child abusers. The health care professional from Connecticut added that media crackdown campaigns send violent parents "the message that they are not accountable for their behavior." Should anticensorship activists criticize parent-on-child violence, since it is such a primary cause of violence and other problems?
- Should raters be asked to break confidentiality agreements and criticize the system via "tell all" writings? Should journalists publicly offer unnamed source status in exchange for information?

Likewise, the rating system—although described as voluntary by the MPAA—enjoys a level of authority akin to law. Therefore, action at the highest level is needed along with discussion. Tell your Senators that you want justices appointed to the U.S. Supreme Court who have opined that obscenity (as defined in the disastrous cluster of 1973 Court rulings informally called *Miller vs. California*) is protected by the First Amendment. Oregon's Supreme Court affirmed such protection in 1986. An overturn of the High Court's anti-obscenity precedents would prevent future prosecutors from legally denying adults access to unrated, NC-17, and X films in all fifty states.

It is also imperative that, as more and more control is concentrated in fewer and fewer hands, enlightened consumers express their concerns about the rating system's negative effects to as many film-related corporations as possible. Comment cards, prepaid and preaddressed, are available at retail sites. Letters should ask cineplexes and retailers to offer NC-17 films. If a new film has been cut, a letter to the editor should point it out. Misstatements by pro-censorship leaders, columnists, clergy, politicians, and academics also need to be corrected whenever made.

In *How it Works*, the MPAA's Jack Valenti declares that movies are the "most creative of art forms." In a 1996 issue of *Columbia-VLA Journal of Law and the Arts*, attorney Jacob Septimus observes that films "may be the single greatest cultural influence on the collective American psyche." However, the right to create, exhibit, or watch a film is only a quaint abstraction if marketplace practices and conditions prevent people from doing so.

Since movie theater attendance figures and home-video sales indicate growing interest in films, there should be growing interest in their First Amendment protection. Through a coordinated and comprehensive grassroots effort, We the People can succeed in promoting and protecting a diverse marketplace of ideas on screen. Until then, the screen is not free.

A shorter version of this article first appeared as the cover story of the January/February 2000 issue of *The Humanist*. Chris Roth is a board member of the American Civil Liberties Union chapter in Milwaukee, Wisconsin. The author welcomes your comments by e-mail at ChrisRoth@Hotmail.com or PO Box 170121 Milwaukee WI 53217-8011 USA. Copyright 1999, 2000, 2001 by Chris Roth. All rights reserved.

What do the rating symbols mean?

G General Audiences—All ages admitted. Signifies that the film rated contains nothing most parents will consider offensive even for their youngest children to see and hear. Nudity, sex scenes, and scenes of drug use are absent; violence is minimal; snippets of dialogue may go beyond polite conversation but do not go beyond common everyday expressions.

PG Parental Guidance Suggested—Some material

may not be suitable for children. Signifies that the film rated may contain some material parents might not like to expose to their young children—material that will clearly need to be examined or inquired about before children are allowed to attend the film. Explicit sex scenes and scenes of drug use are absent; nudity, if present, is seen only briefly; horror and violence do not exceed moderate levels.

PG-13 Parents Strongly Cautioned—Some material may be inappropriate for children under 13. Signifies that the film rated may be inappropriate for preteens. Parents should be especially careful about letting their younger children attend. Rough or persistent violence is absent; sexually oriented nudity is generally absent; some scenes of drug use may be seen; some use of one of the harsher sexually derived words may be heard.

R Restricted—Under 17 requires accompanying parent or adult guardian (age varies in some jurisdictions). Signifies that the rating board has concluded that the film rated may contain some adult material. Parents are urged to learn more about the film before taking their children to see it. An R may be assigned due to, among other things, a film's use of language, theme, violence, sex, or its portrayal of drug use.

NC-17 No One 17 and Under Admitted. Signifies that the rating board believes that most American parents would feel that the film is patently adult and that children age 17 and under should not be admitted to it. The film may contain explicit sex scenes, an accumulation of sexually oriented language, and/or scenes of excessive violence. The NC-17 designation does not, however, signify that the rated film is obscene or pornographic in terms of sex, language, or violence.

—from *Everything You Always Wanted to Know About the Movie Rating System*, published by the Motion Picture Association of America and the National Association of Theatre Owners in association with local theaters.

Edited for "the System"

Many films are known have been edited to avoid the most restrictive rating. In the July 18, 1999 issue of *The Los Angeles Times*, Amy Wallace reported that "last year the board initially gave an NC-17 rating to 154 films for sex and language, compared with 174 films for violence" and a "vast majority of the filmmakers opted to cut their films in order to get an R."

This partial list of films edited to avoid an X or NC-17 rating—presented here together in one place for the first time (with their director in parentheses)—is long, beginning soon after the rating system took effect and peaking in 1999:

- *If...*, 1968 (Lindsay Anderson)
- *The Wild Bunch*, 1969 (Sam Peckinpah)
- *The Magic Garden of Stanley Sweetheart*, 1970 (Leonard Horn)
- *Soldier Blue*, 1970 (Ralph Nelson)
- *Part Time Virgins*, (previously known as *Interplay*) 1970 (Albert T. Viola)
- *Straw Dogs*, 1971 (Sam Peckinpah)
- *The Bang, Bang Gang*, 1971 (Van Guylder)
- *Getting High* (previously known as *Loving and Laughing*, 1971), 1973 (John Sone)
- *Tis a Pity She's a Whore* (also known as *Addio, Fratello Crudale*), 1973 (Guiseppe Patroni Griffi)
- *The Street Fighter* (also known as *Gekitotsu! Satsujin ken*), 1974 (Shigehiro Ozawa)
- *The Naughtiest Show on Earth*, 1975 (director not known; distributor was William Mishkin Motion Pictures)
- *Fingers*, 1978 (James Toback)
- *Dressed to Kill*, 1980 (Brian De Palma)
- *The Postman Always Rings Twice*, 1981 (Bob Rafaelson)
- *Scarface*, 1983 (Brian De Palma)
- *Crimes of Passion*, 1984 (Ken Russell)
- *9½ Weeks*, 1986 (Adrian Lyne)
- *She's Gotta Have It*, 1986 (Spike Lee)
- *Angel Heart*, 1987 (Alan Parker)
- *RoboCop*, 1987 (Paul Verhoeven)
- *Damage*, 1992 (Louis Malle)
- *The Lover*, 1992 (Jean-Jacques Annaud)
- *Basic Instinct*, 1992 (Paul Verhoeven)
- *Body of Evidence*, 1993 (Uli Edel)
- *Hard Target*, 1993 (John Woo)
- *Sliver*, 1993 (Philip Noyce)
- *The Advocate*, 1994 (Leslie Megahey)
- *Natural Born Killers*, 1994 (Oliver Stone)
- *Bliss*, 1997 (Lance Young)
- *Boogie Nights*, 1997 (Paul Thomas Anderson)
- *Two Girls and a Guy*, 1997 (James Toback)
- *American Pie*, 1999 (Paul Weitz)
- *But I'm a Cheerleader* (also known as *Make Me Over*), 1999 (Jamie Babbit)
- *Coming Soon*, 1999 (Colette Burson)
- *Summer of Sam*, 1999 (Spike Lee)
- *Eyes Wide Shut*, 1999 (Stanley Kubrick)
- *South Park: Bigger, Longer & Uncut*, 1999 (Trey Parker)
- *Black and White*, 1999 (James Toback)
- *The Idiots*, 1999 (Lars von Trier)
- *American Psycho*, 2000 (Mary Harron)
- *Storytelling*, 2001 (Todd Solondz)

Reports of a rating disagreement can increase awareness of an upcoming film. Sometimes a "director's cut" or unrated home video version of a film that has been edited for theaters is released for the U.S. market. But this is not always done. For example, according to the March 23, 2000 *USA TODAY*, the domestic home video version of "Eyes Wide Shut" has some imagery digitally obliterated, even though Europeans can purchase the unmodified version. Note how many of the films on the above list are major motion pictures by critically acclaimed directors who had deals with major studios. If someone as securely positioned as Brian De Palma or the late Stanley Kubrick could not place their films in any domestic theaters or households without edits, then who can? Even a record of commercial success is useless.

ALTERNATIVES

Libraries as Media:
The Struggle against Corporate and Government Indoctrination in American Schools and Universities, and in Daily Life
by Charles Willett

Charles Willett is founding editor of *Counterpoise*, a review journal, 1997– ; founding editor of *Librarians at Liberty*, a magazine, 1993– ; founder and publisher of CRISES Press, Inc., 1991– ; and co-founder, board member, and treasurer of the Civic Media Center and Library, Inc., Gainesville, 1993– . He has worked in acquisitions and collection management at three large research libraries (1968–85) and is past chair of the Alternatives in Print Task Force of the Social Responsibilities Round Table of the American Library Association (1993–99).

This article grew out of three talks he gave in November and December 2000, just before and during the national election crisis, with its unexpected focus on Florida: "Independent Learning Communities and Libraries," at the "Florida Coalition for Peace and Justice" conference (Winter Park, Florida, 4 November 2000); "Libraries as Media," at the "Vienna 2000" conference of progressive librarians (Vienna, Austria, 18 November 2000); and "Alternative Libraries and Infoshops," at the "Florida Youth Liberation Conference 2000" (Gainesville, Florida, 17 December 2000). An earlier version of this article, "Alternative Libraries and Infoshops," appeared in Librarians at Liberty, *vol. 8, no. 1–2 (December 2000).*

Libraries as Media

In common parlance the word "media" refers collectively to the organizations that gather and present news to the public. Thus, the *American Heritage Dictionary* (1969 edition) defines it as **"a means of mass communications, such as newspapers, magazines or television."**

Webster's 3rd New International Dictionary (unabridged, 1976) casts a somewhat wider net. It defines "media" as **"a channel, method or system of communication, information or entertainment,"** and cites an illustration from the *Saturday Review*: "'A book needs the widest possible discussion in the reviewing media of the country —whether magazine, newspaper, radio, television, or public platform'." Here "information" and "entertainment" have been added to the content of media, and "public platform" to the means of delivery.

Those definitions of "media," however, were written before the consolidation of the mass communications industry during the 1980s and 1990s. Where there used to be hundreds of independent publishers, here and abroad, that produced English-language books and periodicals, only a few remain. Most have been swallowed by global conglomerates that include print and broadcast news media, movie studios, and other sources of content, as well as global electronic systems that manipulate, package and deliver these "products" to "consumers." as Ben H. Bagdikian, author of *The Media Monopoly*,[1] described in April 1998 in his Preface to the fourth edition of *Alternative Publishers of Books in North America*:

> As of this writing, eight major conglomerates dominate the English-language book market. The number "eight" conceals a larger reality. Within each of those eight multi-national conglomerates (three belong to parent firms headquartered outside the United States), their current main house brand includes more than forty formerly independent imprints. Bertelsmann, based in Germany, may be known mostly for owning Random House, but Bertelsmann also owns the imprints Doubleday, Anchor, Bantam, Dell, Delacorte, Pantheon, Ballantine, Times, Vintage, Fawcett, Fodor, and Knopf (alas, poor Knopf, we knew it well). Rupert Murdoch's Australian-based News Corp. owns HarperCollins, which is itself a gene-spliced offspring of former houses that had already merged in the past. One firm, Viacom, formerly known mostly to telecommunications investors, was unknown to the book business until recently, when it bought Simon & Schuster, Scribner, Macmillan and others that were once

> **"The current actions of large multi-media, multi-national conglomerates have a special influence on their book subsidiaries. The new corporate strategy is to control every step in the mass media process, from purchasing the firms that originate content—movie studios, TV networks, newspapers, book publishers, etc.; and then the national delivery systems—cable, radio and television networks; and finally the entry to each home—telephone and cable lines or satellite dishes. These all-inclusive systems have given each company more communications power than any nation or dictator in history."**
> —*Ben H. Bagdikian*

separate houses (Viacom's new publishing president said the line between publishing and entertainment is now going to be more blurred than ever).

The current actions of large multi-media, multi-national conglomerates have a special influence on their book subsidiaries. The new corporate strategy is to control every step in the mass media process, from purchasing the firms that originate content—movie studios, TV networks, newspapers, book publishers, etc.; and then the national delivery systems—cable, radio and television networks; and finally the entry to each home—telephone and cable lines or satellite dishes. These all-inclusive systems have given each company more communications power than any nation or dictator in history. Furthermore, books become seen not just as books but as content usable in other forms in the conglomerates' exclusive, all-purpose systems. [2]

The power of these giants, in turn, has led to the tremendous growth of the mainstream public relations and advertising industries. Every corporation, every government office, every institution that wants to attract the attention of large numbers of people must employ public relations and advertising specialists in order to be able to shape positive messages about its products and services and buy access to appropriate subsidiaries of these conglomerates. Huge amounts of money are spent in this way. It is estimated, for example, that the Democratic and Republican parties together spent three billion dollars on the 2000 presidential campaign.

In recognition of these changed circumstances, the definition of "media" might be revised as follows: **Institutions that define and interpret reality for large numbers of people, including the mass communications, entertainment, public relations, and advertising industries; book publishing and distribution; corporate and government information offices at all levels; and the administrative offices of all cultural, scientific, educational, professional, religious and philanthropic organizations.**

In a recent paper on the uses of language in the field of international relations, barb howe, a graduate student in political science at the University of Florida, made these observations about the nature of reality:

> "Language is power because it categorizes reality, and any categorization of reality, while being a useful 'convenience of the mind,' also reflects the prejudices and world view of the language-user. Language not only shapes thought; it is thought. It creates categories, subjects and abstractions that then become reified. Human beings create their worlds through language. Language creates our realities, and by asking who controls the language that shapes and influences us, we are also asking who controls reality. For this reason it is immensely important to look at who controls the language of any given field....
>
> "When we think about language and its pervasive influence in our lives, in our interactions with other people and in the way we perceive the world, we cannot help but recognize the importance of examining who controls language. 'In a participatory universe, there are no neutral observers.' Reality is not only a noun, it is also a verb. We are in the process of creating our realities every day, and we create those realities with words. In order to come to as accurate and representative an understanding of reality as we can, we must ask whose words are being heard, who controls the language, and how that affects the picture of reality they are painting of and for the rest of the world. In this light, the Quaker saying 'Speak truth to power' has all the more urgency." [3]

The reality that media perceive and promulgate is based on words carefully brought together into language that is widely understood and accepted by the empowered elements of society. And central to establishing that reality for all media are their resources and networks—their in-house or externally accessible libraries, which acquire and organize information and knowledge and make it available for use.

All libraries are linked together—through common acquisitions, cataloging, reference, circulation, collection management, and electronic systems procedures; through international rules and standards; through accredited institutions offering the MLS degree; through local, state, regional, national and international professional associations, through national libraries; through many specialized print and online publications; through a myriad of meetings and conferences on every conceivable topic; and through ongoing correspondence utilizing every possible means of communication—into elaborate groups and subgroups categorized in almost every way that professional information organizers can devise. Thus libraries are fundamental to all media and are themselves a form of media.

All libraries are linked together—through common acquisitions, cataloging, reference, circulation, collection management, and electronic systems procedures; through international rules and standards; through accredited institutions offering the MLS degree; through local, state, regional, national and international professional associations, through national libraries; through many specialized print and online publications; through a myriad of meetings and conferences on every conceivable topic; and through ongoing correspondence utilizing every possible means of communication—into elaborate groups and subgroups categorized in almost every way that professional information organizers can devise. Thus libraries are fundamental to all media and are themselves a form of media.

Problems of Acquisitions

Libraries fail to meet many users' needs. One problem is funding. The steep rise in the cost of books and periodicals, and the enormous increase in worldwide publishing output over the past several decades have reduced the collections at even the largest research libraries to an ever-shrinking portion of available knowledge and information. In September 2000 Duane E. Webster, Executive Director of the Association of Research Libraries, which represents the interests of 121 of the largest research libraries in North America, wrote a letter to the Antitrust Division of the Department of Justice protesting the acquisition by Reed Elsevier of Harcourt General for an estimated 5.6 billion dollars. As background, Webster presented the following information about funding research library collections:

> "In the aggregate, ARL libraries spend over $900 million a year on books and journals to support the information resource needs of faculty, students and the public. But these dollars have been unable to keep up with the inflation in the cost of library materials. Librarians make their purchase decisions by broad subject categories, evaluating titles by price, quality and anticipated use. They purchase as many titles in each subject area as their budgets will allow. The more titles in a subject area a publisher owns, the greater its market share and power. Of particular concern over the past 15 years have been the high prices of journals in science, technology and medicine (STM), an area of publishing increasingly dominated by a few large commercial companies.

> "According to Library Journal, STM journals have increased in price about 11% a year between 1990 and 2000. The 2000 subscription price for an STM journal averaged $974. This is over 5 times more expensive than a title in the humanities ($188) and almost twice as expensive as a title in the social sciences ($504). Moreover, recent studies show that the prices of STM journals published by commercial firms are far more expensive than those published by not-for-profit society and association publishers. A study conducted at the University of Wisconsin, Madison, found that commercially published journals in physics were, on average, 2.5 times more costly than not-for-profit journals, and in neuroscience, they were 6.5 times more expensive. [www.library.wisc.edu/projects/glsdo/cost.html]

> "The high prices of STM journals have had a devastating effect on libraries' ability to support the information needs of their communities. According to statistics collected by ARL, between 1986 and 1999 the typical research library has had to cut journal subscriptions by 6% and decrease the purchase of books by 26%, all while spending 170% more on journals and 34% more on books. At the same time, worldwide publishing output increased over 50%. Libraries cannot even afford the same number of resources acquired in 1986, let alone the same proportion of published knowledge.[4]"

I can amplify Webster's figures by my own experience in acquisitions and collection development at three of those ARL libraries from 1968 through 1985. The enormous expansion of library collections that began with federal aid to education after Sputnik (1957) peaked about 1971. By the second half of the 1970s and the early 1980s, most large research libraries were already cutting back their book and journal collections.

Webster notes that the three major factors in determining where to cut are "price, quality and anticipated use." Libraries spend their limited funds on materials assumed to be most heavily used. The areas most ruthlessly cut, therefore, are those least strongly defended. This especially hurts the alternative press, which administrators—who usually are unfamiliar with it—reject for alleged high cost (because there is so much of it), poor quality (though many alternative publications are very well done), and low anticipated use (a circular argument: what is not known is not used and therefore is not known and so is not used. . .).

Second-tier universities and colleges, many of them founded during the educational boom years of the 1960s, were especially badly hurt when funds were cut back in the '70s and '80s. Their collections of current foreign and alternative press materials, never strong to start with, became almost non-existent by the 1990s. In a study of alternative press holdings at 45 general academic libraries in the Southeast in 1988, I found that the six large research libraries in the group held 60 to 89 percent of the 32 recommended new books in the sample, but the remaining 39 smaller libraries held few or none of them, as follows:[5]

> **The high prices of STM journals have had a devastating effect on libraries' ability to support the information needs of their communities. According to statistics collected by ARL, between 1986 and 1999, the typical research library has had to cut journal subscriptions by 6% and decrease the purchase of books by 26%, all while spending 170% more on journals and 34% more on books. At the same time, worldwide publishing output increased over 50%. Libraries cannot even afford the same number of resources acquired in 1986, let alone the same proportion of published knowledge.**
> —Duane E. Webster

PERCENT OF SAMPLE	NUMBER OF LIBRARIES
90–100	none
80–89	2
70–79	2
60–69	2
50–59	none
40–49	1
30–39	1
20–29	3
10–19	7
1–9	15
0 percent	12

Several of these smaller academic libraries did not have a single book by Noam Chomsky, the world renowned linguist and outspoken critic of U.S. foreign policy and the mass media, who has been cited more often than any other living scholar by *Arts and Humanities Citation Index*.

Another reason why libraries fail to acquire what users need is ignorance of what is available. Selection decisions are highly dependent on how much money publishers spend on marketing their materials. As Byron Anderson, editor of *Alternative Publishers of Books in North America*, has written,

> Librarians would be fortunate to be aware of even 10 percent of the publishers publishing today. The other 90 percent remain obscure. Library collections represent only a fraction of the true diversity of books available. While a library cannot collect everything, most librarians are not even aware of many publications available in their effort to build a collection. Examples of alternative publications generally absent from library collections include:
> - Translated works about the Third World by indigenous writers.
> - Topics of anarchism, poverty, labor, erotica, human rights, and peace studies.
> - Most books of poetry.
> - The writings of many new and lesser known authors.

There is a persistent myth that publications from small presses are the leftovers or rejects screened out by the "rigorous" editorial standards set by editors at mainstream presses. If a manuscript can't cut it with the big houses, the authors submit to the smaller houses. With some exception, this is simply not true. In mainstream presses, decisions to print are market-based, that is, books are based on profit potential. In independent presses, especially progressive presses, decisions to print are topic-based or based on literary merit, that is, books are mission-driven or have something to say.[6]

Problems of Cataloging

Not only the failure to acquire publications denies users access to materials they need; how acquired materials are organized in library collections does also. The Library of Congress (LC) maintains the Dewey Decimal and LC classification systems, used by virtually all American and many foreign public and academic libraries, and also a complex structure of authorized subject headings. As new titles appear, LC classifies and catalogs them, assigning subject headings based on these rules. Commercial bibliographic utilities like OCLC then transmit these authorized catalog entries electronically to libraries that acquire these titles, and the libraries download them automatically into their online databases. Nothing prevents individual libraries from changing or enhancing these original LC records, but in fact very few do so.

The most celebrated critic of LC's cataloging policies and practices for the past quarter century has been Sanford "Sandy" Berman, for 26 years head of the Catalog Department at Hennepin [Minnesota] Public Library until he was forced into retirement in 1999.[7]

Berman and his staff of original catalogers often changed LC subject headings (LCSH) from abstruse terms to those in common use and established new headings and subdivisions where none existed. They documented these changes in HCL's bimonthly *Cataloging Bulletin* and sent copies to other interested librarians for their information.

> **Librarians would be fortunate to be aware of even 10 percent of the publishers publishing today. The other 90 percent remain obscure. Library collections represent only a fraction of the true diversity of books available. While a library cannot collect everything, most librarians are not even aware of many publications available in their effort to build a collection. Examples of alternative publications generally absent from library collections include:**
>
> - **Translated works about the Third World by indigenous writers.**
> - **Topics of anarchism, poverty, labor, erotica, human rights, and peace studies.**
> - **Most books of poetry.**
> - **The writings of many new and lesser known authors.**
>
> —*Byron Anderson*

The most celebrated critic of LC's cataloging policies and practices for the past quarter century has been Sanford "Sandy" Berman, for 26 years head of the Catalog Department at Hennepin [Minnesota] Public Library until he was forced into retirement in 1999.[7]

Berman and his staff of original catalogers often changed LC subject headings (LCSH) from abstruse terms to those in common use and established new headings and subdivisions where none existed. They documented these changes in HCL's bimonthly *Cataloging Bulletin* and sent copies to other interested librarians for their information.

In 1992 Sandy visited LC, met with members of LC's Regional and Cooperative Cataloging Division, and arranged to send them a subscription to HCL's *Cataloging Bulletin*, highlighting each new HCL term that was being recommended for addition to LCSH. He then scanned *LC Subject headings Weekly Lists* to see if HCL's recommendations were being accepted. At first he found a quite a few HCL-originated terms, but then they appeared much less frequently. So in 1994 he wrote a letter to Sarah Thomas, then Director of Cataloging at LC, summarizing LC's cataloging deficiencies. The letter was published in full in an article he wrote in 1998, "Jackdaws Strut in Peacock's Feathers: The Sham of 'Standard' Cataloging,"[8]. Among twelve categories of shortcomings noted, he especially emphasized the following:

1. Subject headings: awkward/bizarre vocabulary. Some of the terms that Berman reports LC has declined to change are the following:

    AMICICIDE (MILITARY SCIENCE) instead of
FRIENDLY FIRE CASUALTIES

MEDICINE, MAGIC, MYSTIC AND SPAGIRIC instead of OCCULT MEDICINE

SPAIN. EJERCITO POPULAR DE LA REPUBLICA. BRIGADA INTERNACIONAL, XV instead of ABRAHAM LINCOLN BRIGADE

ABNORMALITIES, HUMAN instead of BIRTH DEFECTS

2. Subject headings: needed but unrecognized topics and genres. some of the terms that Berman reports LC has declined to recognize are the following:

    FAMILY PLANNING (encompassing child spacing, birth control, infertility and adoption among other sub-topics)
CLASSISM
SEX MANUALS
FAMILY MENTAL HEALTH
FAMILY STRESS
HANDICAPISM (or ABLEISM)
LOOKSISM**
ANTI-ARABISM
ETHNOCIDE
HOLOCAUST, ROMANI (1933–1945)**
HOLOCAUST, NATIVE AMERICAN (1492–1900)
SKINHEADS**
VIOLENCE AGAINST MINORITIES
VIOLENCE AGAINST GAY MEN AND LESBIANS
VIOLENCE AGAINST WOMEN
MOVE BOMBING, PHILADELPHIA, PENNSYLVANIA, MAY 13, 1986
GAY AND LESBIAN RIGHTS**
GAY AND LESBIAN STUDIES**
GAY AUTHORS
GAY-OWNED BUSINESSES
LESBIAN BATTERING
LESBIAN-OWNED BUSINESSES
LESBIAN SEPARATISM
BUTCH AND FEMME (LESBIANISM)
CHILD LABOR EXPLOITATION
CHILDREN OF UNEMPLOYED PARENTS
DEMOCRATIC SOCIALISM
ECONOMIC DEMOCRACY
HOMELESS FAMILIES
HOMELESS MENTALLY ILL PERSONS
HOMELESS PEOPLE IN ART**
HOMELESS TEENAGERS
INTERCLASS FRIENDSHIP
POOR FAMILIES
RIGHT TO SHELTER
VIOLENCE AGAINST POOR PEOPLE
CORPORATE POWER
EMPLOYEE LIE DETECTOR TESTING
EMPLOYEE WELLNESS PROGRAMS**
EMPLOYEE WORK MONITORING
EMPLOYER NEGLIGENCE
FRUIT PICKERS
LABOR ORGANIZERS
LABOR PERIODICALS

LABOR POSTERS
LABOR REPORTERS
WORK QUOTAS
WORK SPEEDUPS
WORKING CLASS CHILDREN
WORKING CLASS CULTURE
WORKING POOR PEOPLE
AFRO-AMERICAN FEMINISM
ANARCHA-FEMINISM
ANTIFEMINISM/ANTIFEMINISTS
BIOLOGICAL DETERMINISM
CHILD SUPPORT ENFORCEMENT
GYNOCIDE
RADICAL FEMINISM
SOCIALIST FEMINISM
WOMEN'S MOVEMENT
WOMEN'S POWER

3. Subject headings: biased vocabulary. Berman notes that many LC headings may bias users for or against certain materials. "For example, LCSH continues to describe the 1942–1945 mass internment of Japanese Americans as merely an 'evacuation and relocation,' which makes the event sound almost benign, if not also voluntary. Similarly, LC recently announced a regressive change from the heading INDIANS OF NORTH AMERICA—REMOVAL to INDIANS OF NORTH AMERICA—RELOCATION. Again, the likely inference is that what transpired was essentially helpful, much as British children during World War II were 'evacuated' and 'relocated' from urban to rural locales for their protection."

4. Subject headings: needed but unrecognized cross-references and subdivisions. Berman pointed out that subheadings for certain facets or concepts within larger topics would prove useful; for example:

LOBBYING (under names of groups or movements)

EMPOWERMENT and RIGHTS (under names of occupations and classes of people like BATTERED WOMEN, INDIGENOUS PEOPLES, POOR PEOPLE, and WOMEN WORKERS)

INTERVENTION (under a host of "social problem" forms, such as ALCOHOLISM, SUICIDE, and FAMILY VIOLENCE)"

SUBLIMINAL METHODS (applicable to a multitude of audiotapes under primary forms like STUDY METHODS and RELAXATION)

COMMERCIALIZATION (e.g. under RELIGION, CHRISTMAS, CULTURE, SCHOOLS, and LIBRARIES)*

LABOR PRACTICES (under names of firms or organizations, like NIKE—LABOR PRACTICES and WAL-MART—LABOR PRACTICES.*

NOTE: In 1999 Berman added some of these examples to his earlier list.

Looking back in 1998 at the results of his efforts to make LC subject headings more user-friendly, Berman noted some successes. Items above marked with a double asterisk have been added to LCSH, though sometimes in an odd, unhelpful fashion, such as GYPSIES—NAZI PERSECUTION instead of the more accurate and direct HOLOCAUST—ROMANI. A great Berman victory was LC's recognition of HUMAN BEING, replacing MAN.

But most of the changes that Berman and his staff made in the Hennepin catalog have not yet been accepted at LC. At the end of "Jackdaws" Berman concludes:

> Well, what can be done to make catalogs more effective and user friendly? At the national level, LC should be pressured to do what's needed. Individual librarians and systems should send that message to Washington. And so should our thus far toothless "watchdog" committees within ALA. Locally, catalogers themselves could hugely remedy many of the ongoing mistakes and omissions within "standard" records, providing—in this period of brainless downsizing and outsourcing—that there *are* any local catalogers left and that they're empowered to "deviate" from the divine and largely dysfunctional norms of AACR2 [Anglo-American Cataloging Rules, 2nd edition], DDC [Dewey Decimal Classification] and LC practice.... Until such reforms happen at either the national or local level, catalogs will be much less valuable than they could be, and users will be denied access to the vast stores of information, ideas and inspiration that a functional catalog might have revealed. At present, what passes for "cataloging" is a fraud and an embarrassment.

Commercialization of Schools and Libraries

One of the math problems in a middle-school textbook titled *Mathematics: Applications and Connections* reads, "The best-selling packaged cookie in the world is the Oreo cookie. The diameter of an Oreo cookie is 1.75 inches. Express the diameter of an Oreo cookie as a fraction in the simplest form." Lynn Waddell wrote recently in Tampa's alternative *Weekly Planet*:[9]

> ... The book is liberally peppered with mentions and pictures of Nike shoes, Burger King and McDonald's food, Kellogg's Cocoa Frosted Flakes, Sony PlayStations, Gatorade, and Disney characters and theme parks....
>
> More than 83,000 copies of the McGraw-Hill textbook have been sold to Florida schools. It's been a success nationally. And while it's not the only school textbook to contain commercial references or ads, it has by far received the most national attention.
>
> In response to the book's release, Californians voted to ban textbooks with advertising.

Waddell reports that in 1999 advertisers spent $12 billion on ads to children, nearly twice as much as in 1992. In 1989

Channel One entered the school market bringing a news TV show with ads into classrooms, which caused a stir among parents and educators. Since then "marketers have become more adept at cloaking their self-promotion as incentive programs, educational materials, and fundraising opportunities," Waddell says. "Marketing magazines report that children ask their parents for products by brand name 90 percent of the time. According to U.S. Department of Commerce statistics, children between the age of 4 and 12 are estimated to spend or influence the spending of $500 billion in goods and services a year."

The Internet is also being used at some schools for commercial access to students. The Internet home page at Hillsborough High and Tampa Technical High is covered with banner ads, and every move students make online is tracked by ZapMe!, the computer/marketing company that supplies the computers. The ZapMe! contract requires that students, collectively, be online four hours a day and that the school get ZapMe!'s permission to add new software to the computers. ZapMe! makes money off the Web site ads and also profits by tracking the students online and selling that information to marketers. Waddell says:

> In the past year and a half, ZapMe! grew from having contracts with 500 schools to having contracts with 1,800. And that's despite having come under attack for introducing ads and conducting market research in the classroom. Consumer advocate Ralph Nader called ZapMe! "borderline child abuse." Nader's Consumer Alert in February sent letters to all governors protesting ZapMe!. Since then, ZapMe! has reevaluated its advertisers and added public service announcements.

After all this happening in schools for the past decade, it should come as no surprise that corporations are beginning to market directly to public libraries. A company named Library Marketing Network of West Chester, PA claims to have approached 4,000 U.S. libraries to join

> ... a *voluntary* marketing alliance of libraries acting on the basis that cumulative impact of many libraries would be of more interest to Corporate America than they would be individually. This *no-cost* membership organization acts as an information and marketing channel for marketing programs developed by LMN with input from its members. LMN sells these to corporations for sponsorship. Libraries share in the sponsorship revenue and benefit from various publicity and awareness activities which are part of each marketing plan....
>
> The initial program is *The Learning Center*™. In exchange for a small amount of space, a limited number of free standing or wall mounted displays are set up profiling selected books related to the sponsor's industry or a special topic. This incorporates a synopsis of the book, a sponsor's communications, and a take-one related to the sponsor's business.
> • The books are selected by our library committee, we purchase 3 copies of each title, the titles are changed monthly, and all books are donated to the library.

• Estimated <u>minimum</u> revenue is $3,000 per year, per display.
• Additional financial benefits are to be gained if a majority of a county, district or state chooses to participate as a group.
• The participating library receives marketing support promoting their programs and activities in the community.[10]

> **"The initial program is *The Learning Center*™. In exchange for a small amount of space, a limited number of free standing or wall mounted displays are set up profiling selected books related to the sponsor's industry or a special topic (see prototypes). This incorporates a synopsis of the book, a sponsor's communications, and a take-one related to the sponsor's business.**
> • **The books are selected by our library committee, we purchase 3 copies of each title, the titles are changed monthly, and all books are donated to the library.**
> • **Estimated <u>minimum</u> revenue is $3,000 per year, per display.**
> • **Additional financial benefits are to be gained if a majority of a county, district or state chooses to participate as a group.**
> • **The participating library receives marketing support promoting their programs and activities in the community."**[10]
> —*Leslie R. Wolff, CEO*
> *Library Marketing Network*
> "Developing marketing programs for Corporate America to benefit libraries"

In September 2000 the CEO of Library Marketing Network, Leslie R. Wolff, wrote me that libraries in New Jersey, Pennsylvania, Illinois, Kentucky, Texas and Virginia had signed up for the program. Advertising and PR agencies such as Grey, DDB, FCB, and Leo Burnett were discussing LMN with clients for their 2001 marketing plans, and many potential sponsors had expressed interest, including Pfizer, AstraZeneca, Novartis, Roche, Bristol Myers Squibb, AXA, Discover, Merrill Lynch, New York Life, HCFA, and the U.S. Army.

Political Indoctrination in Libraries

A few weeks before the 2000 U.S. national election, an e-mail message was forwarded to me by chance containing the text of a letter that an experienced local librarian had written to the *Gainesville Sun* with what was meant to be helpful advice about how to inform oneself about issues and candidates. From the mainstream point of view, it was an excellent letter, leading voters to what are generally believed to be reliable sources of information. The *Sun* did not print the letter, but I would like to publish it here anonymously as a good illustration of how libraries and librarians indoctrinate the public politically, without even being aware that they are doing so.

To the editor:
We frequently read or see ads or other statements during this election season, presenting a point of view about one or another candidate. And we hear the candidates themselves presenting not only their own points of view, but putting views of their opponents into their own words. How do we check out these obviously, or not so obviously, biased statements? Where can we compare what is being said and check out the facts? As a librarian working each day to help people find information, I'd like to present a few ideas.

An easy way to get started is to log on to the web site of Project Vote Smart at http://www.vote-smart.org or call their toll-free Voter's Research Hotline at 1-800-VOTE-SMART. This non-partisan citizens project has information on over 40,000 candidates, including Florida candidates for United States House and Senate races, Florida House and Senate, and the Presidential race, and is endorsed by the American Political Science Association. Conservatives and liberals have joined to compile voting records, campaign finances, position statements, backgrounds, and evaluations done by special interest groups. A Political Awareness Test allows you to choose to answer either a long list of questions about issues, or just a few questions about a certain category, say the environment, and then the computer compares your answers with those which have been given for the same questions by the candidates to find which candidates produce the best match for your views. Another section features Presidential Candidates' Public Statements, all searchable by key words, so that you can search for statements by the candidates themselves on issues you are most interested in.

The second step is to get an analysis of the issues and platforms, which needs to come from a variety of sources in order to provide different points of view and provide some balance. The Lexis-Nexis database at the University of Florida Libraries offers access to an easy way to target your reading. Go to the News section of this service, which provides online access to full text of newspapers and news magazines, and you can enter keywords "Bush and Gore and Nader" and then narrow your search with the word "analysis" or any of the specific issues such as "education," "health," "environment," or "death penalty." You can then read a collection of articles from major newspapers, or from magazines including *Newsweek* and *U.S. News and World Report*, or from regional sources such as newspapers of the southeast, including such papers as the *Miami Herald* and the *Atlanta Journal and Constitution*.

I believe that using Project Vote Smart to check what the candidate's views are, and then using a variety of analytical news sources, provides the kind of information necessary to making our own informed decisions about the upcoming election.

(signed)
(name deleted)

Earlier this year the American Library Association issued thousands of copies of *Smart voting starts @ your library*, a glossy, 16-page pamphlet with the American flag on the cover and at the top of every page. Under "**Selected Resources: Web Sites**" the following entry appears:

www.vote-smart.org
Site of Project Vote Smart, an organization that partners with the American Library Association, where users can find candidates by entering their zip codes. Also included is information on where to vote, voter registration details, and national and state candidate profiles, including positions and voting records.
Libraries can register with Project Vote Smart to receive a free resource book, a Web site guide, a reporter's source book, and a toll-free service that puts them in touch with a researcher. To register, see the Project Vote Smart Web site or contact the organization at Project Vote Smart, One Common Ground, Philipsburg, MT 59898. Telephone 406/8590-8683. E-mail: libraries@vote-smart.org
[Italics are in the original, ed.]

I looked up Project Vote Smart on the Internet a few days before the election. Its home page said it is "Praised by the *New York Times*, *CNN*, *PBS* and virtually every other major media outlet as the most trusted and comprehensive source for information on candidates and issues."

At their annual national convention, the American Political Science Association honored PVS as "The Best source for accurate political information on the World Wide Web." The APSA president told PVS that it was selected unanimously by each region. "We cancelled our final selection committee meeting to pick the award winner," the APSA president said. "It simply became a no-brainer."

Another page, "What's new at Project Vote Smart" said that on 5 September 2000, at their annual national convention, the American Political Science Association honored PVS as "The Best source for accurate political information on the

World Wide Web." The APSA president told PVS that it was selected unanimously by each region. "We cancelled our final selection committee meeting to pick the award winner," the APSA president said. "It simply became a no-brainer."

Then I looked up my candidate, Ralph Nader. The first page, Biographical, gave Nader's name, date and place of birth; a brief summary of his education and professional experience; a list of nine organizations he founded; the fact that he had been a presidential candidate in 1996, and his address, phone, fax and web site. At the top of all this data appeared the following:

Current Office:
Challenger
Name: Mr. Ralph Nader
Party: Green Party
Candidate Public Statements (blank)

This page was followed by four others in standard PVS format: Campaign Finances, Issue Positions (NPAT), Special Interest Groups, and Voting Record. Three simply said that no information was available on this person. The Issue Positions (NPAT) page read as follows:

2000 Presidential National Political Awareness Test Results

Results for Candidate Nader:

Candidate Nader was contacted on 6 separate occasions over seven weeks and asked to complete the National Political Awareness Test, which is designed to evaluate candidates' willingness to provide voters with information regarding their intentions in 17 issue areas. Project Vote Smart and prominent national leaders all requested that Nader do the right and honorable thing by providing citizens with this critical information in the national interest. Those contacting Nader included:

Geraldine Ferraro, Michael Dukakis, Mark Hatfield, Jim Leach, and Bill Frenzel.

On each occasion Nader failed to provide voters with the critical information.

Now I don't know how other people who visited this site would interpret that statement. To me, it says that despite repeated, earnest appeals "in the national interest" by wonderful PVS and "prominent national leaders," Ralph Nader **disdainfully, unpatriotically, wrongly and dishonorably refused to come clean to the American people about his political intentions in 17 critical issue areas.**

Compare the thrust of that statement with the following item on the "What's new at Project Vote Smart" Web page:

Project Vote Smart Fills Out the National Political Awareness Test (NPAT) FOR Bush and Gore— After 30 attempts over the last months to get these two front runners to provide voters with crucial information on how they may handle the tough issues if elected, our researchers did it for them, in the national interest.

Now I don't know how other people who visited this site would interpret that statement. To me, it says that despite repeated, earnest appeals "in the national interest" by wonderful PVS and "prominent national leaders," Ralph Nader *disdainfully, unpatriotically, wrongly and dishonorably* **refused to come clean to the American people about his political intentions in 17 critical issue areas.**

Compare the thrust of that statement with the following item on the "What's new at Project Vote Smart" Web page:

"Project Vote Smart Fills Out the National Political Awareness Test (NPAT) FOR Bush and Gore— After 30 attempts over the last months to get these two front runners to provide voters with crucial information on how they may handle the tough issues if elected, our researchers did it for them, in the national interest."

So who and what, exactly, is Project Vote Smart? Its Web site has a letter from its president, Richard Kimball, on letterhead giving a partial listing of about thirty "Founding Board Members," leading off with Gerald Ford, Jimmy Carter, Barry Goldwater, and George McGovern, and including some former senators, former attorney generals, former officials, a political scientist, a historian, and even Newt Gingrich. The page includes a color photo of young, clean-cut, white staff members at work, and also a photo of PVS's beautiful location in Philipsburg, MT, with a snow-capped peak not far away. Kimball writes,

"Picture this: at an extraordinary research facility high in the Rocky Mountains hundreds of idealists— conservatives and liberals alike—volunteering together, spending thousands of hours researching the backgrounds and records of over 12,000 candidates for public office. Forcing them, with or without their cooperation, to fill out a detailed application of employment.

"Their voting records, campaign finances, position statements, backgrounds, and the evaluations done on them by over 100 competing special interest groups. Research that will defend the people's right to abundant, accurate, relevant information and enable them to check the credibility of the often misleading claims candidates make. The kind of information that is essential to prudent decision-making in the voting booth. Information that will ensure that tolerance is no longer the only option available to the millions of us who are tormented by the issueless personal attacks that have come to dominate our elections. Information that is made easily available to every American free of charge by simply picking up a phone and calling one of the hundreds of trained volunteers and student interns on our toll-free Voter's Research Hotline, or through our Vote Smart Web site and publications."

I found Philipsburg, Montana in my atlas. It's a small town and county seat located on the Flint River in a valley just west of the Continental Divide, about midway between Missoula and Butte on Route 1, designated as a scenic highway, close to national forests, camping areas, and a ski resort. The *World Guide to Libraries*, 10th ed. (1991) listed no public or academic library in Philipsburg, Montana. A librarian from Missoula told me that many Mormons live there. I wonder how many people of color live there, how many poor people, how many elderly people, how many single mothers with children, how many street people, how many socialists and anarchists. I wonder if there are big private estates nearby. I wonder if people work in factories and mills in Philipsburg. I

I found Philipsburg, Montana in my atlas. It's a small town and county seat located on the Flint River in a valley just west of the Continental Divide, about midway between Missoula and Butte on Route 1, designated as a scenic highway, close to national forests, camping areas, and a ski resort. According to the *World Guide to Libraries*, there is no public or academic library in Philipsburg, Montana.

wonder how big its police force is and whether they have been outfitted with chemical weapons and rubber bullets and dogs and helicopters since the WTO protests in Seattle. I wonder if people demonstrate in the streets of Philipsburg, Montana when the United States of America time and again violates the Universal Declaration of Human Rights.

I did not follow the rest of the Gainesville librarian's instructions. I did not go to the Lexis-Nexis database at the University of Florida Libraries and "get online access to full text of newspapers and news magazines." I could already guess what their corporate fix on the forthcoming U.S. national election would be. Similarly, I did not "read a collection of articles from major newspapers, or from magazines including *Newsweek* and *U.S. News and World Report*, or from regional sources such as newspapers of the southeast, including such papers as the *Miami Herald* and the *Atlanta Journal and Constitution*." I knew what they would say, but I did not believe them, and I would never believe them again.

Alternative Libraries for the Alternative Press

"We started Z because the New York Times, the Washington Post, Time, Newsweek, and all the rest lie. We started Z because NYU, Harvard, Berkeley, Michigan State, Loyola and all the rest teach only what reinforces the status quo."
—Z Magazine flyer, 1992

In his essay "Democratic Media"[11] Edward S. Herman divided media into three sectors—corporate, government and civic. He urged the vigorous development of community-based, democratic, civic media in order to offset the immense power and frequent bias of the corporate and government media sectors. Because of the importance of this essay (the Civic Media Center and Library found its name and some of its inspiration here), I am quoting from it at length.

"As regards function, a democratic media will aim first and foremost at serving the informational, cultural, and communications needs of the members of the public which the media institutions comprise or represent. The users would determine their own needs and fix the menu of choices either directly or through their closely controlled agents, and debate would not be limited to selected voices chosen by corporate or government gatekeepers. The sovereign listeners [and readers —ed.] would not only participate in choosing programs and issues to be addressed, they would be the voices heard, and they would be involved in continuous interchanges with other listeners. There would be a horizontal flow of communication, in both directions, instead of a vertical flow from officials and experts to the passive population of consumers.

"At the same time, a democratic media would recognize and encourage diversity. It would allow and encourage minorities to express their views and build their own communities' solidarity within the larger community. This would follow from the democratic idea of recognizing and encouraging individual differences and letting all such flowers bloom irrespective of financial capability and institutional power. This is also consistent with the idea of pluralism, part of mainstream orthodox doctrine but poorly realized in mainstream practice....

"A democratic media would encourage people to know and understand their neighbors, nearby and at a distance, and to act and participate in social and political life. This is likely to occur where media structures are democratic, as these media will be open to neighbors who want to communicate views on problems and their communal resolution....

"For real progress in democratizing the media a much larger place must be carved out for the civic sector. This is the nonprofit sector organized by individuals or grassroots organizations to serve the communications needs of the general population (as opposed to the corporate community and government). A top priority must be given to building this sector, because only out of such democratically rooted structures are we likely to get a truly democratic communications service. Furthermore, the very process of building a media civic sector is important in the learning process of democracy and as part of community mobilization....

"We are not living in an era of democratizing media. Instead, the main drift in the West has been toward increasing media centralization and commercialization, and a corresponding weakening of the public sector. The civic sphere of non-government and non-commercial media has displayed considerable vitality but has been pressed to defend its relative position overall.

"For real progress in democratizing the media a much larger place must be carved out for the civic sector. This is the nonprofit sector organized by individuals or grassroots organizations to serve the communications needs of the general population (as opposed to the corporate community and government). A top priority must be given to building this sector, because only out of such democratically rooted structures are we likely to get a truly democratic communications service. Furthermore, the very process of building a media civic sector is important in the learning process of democracy and as part of community mobilization....

"We are not living in an era of democratizing media. Instead, the main drift in the West has been toward increasing media centralization and commercialization, and a corresponding weakening of the public sector. The civic sphere of non-government and non-commercial media has displayed considerable vitality but has been pressed to defend its relative position overall."

—*Edward S. Herman*

"I have argued that the civic sector is the locus of the truly democratic media and that genuine democratization in western societies is going to be contingent on its great enlargement. Those actively seeking democratization of the media should seek first to enlarge the civic sphere by every possible avenue, to strengthen the public sector by increasing its autonomy and funding, and lastly to contain or shrink the commercial sector and try to tap it for revenue. Funding this sector properly is going to require government subvention. Media democrats should be preparing the moral and political environment for such financial support, while doing their utmost to advance existing democratic media."

The Alternative Press Index[12]

Alternative media have been growing steadily. When the Alternative Press Center started the *Alternative Press Index*[11] in 1969, it indexed 72 periodicals. Now it has about 300. Theoretical perspectives include feminism, Marxism, critical theory, structuralism, poststructuralism, critical race theory, and queer theory. *API* titles document dozens of political and social movements, including the efforts of women, people of color, workers, environmentalists and student groups spanning the globe.

Annotations[13]

In 1999 the APC brought out a revised second edition of *Annotations: A Guide to the Independent Critical Press*, listing 328 periodicals. The Introduction, written by Beth Schulman with Charles D'Adamo, points out,

> ...[P]rint persists as the medium—despite the proliferation of all-news cable channels, talk radio and the now ubiquitous Internet—where we begin to describe and name public problems, where we undertake the first discussion of issues that shape the daily lives of ordinary people. And while mainstream newspapers and magazines may participate in this process, feisty independent publications tend to generate the most innovative reportage, analysis and debate. Investigative reporters, academics, policy specialists and other advocates for change do their most original work in these pages. There they know they can expect to engage the readers they encounter—even through the smallest of these publications—in the kind of spirited exchange necessary to refine and sharpen a new idea. These conversations, all too often ignored or pushed to the margins, can go on to become the cornerstones essential to building new public policies and new ways of thinking. [14]

APBNA[15]

Alternative book publishing is also increasing. The current, 4th edition of *Alternative Publishers of Books in North America*[14] (1999) describes 148 publishers, as compared with 75 in the first, 1994 edition. In the Foreword to the 4th edition, the late Herbert I. Schiller wrote,

> Business-influenced culture is an old story in the United States, but today it has reached an ominous

dimension. But powerful and expanding as this influence is, happily it has not yet taken over the entire cultural terrain. In publishing, for example, there is a considerable body of work by those who are outside the commercial loop.. There are also readers who are curious and open to sampling work produced free of the fetters of commercialism.

To assist in bringing these groups together—and librarians can help in making the connection—the publication of a directory of "Alternative Publishers of Books in North America" is a modest but worthy contribution. In this publication are located many, not all, of the small presses and publishers, the non-conglomeratized defenders of independence, diversity and unorthodoxy in book publishing.

As the twentieth century draws to a close, the corporate seizure of the public's space, attention and thought has reached dismaying levels. Still, it is a source of hope and satisfaction that alternative voices continue to express themselves, and brave efforts are made to bring their expression to wider audiences. [16]

> "Print persists
> as the medium—
> despite the proliferation
> of all-news cable channels,
> talk radio, and
> the now ubiquitous Internet—
> where we begin
> to describe
> and name
> public
> problems,
> where we undertake
> the first discussion of issues
> that shape
> the daily lives
> of ordinary people."
> —Introduction to *Annotations*

Review Journals for the Alternative Press

There are also two review journals for the alternative press, *Alternative Press Review*[17] and *Counterpoise*.[18]

The Internet

The Internet is also maturing. I subscribe to about a dozen lists, and friends regularly forward additional items of interest to me. A successful effort to get a wide range of new essays before the public very quickly, without the delays of print publishing, has been achieved by Michael Albert, co-editor of *Z Magazine*. For a modest subscription I receive every evening a polished essay on a matter of national or global concern. In December, these ZNet (http://www.zmag.org) Daily Commentaries, ordinarily available only to ZNet Sustainers, were also sent to all 44,000 ZNet Free Update recipients. The following paragraph is from the ZNet Commentary "Silent Democracy"[19] by David Cromwell and David Edwards, received on 24 October:

> During last year's 78-day NATO bombing campaign of the former Republic of Yugoslavia (FRY), Guardian columnist Jonathan Freedland wrote, "Future historians will spend long hours and write fat books working out this phenomenon. Why have the Serbs not risen in outrage at the unspeakable horrors committed in their name?"
>
> Future historians, in fact have already examined Freedland's "unspeakable horrors" and found them to be pure fantasy, the product of the overheated imagination of NATO warmongers and credulous journalists. It is now clear that in the twelve months prior to the bombing, between 1,000 and 2,000 people were killed on both sides of the conflict, with deaths running at an average of one per day in the weeks running up to the attack—appalling, but hardly genocidal. In its examination of 30 mass grave sites the FBI unearthed a total of some 200 bodies. In Ljubenic, a mass grave alleged to contain some 350 bodies was found to contain just seven. In town after town, alleged mass graves were found to be empty or contained only one or two bodies. . . .
>
> The real question, not just for future historians, but for all thinking people, is how so many respected journalists, like Jonathan Freedland, could yet again be so readily taken in by the deceptions of power? Spokespeople for state power have always insisted that they are acting for the good of all humanity, and respected commentators have always accepted their words at face value as though they were born, if not yesterday, then since the previous set of lies had been exposed as utterly fraudulent. This happens with such consistency that there is clearly something more than random chance at work. Noam Chomsky explains how the selection process can best be understood: "In any society, the respectable intellectuals, those who will be recognized as serious intellectuals, will overwhelmingly tend to be those who are subordinated to power. Those who are not subordinated to power are not recognized as intellectuals, or are marginalized as dissidents, maybe 'ideological'. . . . The tendency is just as obvious as the fact that corporate media serve corporate interests."

The same dynamic holds true for libraries as for other media. The words and works of "respectable intellectuals," subordinated to power, are acquired, cataloged, circulated and preserved, but those of marginalized dissidents are shut out—except in very large research institutions (where a few are acquired and buried among mainstream titles) and a handful of special collections, like zoos.

Let's invert the equation. Let's put civic democracy into practice. Let's seek out alternative publications and points of view. Let's respect and call attention to marginalized writers and dissidents. Let's set up and support many alternative libraries and infoshops like the Civic Media Center.[20]

1. Ben H. Bagdikian. *The Media monopoly*, Boston, MA: Beacon Press, 1983 and subsequent revised editions.

2. *Alternative publishers of books in North America*, 4th edition (CRISES Press, 1999), Preface, pp. 6–7

3. barb howe, unpublished paper: "Whose IR? Voices of the South in the Study of International Relations," October, 2000

4. Letter from Duane E. Webster, Executive Director, Association of Research Libraries, Washington, D.C. to Susan Edelheit, Assistant Chief, Civil Task Force, Antitrust Division, Department of Justice, dated September 18, 2000, protesting the acquisition by Reed Elsevier of the Worldwide Scientific, Technical, and Medical Group of Harcourt General. Companies included are Academic Press, W.B. Saunders, Mosby, and Churchill Livingstone. Under the terms of the agreement, Reed Elsevier will buy Harcourt outright in a transaction estimated to be worth $5.6 billion. Reed will retain Harcourt's STM businesses, in addition to its grade- and high-school text-publishing divisions. Reed will sell the college textbook businesses and most of the corporate and professional-service segment to Thomson for $2.1 billion.

5. Charles Willett. "Politically Controversial Monographs: Roles of Publishers, Distributors, Booksellers, *CHOICE* Magazine, and Librarians in Acquiring Them for American Academic Libraries," *Building on the First Century. Proceedings of the Fifth National Conference of the Association of College and Research Libraries*, 1989: pp. 238–241.

6. Byron Anderson. "The Other 90 Percent: What Your MLS Didn't Teach You," *Counterpoise*, vol. 3, no 3/4 (July/October 1999): 11-12.

7. See *Librarians at liberty*, vol. 7, nos. 1 & 2, December 1999, 52 pages: "Special Double Issue: Sandy Berman's Forced Retirement from the Hennepin County Library, Minnetonka, Minnesota; a series of documents, followed by letters of support and a petition on the Internet"

8. "Jackdaws Strut in Peacock's Feathers," *Librarians at liberty*, vol. 5, no. 2 and vol. 6, nos. 1 & 2, June 1998, pp. 1, 4–24.

9. This information about commercialism in public schools is drawn from the article "Reading, 'Riting and Retail" by Lynn Waddell, *Weekly planet* (Tampa, Florida; tabloid), 23–29 November 2000, pages 22–28

10. Personal letter dated September 1, 2000 to the author from Leslie R. Wolff, CEO, Library Marketing Network, P. O. Box 1242, West Chester, PA 19380, 800/531-5202 or 610/436-6774; librarymarketing@mindstring.com

11. Edward S. Herman. "Democratic Media," *Z papers*, vol. 1, no.1, 1992, pages 23–30

12. *Alternative press index*. Baltimore, MD : Alternative Press Center, 1969– , ed. by Charles D'Adamo, Les Wade et al. 200p. ISSN 0002-662X Quarterly. 4th issue cumulates. 1,000 pages. Inst.: $300; Indiv.: $75. Discounts for social change groups. API 1991–1995: Inst.: $175, Indiv.: $35. 1969–1990: Inst.: $125, Indiv.: $35. The most comprehensive and up-to-date guide to alternative and radical magazines and journals. Articles from roughly 300 popular and scholarly periodicals are indexed. 20,000 records are added each year. Ninety percent of API's coverage is not found in *Reader's Guide* or *Social Sciences Index*. http://www.altpress.org/api.htm

13. *Annotations: a guide to the independent critical press*, 2nd updated ed. Edited by Marie Jones (General Editor), Charles D'Adamo, Robert Rosenthal, Beth Schulman, and Les Wade. Baltimore, MD: Alternative Press Center, 1999; San Francisco, CA: Independent Press Association, 512p. index. ISBN 0-9653894-2-1 paper $24.95 http://www.altpress.org/annotate.html http://www.indypress.org/order/annotations.htm

14. *Ibid*, page 7

15. *Alternative publishers of books in North America*. American Library Association, Social Responsibilities Round Table, Alternatives in Print Task Force. Byron Anderson, editor and compiler. 4th biennial edition, revised and enlarged, 1999-2000. With a foreword by Herbert I. Schiller and a preface by Ben H. Bagdikian. Gainesville, FL : CRISES Press, 1999. 150p. Bibliographical references, webography and indexes. ISBN 0-9640119-8-0, paper, $20. A directory of 148 significant presses selected by members of the Task Force. Available from CRISES Press, 1716 SW Williston Road, Gainesville, FL 32608. 352/335-2200 willett@gnv.fdt.net http://www.LibLib.com

16. *Ibid*, page 5

17. *Alternative press review*. Columbia, MO : C.A.L. Press, 1993– Edited by Jason McQuinn. 84p. ISSN 1072-7299 Irregular. Standard class: $16/year. Articles, essays, and reviews spanning the genre from scholarly journal to radical zine. C.A.L. Press, P. O, Box 1446, Columbia, MO 65205. 314/442-4352 apr@flag.blackened.net http://flag.blackened.net/apr/

18. *Counterpoise: for social responsibilities, liberty and dissent*. Edited by Charles Willett and a volunteer staff of subject specialists; published by CRISES Press. 1997– 65p. ISSN 1092-0714. Quarterly. International journal for the alternative press: reviews, letters, essays. Indexed. Inst. $35, Indiv. $25. Low income $15. Back issue $9. Counterpoise, 1716 SW Williston Road, Gainesville, FL 32608. 352/335-2200. willett@fdt.net http://www.LibLib.com/Cpoise/Cpoise.html

19. "Silent Democracy" by David Cromwell and David Edwards. *ZNet commentary* <znetcommentary@tao.ca> 24 October 2000

20. James Schmidt.. "How to Maintain an Alternative Library: The Civic Media Center Six Years On." *Creating learning communities*, edited by Ron Miller, Brandon, VT: Foundation for Educational Research, 2000

A QUESTION OF BALANCE: THE ROLE OF LIBRARIES IN PROVIDING ALTERNATIVES TO THE MAINSTREAM MEDIA

Based on a Presentation before the SRRT/Alternatives in Print Task Force
at the American Library Association Annual Conference
New Orleans, LA, June 27, 1999
by Nancy Kranich
Associate Dean, New York University Libraries, and
President-elect, American Library Association

Walk into any Barnes and Noble superstore and customers will be reading intently in settings not unlike those in our libraries. Many people now spend their days in these stores, undisturbed, conducting research or simply curling up with a good book. Others come to hear a multitude of authors speak, to meet friends, to sip cappuccino, or to pick up the latest issues of their favorite magazines. Renee Feinberg visited several of these stores in New York City last year and interviewed various customers, including students from New York University, who told her that the store adequately met their research needs. Remarked Feinberg, "the library has information, but B&N has books. The library is still involved with good reading to make good people, while B&N is willing to suspend 'good' and to stretch the limits."(1)

Big chain bookstores not only serve many of the research and recreational needs of residents and students alike, but they also exert enormous influence over what gets published. They make big profits with best sellers. They use their ambiance to effect sales. Yet, they have few staff to guide customers, making it difficult to sell less popular titles. So what distinguishes these superstores from the libraries that they appear to imitate so well?

The Library Marketplace

In the United States, we have 115,000 school, public, academic and special libraries. Last year alone, these libraries spent more than $5 billion for books—10% of publishers' revenues overall, but 50% to 90% of sales of reference books, specialized materials, children's books, poetry and non-fiction. Nevertheless, librarians are often an invisible market to publishers, since most of our purchases are through wholesalers rather than direct from the publisher. In an article in *Library Journal,* Barbara Hoffert noted, however, that: "Publishers are beginning to realize that although they create the books, librarians have tremendous power to influence readers."(2)

The U.S. Publishing Industry

In this country, we have 20,000 publishers, including trade, professional, journal, electronic, textbook, university press, reference and mass-market paperback. Together, these publishers produce 50,000 imprints annually. Yet a mere 2% of them account for 75% of the output. Less than 6,000 titles are reviewed each year, most of which are published by fewer than 200 publishers—the largest publishers. Since the passage of the Telecommunications Act of 1996, a single corporation may now own not only book publishing, but also radio, TV, newspapers and Internet services—all in the same market area and up to a one-third market share nationally. This means that the dozen major corporations dominating media output today could further consolidate to three or four in the next decade. In 1998, mergers and acquisitions activity in the publishing/information sector was up 59% to $33.4 billion. The number of deals climbed to 439 from 390. Among the largest: Pearson purchased Simon and Schuster from Viacom for $4.6 million. Thomson completed the largest number of acquisitions: 29. Reed Elsevier completed the largest number of divestitures.(3) Since the 1920's, the average profit of a U.S. publishing house was around 4%. These houses sought to balance profitability with responsibility. Today, conglomerates look for a 12-15% return on their investment. Periodicals publishers like Elsevier average in the 25%+ range.

Reprinted with permission from *Counterpoise* (1716 SW Williston Road, Gainesville, FL 32608), v. 3, nos. 3/4 (July/October 1999), pp. 7–10.

André Schiffrin, director of The New Press, recently reviewed the lists of the three largest publishers: HarperCollins, Simon and Schuster, and Random House. Out of a total of 400 titles, the three lists included only four books on current politics, one of which was by an ideologue who is among Rupert Murdoch's favorite political thinkers. There was not a single work of serious history, no work of scientific inquiry, and no translations. "Of course the remaining independent presses and university presses are doing their best to publish the books that have disappeared from the conglomerate lists. But as the investment of the major publishing houses, which control 80% of sales, continues to shift to more commercial fields, the choice of ideas presented to American readers will continue to dwindle."(4) Like publishing, book distribution is also dominated by only a few companies: Ingram and Baker & Taylor. These big distributors tend to be very slow in making payments, not a problem for conglomerates but this really hurts small publishers. Stated one, "They feel you can't do business without them. But we can't stay in business if we keep dealing with them."(5)

As the mainstream media continues its gold rush to acquire and merge with other media companies, they are neglecting their public interest obligation to advance knowledge and the public's right to know. More and more, homogeneity is creating a monoculture in this country where we are bombarded with celebrity news, infomercials and titillation. We alternate between sex and violence: from Monica Lewinsky and Paula Jones to atrocities in Kosovo and Littleton. As Neal Postman has stated, we have become the "best entertained, least informed society in the world."(6) Increasingly, Americans are more ignorant about public and international affairs and alienated from social issues.

In the publishing arena, conglomeration has resulted in the inclusion of financial and marketing people in the editorial process. If a book does not look as if it will sell a certain number—and that number increases every year—these "numbers" people will argue that the company simply cannot afford to undertake the project. Market censorship is increasingly in force in a decision-making process that is based on whether there is a pre-existing audience for a particular title. Books by well-known authors or obvious successes are preferred; new authors and critical viewpoints are increasingly rejected by the major houses. In short, states Peter Phillips, Director of Project Censored, "The U.S. media has lost its diversity and its ability to present different points of view."(7)

Perhaps the most dangerous aspect of the current increase in conglomerate media power is that it has gone largely unchallenged by the public in general and librarians in particular. Antitrust legislation is rarely discussed, and other forms and structures of media ownership are hardly contemplated. While the small, independent presses provide an alternative, their share of the market is just 1% of total book sales. Moreover, they do not have the strength or resources of the major firms, and they do not have anywhere near as ready access to bookstores.

The Alternative Press

Often absent from the review media, standard bibliographic tools, and conference exhibits are the alternative, small and/or independent publishers. While none of these labels is satisfactory, the term "alternative" is most apt because these publishers counterbalance the corporate media. Too often, however, they are outside the mainstream of traditional distribution channels and the peripheral vision of libraries. Some are even unaware of the potential of selling to libraries. Others are confused how to do so. This is unfortunate. Alternative publishers are on the cutting edge of important literature and issues. They make an important cultural and literary contribution. And, they are an essential part of the community of publishers with whom librarians must interact.

Little money, influence or prestige backs alternative publishers. They are small, and their authors and editors are rarely known. Often, Library of Congress cataloging is minimal or non-existent for their publications. Booksellers omit them from approval plans, making it difficult for libraries to acquire their titles efficiently. Librarians have to work hard to seek out their titles. Nevertheless, we have a duty to guide users to the full range of relevant facts and opinions; therefore, we must pursue these publishers, who can provide us with more obscure fiction and literature as well as vital information about our communities and diversity.

The Role of Libraries in Supporting the Alternative Press

Unfortunately, alternative publishers do not always see librarians as their alternative. They simply do not look to us as outlets for their resources. They do not understand how to work with us. They do not see us as natural allies. With media wealth so concentrated, so solidified, and so integrated into the corporate-government elite, what role can libraries play to ensure the public a more democratic flow of ideas and offer alternatives to the narrow, corporate-media view of the world? How can we create real access to information and participation for all sectors of our communities? How can we counteract the market censorship that is shifting formerly reputable publishers' lists from serious titles to hype?

Libraries could and should be that community-based information sanctuary that offers diverse voices the right to read, view, listen and discuss ideas. But library collections are increasingly looking more and more alike. According to Milton Wolfe and Marjorie Bloss (8),

> librarians have put their library clientele on a core collection starvation diet, depriving them of those nutritious sources that distinguish one library from another, those materials that enable thinking outside the box of commercially purveyed pabulum. The fast-food collecting syndrome, which focuses on the core at the expense of the periphery, is threatening library users with a severe case of content-deprived anemia. . . . In truth, there is a well-entrenched, global commercial monopoly on the distribution and approval of ideas, and we, as selectors, often contribute to its hegemony by our slothful collection habits. "Content," too often, has become what our commercial enterprises define and distribute, and we often unwittingly purchase–largely because few institutions now devote the number of hours required to the time-consuming, professional job of selection.

Among Wolf and Bloss's recommendations are that we "put our always limited funds toward our overarching visions: to ensure that we have cooperative, just-in-case repositories and archives, which have purposely targeted the peripheral, the non-mainstream, the non-corporate information to serve the just-in-time needs of our clientele."

A study of ARL libraries undertaken by Anna Perrault in the late 1980's reinforces Wolfe's and Bloss's concerns about collection homogeneity. Perrault found that there was "a decrease in the percentage of unique titles in many subject areas, and an increased concentration on core materials."(9) Another collection development study by Stephen L. Hupp in Ohio libraries concluded that "the state's libraries have done a poor job in collecting controversial political materials."(10) His follow-up study found that holdings of alternative periodicals lagged behind holdings of liberal or conservative titles.

Another study by Markinko and Gerhard published in *College and Research Libraries* (11), which examined the holdings rates of alternative press titles in U.S. research libraries, determined that alternative press titles are not widely held in these libraries. The authors concluded that these rarely-indexed periodicals were less likely to be purchased. Likewise, these periodicals are not cited because they are difficult to obtain. Therefore, they are often not utilized by scholars and are, consequently, less likely to be purchased by librarians.

Policies Supporting Diversity of Sources

Over the years, the library community has developed and endorsed numerous policies that recognize and support the importance of a diversity of sources in our libraries.(12) Our *ALA Intellectual Freedom Manual* states that: "Librarians have a professional responsibility to be inclusive. . . ." And our Library Bill of Rights maintains that: "Libraries should provide materials and information presenting all points of view on current and historical issues. Materials should not be proscribed or removed because of partisan or doctrinal disapproval." ALA's Telecommunications Policy, which was passed in the early 1990s, reinforces these ideals for the information superhighway: "The NII should support and encourage a diversity of information providers in order to guarantee an open, fair and competitive marketplace, with a full range of viewpoints." The related Freedom to Read Statement endorsed by both ALA and the American Association of Publishers says that:

> It is in the public interest for publishers and librarians to make available the widest diversity of views and expressions, including those which are unorthodox or unpopular with the majority. . . . It is the responsibility of publishers and librarians to give full meaning to the freedom to read by providing books that enrich the quality and diversity of thought and expression. . . .

It is impossible to have a meaningful discussion on issues of the day without access to a broad representation of the viewpoints held in society at large. Yet, information is no longer referred to as a public good but a marketplace commodity. This creates a major dilemma for librarians concerned with ensuring the public's right to know in a commercially-driven information age.

What Librarians Can Do to Ensure a Healthy Alternative Press

As we explore ways to help the alternative press flourish, we must realize that, too often, these publishers are unfamiliar with libraries and librarians are unfamiliar with them. We have an insufficient involvement with the publishing industry, particularly the alternative press, even though we are highly interdependent. Nevertheless, there exists a natural synergy between a healthy publishing industry and healthy libraries, both of which are essential for a democratic society. We must decide where and how we want to weigh in on the impact of the corporate media and the role of the alternative press.

First, we must counter the illusion that the current media offers more choice. We should conduct studies on the impact of conglomeration and document harm to the free flow of ideas. We should focus on antitrust issues, not just legislative action. We should become much more media literate and recognize the synergy between the communications and library communities. We should join forces with the many groups who are speaking out about the impact of media conglomeration on intellectual freedom and the public's right to know.(13)

Second, we need to prioritize the acquisition and cataloging of alternative press materials. We should encourage the indexing of alternative press publications and buy alternative press indexes. We should establish standing orders with independent presses and encourage distributors to handle more small publishers. Because these publishers prefer direct sales which pay much faster, they may be willing to offer libraries a higher discount for direct purchases. By seeking out alternative publishers, we can help guarantee them a more predictable market. We can also help to market their lists by showcasing them at programs, book parties, and lectures, as well as adding their archives to our special collections.

Third, we can encourage our professional associations to promote the alternative press more actively. They can feature their publications more prominently in advertising and exhibits and offer more programs about these resources at conferences. We should also mainstream discussions about the alternative press within ALA; all collection development specialists should be concerned about these publications. ALCTS should cosponsor programs with several of the roundtables and focus more attention on the issues surrounding corporate media.

Fourth, we should adopt alternative publishers. They need our help to thrive, and they simply do not know how to get to our market. We should go to their meetings and develop and distribute guides about working with libraries. We should also produce guides to help librarians work with alternative publishers. A slight increase in our business can mean a big difference in their survival rates. According to one small publishers, if every librarian simply bought just 10 independent press titles this year, the marketplace would boom. Many titles such as literature in translation and short stories published by the alternative press sell almost exclusively to libraries. Library sales can make a big difference for small publishers whose average press run is 5000 copies; some are even smaller. We must recognize that the marketplace is as much a censor as those who purge information from our airwaves, libraries, publisher's lists, or the Internet.

Libraries are sanctuaries for alternative voices. If the mainstream press ignores, under-covers, or diminishes hard-hitting, essential stories, our libraries and our databases are unlikely to pick them up. On a recent Pacifica radio show about Project Censored, I was asked: "Can't someone who just searches Nexis/Lexis pick up on these stories?" I responded: "No, if they are not printed in the mainstream press, the mainstream indexers are not going to cover them." In the library community, we have an obligation to build balanced collections. Given the trends in publishing, we cannot build these balanced collections without heavily investing in alternatives to the mainstream press. It is time we recognize our own values and ensure we have diverse collections that truly represent the full spectrum of published opinion and thought. Otherwise, Barnes and Noble will eclipse us as the community's primary information resource.

NOTES.

1. Renee Feinberg, "B&N: The New College Library?" *Library Journal* 123, #2 (February 1, 1998): 49-51.

2. Barbara Hoffert, "Publishers are Looking at You," *Library Journal* 116, #3 (February 15, 1991): 146-154.

3. See *Who's Buying Whom: Highlights of Publishing/Information/Training Acquisition Activity,* NY: Whitestone Communications, 1999.

4. See André Schiffrin, "Bucking the Monoliths: Publishing with a Mission," *American Libraries* 30, #5 (May 1999): 44-46; "Publishers' Spring Catalogues Offer Compelling Reading About the Market for Ideas, *The Chronicle of Higher Education* (March 19, 1999): B8-B9; and "Random Acts of Consolidation," *The Nation,* (July 5, 1999): 10.

5. Mark Crispin Miller, "The Crushing Power of Big Publishing," *The Nation* 264, #10 (March 17, 1997): 11-18.

6. Neil Postman, *Amusing Ourselves to Death: Public Discourse in the Age of Show Business.* (New York: Penguin Books, 1985)

7. Peter Phillips, "Building Media Democracy," in *Censored, 1999: The News that Didn't Make the News* by Peter Phillips and Project Censored.. (New York: Seven Stories Press, 1999): 129-135.

8. Milton Wolf and Marjorie Bloss, "Without Walls Means Collaboration," *Information Technology and Libraries*, 17, #4 (December 1998): 212-215.

9. Anna H. Perrault, *The Changing Print Resource Base of Academic Libraries in the United States: A Comparison of Collection Patterns in Seventy-two ARL Academic Libraries of Non-Serial Imprints for the Years 1985 and 1989.* Florida State University doctoral dissertation, 1994. P. xi.

10. Stephen L. Hupp, "The Left and the Right: A Preliminary Study of Bias in Collection Development in Ohio Libraries," *Collection Management* 14, #2 (1991): 139-54. And " The Left and the Right: A Follow-Up Survey of the Collection of Journals of Public Opinion in Ohio Libraries," *Collection Management* 18, #2 (1993): 135-52.

11. Rita A. Marinko and Kristin H. Gerhard, "Representation of the Alternative Press in Academic Library Collections," *College and Research Libraries,* 59, #4 (July 1998): 363-377.

12. For a compilation of statements and interpretations, along with a history and guidance for action, see *Intellectual Freedom Manual,* 4th ed. by the American Library Association, Office for Intellectual Freedom, (Chicago: American Library Association, 1992) and "Principles for the Development of the National Information Infrastructure," (Washington, DC: American Library Association Washington Office, 1993).

13. For an extensive list of groups working to democratize the media, see *The Progressive Guide to Alternative Media and Activism.* (New York: Seven Stories Press, 1999) and *Censored, 1999: The News that Didn't Make the News* by Peter Phillips and Project Censored. (New York: Seven Stories Press, 1999): 271-323.

The Other 90 Percent: What Your MLS Didn't Teach You

Byron Anderson

This paper is based on participation in the panel discussion, "Alternative Press and Intellectual Freedom," sponsored by the Alternatives in Print Task Force presented June 27, 1999, as part of the American Library Association's Annual Conference, New Orleans, Louisiana.

In order to understand today's book publishing industry, it is helpful to understand some statistics and definitions that go along with the industry. All figures presented are approximate and gathered from reliable sources. More than 600 mergers and acquisitions have been reported in the U.S. book industry since the 1960s, a long-term trend expected to continue. Each year during the 1990s, approximately 65,000 titles were published in the United States. Eighty percent of all trade titles came from the five largest publishing conglomerates. The term "trade books" is imprecise and generally taken to mean adult fiction and nonfiction, paperbacks, and children's books, intended for the general public, and marketed through bookstores, including online sales, and libraries. They are distinct from textbooks, subscription books, book clubs, etc. The 1990s had some revolving at the top among the five largest publishing conglomerates, but generally included Bertelsmann AG, S. I. Newhouse (Advance Publications), Viacom, von Holtzbrink, and Pearson. With the purchase of Random House from the Newhouse family, the Bertelsmann Group alone is responsible for more than 30 percent of the U.S. trade books and close to 40 percent of the best sellers.

There are several terms used to describe the small press, and these are often used interchangeably. The term "independent press" has gained in popularity and is commonly used in lieu of "small press." Independent publishers are independent of corporate ownership and make up more than 53,000 presses in the United States. Independent presses are not necessarily small, for example, Grove Atlantic and W. W. Norton publish more than one hundred titles per year. Publications from independent presses cover a wider range of subjects do than publications from corporate-controlled presses. The publications come from a greater variety of places than do mainstream publications, and include academic institutions, associations, literary groups, home-based and one- person operations, hobbyist or collector's clubs, and think tanks. A subset of the independent press is called the alternative or progressive press. Though difficult to define, the uniqueness of progressive presses lies in giving voice to marginalized groups, emerging writers and poets, thought-provoking and sometimes thought-disturbing ideas, and translations of international writers.

Unless aggressively pursued, librarians would be fortunate to be aware of even 10 percent of the publishers publishing today. The other 90 percent remain obscure. Library collections represent only a fraction of the true diversity of books available. While a library cannot collect everything, most librarians are not even aware of many publications available in their effort to build a collection. Examples of alternative publications generally absent from library collections include:

- Translated works about the Third World by indigenous writers.
- Topics of anarchism, poverty, labor, erotica, human rights, and peace studies.

Reprinted with permission from *Counterpoise* (1716 SW Williston Road, Gainesville, FL 32608), v. 3, nos. 3/4 (July/October 1999), pp. 11–13.

- Most books of poetry.
- The writings of many new and lesser known authors.

There is a persistent myth that publications from small presses are the leftovers or rejects screened out by the "rigorous editorial" standards set by editors at mainstream presses. If a manuscript can't cut it with the big houses, the authors submit to the smaller houses. With some exception, this is simply not true. In mainstream presses, decisions to print are market-based, that is, books are based on profit potential. In independent presses, especially progressive presses, decisions to print are topic-based or based on literary merit, that is, books are mission driven or have something to say.

The failure of librarians to consider the independent press as an entity worthy of collecting begins in the curricula for library and information science (LIS). In collection development coursework, students are introduced to basic tools used in building a collection. The critique here is not in what students are taught, but in what they're not taught. Textbooks used in collection development classes, such as Elizabeth Futas' *Collection Development Policies and Procedures*, 3rd ed. (1995), lack certain headings in the subject index, for example, small press, independent press, alternative press, or progressive press. More surprisingly, the index has no listing for publishers, presses, vendors, distributors, or wholesalers. There is only one-page devoted to approval plans. This strongly indicates that students are not introduced to the publishing industry, including how publishers and librarians should interact with each other.

G. Edward Evans' *Developing Library and Information Centers*, 3rd ed. (1995), presents a number of guidelines to use when developing collections. First, select items useful to clients. There is no explanation of what is "useful." It would be better to teach librarians how to develop a diverse collection and let patrons decide what is of use to them. Second, select only items of lasting, literary or social value. Without exposure to alternative presses, librarians are likely to select materials that reflect mainstream values. Third, select based on the demand for the material. Even reader preferences can be rigged to create demand, for example consider the Princess Di publication industry. Librarians need to realize that there will be little or no demand for small press items. It's up to librarians to make these publications available.

For libraries maintaining collection development policies, criteria for selection will include components such as, first, suitability of subject and style for intended audience. Progressive publications are rarely targeted to suit reader tastes, but rather are challenging and thought disturbing. Second, collect based on the reputation or significance of the author and publisher. Small presses will rarely have a "reputation," and most of authors will be unknown. Third, collect based on popular appeal. Alternative press publications are not trying to compete with popular best sellers. The writing and content are not trying to suit mass market mentalities. Finally, collect based on the number and nature of requests from patrons. Patrons will not request what they don't know, and most will be unaware of small press publications.

Collection development policies can contain criteria worthy of consideration in any library. Examples include, first, collect based on insight into human and social conditions. Second, collect based on relevance to the experience and contributions of diverse populations. Third, collect based on representation of a minority point of view. Finally, this statement from the Greenville County (SC) Public Library:

> The library does not act as an agent for or against a particular issue. The disapproval of materials by one individual or group should not be the means of denying those materials to all groups if by library selection standards, they belong in the collection.

The above criteria is a basis for the consideration and purchase of progressive publications.

Collection development textbooks will recommend bibliographic tools useful for selecting materials. These tools often begin with *Books in Print*. While expansive, this title misses many presses and their publications. Even Len Fulton's *International Directory of Little Magazines and Small Presses*, while significant for building collections, lists approximately 6,000 presses, a small fraction of worldwide presses. Second, textbooks will typically recommend that librarians follow through on publisher's catalogs, flyers and advertisements. Independent presses cannot afford to market heavily, if at all, and corporate publishing houses are prolific mailers and advertisers. Often, they set out with a marketing plan in mind designed to create a demand for their materials. Third, an item being considered for selection should have been favorably reviewed in two or more sources. Of the 65,000 or so items published in the United States each year, approximately 10 percent are reviewed, and most of these books are published by fewer than 200 presses. Finally, "recommended" or "best" lists should be used in developing a collection because the "leg work" has been done in singling out worthwhile titles. The compilation of these lists rarely reviews titles published by progressive presses. For example, the "Best Books of 1998" list in the *Bowkers Annual Library and Book Trade* (1999), put together by the Notable Books Council of the Reference and User Services Division of ALA, has five categories covering from fiction to children's books totaling 159 titles. Of these, four titles, all children's books, were from two alternative presses that were profiled in the *Alternative Publishers of Books in North America*, 4th ed. (1999). The directory contains profiles of 148 significant alternative presses that total published hundreds of titles during 1998. Surely, many titles worthy of consideration were missed as part of the Best Books recommendations.

To examine what library and information educators say about the current state of their profession, one can turn to the American Library Association co-sponsored Congress on Professional Education <www.ala.org/congress/lis-ed.html>, held April 30–May 1, 1999 in Washington, DC. Keywords and phrases taken from the Statement on LIS Curricula for the ALA Congress in Professional Education includes leadership and management skills, recognize the fluidity of information channels, marketing, entrepreneurship, grant writing, multitasking, strong technical abilities, webmasters, digital preservation, and systems design. New topics for LIS course development were also identified in the five-year study funded by Kellogg and conducted by the Association for Library and Information Science Education, 1996–2000. Courses identified were advanced information technology design and analysis; advanced studies in Intranet and Internet design and development; data mining; digital libraries; electronic commerce; and information policy. While the profession is headed in many of these directions, what's interesting is in what's missing. Besides lacking the word service (a separate concern), there is no mention of publishers or the publishing industry—print, online or otherwise.

The LIS curricula should have instruction in the publishing industry. Students should know something about marketing techniques of the publishing industry and distribution channels for books. In a book chapter by Patricia Glass Schuman and Charles Harmon entitled, "The Business of Book Publishing" in the ALA publication, *Understanding the Business of Library Acquisitions*, 2nd ed. (1999), Karen A. Schmidt, editor, these concerns are listed:

- Librarians and publishers as professions are frequently unaware of the methodologies, economics, impacts, and policies of the other.
- There are few formal education programs for those in the publishing industry.
- Few library education programs offer courses about the publishing industry.
- Libraries are somewhat of an invisible market for many publishers since a majority of libraries purchase books and journals through wholesalers rather than directly from publishers.

A key to diverse library collections is publisher relations. Get to know who's publishing what and how to seek out small presses. Understand a library's acquisition process, including approval plans and standing orders, and the process used to add a particular item to a collection. Know how to order publications from small publishing houses, especially those with no distributor. Realize that most small presses will never find a library or bookstore market for their publications, nor are they trying to. Ensure by policy that small press material is represented in the collection. These ideas should be taught in the classroom and put to work in every library.

Actions can be taken to create a link between libraries and the independent press. First, become aware of organizations working to get small press materials into libraries and bookstores, for example, the Independent Press Association <www.indypress.org>, Small Press Distribution <www.spdbooks.org>, the Alternative Press Center <www.altpress.org/api.html>, and the Women's Presses Library Project <www.litwomen.org/wplp.html>. Second, join ALA committees committed to creating an awareness of the independent press and promote its use in libraries. Especially valid is the Social Responsibilities Round Table's Alternatives in Print Task Force <libr.org/AIP>. Third, advocate for issues surrounding progressive literature, particularly intellectual freedom, the freedom to read, and the right to access. Read through ALA's An Interpretation of the Library Bill of Rights <www.ala.org/work/freedom/interprt.html>. Finally, advocate for library collections that reflect the true diversity of society.

Taking the (Bad) News with the Good: Alternative Publications Build a Movement on the Margins

Abby Scher

On a recent summer day, I found myself walking along Malcolm X Boulevard in Bedford Stuyvesant in search of the editor, publisher, lead writer and advertising director of *Our Time Press*, a monthly newspaper distributed largely in central Brooklyn. I was visiting David Greaves, the one-man band whose energy and vision keeps this local, radical newspaper—circulation 25,000—going. His office was stuffed in the back of a used furniture store, and the brand new computer on his desk was only recently purchased using a loan from Accion International, the nonprofit loan operation working in poverty stricken areas of the world, including Brooklyn.

I discovered *Our Time Press* while retrieving cash from my bank in downtown Brooklyn, taking an issue from a pile stacked high near the ATM machine. Every month, Greaves combines articles and photos of local interest with his political essays and reporting. The July issue, for example, published a four-column photo of Brooklyn Boy Scouts marching. Right next to it in the left hand column, Greaves reprinted a letter written by a friend of Gary Graham/Shaka Sankofa, describing the condemned man's struggle against being removed from his regular cell for transport to Texas' death row. Inside Greaves ran Sankofa's last words before his execution, plus Fidel Castro's statement on his death (printed in a box right under the regular pro-entrepreneurial column "Black Business Roundup").

I love *Our Time Press*. Already five years old, it is probably one of the most important progressive publications out there, but it fails to receive credit for the same reason it is so important: because it is locally written and distributed. The tag line under its masthead reads "The local paper with the global view," and it is true that a new community—Central Brooklyn—is being informed and formed by a paper operating in an internationalist, black, frame of reference.

I'd be interested to know how many other *Our Time Press*es there are out there. In New York, other publications targeting communities of color have a political edge. Among the four Haitian newspapers in NYC, one, *Haiti Progres*, is explicitly radical. (As a former coeditor of *Dollars and Sense*, I was thrilled to discover it recently ran a translation of a *D&S* article, "The ABCs of the Global Economy.") The often-free distribution favored by the newer local papers bypasses the perennial problem faced by the left press—distribution. The consolidation of bookstores and the demise of the independent bookseller has diminished the reach and usual outlets for

---

Expanded and corrected version of an article published in *Resist* (259 Elm St., Suite 201, Somerville, MA 02144), v. 9, no. 1 (August 2000), pp. 1–2, 7. Reprinted with permission.

our press. Nurturing the resurgence of local radical papers can only help it.

Role of Alternative Media

At its best, the alternative press presents different voices of analysis to different constituencies. When successful, a publication rests on the shoulders of a movement, past, present or future. Each historical moment throws up a publication or two that may survive its time and perhaps contribute to the next eruption, or even influence the framing in the corporate media. Greaves was shaped by the 60s, and worked as a filmmaker before taking up his present calling to speak to Brooklyn in the year 2000.

Another much loved publication very much of this moment is *Blu*, a political hip hop magazine with a CD glued to its pages that is put out by the Bruderhof community in New Paltz, New York. None of Blu's eight staff people are paid, and six are members of (and supported by) the Bruderhof's Christian commune. Only recently published on a regular basis, Blu is now bimonthly. A network of volunteers promotes the pub across the country, and it sells out quickly from places like Tower Records. With a 7,000 issue print run, *Blu* records a phenomenal 80% to 90% "sell through" rate on the newsstand. *Blu*'s managing editor, Pete Mommsen, told me they aim to build a bridge between the 1960s movements and today's young people who know little about the past. They do that, for example, by running interviews with Black Panther Asaka Shakur.

Pressing Past the Usual Suspects

The "alternative" publications like these do not preach to the converted, especially among the young. Young people are dropping away from regular newspaper reading in droves, yet youth-led publications—particularly underground and student papers—are a growth area. These newspapers often draw on the national left press or leftwing think tanks on the web for information which they reframe in their own language.

Student publications often take more initiative and cover political issues that the mainstream media skip over. For example, while on the streets of Washington DC protesting the IMF and World Bank, "the corporate media managed to ignore us," reports Gary Grant and Dr. Ridgely Mu'min of the Black Farmers Association, which has been challenging racist practices at the USDA. "We were giving an interview to a college newspaper right next to a CNN set up. We noticed the CNN reporter listening to our conversation and thought that they may turn their cameras on us and interview us next. However, by the time we finished the interview with the students, they were gone, poof!"

Many of the alternative publications formed in the past ten years seem to take a cultural bent—*New Directions for Women* may be long gone, and *Ms.* struggling to find an audience, but *Teen Voices* and *Desert Moon* offer feminist parents popular non-sexist alternatives to the dominant kids magazines. The most famous of the newer cultural magazines is *Adbusters*, a bimonthly out of Vancouver that sponsors "Buy Nothing Day" to protest rampant commercialism and runs counter-ads riffing on corporate advertising.

But *Adbusters* is in an usual situation since it receives subsidies from the Canadian government. In the face of burn-out, low pay, and ever-dry revenue streams, many other "alternative" publications come and go. A former favorite, *Profane Existence*, was an anarchist punk magazine with maybe 7,000 circulation at its height that started around the same time as *Adbusters* in the late 1980s. After 10 years, the small collective just couldn't do it any more. Chuck D'Adamo of the Alternative Press Index reports that since the API's founding in 1969, it indexed a changing roster of popular and academic left publications totaling about 900 (now the index covers about 300). Even some long-established publications disappear or become irregular to the point of nonexistence—*Radical America* where are you?

Fighting Commercialism

The survival of any noncorporate-owned, noncommercial enterprise is usually due to heroic effort and sacrifice, because the magazines do not benefit from the advertising that keeps commercial enterprises not just afloat but highly profitable. Foundations, which help support much of the rest of the nonprofit sector, loathe to give nonprofit publications any money. Tight money margins and minimal means to pay authors mean that publications often rely on academics to write for them, who may not communicate in the most popular or user friendly language, restricting their readership further.

The older publications that survive, like *The Nation*, *Mother Jones*, *The Progressive* and *In These Times*, tend to have a wealthy patron or two so they can stay afloat in times of stagnant or declining circulations. Others become entrepreneurial—20% of the operating revenue of the economic justice magazine *Dollars and Sense* comes from fundraising, but 40% comes from its seven economics readers used in college classrooms. *Blu* holds fundraising concerts. *E magazine*, a 40,000 circulation environmental bimonthly out of Connecticut, devises special issues as far as a year in advance and raises money from environmental foundations to help pay for them.

Still, the magazines survive on slim margins. And they wonder, like Deborah Thomas, publisher of the media watchdog magazine *EXTRA!*, whether their audience will ever extend beyond the usual 200,000 or 300,000 suspects who flow through the readership of the national magazines. The left press has always depended on underlying social movements for its health and in periods of relative demobilization it tends to stagnate.

The Importance of the Left Press

The left press develops in waves. In the late 60s and early 70s, "there were all these left academic publications forming, like *Review of Radical Political Economy*," recalls D'Adamo of the Alternative Press Index. Every city had an underground newspaper. Then in the mid-70s, the "underground" papers became "alternative" and sanitized, promoting music more than politics. Another wave came in the mid- to late-1980s with the interest in criticism—that's when *EXTRA!* formed, along with the *Baffler*, an irregularly published journal investigating the production of culture, and *Adbusters*. The 'zines young people started putting out in the late 1980s and early 1990s were driven by individuals and rarely became community enterprises.

All the while, the corporate press was changing too, becoming more consolidated and less local. Left-wing publications became independently owned islands in an increasingly corporate sea. At last count, 86% of newspapers are now owned by corporations. Competition between the types of media—television, print and movies—pushing conglomeration within each type of medium and fusion across media.

The print media is more profitable than ever even as it cuts back on news gathering—a trend even decried by mainstream editors like Gene Roberts of the *New York Times*. The newspapers' legitimacy erodes as its role in presenting the "news" erodes. Circulation is stagnant or down. The whole premise of liberal journalism asserted at the beginning of the 20th century—unbiased, giving two sides of the story—is in decline. Still, the editors at big papers are well remunerated, making $250,000, with bonuses alone averaging $56,000 annually. FAIR released an interesting survey a few years ago showing that Washington journalists are more conservative on economic issues and more liberal on social issues than most of the public. While 77% of the public polled thought corporations have too much power, only 57% of these journalists did. This gap in perception between editors and parts of the public paves the way for community publications to take on big media against the odds.

Context Asks Why Not What

That said, I also think there is an essential fallacy in some off-the-cuff criticisms of the corporate media—if only we could deliver the right information to more people, then the people would "be with us." In fact, one of the largest problems with the news that the media critic George Trow pointed out long ago is that it is decontextualized information. It ignores the larger social contexts. It accepts the "facts" neatly gathered as a closed and dehistoricized universe that comes out of nowhere, rarely asking why something is the case or how we got to this state of affairs.

As critical theorist Herbert Marcuse argues, we must analyze the "facts" so they no longer seem inevitable or obvious, and situate them in a larger frame that we've thought a lot about. It can be a historically aware frame or a theoretically informed one. Merely delivering the "right" facts is not truly an alternative.

This is especially true because the "brute facts" are ever more accessible to the motivated person—the reports once requiring special access are now widely available on the web to those who know to look at the Economic Policy Institute web site or that of Global Exchange.

Our Effectiveness/Impacting Mainstream Media

The type of media that is interesting and growing is controversial media, as can be seen by the voracious media networks on the Right. The Right's exposes—most famously about Clinton's sex life—are powering controversies in the mainstream media. At one time, Bob McChesney pointed out to me, *Ramparts* played that role. It's left wing exposes on the Vietnam War and 1960s politics provoked national press attention. Now, he argues, the two or three meaty exposes a year by the *Progressive* are never picked up, not to mention the list of stories issued yearly by Project Censored.

This suggests that we cannot measure the effectiveness of the left press these days by the level of mainstream attention. We are marginal and ignored. When our issues do make it into the pages of the mainstream press, they do not get sustained attention, unlike the vapid campaigns of the corporate party candidates, for instance. And spending too much creative energy trying to capture the mainstream press's imagination can be risky, since it can distort the goals of our movements and reduce our politics into imagemaking.

Where Are We Going?

Does that mean we should just be grateful that our press nurtures the movements out of which they grew and forget about the corporate media? Activists like Bob McChesney and even Ralph Nader are not waiting to see whether our marginal publications grow a little here and there. They are pushing for the left to take on media democracy as a major political goal. They have not given up on challenging corporations' control of the mainstream media. "The core principle is that control over communication has to be taken away from Wall Street and Madison Avenue and put in the hands of citizens, journalists, and others whose concerns are not limited to the bottom line," writes McChesney in *Rich Media, Poor Democracy*.

First, according to McChesney, the labor movement needs to give money to community and nonprofit media while accepting that its money will not buy them editorial control. The government can also lower mailing costs for nonprofit publications. Second, McChesney calls for restructuring public broadcasting into a system that cannot accept grants from corporations. This means the U.S. government must subsidize local, independent, public access and national networks on the order of $5 billion to $10 billion a year, as is done in Japan and Britain. Fourth, the government must hold commercial broadcasters to high public service standards instead of handing the public airwaves over to them. Deregulation has meant half of radio airtime is now dedicated to advertising. Allow them only 18 to 20 hours of broadcasting a day, with the rest of the "liberated" time going to public affairs and children's shows. Finally, enforce antitrust laws and break apart the media monopoly chains that are blanding newsfare.

The Left and Labor parties abroad put such politics in their platforms as a matter of course, but here only the Green Party is campaigning on these issues, albeit with a less detailed and radical agenda than McChesney. Like many media activists in local alliances, the Greens focus on the ever more commercial airwaves not print. It is vexing to devise a true reform agenda for the print oligopolies.

Some of us long for a national leftwing newspaper—let's add that to McChesney's list of activist solutions. Or, better than creating a single outlet, let's get more money to the Pacific and Inter Press news services so what remains of the independent community press can get some comprehensive coverage from the left. Funnel in reporting from *Labor Notes*, *Dollars and Sense*, and *Color Lines* to round out their offerings. Spread around our work so it's read by more than the usual suspects and we are forced to write in a way more people can read and engage with. And, while we are being utopian, why not build up a truly alternative news world so more of us are reading the reporting of the community newspapers on the left, particularly in communities of color. It's past time but unfortunately we are not past the time when money limits what we can do.

Abby Scher, former editor of *Dollars & Sense*, currently works at the Independent Press Association in New York. This is an expanded version of an article that appeared in the Resist Foundation newsletter of August 2000.

The Alternative Media: Open Sources on What's Real

Daniel C. Tsang

Wake Up Call

America—and the world—woke up one December 1999 morning to a new reality. No, I'm not talking about the start of the new millennium. I mean the World Trade Organization (WTO) protests in Seattle, Washington, which saw a resurgence of 1960s-style protests but more importantly, new formations among previously unaffiliated groups. For the first time, labor marched with environmentalists and with indigenous rights activists. NGOs featured prominently in the protests. And the young and idealistic marched with the old and seasoned. While the mainstream media focused on the ensuing "riots," blaming the disturbances that closed down the World Trade Organization parley on black-shirted and -hooded "anarchists," the alternative media tried to present what really went on in the streets of Seattle. Mastering the Internet, activist groups presented daily reports of the "direct action" to a global audience on the Web; encoded on RealAudio—and initially on MP3 as well—a collaborative Web-site (http://www.corpwatch.org/trac/wtw/index.html) encouraged free duplication and broadcasting on local radio stations, spreading the alternative perspective.

One ignores the alternative media at one's own peril. The Cold War may be over, Stalinist-state systems long dead, and multinational conglomerates rule the world, but the counterculture and resistance movement are still alive and kicking. They've just moved to another arena. Activist groups still issue their print manifestos and analyses, much of it highlighted by activist review media such as *WordViews* (contact info: http://www.igc.apc.org/worldviews/magblurb.html), *MSRRT Newsletter* (http://www.cs.unca.edu/~davidson/msrrt/), *Counterpoise* (http://www.liblib.com/Cpoise/Cpoise.html), *Factsheet Five* (http://www.factsheet5.com/) and *Zine Guide* or anarchist publications like *The Fifth Estate* and *Anarchy*; or they are among the 200-plus publications indexed by the Alternative Press Center's *Alternative Press Index* (for its listing of alternative titles, see: http://www.altpress.org/direct.html).

Access to Resources

In particular, *WorldViews* has focused on the grey literature emanating from Third World NGOs in environmental, justice, women's, indigenous, peace and liberation theology movements. The University of California, Irvine, Libraries recently acquired WorldViews' collection of hundreds of such pamphlets, broadening the scope of UCI's Political Literature Collection in the libraries' Special Collections Department, already strong in left and labor history. Increasingly, such grey literature is appearing with its full text online, accessible with a click of the mouse. The Zapatistas in Chiapas, Mexico, perhaps, are the revolutionary group most prominent on the Web (http://www.ezln.org/), but guerrillas and activists of all sorts have taken technology in their stride and mastered Web-authoring to bring their voices and concerns to the rest of humanity.

On rare occasions, these voices manage to penetrate past the ideological gatekeepers of the mainstream media. A *60 Minutes* variant presented the "anarchists" from

Oregon who caravanned to Seattle to protest the WTO (Pelley, 1999), while the *New York Times* waxed about their "intellectual cheerleader," John Zerzan (Verhovek and Kahn, 1999). And the *Sunday Times* warned that the "Eugene anarchists" were ready to invade England (Rhodes, 1999). Yet how many libraries had bothered to collect Zerzan's works? A search in *WorldCat*, the database of OCLC, a cataloging consortium for public and most academic libraries, shows that his 1994 book of essays, *Future Primitive*, jointly published by Autonomedia in Brooklyn and Anarchy in Columbus, Missouri, was owned only by some two dozen libraries in just a few states. A new collection edited by him, *Against Civilization* (Uncivilized Books, Eugene, 1999) appears in fewer than ten libraries. As did another collection of his own essays, *Elements of Refusal* (Left Bank Books, Seattle, 1988), garnering only fewer than 20 library holdings. An earlier work he co-edited, *Questioning Technology* (New Society Publishers, Philadelphia, 1991 and Freedom Press, London, 1988) did manage to get into more libraries in its two editions.

It goes without saying that an educated public will survive better in the new millennium. Yet even the CIA is now floundering in the wake of the fall of the Berlin Wall and the end of the Cold War (both events blindsiding the intelligence analysts). Indeed, there are increasing calls for ridding the CIA of its covert-action focus or its quest for uncovering state secrets. Instead, reformers from across the political spectrum are now calling for the national security establishment to focus more attention on "open sources," to provide the ingredients necessary for making informed policy decisions, including Robert Steele, CEO of Open Source Solutions, Inc. (Steele, 1999). The alternative media, of course, form an important component of such open sources.

Then and Now

Over two decades ago, the US government (through the then–US Office of Education) funded the Alternative Acquisitions Project at Temple University, for which I served as the Research Librarian. Traversing the country on a Greyhound, I tried to spread the alternative press gospel to college libraries (see my essays in Danky and Shore, 1982). We were then concerned about the lack of alternative materials appearing in many library holdings. Today, while some movements have gained mass media attention (e.g. that of gays and lesbians aspiring to the mainstream), other, less assimilated movements or more hidden portions of those movements remain largely invisible to a public that is served a daily diet of MTV and corporate pap. We risk raising a new generation of post-Gen-Xers expert at computer chats and Web design but lacking the skills to critically analyze world events. (Parenthetically, libraries go down a dangerous road by just hiring as bibliographers newly graduated librarians who know how to search the Internet, but lack any subject knowledge.) Arguably, one reason this country got bogged down in the Vietnam War morass was the absence of any Vietnam specialists in the State Department at the start of the conflict, a consequence no doubt of the McCarthy era. Other empirical studies since the Alternative Acquisitions Project have shown similarly dismal results in terms of incorporating alternative viewpoints into library collections.

Charles Willett, an acquisition librarian turned-alternative press crusader as editor of *Counterpoise*, found that holdings of some 45 academic libraries in Alabama, Georgia and Florida lacked a "representative sample" of 32 English-language monographs from these small presses: Africa World Press, Amana, Claremont, Cleis, Earth Resources Research, Latin American Bureau, Lawrence Hill, Marram, Monthly Review Press, Orbis and Zed. No library in the sample had 90 percent or more of the titles, and only two had over 80 percent. Twelve libraries had none of the titles. Only three of the presses marketed to libraries through approval plans (Willett, 1991/92), suggesting to me that bibliographers need to be more pro-active in acquiring the titles from small, political presses.

Charles D'Adamo, of the Alternative Press Center found out, for example, that while critics of US foreign policy like Noam Chomsky, Edward Herman, and Alexander Cockburn are well covered in the alternative press, their work appears in publications largely not indexed or underindexed by a major index found in libraries. Indeed, he argues that countries of importance to foreign policy critics, such as Cuba and Haiti, were well covered in the alternative media, and largely ignored by mainstream publications, for what he argues may be ideological bias against the left. These Third World countries (including Haiti under Aristide), he posits, "represented potential economic and political alternatives to unregulated capitalism and liberal oligarchy, which could serve as models for other Latin American nations, thus making them 'enemies' of the US foreign policy establishment" (D'Adamo, 1999, p. 41).

Role of Libraries and Repositories

Yes, much of the grey literature from the political left (and for that matter, the political right) are showing up on the Web. But a passive library collection building policy ("Oh, they'll find it through altavista!") is hardly sufficient. Granted, E-text Archives, http://www.etext.org/index.html is a valiant effort to preserve electronically the textual content of political missives. Libraries need to begin to link these alternative sources to their subject home pages, but beyond that, bibliographers need to continue to acquire print versions of these political tracts, and subscribe to political zines and journals, so as to ensure that the content does not just evaporate into ethernet sometime during this millennium. Activists, after all, are rarely archivists. Although some micropublishers have paid attention to the alternative press (see Tsang, 1993), librarians must begin a discussion (paying due attention to intellectual property rights of authors) with alternative publishers about the need to archive, electronically as well as in paper) the voluminous output that forms the alternative grey literature.

References

D'Adamo, C. (1999) "Searching for 'the enemy': alternative resources on US foreign policy," *Progressive Librarian* Vol. 16, pp. 37–50. Progressive Librarian e-version: http://libr.org/PL/contents.html

Danky, J.P. and Shore, E. (Eds) (1982), *Alternative Materials in Libraries*, Scarecrow Press, Metuchen, NJ.

Pelley, S. (co-host), (1999) "The new anarchists: anarchists at Seattle riots are part of a movement developing in Eugene, Oregon," *Sixty Minutes II*, December 14, on CBS.

Rhodes, T. (1999) "Seattle Seattle's army of anarchists heads for UK," *Sunday Times*, December 5.

Steele, R.D. (1999) "Smart people, stupid bureaucracies: a tough look at US spies, satellites and scholars," December 21, Web-published at: http://www.oss.net/Papers/white/SmartPeople.doc

Tsang, D.C. (1993) "Preserving the US underground and alternative press of the 1960s and 1970s: history, prospects and microform sources," in Wachsberger, K. (Ed.), *Voices from the Underground*, Vol. 2, Mica Press, Tempe, AZ, pp. 81–128.

Verhovek, S.H. and Kahn, J. (1999) "Talks and turmoil: street rage; dark parallels with anarchist outbreaks in Oregon," *New York Times*, December 3, p. A12.

Waldman, P. (1999) "An anarchist looks to provide logic to Coterie at core of WTO vandalism," *Wall Street Journal*, December 6, p. A17.

Willett, C. (1991/92) "Politically controversial monographs," *Progressive Librarian* No. 4 (Winter, 1991/92), pp. 28–37.

Daniel C. Tsang has been, since 1986, economics and political science bibliographer and Data Services Librarian at the University of California, Irvine and a former coordinator of the American Library Association's Task Force on Alternatives in Print. He also serves on the advisory board for the Alternative Press Center. Since 1993, he has hosted "Subversity," a weekly alternative radio interview program on KUCI that is also Web-cast (http://go.fast.to/sv). His WWW News Resource Page (http://go.fast.to/news) has links to hundreds of alternative online publications. He can be contacted at dtsang@uci.edu

Independent Publishing Matters

Beth Schulman

Vital public discourse starts small. That's why independent periodicals with modest circulations—exemplified by the members of the IPA—matter just as profoundly in 1999 as they did a century ago. The practice of democracy, everywhere in the world, depends on media outlets like these.

Despite the proliferation of all-news cable channels, talk radio and the now ubiquitous internet, print persists as the medium where we begin to describe and name public problems, where we undertake the first discussion of issues that shape the daily lives of ordinary people.

And, while mainstream newspapers and magazines may participate in this process, feisty independent publications generate the most innovative reporting, analysis and debate. Investigative reporters, academics, policy specialists and other advocates for change do their most original work in these pages. There they know they can expect to engage the readers they encounter—even through the smallest of these publications—in the kind of spirited exchange necessary to refine and sharpen a new idea. These conversations, all too often ignored or pushed to the margins, can grow to become the cornerstones essential to building new public policies and new ways of thinking.

Many of the periodicals in the IPA take it as their mission to move readers beyond conversation to action. The independent, "alternative" press is organically connected to social movements. Publications rise, fall or subsist in circumstances that parallel the movements they represent. Such periodicals serve as forums for debating strategic approaches, for finding common cause among seemingly disparate, often geographically diffuse, constituencies, and, in hard times, for relentless critiques and attempts to resolve factional quarrels.

When, in the spring of 1776, Thomas Paine used a self-published pamphlet called *Common Sense* to argue that rebellion against the crown was a legitimate response to oppressive conditions, he directly challenged the prevailing public sentiment that acts of rebellion were beyond the boundaries of responsible civic behavior. By the summer of 1776, Paine's radical argument had evolved into a new conventional wisdom.

In a series of 1862 articles in his small circulation *Douglass Monthly*, Frederick Douglass argued that the best way to disrupt the Confederacy was to take southern blacks out of slavery and put them into Yankee uniforms. Douglass' arguments crystallized new but growing recognition throughout the Union leadership that slavery had become an obstacle to preserving the Union. The *Douglass Monthly* and Frederick Douglass himself deserve much of the credit for persuading Abraham Lincoln to sign the Emancipation Proclamation.

Ida Tarbell, Ray Stannard Baker and the other muckrakers exposed "the underside of American capitalism" in the pages of *Colliers'*, *McClure's* and other popular magazines. Before these crusading journalists were silenced by new, industry-friendly, magazine owners, they had facilitated the passage of some of the Progressive era's most effective regulatory reforms.

Writing in *The Revolution*, a nineteenth century journal whose circulation never exceeded 2,500, Susan B. Anthony began a critique of gender-based civil discrimination that galvanized the movement for universal suffrage. A century later, her successors, in the pages of still-extant periodicals like *Feminist Studies* and *Off Our Backs*, offered the analysis that has expanded the definition of feminism to include militancy against rape, domestic violence and the poverty of single mothers.

In the Cold War era, analysis appearing in the pages of *Monthly Review*, *Latin American Perspectives*, *The Bulletin of the Atomic Scientists* and dozens of other journalistic and scholarly titles fundamentally informed organized efforts to influence US policy on nuclear weapons, Vietnam, and Nicaragua.

Reprinted with permission from *Library Juice* (http://libr.org/Juice), v. 4, no. 19 (May 23, 2001).

Challenging conventional wisdom. Speaking truth to power. Exposing unpleasant realities. Giving voice to the silenced. These are the sacred priorities of advocacy journalism. Throughout the twentieth century, oppositional and minority movements, including people of color, the disabled, gays and lesbians, workers and welfare mothers, have used small-circulation periodicals to develop the vision and power their struggles have required.

Excerpted from the introduction, co-authored by Chuck D'Adamo, to *Annotations: A Guide to the Critical and Independent Press*, new from the IPA and the Alternative Press Center. IPA: http://www.indypress.org

Pursuing Small, Independent Book Publishers

Byron Anderson

In 1999, the Book Industry Study Group issued a report entitled, *The Rest of Us: the first study of America's 53,000 independent, smaller book publishers*. The study is an important benchmark measuring small publishers that are independent of corporate control. While most independents are small, a few are large, for example, W.W. Norton, and others are more ambiguously medium-sized, for example, Health Communications publisher of the ubiquitous Chicken Soup series. Small is a relative term and can include presses that publish one hundred or more titles per year. Small also includes what is sometimes referred to as micro-presses, commonly one-person, part-time presses that publish one new title every two or three years. Micro-press activity is commonly based on a press's resources—publishing happens when there is time and money to do so. In addition to the above count, it has been estimated that approximately 7,000 new book presses start up each year. Most are independent presses, though some can be new imprints of established presses.

Missing from the above book study count is an unknown, much smaller number of other independent presses. These presses are difficult to track because they're very small and elusive and do not participate in programs established to track current publishing activity. Examples of these programs include, first, the International Standard Book Number, a registry that annually assigns more than 10,000 new ISBN publisher prefixes. The IBSN serves as a tracking mechanism for publishers and books. Second, the Library of Congress registry, a program that requires two copies of each new title be sent to the Library of Congress. These titles are then classified creating a national cataloging record for the work. Finally, *Books in Print*, an annual publication or online database from Bowker that records titles in print from publishers who supply the information. The 2000/2001 edition has 66,000 publishers, including international publishers that distribute in the United States.

There are different reasons why a press is not included or does not participate in the tracking mechanisms designed for books and publishers. For example, publishers may not be aware of these programs or how to participate in them. Also, they may not want the government or an organization tracking and recording of their publishing activity. This would hold true for certain radical presses or maverick publishers. Further, a number small publishers do not work with a distributor, that is, businesses that promote and distribute books to the trade, mostly bookstores and libraries. Distributor services can cost 45 to 55 percent of the cover price of a book, making it difficult for some small publishers to participate. Rather, these publishers self-promote their works and rely on word of mouth. Often knowledge of their titles are limited to a small geographic area.

Complicating the above numbers is the fact that most small presses do not make it beyond their first year or title. It has been said that publishing is an easy business to get into, but a grueling business in which to survive. Currently, there is no method to track presses that go out of business each year. *Publishers' Weekly* and other trade magazines make mention of some presses that cease operation, but most fade away with no mention anywhere. Few notice that they're gone. Complicating this are the presses that lie dormant for several years with no publishing activity. Some resume publishing, some do not.

There are many different reasons that a press can go

Reprinted with permission from *Counterpoise* (1716 SW Williston Road, Gainesville, FL 32608), v. 4, no. 3 (July 2000), pp. 17–19.

out of business. It's been said that publishing is an accidental profession, especially true for many small presses. Those entering the publishing field want to see certain writing brought into print, but they may lack the business sense to do so. They may not give much thought to the financial and marketing skills required. Also, some small presses are dependent on one dedicated person, and the business is a labor of love. Publishing becomes a passion. When these individuals move on or retire, there is seldom anyone able or willing to continue the labor of love.

There is one other category of publications that can prove elusive, namely those works that come from associations and organizations. Associations and organizations run in size from large and global to small and local. They number in the tens of thousands and many publish books. Some have formalized publishing programs, but others find do not view themselves as being in the publishing business. Rather, they just want to get certain information distributed to a wider audience, and books are the medium of choice.

It should be evident from the above that there are many independent presses, and new ones are starting up all the time. Independent book presses cover a wide spectrum of interests and represent many points of view. Most independent presses have a unique publishing niche(s), and many are run by individuals or organizations dedicated to a cause. Singling out presses and titles of interest can be a tedious process, but the rewards are great. The authors and publishers can bring great conviction to their work, and their publications can be an ideal fit for one's particular needs, beliefs and values. They greatly expand the bounds of intellectual freedom.

So, how does one get started? Developing a greater awareness of independent publishers is the first step. There are reference sources that can help by providing profiles of many presses, including independents. These sources are useful as verification tools, for contact information, or furthering awareness. The information provided will vary between sources and some will tend to overlap in coverage. The below reference sources may combine independent and corporate presses, book and periodical presses, or have international coverage. Some sources will have broad coverage and others will focus on specific presses, for example, alternative or literary. Each source will need to be personally culled for the information sought. There may be a subject index or keyword access that can help focus a search. Web sites will frequently provide links to publisher homepages. While many independent presses are represented, the sources are not comprehensive. Given the dynamics of the publishing industry, it would be prove nearly impossible to have a complete list. This is a starting point. Pursuit of the independent press is a lifelong venture, but well worth the effort.

Sources for Locating Independent Book Publishers

REFERENCE BOOKS

Alternative Publishers of Books in North America, 4th ed. Edited and compiled by Byron Anderson. Gainesville, FL: CRISES Press, 1999. Biennial.
Profiles 148 alternative presses that are small, not driven by profit, and either publish books that are politically progressive or are literary and deliver oppositional thought through fiction, short stories, or poetry.

The American Directory of Writer's Guidelines, 2nd ed. Clovis, CA: Quill Driver Books, 1999.
A compilation of information for freelancers from more than 1,300 magazine editors and book publishers.

Books in Print and *Subject Guide to Books in Print*. New York: R. R. Bowker, 1988–. Annual.
BIP is a master reference to titles, authors and publishers currently in print. The publisher volume has address and contact information, including email and Web sites when available. Indexes include new publishers, wholesalers and distributors, and inactive and out-of-business publishers.

The Directory of Poetry Publishers, 16 edition, 2000/2001. Paradise, CA: Dustbooks. Annual. www.dustbooks.com
Feature some twenty-one pieces of information on each of the more than 2,000 book and magazine publishers of poetry worldwide, including university presses and e-zines. Includes editorial biases, percentage of submissions published, contest information and reporting time.

The Directory of Small Press/Magazine Editors & Publishers, 31st edition, 2000/2001. Paradise, CA: Dustbooks. Annual. www.dustbooks.com
More than 7,500 listings of editors and publishers, along with their associated publishing companies, their addresses, phones, e-mail addresses and Web pages. Includes self publishers.

The International Directory of Little Magazines & Small Presses, 36th edition, 2000/2001. Edited by Len Fulton. Paradise, CA: Dustbooks. Annual. www.dustbooks.com
Called "the bible of the business," the directory contains nearly 5,000 short profiles book and magazine publishers of literary, avante garde, cutting-edge contemporary, left wing, right wing, radical chic fiction, and mainstream areas such as photography and travel.

Literary Market Place. New Providence, New York: R. R. Bowker, 1988–. Annual.
Directory of the book publishing industry, including publishers, literary agents, editorial services, trade associations and foundations.

Publisher's Directory. Detroit, MI: Gale Research, 1984–. Annual.

Describes over 20,000 publishers and distributors that offer a wide variety of formats, including books, calendars, CD-ROMs, and software. Indexes include subject, geographic, and publishers, imprints and distributors.

Publisher's International ISBN Directory, 26th edition, 1999/2000. Muchen, Germany: K. G. Saur; New York. R. R. Bowker.

Divided into two parts: Geographical Section and an Alphabetical Section. These can be used to verify a press's ISBN and country of origin.

WEB SOURCES

AcqWeb's Directory of Publishers and Vendors acqweb.library.vanderbilt.edu
Access to many presses through alphabetic, geographic or subject directories.

AK Distribution www.akpress.org
Sells books and magazines by mail on radical politics from publishers.

Booksense www.booksense.com
A Web site created by the American Booksellers Association to represent independent booksellers. It is meant to rival the online booksales of Amazon.com and barnesandnoble.com. There is also an alternative "bestseller" list and recommended reading by independent booksellers.

Bookwire www.bookwire.com/index/publishers.html
Online information source for the publishing industry. Seventeen publisher indexes, e.g., Associations, Mystery, Science Fiction, provide links to many presses.

Consortium Book Sales & Distribution www.cbsd.com/cbsd_pubs.cfm
Distributor of more than sixty small, alternative presses in the areas of poetry, lesbian and gay studies, theater, art, Latin American studies, multicultural literature, and women's studies. Presses are annotated and linked.

Left Bank Books Collective www.leftbankbooks.com
A collectively owned and operated not-for-profit umbrella organization for anarchist projects and literature distribution—books, pamphlets, periodicals, zines, comix, other.

NewPages Online—Alternatives in Print & Media www.newpages.com
Annotates and links to independent publishers, alternative periodicals, literary periodicals, reviews, alternative newsweeklies and independent bookstores. The NewPages Resource Library expands to provide links to activist organizations, media criticism, radio, and other.

Omicrom Inforium—Small Press Connection www.booknotes.com/connect/
Organizations and publishers.

Publisher's Catalogues www.lights.com/publishers
Keyword search by publisher or city or browse by location, topic or type of material, i.e., books or magazines. Entries include a brief description and links to publisher homepages. Over 6,000 publishers.

PubList www.publist.com/indexes
Publishers pages searchable by title, subject and publisher.

Street Librarian: Independent & Non-corporate Media www.geocities.com/SoHo/Café/7423/altpress.html
Divided into categories of organizations, directories, reviews, etc.; notable press and media; some magazines and newsletters; zines on the web; distributors; multimedia.

Small Press Center www.smallpress.org
A nonprofit institution dedicated to independent publishing. Promotes interaction between the public and small independent book publishers. Co-sponsor of Small Press Month during the month of March. Site has a publisher member directory with full address listings.

Small Press Distribution www.spdbooks.org
The mission of this nonprofit organization is to nurture a cultural environment in which the literary arts are valued and sustained. Provides services to literary audiences, writers and publishers via its book and magazine distribution activities, public programming and advocacy efforts.

Women's Press Library Project www.litwomen.org/wplp.html
A coalition of women-owned independent presses that produce books addressing a range of subjects and concerns for women and girls not regularly dealt with by the mainstream houses.

SOURCES FOR SMALL PRESS REVIEWS AND AWARDS

Broken Pencil: the guide to alternative culture in Canada. Toronto, ON: Broken Pencil, 1995–. Semiannual. www.brokenpencil.com
Approximately 200 reviews of zines, books, CDs and tapes published in Canada. Also, interviews, zine excerpts, cartoons, and short sections focusing on e-zines, music and books.

Counterpoise. Gainesville, FL: CRISES Press, 1997–. Quarterly. www.LibLib.com/Cpoise/Cpoise.html
Publication describes itself as "for social responsibilities, liberty and dissent." Primarily reviews alternative books, magazines, pamphlets, and videos, in addition to publishing a few articles, bibliographies and essays.

Firecracker Alternative Book Awards 209.245.245.74/Merchant/fabwinners.html
Honors books which "toss a firecracker down the shorts of the mainstream." Awards are given annually in the categories of fiction, nonfiction, poetry, politics, sex, drugs, music, art/photo, graphic novel, zine, kids, outstanding independent press of the year, and special recognition/wildcard categories.

ForeWord Magazine Traverse City, MI: ForeWord Magazine, Inc., June 1998–. Monthly. Also, **ForeWord Online** www.forewordmagazine.com
Provides news about independent and university presses. Each issue has a number of well written reviews. Sponsors the Book of the Year Awards that honor excellence

in independent publishing covering wide variety of publishing categories.

Independent Publisher Online www.independentpublisher.com

News and editorials about the independent press industry written for authors and others. Also, product resources, numerous short book reviews, and the Independent Publisher Book Awards. The IPPY Awards lists the two finalists in each of 48 categories, plus the ten Outstanding Books of the Year.

Publisher's Weekly. New York: R. R. Bowker, January 18, 1872–. Weekly.

A primary source of news for the publishing industry, including many short book reviews of works from independent presses. Also, an good source for keeping up with mergers, acquisitions, and some of the presses that go out of business.

Rain Taxi Review of Books. Minneapolis, MN: Rain Taxi, 1995–. Quarterly. www.raintaxi.com

Rain Taxi is a nonprofit corporation dedicated to spreading the work about the best in contemporary literature. The magazine and online counterpart focuses on literary fiction, poetry, and nonfiction with an emphasis on works that push the boundaries of language, narrative, and genre. Press profiles, interviews, and in-depth reviews reflect *Rain Taxi's* commitment to the kind of innovative publishing that so often falls outside the spotlight of the other review media.

Small Press Review. Paradise, CA: Dustbooks 19—. Bi-monthly. www.dustbooks.com

A newsprint magazine with review columns, information and helpful hints on getting published.

Letters & Messages

Minneapolis Community & Technical College Alternative Press Collection

Minneapolis Community & Technical College (MCTC) is a medium-sized (9,500 students) comprehensive two-year college. Like most community & technical colleges we are a tuition dependent institution and are always struggling for adequate resources. However, our college does have a few qualities that set it apart from other colleges in the state of Minnesota. We are the only urban inner city college in the state. Located in downtown Minneapolis, we have the most diverse student population in Minnesota. Our student body is made up of 35% people of color. The state of Minnesota has a total minority population of 9%. Another unique characteristic of our college is that a large percentage of our students come from working class families. As a result, most of the faculty and staff at the college are people committed to teaching in a diverse urban environment.

Because of all these factors the library at MCTC has historically collected materials that critically examine political, cultural and economic issues. Over the years we have purchased material from the alternative press, but had made no attempt to systematically collect alternative press resources. All this changed three years ago as a result of additional monies provided to libraries in the Minnesota State College and University System by the state legislature. With this money came the stipulation that each library in the system use 20% of the money to build collections in unique subject areas. The MCTC Library chose to collect in the areas of the alternative press, multicultural and global issues, and media and information studies.

As a result of the extra money, and other decisions made by the staff, our library now devotes 10% of its total annual materials budget to collecting alternative press books, journals, and video and audio tapes. All these resources are cataloged in our statewide automated library system and are available to people throughout the Minnesota, North Dakota, and South Dakota regional lending area. In addition to the 10% annual materials budget spent on the alternative press, we have also raised $25,000 from licensing our Information Literacy Tutorial to out state library network. All this money has been placed in a special fund that is used for the exclusive purchase of alternative press resources. We are working with our faculty to assist them in integrating alternative press material into their courses. The issues raised by the alternative press are also integrated into our Information Literacy courses. We teach 25 sections of this course each year, reaching about 600 students.

As a result these students are exposed to a wealth of ideas and points of view as they learn the practical and theoretical aspects of information searching and evaluation. For those students who express an interest in exploring "non-mainstream" ideas further, we offer two additional courses in our Information Studies program, *Necessary Illusions: A Critical Introduction to the Information Age*, and *Alternative Knowledge: How Radical Ideas are Communicated in Society*.

The wonderful thing about all we have accomplished is that it has developed quite organically from our college and library mission. We are not treating our alternative press material differently than our other resources. The alternative press material is interfiled with the rest of our collection and has the same loan periods.

We have only just begun our collection and look forward to years of building the collection into a unique regional resource. In addition to the published alternative press material, we have begun to collect zines—those self-published ephemeral resources that seem to be so hard for libraries to acquire. We have only begun the collection and are actively soliciting donations. We plan to index the zines and provide author/editor, title and broad subject access. The zines will be filed by title and the zine database will be mounted on the web and a link made available from our library web site.

And lest the reader get the idea that we must have a huge library staff to accomplish all this, you may be surprised to know we do all this with a staff of 4.5 faculty librarians and 2 library technicians. What makes it all work is the fact that the entire library staff is committed to the mission of the library and the college. It is also helpful that we are a peer-based collegial department. We have no library director and all decisions are made by consensus. Sometimes our staff meetings get a bit long, and on occasion we enter into spirited debates, but the entire library staff is invested in the process and we keep each other honest.

I would like to thank Charles Willett and all the reviewers of *Counterpoise* for all their hard work. They have made our job of collecting alternative press material much easier.

If any of you would like to find out more about what we are doing at MCTC, please visit our library home page at <http://www.mctc.mnscu.edu/academicAffairs/library/index.html>. There you will find an overview of our alternative press collection, our collection development policy with an appendix devoted to the alternative press material, and all the support material for our Information Studies courses. If you have questions on anything we are doing, please feel free to write, email or call me.

Sincerely,

Tom Eland
Instructor/ Librarian
Minneapolis Community & Technical College
1501 Hennepin Avenue
Minneapolis, MN 55403
<elandth@mctc.mnscu.edu>

Reprinted with permission from *Counterpoise*, v. 4, no. 3 (July 2000), p. 2.

Continuing a Legacy: Collecting for a Special Collections Library

Julie Herrada

The Birth of a Legacy

Special Collections Libraries are often filled with the whims and fancies of generations of library directors, curators, and donors. Each collection, large or small, has its own story, just like each item in an antique shop. As the collections are processed, moved, or added to, and as employees move on, these stories often become lost or watered down, their provenance forgotten. However, each collection means something special to the person who worked most closely with it, either through contact with the donor, the physical obtaining of the collection, which could often mean distant travel or hours or days spent packing materials in someone's home, or the processing of the collection, wherein precious treasures are discovered. Curators hold these stories in their heads and hearts, and learn details no one else knows. Therein lies the wealth of a Special Collections Library; not just the collections themselves, but the stories behind them, the stories that impassion the hearts of curators.

The Labadie Collection at the University of Michigan was established in 1911 when Joseph A. Labadie (1850–1933), an anarchist and printer, donated his substantial collection of materials to the University Library. Labadie, an early trade union pioneer in Michigan, used his printing press, assisted by his wife, Sophie, to create little booklets containing his essays and poetry and those of his friends and other writers. He also wrote a regular newspaper column called Cranky Notions, and published several labor newspapers in Detroit in the late 1800s. Labadie corresponded with scores of people active in the turbulent labor, socialist, and anarchist movements of the period. In addition to materials from his printing press and his vast correspondence, there were pamphlets, newspapers, newsletters, announcements, photographs, posters, and badges from the days of Labadie's activism. For quite some time after the materials were deposited in the Library, nothing was done with them. Inquiring researchers would be given a key and sent into a caged area on their own, left with boxes of unaccessioned, unprocessed and uncataloged material. Items undoubtedly disappeared.

A Curatorial Debut

This might have remained the fate of the materials had it not been for a wealthy Detroit radical, Agnes Inglis (1870–1952), who began doing research in the Labadie Collection in the early 1920s. Inglis had been involved in radical political activities, organizing lectures, rallying support for labor and civil liberties causes, and assisting and even putting up bail money for World War I draft law violators and political prisoners. She knew Joseph Labadie, and knew of his donation to the Library. Her first encounter with the Labadie Collection was like everyone else's, but Inglis's inherent organizing instincts took over, and she stayed to "sort out" the materials and bring some order to the chaos. This decision changed her life, for she stayed at the Labadie Collection until she died at the age of 81.

Explaining the history of the Labadie Collection would not be possible without discussing Agnes Inglis. Her work (initially as a volunteer) brought the archive to the forefront of "labor" libraries, as she called it, and during her tenure she increased its size dramatically. Her own correspondence with political and labor activists is extensive, and is contained in the Agnes Inglis Papers. Her papers also contain notes and biographical information on many activists and writers of her era. It is a valuable resource in itself, as are all of the print and visual materials she collected and painstakingly preserved, bound, referenced, analyzed, and cataloged, in her own idiosyncratic way. She remained active throughout her life in political circles, writing letters, and organizing lectures and other events. The longer Inglis worked in the Library, the more people she met, the more she learned about social movements, and the more materials she was able to collect. Her extensive research into people and events uncovered more sources for materials. She scouted out materials like a sort of polite snoop, as evidenced in her copious notes, and by so doing was able to preserve history, which would otherwise have probably been lost forever. She asked her radical friends who were active at that time to donate items, and they did, with gusto. Diaries, journals, artwork, letters, autobiographies, photographs, posters, scrapbooks, as well as masses of books, journals, and newspapers, came flowing into the Collection. She spent her days, and many nights as well, reading, writing, processing, and caring for the materials she knew were going to document the history of social protest. The notes Inglis kept tell us she always made time for researchers in the Labadie Collection, and even today I encounter people who were lucky enough to have made her acquaintance there.

A Paragon Successor

Inglis died in 1952, and for many years the Labadie Collection operated without a curator. It would take a dedicated, knowledgeable, plucky person to take over the job, and in 1964 Edward Weber, a reference librarian from the Social Sciences Department, was chosen. Although the characters and causes were changing, the times were similarly turbulent, and Weber's work in continuing the collecting of social protest materials was cut out for him. During that period, the Collection was not affiliated with any University Library department, and didn't even have an acquisitions budget. It also suffered from over a decade of neglect, even abuse, at the hands of a library director who thought some of the materials ought to be distributed to other parts of the library, or even to other libraries outside the University. Due to this disbursal, Inglis's precise filing and locating system was lost forever (though her cards, mostly handwritten with notes and analytics, are still in use today, filed in an old card catalog). Weber's ingenuity and connections both within and outside the Labadie helped him bring in materials not many other institutions were collecting at that time: pamphlets and posters from the student, gay, civil rights, anti-war and black liberation movements, as well as underground newspapers, leaflets, political buttons, and other items. Weber applied a broader interpretation to the Collection to reflect changing times and movements. Gay liberation, feminism, communism, civil rights, and, at the behest of the library director, radical right materials are now included in its range.

In 1970 the Labadie Collection became part of the University's Special Collections Library and was finally granted the respect it deserved, in the form of a budget for acquisitions and supplies, more space, and eventually a small staff. In the early 1970s a new wing was built on the Graduate Library and Special Collections was given an entire floor. These new benefits, however, brought with it some administrative responsibilities, such as monthly reports, budget proposals, and year-end spending, duties which Weber found unpleasant. Up to that point he had free rein over most decisions pertaining to the Labadie Collection, but now it was a trade off, and he adapted to his new place in the hierarchy. Weber, armed with his new acquisitions budget, began making documented purchases of underground newspapers, self-published pamphlets, and other material. Most of these items cost very little at that time, since they were not yet seen as collectibles, and were usually obtained directly through the publishers. Now, retrospective publications purchased through book dealers can cost up to thirty times their original price. That's why it is financially prudent to purchase newly published items, even though it often takes an educated guess to ascertain what might be valuable to future researchers.

The label "social protest" can be widely interpreted. For this reason, the lines of our collecting policies have been blurred and stretched in ways that sometimes seem difficult to define. This broad subject range naturally makes it challenging to weed out and keep up with the processing of incoming materials. Since our collecting scope is not limited by date, we often are faced with contributions of many boxes of serials and books pulled out of people's attics, basements, and garages, sometimes moldy and usually dusty. Rarely a week goes by without someone calling to offer us a gift of "old magazines," or similar items. At times (about once per year) these are very large donations, taking weeks to process. This is more a benefit than a nuisance, however, since without these generous packrats, much of this history would be lost.

The question always arises as to what to include in a collection such as ours. Although Labadie's wide-ranging collecting policy makes it easy to accumulate materials, subject matter, such as labor organizing or gay liberation, which was once considered controversial or radical, may not necessarily be so today. Many movements and ideas of the past have moved into the mainstream, but does that mean we should stop collecting them? If so, we could make more room for new radical materials, in keeping with the contemporary issues of the day. On the other hand, abruptly ceasing the collecting in an area leaves only a part of the story, and may do a great disservice to our current and future researchers. Decisions like these always face a curator and having autonomy in decision-making, as well as the encouragement and backing of the library administration when needed, is extremely important in my job.

The Legacy Continues

I began working at the Labadie Collection in 1994. Prior to that time, I was active in a variety of different local and national, and even international progressive and environmental campaigns. Through those activities I met many people, much as Inglis had. Although full-time, professional employment has restricted my ability to be involved to the extent I once was, I continue to maintain my contacts, and, indeed, have broadened them through my work. My political activism before I became a professional turned out to be an asset to the Labadie Collection, because I came to the job with my own contacts, collecting base, and knowledge of many social movements.

In order to maintain these connections and continue an aggressive collecting program, I attend various political conferences, book fairs, and other events where I meet people and obtain literature, and visit with donors (both established and prospective). Many of those attending these events are pleasantly surprised when I tell them I'm collecting materials for a library. Some of this is done on my own time, but for me the distinction between work and pleasure is often hazy.

I have a different mission now: to preserve and make accessible the history of radical social movements, which is so often distorted or concealed, from textbooks and the media. My knowledge of the subjects we collect has expanded greatly since I was hired, and my passion for the materials for which I am responsible and what they convey gives me the sense of a true calling.

Additional Resources

Anderson, Carlotta R. *All-American Anarchist: Joseph A. Labadie and the Labor Movement.* Detroit: Wayne State University Press, 1998. This critically acclaimed biography of Joseph Labadie, written by his granddaughter, is an informative and exciting history of pre-auto industry Detroit.

Herrada, Julie and Tom Hyry, "Agnes Inglis: Anarchist Librarian" *The Progressive Librarian*, Special supplement to #16, Fall 1999. Two archivists who have worked in the Labadie Collection tell Inglis's story from a professional perspective.

Miles, Dione, "Agnes Inglis: Librarian, Activist, Humanitarian." *The Dandelion*, 3:12, Winter 1979. A well respected (now retired) archivist from the Walter Reuther Labor History Archives tells a revealing and inspiring story of Inglis's life.

Julie Herrada is the Curator of the Labadie Collection at the University of Michigan. jherrada@umich.edu. She received her MLS and Certificate of Archival Administration from Wayne State University in 1990.

DON'T DISCUSS SECRETS ON THE TELEPHONE

"They Sure Got To Prove It On Me:" Millennial Thoughts on Gay Archives, Gay Biography, and Gay Library History

James V. Carmichael, Jr.

The American Library Association's Gay, Lesbian, Bisexual and Transgendered Round Table (GLBTRT)* justly takes pride of place as the first professional gay organization in the world.[1] While the ALA itself ended discrimination based on sexual orientation in 1974, antipathy to gay issues within the profession is by no means dormant. At the same time, the growth in gay archives and gay studies in the past twenty-five years has been phenomenal. Gay librarians and archivists can continue to play an increasingly important role in promoting these collections and their use, but only if they understand the full range of problems that gay history and biography present. Where appropriate, library historians should also chronicle the achievements of gay library worthies.

Apologia Pro Vita Sua

From 1970 to 1976, I worked as a Trust Administrative Assistant at an Atlanta Bank, a job for which I was temperamentally and intellectually ill-suited. In addition to learning how foolishly some widows and orphans spend their money, and how easily private foibles become common public knowledge anywhere that money is involved, I began to sense that all of the gray suits and silence in the world would never save me from who I was, a gay man. I was the shortest, least muscular, and most troubled member of the twenty or so young men who ran up and down stairs all day long to do the bidding of trust officers on the second floor—opening estates and spendthrift trusts, drafting checks in amounts that represented the lifetime earnings of most trust department employees, sorting through papers, jewelry, and financial records of the recently-deceased, and occasionally holding the hand of a widow who wanted to spend an afternoon complaining about the quality of available domestic help on bank time.

One estate that arrived along with a box of papers

---

*Formed as the Task Force on Gay Liberation (shortly thereafter the Gay Task Force), the name of the group was extended to th eGay and Lesbian Task Force in 1986, the Gay, Lesbian, and Bisexual Task Force (GLBTF) in 1995, and the Gay, Lesbian, Bisexual and Transgendered Round Table in 1999.

Reprinted with permission from *Libraries and Culture*, v. 35, no. 1 (Winter 2000), pp. 88–102. Copyright © 2000 by the University of Texas Press.

was unforgettable—that of a retired professor. In the box, along with a truly remarkable collection of early-nineteenth-century cryptograms, was private correspondence to the professor from his best friend, interspersed with some titillating although not raunchy gay pictorial pornography. What I remember now about that experience is the all-male guffaws about the illegality of the material, speculations about the depraved professor, and comments about how sick the letters were. Thinking back on those touching, tender, and outrageous letters, I surmise that they were minor literary masterpieces. The professor and his friend addressed each other as "Mary Ann" and "Emily" and alluded in a parody of finest nineteenth century ellipsis to racy encounters with attractive males, to the price of fine linens, mundane household matters, and legal quagmires of gay males who were even in the 1970s still being entrapped by the Atlanta police. What struck me was the fact that Mary Ann and Emily really cared for each other under their campy disguises, and I resented the dehumanizing banter around me, even if it would be several more years before I cut myself off from that workaday world of testosterone-laden coffee-breaks which often assumed the ambience of a pack of dogs pursuing a bitch in heat. It is a shame the letters were destroyed like disease-bearing rags.

This memory resonates with me today because I wrote many such letters myself to my friend John when he and his lover Gary moved to upstate New York in the early 1990s. During the difficult period when I was struggling to achieve tenure, and John was establishing a practice as a gay substance-abuse counselor in his home state, the letters provided a focus for all of the pent-up professional anger, romantic frustration, fears of living alone and dying alone, self-pity and impatience that any normal forty to fifty year old gay man feels from time to time. The letters were spiced with gossip about mutual acquaintances in Chapel Hill, and flights of sheer imagination, hyperbole, and overstatement that had more than a kernel of truth to them. They were invariably signed by obscure female personages, some librarians, with elaborate Victorian names—which would send one or both of us to the library to look that one up and come back with an even more hilarious example. John understood my feelings. He had come out to me at age 31 while he was still married; he had been through rigors of a doctorate at Notre Dame. He was the best looking man I ever saw, bar none, with his rugged rangy body and the black Irish twinkle in his eyes when he recited "Dangerous Dan McGrew" in faultless County Cork brogue.

The night John called me to tell me he had AIDS in October of 1993, I had just seen the AIDS Quilt for the first time. When I got home from work in May of 1994 to find a message on the phone from Gary saying that John had just been removed from his house in a body bag, I could not believe that we were not ever going to write those letters again. They had kept me going for five years. I suppose I had been more than just a little in love with him. His family made me much more a part of his memory than I deserved, based on our short but intense friendship, but I sent them my letters from John, since they had already discovered the other half of the correspondence, and had repeatedly expressed their appreciation of our relationship. I sent the originals with no hope of ever seeing them again because somehow, the letters were secondary to the feelings that produced them.

The Growth of Gay Literature and Gay Consciousness

Great progress has been made in the quantity and quality of historical and biographical studies in lesbigay history over the past quarter-century. In 1995, the high-water mark of gay publishing to date, over 244 nonfiction monographs were published of which at least 27 were historical or biographical.[2] Compare this figure to only twenty-seven monographs in 1970 (one historical plus two literary histories), thirty in 1981 (three historical plus two literary histories), and forty-three in 1985 (no history per se but two literary histories), and one begins to appreciate what the numerical trends say about the growth of gay studies in the past decade. These monographs correspond to a growth in the number of theses and dissertations on gay themes in the same period. In spite of the fact that these figures do not include exclusively lesbian monographs, they indicate clearly that gay studies have become a desirable specialty in some academic settings—even if some researchers in narrative history would maintain that as soon as any subject becomes entrenched in the academy, its research product becomes irrelevant to the ongoing concerns of the population under investigation. One can't have the same sort of confidence in analysis of gay archival collections, because only a fraction of relevant collections are cataloged online.

Fairly detailed accounts of the gay movement in America have emerged, not only of the post–Stonewall era "revolution" but also inclusive of Victorian and Colonial antecedents that could have scarcely been imagined when Jonathan Katz first published his groundbreaking documentary history.[3] Some important urban centers as well as discernible regions have been studied, and the biographical and autobiographical genres have flourished, particularly since the advent of AIDS.[4] Gay biographical studies are more problematic, perhaps. Here, too, although no writer has achieved a totally satisfactory "outing" of Walt Whitman, Gertrude Stein, or Henry James, whose surviving papers still remain opaque as far as explicit discussion of sexual detail, some authors deploy more sophisticated historical analysis to contextualize "gay behavior" in other eras.[5] Of course, there is repetition: the 1990s heralded still another interpretation of Oscar Wilde's fall, one that basically adds little but explicit sex, more elaborate period detail, and Stephen Fry's uncanny resemblance to the Irish playwright, to Robert Morley's and Peter Finch's earlier interpretations (both released in 1959). At any rate, one can point to the compilation of numerous biographical dictionaries and almanacs from which beginning researchers can peruse the list of famous gay men and lesbians as signifying greater awareness of the importance of gay history.

Most encouraging of all is the growth and development of over sixty U.S. and Canadian repositories for specialized gay archives from which are drawn the raw materials of gay historical research.[6] The WorldCat database now includes at least 125 entries for archival material, plus another 100 or so entries that would qualify as special collections material, and these merely give a rough indication of the growth of primary materials that support gay history. Among the most notable of these gay collections are the James Mariposa Human Sexuality Archives at Cornell University, the International Gay and Lesbian Archives, the James Hormel Collection of the San Francisco Public Library, the Gebner-Hart Archives in Chicago, the Lesbian Herstory Archives, and the New York Public Library. Gay historian and educator James T. Sears has promoted the formation of similar archives throughout the Southeast, and Duke University is only the latest recruit to the expanding gay archives field.

Thistlethwaite brilliantly describes the manner in which archivists and librarians of past eras squelched research into gay and lesbian topics by destruction of records, creation of byzantine and pejorative (not to mention, blatantly inaccurate) subject headings, inventory descriptions that euphemize sexual relationships and others which fail to mention them at all, and a compulsive recalcitrance to deal with sexuality of any sort in the profession (in this, librarians, as always, have reflected the social mores of the eras in which they lived).[7] The new collections supposedly augur an era of social acceptance for homosexuality, one that Thistlethwaite is at pains to remind the profession may only run skin-deep.[8] Without putting too fine a point on recent findings which suggest that, even in urban collections, gay literature and gay studies have received uneven treatment or recent evidence of a backlash against social responsibilities as a part of the librarian mandate, it is probably no exaggeration to claim that gay studies have progressed in spite of librarianship as well as because of it.[9]

The Task Force on Gay Liberation (TFGL) of the American Library Association, formed in 1970 at the height of the social revolution and activism of the Vietnam Era, was the first gay professional association in the world. That it was established by Israel Fishman mainly as a means for its founder to meet available gay men,[10] and developed only secondarily into an organization for redress of professional and publishing inequities, a forum for discussion of gay issues impacting library service, and a vehicle for recognizing quality gay fiction and non-fiction for both younger and adult audiences, should confirm what we understand about a population whose entire being was defined in terms of its sexual behavior. Only when Barbara Gittings, a longtime lesbian activist sans library credentials, took over leadership of the Task Force in 1971 and began to plan programs that reflected larger concerns within librarianship and the gay community at large did its coherence and visibility as an established organization increase. Ironically, like so many other social minority groups within librarianship, the Gay, Lesbian and Bisexual group did not achieve more than Task Force status for a quarter-century (because the task of liberation was still ongoing?) and three nomination attempts have failed to win for Gittings an intellectual freedom award for the sixteen years of leadership she provided gratis to librarians.[11]

Perhaps the most damning qualification to be placed on librarian involvement in the gay movement is the relative paucity of historical literature about gays in libraries. While we now have several negative examples of how libraries participated in the persecution of homosexuals in the pre–Stonewall Era,[12] examples of positive librarian influence are nearly nonexistent. Both Gittings and Marie Kuda, non-librarians who have made significant contributions to the GLBTF and bibliography, are cited in standard historical and biographical sources, but only one librarian, Jeanette Howard Foster (author and one-time[13] librarian of the Kinsey Institute, among many library jobs she held) is included in a recent gay and lesbian encyclopedia.[14] Foster was the third winner of the ALA Gay Book Award, although she is virtually unknown to the current generation of librarians, straight or gay/lesbian.

The 1990s have seen the publication of three important gay library titles, Cal Gough and Ellen Greenblatt's pioneering *Gay and Lesbian Library Service*, Norman Kester's collection of personal essays, library anecdotes, and coming-out stories from lesbian and gay librarians (*Liberating Minds: The Stories and Lives of Lesbian and Gay Librarians and Their Allies*); and my own collection of essays on the challenges of writing lesbigay library history (*Daring to Find Our Names: The Search For Lesbigay Library History*). One may applaud these efforts while excoriating ALA's lack of leadership in bringing gay and lesbian issues into the grand design of the organization. Granting a minority organization round table status is one way to squelch rebellion without ceding power; but as some blacks within ALA have discovered, task forces, round tables, and caucuses do not engender the kind of solidarity necessary for coherent social programs and professional self-development. The formation of the Black Librarians Association in 1994 reflected a discontent of several decades with ALA's tepidity on racial issues. It is doubtful that lesbians and gays will register a similar degree of alienation from the professional organization, especially because many are so used to compromising their identities that any recognition strikes them as amazing, because the organization does provide them with some funding, and because a more radical agenda threatens the invisibility that the gradualist agenda affords. External signs of encouragement from ALA arrive none to early: the twenty-fifth anniversary celebration of GLBTF was attended by two ALA past presidents, the current president, and at least one nominee for president-elect, yet in twenty-five years, only one ALA president has ever explicitly defended gay rights.[15] Still, the programs of GLBTF of the 1990s emphasized a positive social and publishing climate, signaled most significantly, perhaps, by the summer 1999 program that focused on gay archives ("Daring to Save Our History: Gay and Lesbian Archives," 26 June 1999, New Orleans).

This "boom" in gay archives and collections arrives at a felicitous moment when the availability of online technology has precipitated a new awareness of the accessibility of archives among professionals in the field. Scholars no longer necessarily have to travel thousands of miles or spend hours on the telephone to ascertain what the holdings of archives are: many inventories and descriptions of archives are now accessible online. Who knows, one day library directors may come to realize that weekends are the most convenient time for most academic researchers to do their work and support weekend staffing of the archives accordingly.

In spite of the numbers, there are at least three problems that challenge gay archivists and historical researchers that will be more difficult to resolve by fiat. The first, "mothball outing," consists of the "outing" of historical personages who may have never identified themselves as homosexual, who merely may have been unmarried, or who left no trace of their personal passions on paper. Gay historians, in their eagerness to create a lesbigay pantheon from which struggling young gay people may gather inspiration, sometimes ignore normal rules of historical evidence in favor of more circumstantial cases for their subjects.

CIRCUMSTANTIAL EVIDENCE AND AMBIGUITY

While the growth of gay archives over the past twenty or thirty years seems nothing short of miraculous, the application of historical principles to the stories of lesbians and gays, blacks, Native Americans, and Latinos, to name only a few minorities deserving of revisionist interpretations, has been inconsistent. While it is true that historians of the nineteenth century, in their frenzy to apply "scientific" principles to what was basically a literary form (historical narrative) almost succeeded in killing narrative interest (storytelling ability) entirely with narcotic chronologies, facts, and footnotes, in the late twentieth century, post–Warhol fame game, the rigors of evidentiary protocols have been loosened to include speculation and insinuation. Apologists defend the practice of "outing" Eleanor Roosevelt and her secretary Lorena Hitchcock, although clearly Roosevelt would never have made a public pronouncement on her sexuality, period, since sexuality according to her time, tradition, and station of birth was an unmentionable subject outside of a lover's arms. Revisionists defend this practice on the grounds that (as one writer put it in *The New Yorker*) the possibility that such a relationship existed has more importance to the future of the gay movement than any squeamishness about evidentiary value can have to the case for acceptable historical standards.[16] Rose Gladney discussed the problems of generational differences between lesbians at the 1995 meeting of the American Library Associations Gay, Lesbian, and Bisexual Task Force, where she described her difficulty in probing the nature of the Lillian Smith/Paula Snelling ménage by engaging Snelling in a conversation that women of her generation never had.[17] Other than for hypocrites like federal prosecutor Roy Cohn, who prosecuted lesbigays during the McCarthy era while hiding in his own closet, outing anyone against their will is a perpetuation of the kind of emotional violence to which people of earlier generations were routinely subjected. As Andrew Sullivan noted in one of his most famous reactionary statements,

> In all the recent brouhaha over the "outing" of alleged homosexuals, one fallacy has remained virtually unchallenged. It's the notion of the simple "closet" and the crude assertion that one is either in it or out of it. I know of no one to whom this applies. Most homosexuals and lesbians whose sexualities are developed beyond adolescence are neither "in" nor "out." They hover tentatively somewhere in between.[18]

While one may abhor the damage that closeted lives imply for the gay "movement," gay historians and historians who are gay should never forget that coming out can be a singularly painful experience for many people. In other words, *historical evidence must support the assertion of homosexual activity before one can claim they were "gay" in the modern sense of that term.* This caveat becomes even more essential when no signifying relationships are involved, due to the fact that few writers are equipped to deal with the situation of single people, straight or gay.[19]

Related to this problem is how people from an earlier era regarded their own same-sex attractions:

THE CANONICAL GAY "EXPERIENCE"

Daniel Harris has noted the negative as well as the positive effects of gay liberation in the post Stonewall era.[20] Primary among the negative effects is the narrowing of vision related to the gay experience. The tendency to categorize gays, to assume homosexuality where archival evidence remains ambiguous, to simplify all same-sex affections as homosexual is astounding, even if it represents an understandable tendency, given the centuries-long invisibility of many gay people, and the desire to claim group identity. Yet identity politics also tends to preclude dissent from the politically correct orthodoxy of the moment—it does not leave much room for conservatives like Bruce Bawer or Andrew Sullivan, for example, and even gay conservatives and neo-individualists sometimes feel hemmed in by the political, religious, and social orthodoxies of their nomenclatures.[21]

How orthodoxy, combined with a superficial, tabloid-deep respect for supporting documentation, plays out in gay history is both fascinating and terrifying to behold. One wonders what future gay historians will think when they examine the unevenness of the historical record regarding gays and lesbians one hundred years from now. John Addington Symonds, Oscar Wilde, Greg Louganis, Bessie Smith, Amy Lowell, Elizabeth Bishop—these lives have been documented as lesbigay with very little room for guessing what we mean by "gay," "lesbian," or "bisexual." Yet one will look in vain for confirmation of the sexual orientation of lesser-known gay figures who emerge in some recent reference sources.

George Washington Carver appears as an important gay scientist in the 1995 compilation *Out in All Directions*, but he fails to appear in *Gay and Lesbian Biography*, *The Gay Almanac*, *Completely Queer: The Gay and Lesbian Encyclopedia* or indeed, as a homosexual in standard biographies.[22] In a section tellingly labeled "Queered Science," we are told that Carver was "openly gay all of his life" and "lived for years with his loving successor at Tuskeegee, Dr. Austin W. Curtis, Jr." What the entry does not tell us was that when Curtis joined the Tuskeegee staff as Dr. Carver's research assistant in 1936, Carver was already over seventy years old, and the next year, his health began to decline. While the newly published, widely-hailed *American National Biography* (1999) does not label Carver as homosexual, it does note Carver's "special talent for friendship" with many famous people including Henry Ford, the Roosevelts, and foundation officials, as well as his proposal and near-marriage in 1905 and his several nervous collapses, to which *Out in All Directions* does not allude. The standard biography by Linda McMurry makes it clear that Carver was rarely well enough for Curtis to have been more than his caretaker, and that Carver saw Curtis's appointment in terms of the younger man's professional advancement. In Carver's later years, Curtis was primarily interested in securing increased revenues for patent rights on Carver's inventions. Does the fact that Carver is usually shown knitting in old age mean that he was openly gay? Tailoring was a leading occupation for black men when I grew up in the segregated South, but one would have to search hard for an openly gay black man even in the Harlem Renaissance because of the especially strong social stigma attached to black gay male identity. The *American National Biography* mentions that Carver spoke of Curtis "like a son." Has a doctoral student discovered some new papers, or has Carver's academic relationship with Curtis been proven to include "bumping ugly?" If so, the compilers of *Out in All Directions* should have included footnotes to support hitherto undocumented facts, or drop Carver until more conclusive evidence came to light.

Ditto composer Stephen Foster Collins, who is claimed by both *Out in All Directions* and *The Gay Almanac*, even though no documentation to support such a claim appears in either the recent biography of Foster, or in the research bibliography on Foster that appeared in the 1980s.[23] While there may be some uncertainty about the reasons for his separation from his wife and family several years before he died (were the reasons financial, as some have claimed, or his increasing addiction to alcohol?) the down-at-the heels life he lived in a grocer's barroom in the Bowery, a section of New York where "Nancys," among many others, congregated, hardly constitutes proof that Foster had homosexual relationships and shortchanges the significance of his career, which is a classic American saga of wasted talent and unscrupulous publisher greed.

The central historical tenet that has failed in practice more often than succeeded is the discussion of ambiguity in evidence. A good example of effective discussion of ambiguity is William J. Mann's biography of silent-screen film idol and Hollywood decorator to the stars Billy Haines.[24] Although Mann was prevented from documenting some facts due to Ted Turner's purchase and subsequent sequestration of the MGM archives, he nevertheless presents a more convincing case for the physical relationship of Cary Grant and Randolph Scott than does Boze Hadleigh, whose *Hollywood Gays* devotes two chapters to Grant and Scott based on lengthy (but circumspect and inconclusive) interviews he conducted with both men before Grant died.[25] One of the reasons Mann succeeds where Hadleigh fails is that he has done his background homework, has corroborated information from interviews with extensive double checking, and discusses evidentiary ambiguity ad nauseam. Whatever such attention to detail detracts from narrative and "scoop" value, it certainly adds to credibility. The focus of Mann's biography of Billy Haines, the number one male box office attraction in Hollywood from 1926 to 1931 who lived an openly gay life and sacrificed his career rather than give up his long-time lover Jimmy Shields to pacify Louis B. Mayer, certainly has more to say to the current generation of gays than the incidental screen gossip gleaned by Hadleigh about stars who snuck around for "nookie." Mann employs a larger cast of characters on a much broader sociohistorical palette, and introduces names to the lesbigay celluloid closet that are often ignored—Claudette Colbert, Elsa Maxwell, and Rod La Rocque, among many less famous others. Of course, theater and film are natural subjects for a gay biographer since the arts have been historically associated with people on the fringe and homosexuals in particular. Still, if the stories are told with little reference to theater or studio history, they have little to impart beyond the cheap thrill afforded by any grocery-store rag.

Similarly, Theo Aronson's roundabout portrait of the heir presumptive to the English throne, *Prince Eddy and the Homosexual Underworld*, achieves an authority that few previous accounts of the Cleveland Street Scandal and its aftermath attain.[26] Again, it is not so much the evidence itself that has changed—the Royal family, probably under the direction of Price Eddy's father, Edward VII, destroyed all papers related to the affair shortly after Prince Albert Victor (Eddy) died in 1892. The depth with which existing evidence is examined and analyzed, as well as Aronson's comprehensive look at not only Eddy's relationship to the Cleveland Street Scandal but also unrelated sensations like Jack the Ripper murders, to which he has been in the past been linked, bolster reader confidence. Aronson, incidentally, sums up the plethora of Ripper scholarship deftly and succinctly but relies for his own primary evidence on the files of the director of public prosecutions at the Public Records Office—a nightmare of bureaucratic disorganization if ever one existed—and conducts a thorough examination of periodical and newspaper accounts of the period—no mean task.

Perhaps the most effective lesbigay biographies of recent years are those of Alla Nazimova and Stephen Tennant.[27] Here the evidence is profuse, some oral history sources are still available, and corroborating evidence exists in abundance. Ironically, Nazimova, a failed icon of the stage and screen by the 1930s, is restored to her rightful place in American theater as the premier interpreter of Ibsen to American audiences. Her multiple lesbian love affairs (immortalized perhaps for all time when her love nest became The Garden of Allah, that seediest and coziest of gathering places for the Hollywood glitterati of the 1930s), as well as those of her arch-rival, Eva La Gallienne, are secondary to the persistence of her professionalism. On the other hand, Stephen Tennant, relatively unknown even to gay cognoscenti as the lover of poet Siegfried Sassoon, was so excessive even as an outrageous member of the minor nobility, "in an electric brougham wearing a football jersey and earrings," for example, as The Daily Express described his arrival at a 1927 society ball, that he became an icon of eccentricity more than of fagdom.[28] Like Nazimova, he is a person about whom so much documentary evidence exists that the biographical quest becomes one of weighing what is fair and just about the person more than it is reconstituting shavings of sexual scandal into shards of pseudo-history.

Discretion about sexuality may not be, as many writers maintain, solely a protective device. It may simply be the better part of taste and "common sense." Gore Vidal condemns gay nomenclature as too limiting of the range of human experience, nor is the gay movement his sole source of dissatisfaction with sexuality in America.[29] Even Ma Rainey's notorious lesbian blues of 1928 echo the defiance of a sexual nonconformist who refuses to be categorized: *They say I do it / Ain't Nobody caught me /They sure got to prove it on me*.[30] Certainly history, with its century-old emphasis on evidence, is an appropriate place to apply stringent qualifications and definitions, whatever the political needs of the moment.

The final historical sin results from willful ignorance as well as the inevitable toll of three decades of identity politics.

THE VARIETIES OF GAY EXPERIENCE

Whose papers get collected? Which gay dissertation director decides who gets written about? In the WorldCat records one finds a preponderance of information not only about the Religious Right but also about mainstream denominations and congregations that have rather selflessly examined their collective consciences about homosexuality and stood behind the lines as subrosa allies for these thirty years. The story of these groups and how they have influenced the growth of gay spirituality would make a fascinating document of far reaching historical interest in an era when the word "Christian" has become synonymous with intolerance.[31]

There are many facets of gay lives that remain undocumented because a younger gay generation may well want to ignore reminders of oppression in the gay past, and, of course, every generation is more interested in its own accomplishments than that of some other. Jeb Alexander's diary, *Jeb and Dash*, for example, provides only one less glamorous example of the life of a repressed gay Washington bureaucrat from 1919 to 1945 from which, nevertheless, we gather many significant details about the continuity of gay experience over a span of several decades.[32]

Library historians and archivists are in a unique position to discover and publicize gay archives and particularly findings that new collections reveal. In this they should be pioneers rather than followers in establishing acceptable historical standards in order to curb the unbridled zeal of the converted to any hint of same-sex inclination while addressing professional antipathy to the sexual nature of biographical subjects, period. It is probably not by accident that the first full-length biographical dissertation about a gay librarian was written by a historian rather than a librarian, and while it is true that Laura Bragg is important not only as the first female museum director of a major museum in America but also for her association with the Charleston writers of the 1920s Southern literary renasence, it seems symptomatic of not only homophobia but ahistoricity that librarians did not first claim her as one of their own.[33] There are lesbigay librarians and archivists worthy of inclusion in the biographical canon. How many librarians can cite the achievements of Jeanette Howard Foster? As the fifteen examples included in Jessie Carney Smith's *Notable Black American Women* demonstrate, librarians and archivists play a central role in minority communities and at the point of intersection between those communities and the world beyond.[34] So, finally, before gay librarians and archivists clean up the whole palace of history, they have to air their own rooms.

Let the reader pretend for a moment that by the year 2075 lesbigay identity won't really be a negative tag, that cases of discrimination, victimization, and persecution will be almost nonexistent in Wyoming and Alabama as well as in Israel and Iraq. Given that unlikely scenario, what purpose will gay archives serve other than to document varieties of gender experience? When there's no longer a revolution to fight, will gays look back with pride not only on their ability to march and to champion the causes célèbres but also to be inclusive in their collection and interpretation of those aspects of their experience that are personally distasteful to them? Will all they have to disclose be the fact that they were or were not gay (so what?), and if so, with whom they slept (ho hum), down to what sexual acts were committed (close the door!). Perhaps they merely dropped campy bon mots now and then, overdressed, flipped their wrists, donned leather chaps, marched in a parade, indulged in interior decoration on the grand scale, pierced their nipples, or drove a pick-up truck, thus confirming social stereotypes of gays. Or is there a more fundamental significance to the quality of their lives that make them worthy of study or remembering? With such a standard in view, whether gays are silent or outspoken, they can begin to place their archival efforts in more coherent historical form than prescribed gay collection areas, the magnetic force of celebrity, or the transient sexual mores of the decade. They can literally live their lives from the inside, without undue concern for what posterity may make of the result.

Postscript

As Emma Tennant, Stephen's niece, wrote in her own reckoning with her family's and her uncle's past, "As with the dreams and documents that fed my obsession with the past, there is no way of saying that what is true to me is not also history."[35] Just as the letters themselves can no longer afford me a truer sense of the John Noonan I knew than the postmortem romance I have construed of our friendship, it will take more discerning eyes than mine to sift what is false from what is true in my boasts, using what papers still exist, what witnesses still live, and what background facts our previous histories afford. It will be left to the historian to say what, if anything, any such story has to tell other people about the quality of relationship of these two men who just happened, by the way, to be gay. The words we wrote tried vainly to stab at feelings, some of which escaped the pen and some of which endured in ink. As to what should be made of the evidence we collected of our tenuous and very fleeting past, or whether it has any historical significance at all, one must trust to the laws of historical principle, and the processes of decay.

Notes

1. Throughout this essay, I use "Gay" in its most inclusive sense to embrace lesbians, bisexuals, transsexuals, and "others" whose interests in gay equality are personal. I use "lesbian" when speaking specifically of women who are gay. "Lesbigay" is used to denote gay men, lesbians and bisexuals.

2. The figures come from a forthcoming article: James V. Carmichael, Jr. "Effects of the Gay Publishing Boom on

Classes of Titles Retrieved Under the Subject Headings "Homosexuality," "Gay Men," and "Gays" in the OCLC WorldCat Database," *Journal of Homosexuality* 42(3)(2002), 63–85. Among the notable historical 1995 titles are John Boswell's posthumously published *Same-Sex Unions in Modern Europe*, Gary P. Leup's history of homosexuality in Japan (*Male Colors*), Scott Lively's *The Pink Swastika*, Colin Spencer's *Homosexuality: A History*, and Neil Miller's remarkable *Out of the Past: Gay and Lesbian History from 1869 to the Present*. Biographical subjects include Oscar Wilde, T. E. Lawrence, John Maynard Keynes, David Norris, and Robert Mappelthorpe.

3. The most wide-ranging sampler of these discoveries is contained in Martin B. Duberman, Martha Vincus and George Chauncey, Jr., eds., *Hidden from History: Reclaiming the Gay and Lesbian Past* (New York: New American Library, 1989); Jonathan N. Katz, *Gay American History: Lesbians and Gay Men in the U.S.A.* rev. ed. New York: Meridian, 1992.

4. George Chauncey, *Gay New York: Gender, Urban Culture, and the Making of the Gay Male World, 1890–1940* (New York: Basic Books, 1994); James T. Sears, *Lonely Hunters: An Oral History of Lesbian and Gay Southern Life, 1948–1968* (New York: Eastview Press, 1997); Gean Harwood, *The Oldest Gay Couple in America: A 70 Year Journey Through Same-Sex America* (Seacacus, NJ: Birch Lane Press, 1997). The later writings of Paul Monette epitomize the AIDS memoir, but a fine, lesser-known example is John R. Noonan. *The Singing Bird Will Come: An AIDS Journal* (Latham, NY: Canticle Press, 1997).

5. See Colm Tóbín, "Roaming the Greenwood," *James White Review* 16 (Spring 1999): 3–11, esp. 11. for a thorough, even-handed, and commonsensical critique of "queer readings" of James, in particular.

6. Alan V. Miller, comp., *Directory of the International Association of Lesbian and Gay Archives and Libraries* (Toronto: Canadian Gay Archives, 1987); Lesbian and Gay Archives Roundtable, *Lavender Legacies. Guide to Sources in North America, 1998*, available at www.archivists.org/units/lagar/htm, accessed 21 June 1999.

7. Polly J. Thistlethwaite, "The Gay and Lesbian Past: An Interpretive Battleground," *Gay Community News* (Boston) 4 (Winter 1995):10–11, 24. For a fine example of the degree of specificity and currency needed in gay subject headings, see Dee Michel, *Gay Studies Thesaurus: A Controlled Vocabulary for Indexing and Accessing Materials of Relevance to Gay Culture, Politics, and Psychology* (The Author, 1985). Copies of the thesaurus are available for $15.00 by writing Dee Michel, 2236 Hillington Green, Madison, WI 53705.

8. Polly J. Thistlethwaite, "Gays and Lesbians in Library History," *The Encyclopedia of Library History*, edited by Wayne A. Wiegand and Donald G. Davis, Jr. (New York: Garland Publishing Company, 1994).

9. Eric Bryant, "Pride & Prejudice," *Library Journal* 120 (June 15, 1995), 37–39; Stephen Joyce and Alvin M. Schrader, "Hidden Perceptions: Edmonton Gay Males and the Edmonton Public Library," *Canadian Journal of Information and Library Science* 22 (April 1997): 19–37. For information and documentation of the backlash, see James V. Carmichael, Jr., "Homosexuality and United States Libraries: Land of the Free, But Not Home to the Gay," *Proceedings of the 64th International Federation of Library Associations Conference 1998*, Booklet 7, 136–145, esp. 141.

10. Israel D. Fishman, "Founding Father," in James V. Carmichael, Jr., ed., *Daring to Find Our Names: The Search for Lesbigay Library History* (Westport, CT. Greenwood Press, 1998), 107–112. Fishman, incidentally, has disclaimed this essay, based upon editorial changes I made at the last moment without consulting him.

11. To be fair, Gittings was honored in 1998 with many others at a dinner given by the Intellectual Freedom Committee, and when Philadelphia Free Public Library and PrideFest America honored her at a ceremony at the Free Library on April 27, 1999, ALA Director William Gordon was on hand to note her accomplishments on behalf of the association. See *American Libraries* 30 (June/July 1999): 43. More recently, a gay and lesbian collection at a Philadelphia branch library was named in her honor.

12. For some of these negative examples, see the illustration on page 102 in Molly McGarry and Fred Wasserman, eds., *Becoming Visible: An Illustrated History of Lesbian and Gay Life in Twentieth Century America* (New York: The New York Public Library, 1997), of a report filed in 1899 at the NYPL by a customer who was accosted in the men's room; see also John Howard's detailed account of the 1953 sting conducted by Atlanta police in the men's room Atlanta Public Library using a two-way mirror in "The Library, the Park, and the Pervert: Public Space and Homosexual Encounter in Post World War II Atlanta," *Radical History Review* 62 (Spring 1995): 166–87; and Louise Robbins, "A Closet Curtained by Circumspection: Doing Research on the McCarthy Era Purge of Gays from the Library of Congress," in Carmichael, Jr., ed., *Daring to Find Our Names: The Search for Lesbigay Library History* (Westport, CT: Greenwood Press, 1998), 55–64.

13. Cal Gough and Ellen Greenblatt, eds., *Gay and Lesbian Library Service* (New York: Garland, 1990); Norman Kester, *Liberating Minds: The Stories and Lives of Gay Librarians and Their Allies* (Jefferson, NC: McFarland, 1997; and Carmichael, Jr., ed., *Daring to Find Our Names*.

14. *Completely Queer: The Gay and Lesbian Encyclopedia* (New York: Henry Holt, 1996).

15. Marilyn Miller spoke at the rally of lesbigay librarians protesting Denver's rescission of its anti-discrimination policies. John Berry, Francine Fiakoff, Evan St. Lifer, and Michael Rogers, "Under Protest: ALA Midwinter in Denver." *Library Journal* 118 (March 1, 1993): 32–38.

16. Mark A. Thompson, Letter, *The New Yorker* 70 (September 26, 1994), 14.

17. Margaret R. Gladney, "Biographical Research on Lesbigay Subjects: Editing the Letters of Lillian Smith," 47–54, in Carmichael, Jr., ed., *Daring to Find Our Names*, 51–52.

18. Paul [i.e., Andrew] Sullivan, "Sleeping with the Enemy," *New Republic*, 9 September 1991, 43.

19. Exceptions exist: the novels of Anita Brookner are exemplary; a model of biographical treatment is Victoria Glendenning's *Edith Sitwell: A Lion among Unicorns* (New York: Knopf, 1981), esp. 158–60.

20. Daniel Harris, *The Rise and Fall of Gay Culture* (New York: Ballentine Books, 1999).

21. See for, example, explorations of this topic in Bruce Bawer, ed., *Beyond Queer: Challenging Gay Left Orthodoxy*, (New York: The Free Press, 1996).

22. Lynn Witt, Sherry Thomas, and Eric Marcus, eds., *Out in All Directions: The Almanac of Gay and Lesbian America*, (New York: Warner Books, 1995), 27, 37–8; Michael J Tyrkus and Michael Bronski, eds., *Gay and Lesbian Biography* (Detroit: St. James Press, 1997); *The Gay Almanac* (New York: Berkley, 1996); *Completely Queer: The Gay and Lesbian Encyclopedia* (New York: Henry Holt, 1996); Linda O. McMurry,

George Washington Carver: Scientist and Symbol (New York: Oxford University Press, 1981). See also Carver's biography in *American National Biography* (New York: Oxford University Press, 1999), vol. 4

23. Ken Emerson, *Doo-Dah!: Stephen Foster and the Rise of American Popular Culture*. (New York: Simon and Schuster, 1997); Calvin Elliker, *Stephen Foster Collins: A Guide to Research* (New York: Garland, 1988).

24. William J. Mann, *Wisecracker: The Life and Times of William Haines, Hollywood's First Openly Gay Star* (New York: Penguin Group, 1998).

25. Boze Hadleigh, *Hollywood Gays* (New York: Barricade, 1996), 237–308.

26. Theo Aronson, *Prince Eddy and the Homosexual Underworld* (London: John Murray, 1994).

27. Gavin Lambert, *Nazimova: a Biography* (New York: A. A. Knopf, 1997); Philip Hoare, *Serious Pleasures: The Life of Stephen Tennant* (London: Hamish Hamilton, 1990).

28. Hoare, *Serious Pleasures*, back dust jacket (not cited in notes).

29. Gore Vidal, *Gore Vidal, Sexually Speaking: Collected Sex Writings* (San Francisco: Cleis Press, 1999).

30. Gertrude "Ma" Rainey, *Prove It on Me Blues*, Paramount Records, 12668, June 1928. Reissued on *Ma Rainey: The Complete 1928 Sessions in Chronological Order*, Document DOCD-5156, 1993.

31. John J. Carey's *The Sexuality Debate in North American Churches, 1988–1995* (1995) concentrates on the reactionary backlash of the 1990s.

32. Ina Russell, ed., *Jeb and Dash: A Diary of a Gay Life, 1918–1945* (Boston: Faber and Faber, 1993).

33. Louise A. Allen, "Laura Bragg: A New Woman Practicing Progressive Social Reform as a Museum Administrator and Educator." Ph.D. dissertation, The University of South Carolina, 1997.

34. Jessie Carney Smith, ed., *Notable Black American Women* (Detroit: Gale Research, 1992).

35. Emma Tennant, *Strangers: A Family Romance*. New York: New Directions, 1999), 182.

The Steven J. Schochet Center for GLBT Studies

Becoming a Gay, Lesbian, Bisexual or Transgender Collector

To understand the past, historians rely on pieces of information and personal artifacts that have survived across the years. While some historical periods are more documented than others, few historical periods are documented from the perspectives of all the people who lived during that time. This means the histories available to us are rarely complete.

This problem of documentation is especially true for minority individuals and communities marginalized by the mainstream cultures in which they live. The lives of gay, lesbian, bisexual and transgender people are largely invisible throughout history precisely because of these reasons. There have been few historical periods when individuals involved in primary same-sex relationships or individuals transgressing gender rules could be publicly open about their affections or choices, let alone live as part of a community of identified and like-minded individuals. Additionally, the lives of many historical figures have been rewritten to serve a purpose. Information about sexual experiences or primary committed relationships with same-gender individuals has often been omitted from the historical record to conform to an idea of "normal."

It is a different thing to be gay, lesbian, bisexual or transgender in the contemporary United States now from even fifty years ago. There are more readily defined communities, legal protections and support services than at any time before. At the same time, being out does not mean the same thing or carry the same ease or difficulty across diverse GLBT communities. There are numerous gay, lesbian, bisexual and transgender communities which represent a vast array of cultural experiences, and more communities come into being every day. All of these communities produce a lot of history. Notices of meetings, performances, readings, political actions and social gatherings paper the walls of cafes and bookstores. We are documenting our concerns and celebrations on a constant basis. But how many of us are looking at these notices with an eye to the future and the histories that we are creating?

Future generations will understand our lives by the texts and artifacts we make available to them. We have the power to help someone centuries into the future feel connected to the details of our lives. We do this by collecting materials we produce and working to assure they are preserved.

Preservation is the key word here. There are too many stories of families who, upon dealing with the death of their GLBT sons and daughters, destroy the materials left behind as a way of "hiding the evidence." Even when those artifacts have been carefully gathered and stored— boxes and boxes of newspaper clippings, letters, and programs from social events— and even when the surviving family or friends were not particularly homophobic or fearful— the materials have often been thrown away because they were considered "junk" and no longer useful or worthy of keeping. Each time this material is destroyed, a part of our history dies.

Preservation of all those personal items, ticket stubs, newsletters, monographs, research papers and bibliographies, as well as photographs, works of art, books, magazines, and newspapers, will determine what and who is remembered into the future. This is especially important for members of our communities who are marginalized even from the gay, lesbian, bisexual and transgender mainstream. How many of us have looked at the histories most available— whether general American history or GLBT history— and not seen our faces or concerns reflected? How

---

Reprinted with permission of Steven J. Schochet Center for GLBT Studies (College of Liberal Arts, University of Minnesota, 132 Klaeber Court, 320-16th Ave. SE, Minneapolis, MN 55455).

many of us have picked up glossy national magazines and felt frustrated by our lack of representation? All of us need to collect the artifacts of our lives to guarantee our presence in the historical record. It is particularly important that those of us who continue to be marginalized make a concerted effort to "fill in the blanks" by preserving the materials of our lives.

How do you become a collector? By saving. Everything.
- Are you a part of an organization that creates flyers to advertise its events? Save two or three copies of each flyer. Save copies of your organizational minutes, your grant proposals, successful or not. Save your in-house notices, program proposals and staffing charts.
- Print up and save the email notices or letters you get via the internet. A huge amount of cultural dialogue takes place in cyberspace. This is even harder to preserve than hard text.
- Save the programs for events you attend. Save ticket stubs and theater or movie reviews. Save the promotional postcards for new GLBT films and the flyers for GLBT film festivals or performances.
- Save newspapers. Don't just save GLBT newspapers but save any document or article that is related to GLBT experiences. If you can, don't clip the article, but save the whole paper. This helps with context.
- Save your research papers, even the papers you write the night before it's due when you are bleary-eyed with sleep. Save it even if you think it's horrible.
- Save your personal letters, your love notes and diary entries. These will be as important to historians as they are to you right now.

What do you do with everything once you have saved it? If you have made out a will, specify where you want your materials sent after you have died. There are a number of gay, lesbian, bisexual and transgender archives across the country. In the Twin Cities, we have the Jean-Nickolaus Tretter Collection, which is in the process of being installed at the University of Minnesota. If you don't want the materials to accumulate over the entire span of your life, then periodically have a clean out. Go over what you have saved and gather it together. If you can, it's helpful to index your materials or to have them in some kind of order: newspapers all together by publication, flyers clumped by organization or subject, and so on.

Many archives are willing to work with you on the public aspect of your archives. It is not unusual for benefactors to add a time restriction to their materials; for example, some people ask that the artifacts not be released into public use until a certain time period has passed after a person's death. Others have used more specific restrictions, such as after the death of a parent or grandparent or even a child who doesn't know you are GLBT.

In whatever way you do it, whether you are out to the whole world or only to a few friends, the materials you have collected are a part of our history. Please pass them on so that our struggles and celebrations can teach coming generations.

For further information about the Tretter Archive and how to donate your materials, call the Schochet Center for GLBT Studies at 612-625-3499 or email us at <qstudies@tc.umn.edu>.

This document is available in alternative formats.
The University of Minnesota is an equal opportunity educator and employer.

Interview with David Barsamian of Alternative Radio

Scott Long

Alternative Radio is a public radio program, founded and hosted by David Barsamian of Boulder, Colorado. It is presented locally on 88.5 KGNU FM in Boulder, and on more than one hundred twenty-five other stations in the United States and Canada, as well as to over one hundred other countries, via short-wave. Completely free to the stations via satellite, the only funding for Alternative Radio is provided by listeners purchasing tapes or transcripts of broadcasts. There are no corporate grants or underwriting. This results in programs that present "perspectives and analyses on the environment, media, U.S. foreign policy, racism, economic and trade issues, and indigenous rights." There are only two staff. Some of the many speakers featured have included, but are not limited to: Noam Chomsky, Barbara Ehrenreich, Michael Parenti, Angela Davis, Edward Said, Cornel West, Bobby Seale, Helen Caldicott, Winona LaDuke, Kwame Ture, Ralph Nader, Urvashi Vaid, Holly Sklar, and Howard Zinn.

David Barsamian has also published several books of interviews with Noam Chomsky, the newest of which is titled *The Common Good*, and will soon also be releasing a book with Howard Zinn called *The Future of History*. This interview was conducted by Scott Long in February, 1999, at David Barsamian's home in Boulder.

S: I'm talking with David Barsamian, the producer of Alternative Radio, and one of the staff at KGNU.

D: No, I'm [actually] a volunteer. I was on the staff as the news and public affairs director from 1987 through 1991. I've been affiliated with KGNU as a volunteer since it started back in 1978, which is when I moved to Boulder. It's one of the best community radio stations of its kind. It's a model success story, and communities around the country would do well to emulate it.

S: Yeah, I recently got turned on to KGNU by coming to Boulder and just flipping through the radio dial. It's amazing to me. I mean the fact that it's basically just a collective of people that are so interested in getting the news and alternative programming out.

D: And diverse music, you know, indies ordinarily, not Casey Kasem's top 40. It's not chart stuff. It's not driven by the corporate culture, as such. But most of the electronic media, like the print media, is a vast desert. It's a wasteland. It's chewing gum for the mind. There's no "there" there. It's a poor substitute for what citizens of a democracy need, which is a wide spectrum of opinion. And I'm not saying what I put out is the grail. I don't say that at all. I don't think it is, but it certainly deserves to be heard. A real democracy, a functioning democracy, allows a thousand opinions to bloom. You know, a million perspectives to flower. You have a range from A to Z. But in the current configuration, which is totally driven by corporate interests and bottom line considerations and ideology, the range of opinion is from A to B, maybe. On a good day, you'll get a B.

S: Yeah, and how often is it that B is really just an illusion?

D: Well, yeah. We'll get someone like Ross Perot, or Pat Buchanan, who seem to be saying something different. But once you strip away the veneer that envelops all the media, electronic and print, you come straight up against propaganda. That's the only term to describe it. The genius of the American propaganda system is that it's kind of seamless. There's no one with a truncheon beating you over the head. "Scott, listen to

---

Reprinted with permission from *Skyscraper Magazine* (P.O. Box 4432, Boulder, CO 80306), no. 6 (February 1999), pp. 117–121.

this, you're going to read this book. I'm gonna tie you. I'm gonna put a rope around you. You're gonna read this book. You're gonna repeat it back to me when you finish." You know, those kinds of things. It's much more subtle than that. As is shown in the film "Manufacturing Consent" [a documentary/biography about Noam Chomsky and his theories on media. You must see this film, it's a form of intellectual self-defense] and the book by that same title. The system here is like what George Orwell said. You have a dog in the circus that does a somersault when he's whipped. Now, the really well trained dog does the somersault without even the presence of the master and the whip. Because he knows, he's internalized the propaganda that this is his function. So that's largely what is the function ... you have to ask yourself a couple of questions: "What are the communication needs of a democratic society?," and once you address that, "Is the current system serving those needs?" So, I think the communication needs of a democratic society should present a huge range of diverse opinion from A to Z, as I said earlier. Is this system providing that? Decidedly no, and that really can't be contested. I don't think this is a left-right issue. I think this is an issue about democracy and freedom of expression. It's a First Amendment issue. No one is going to say that radical voices are available easily to most Americans. It's very difficult. You yourself said that you stumbled upon a film about Noam Chomsky.

S: We're talking about the documentary "Manufacturing Consent."

D: Why hadn't you heard of Chomsky earlier? He's very well known in Canada, Europe, and Asia. He just came back from New Zealand. He's known in Japan, in Germany, Spain, where he drew huge crowds. He's recognized as the foremost critic, the dissident voice of America. Or as Bono calls him, from U2, the "rebel without a pause."

S: You pointed out that you got involved with KGNU in 1978, but Alternative Radio didn't come out until...

D: 1986.

S: How did that develop? What caused you to go "I want to produce a segment that will get this information, these views from A to Z, out there"?

D: Well, it's a classic case of thinking locally and then acting nationally, and globally, and internationally. I honed my chops at KGNU. I learned my skills: announcing, use of voice, mic technique, editing. All of these things I learned over a period of years. I made mistakes; I wasn't trained. Part of the genius of KGNU is that it's pretty much on the job training. You learn as you go along. I noticed, starting in the early Eighties, lots of people were asking me, just locally in Boulder, for copies of my program. I was very flattered "Great, you like the show? I'll make you a copy." I'd give it to them for no charge. And then it occurred to me as this expanded, as the demand kept increasing, I thought maybe there's a national audience for the kind of radical stuff I was doing in Boulder. So in 1986, I put up my first programs on satellite. That's how I distribute. I produce the programs in Boulder, and I distribute them nationally via satellite. So I'm able to reach hundreds of stations at once. And since then, well, that was eighteen years ago.

S: Is it difficult to find stations that are willing to carry the program?

D: There are tremendous ideological obstacles to getting Alternative Radio broadcast. That's because most of the gatekeepers that control public broadcasting in the United States are extremely timid. They're milquetoasts. They're afraid of their own shadow. They're not risk-takers. They go against the founding principles of public broadcasting which stated very clearly that the purpose of public radio and public TV in the United States should be to present a wide variety of perspectives. And particularly to give voice to those whose voices may not otherwise be heard. That's almost a direct quote. Now, what they've done over the last, say, twenty-five years of public radio and TV in the United States, is they've homogenized it. They've become very streamlined, very successful, very corporate friendly. They don't take risks, and the station managers and program directors reflect this timidity. They're not interested, generally speaking, in stretching the intellectual, or political, or cultural boundaries of their listeners. They want to give them Bob Edwards in the morning, and Robert Siegel and Noah Adams in the afternoon. Morning Edition, All Things Considered, and then some classical music in between the two. This is very unfortunate. So the biggest obstacle is ideological, because it can't be financial, because one of the things I did very consciously from the beginning was to not charge for the programs. I did not want to give these stations, and I already knew what their political stance was, the opportunity to say something like "Well, you know we admire your work, but our budget doesn't allow, things are a little tight...." So I just pulled that rug out from under them. Look, the program is for free, can you take it or not take it.

S: Exactly. So by removing the economic argument against dissemination of the information, it comes strictly down to philosophical and ideological issues.

D: Primarily, yeah. In some cases, it's formatting. You know where they can say, "We're an all music station. We don't do political programming." But it's mostly ideological. You know, for example, in the past year Alternative Radio is being broadcast in all major cities in Australia. It's also being broadcast, and this is since the 1980s, in all major cities in Canada. In this case, I have to physically make the dubs here and send them to the stations in those countries. Do they know something we don't know? Are their station directors and program directors more sensitive to alternative views and perspectives? I don't know. But in the United States it's very difficult. Take KUT in your hometown of Austin. They won't give me the time of day. I can't even get anyone on the phone. I can't get letters responded to, I can't get email and faxes responded to, it's like the old Soviet Union. They're not interested. They're not interested in diverse opinion which might ruffle the feathers of the university regents [of the University of Texas at Austin] or the political hacks down the street at the state house, or their corporate sponsors, like Archer-Daniels-Midland [ADM], Exxon, Mobil, and any other corporations. So there you have a particular example.

S: Yeah, that's a very concrete example. What we're talking about is a University of Texas owned radio station in Austin, Texas. It's specifically funded by the state.

D: Right, and also listeners become members, and they have corporate underwriting.

S: And they don't want to lose that corporate underwriting. That's more important to them, perhaps, than...

D: Well, it's hard to get into the mind of these managers, because you can't talk to them.

S: No response.

D: Yeah, as I said it's like the Soviet Union of old. You're a non-person. It's not even like "We're not interested. Go take a hike. Get lost." It's like no response.

S: That's disturbing.

D: That's one way you deal with dissidents. Ignore them.

S: I wonder if there's a parallel situation with the new radio station at the University of Colorado at Boulder, 1190 AM.

D: They're doing all music.

S: Yeah. I wonder if there was an attempt to put some information on there, how that would go. That would be an interesting experiment.

D: Well, the programming should be determined by community interests and needs.

S: And see, I would argue that the students of CU have a need to hear dissenting views that I think, in the ideal state, part of the purpose of higher education is to look at different views of situations. But this is the ideal state, as opposed to what's practiced.

D: Well, the educational system is part of the problem. It can not be isolated, just like the media can not be isolated. These are parts of the whole. The function of the educational system is to produce obedient students, people who will follow orders, who will become executives in companies and managers and professionals, and become cogs in the machine of corporate capitalism. Here and there, you might get a rebel, a dissident, someone who asks questions, and they get thrown out. They get Ds. They have "disciplinary problems," they have "adjustment problems." They can't make it through the system, and the system weeds them out. So they may wind up driving cabs, or busses, or working at Dot's Diner.

S: Right, which is why I found interesting what Chomsky said about himself during his public school years, that he basically knew that it was a bunch of bull, but to get where he wanted to go, he had to play the system for a while. But even now, I find it... I assume he's tenured.

D: Yes.

S: But, still, by making a conscious choice to voice his dissent, he marched down a certain path that there's no turning back from.

D: Yeah. He's in a unique situation because he's at a private technical university. It's a scientific university. In science, you don't encounter this ideological bullshit you get at the University of Colorado or any public institution. Or I would say, non-scientific institution. Because, there in the sciences, you just can't have theories, you've got to come up with evidence. It's not like, you know, "all guys with red hair who wear glasses have IQ's of 150." Okay, that's your theory. Now, what's the evidence for that? You've got to produce something.

S: Dissent is part of the process. You're going to be subject to critique.

D: But in the ideological institutions, particularly the humanities, the so-called political "science" departments, which is a total... If ever there was a misnomer, that is it. What is scientific about political science? They should call it the division of propaganda and ideology. Or the journalism department should be called the division of propaganda, and political science should be called the department of ideology. That would be closer to the truth. Naming things by their proper names is very powerful, and strips them of their gloss and veneer. This patina of respectability they have. So, the ideological components at these schools are dominant. It's not true at the scientific one. There, if you say something, you've got to back it up. You have to cross check it, and produce the evidence. Here you can say anything, you can say "All Muslims are fanatics." "All Palestinians are terrorists." You don't have to back that up with anything. "The Soviet Union was the evil empire." "The Sandinistas in Nicaragua were criminals." Anything that is ideologically accepted does not require evidence, because it fits into the popular culture. Like breathing. No one has to tell you to inhale, and then to exhale. You do it. It's a natural thing.

S: And the goal is to get people to consume this

information in such an automated way, without questioning it.

D: Obedience is important, and also the particular characteristic about United States society at the end of the twentieth century is the level of its de-politicization. It's a highly de-politicized society, where people don't care about public issues. It's "me too." It's "looking out for number one." "Shop until you drop." Now this did not come about as a result of some genetic encoding in Americans. This is a direct result of propaganda. This is an outcome that has been directed. Turn people into consumers. Isolate them. "Go to your mall. Stay in front of your TV. Stay in front of your computer. Don't interact. Don't get involved with other people." And particularly, "don't care about your society, the common good, only look out for yourself, you're number one." This ideology, I submit, takes the capitalist ethic to a very barbaric extreme. And it does isolate people. You see, also, in terms of how the society is de-politicized, in the record low voter turnouts.

S: The ones who do vote are the ones who are inherently benefiting from the status quo, for the most part. The ones who would benefit the most from turning out and voting are the ones who either don't or, even if they do, what are their options?

D: Yeah. Well, the Nazis perfected something called the big lie technique. If you repeat a monstrous lie often enough, it starts seeping into the aquifer. People drink the water, and they regurgitate and replicate the lie. In this case, in the U.S. case, the big lie is that there are two political parties, and that they are distinct. They are very different from each other. I think that's a big lie, and I think that it can be demonstrated to be lie, the Clinton impeachment hearings not withstanding. That was kind of a squabble within the ruling class, because an extreme right wing faction of one of the two business parties hijacked that whole process, and ran it. Great people from Texas, particularly, played a lead role—Dick Army, Tom Delay (who's really on "de-lay"), Livingston, Gingrich, mostly right wing southerners. Extreme right wing fanatics. Bob Barr from Georgia. These guys are way over the top and beyond. Livingston from Louisiana, Phil Gramm, on and on. Bailey-Hutchison. So what you find now is the political parties are, in the words of that great political scientist Lewis Carroll, Twiddly-Dum and Twiddly-Dee. Most people understand that, and don't vote. They're not given a reason to vote. Both the Democrats and Republicans, largely speaking, with a few exceptions here and there, represent the interests of the corporate ruling class. Big business. Who are they? It's not a secret. Get *Fortune* magazine, get *Forbes*. Read the *Wall Street Journal*, and find out who the owners and managers of the country are. This is not quantum physics. You don't have to learn the ablative case in Sanskrit to figure this out. It's pretty straightforward. But all of this information is hidden from the American public.

S: Yeah, I was going to say that one of the things that I found amazing about Chomsky's analysis, once I became familiar with it, is how simple, but elegant, his analysis is. This is common sense. He doesn't hide behind a lot of archaic, esoteric terms. He says these are the facts, and in a real democracy this is not what would be occurring. So I guess one of the things that I was curious about is how did you encounter Chomsky? How did your relationship with Chomsky develop?

D: It started in a very innocuous way. I wrote him a letter, and to my amazement, he responded. I was stunned. I didn't think someone of that stature, who is incredibly busy, would reply. Because that had been my experience with others. So we started exchanging letters, and that was in the late 1970s. We did our first interview in 1984. I met him in Boulder in 1986, for the first time. Since then, we've produced a series of radio programs, a series of magazine articles based on the interviews, and a very successful, quite astonishingly successful, set of books. Interview books that have reached large audiences all over the world—they have been translated into many, many languages. I mean, hardly a month goes by that I don't get some foreign version of a Chomsky book that I did. For example, there are Spanish, French, Japanese, Serbian, and Italian versions. There's a wide readership around the world. He is recognized as the premier critic of U.S. foreign and domestic policy, outside the United States. Inside the United States, he's barely visible, for very good reason. In fact, his marginalization is rational, if you want to adopt the lenses of the owners and managers of the media and the country. Why would you prop up or give a lot of attention to someone who is stripping your armor away? That's not in your class interest, in your base class interest. So within that framework, it's perfectly rational. I'm not saying it's right, but in that framework, they are protecting their interests.

S: If you look in the terms of a class war, and you adopt the positions of the elite, of course they're going to take those actions. I think encountering Chomsky, for me, was like an eye opener to that mode of viewing the world. I was curious, were you pursuing these kinds of analyses on your own, before you encountered Chomsky?

D: Yeah. My politics have always been pretty radical. I've always been a skeptic. It probably has to do with my heritage, which is Armenian. My parents were survivors of the first genocide of the twentieth century. In 1915, the Turks conducted an extensive campaign of genocide against the Armenians. We lost everything. We lost our lands, we were deported, we never got any compensation, nothing—and no one knew about it. It's largely fallen down the memory hole.

S: I have to confess I never even heard of it.

D: That's shocking, but not shocking. It was, in fact, the precursor to the holocaust. Hitler knew about it. Germany was allied with Turkey in World War I. There was no punishment of the Turkish genocidists. Hitler commented, just before he launched World War II, "Who today speaks of the extermination of the Armenians?" Because he knew nothing happened to the Turks, he thought, "I can get away with this." So when I was growing up in New York in the 1950s, I was invisible. I grew up biculturally. We spoke Armenian at home. Armenians are Orthodox Christians, so that also set me apart from the other kids. We had our own food, our own holidays and traditions. When I said "Armenian," people were like "what? Is that Bohemian [as I was called] or Albanian." No one had a clue what that was. So, I found myself always trying to explain and educate people. So I think, in terms of my politics, what happened to the Armenians in 1915 was a perfect example of people being caught in the hurricane, in a cyclone, not of their doing, not of their making, and never knowing why it happened. They didn't have the means at their disposal. They lacked information. They didn't know the plans that the Turks were going to exterminate them, and to create a southeastern Turkey, to conduct an enormous campaign, which is called today "ethnic cleansing." I was determined to make sure that it didn't happen to me, even in the New World, in the United States. So I'd say my politics are very much influenced by that.

I went to public schools in New York. I went to college for a year. That's the one blemish on my resume. I wish I hadn't gone at all. I hated it. I hated school in general. Primarily because I felt imprisoned. I didn't feel that I was being trained. I didn't feel my mind was being trained. I felt like I wasn't getting enough nutrition. Maybe some of the other students were, but I didn't feel that the level of nutrition was sufficient for my needs. I dropped out of school. I was involved in some of the first anti-war demonstrations in 1964, in San Francisco. And also the civil rights movement in 1963–1964 in San Francisco. And then I went to Asia, and I was there for five years. That was an eye opening experience, because to view the United States from the third world, one gets an entirely different, and radical, perspective. Not from Europe, but from India, which was just coming out of colonialism. It was just coming out from the yoke, having severed the yoke of imperialism just eighteen or nineteen years before I got there. People had a vivid memory of what it meant to be colonized.

After five years in India, I came back to the States. I studied music, the sitar. I learned the raga system, which is the ancient Indian musical system, and came back to the States. I got involved in a variety of things, teaching English, working for the Indian government, and then I moved to Boulder in 1978. Then things sort of took off. My current career was launched.

S: Let's talk about the new book with Chomsky, *The Common Good*.

D: It's number seven on the *Village Voice* best seller list, number nine on the *Boston Globe* list, which, if you think about it for a minute, is absolutely amazing. There's no advertising. There's no way to find out about this book. There have been no reviews. There's no publicity about it. So I think, again, that's tribute to Chomsky's drawing power, and also word of mouth. People just say, "hey, did you hear about this book? The new Chomsky book," etc.

S: I found that in my own personal experience there are certain gateways to alternative sources of information, and if you didn't know about them, it was like it didn't exist. So whether that was through the punk rock scene, or through the left movement, it didn't really matter where you were coming from. When you encountered one of these specific organizations, like AK Press, or Jello Biafra's Alternative Tentacles label, you don't even know about these things unless somebody tells you. So the fact that it's selling so well is amazing to me.

D: Yeah, and now there are CD's, which reach young people, a youth audience, that know about Tower Records and HMV and small independent stores. They don't listen to public radio. That's not part of their media menu. Public radio is dull. I don't blame them. It's largely dull, where it's Brahms, Beethoven, Bach, and Bob Edwards. You can't get much duller than old Bob in the morning. That's like listening to an undertaker read the news and do interviews. So the idea with the compact discs is to get to another audience that ordinarily do not use the radio. It's working. It's getting out there. And then you've got groups like Pearl Jam, U2, R.E.M., Kronos Quartet, they're all into Chomsky. He's like an icon. Sonny Rollins, who's coming to town in March, he listens to Chomsky all the time. This great tenor sax genius is into it. A lot of people are. But they know it's hard to get any kind of electronic umbilical cord going in the country to link up all these isolated folds, because the corporations control everything—the big media. Sure Jello Biafra can exist, AK Press can exist, Alternative Radio can exist, *Z Magazine* can be published, etc. But it doesn't have that kind of national coverage.

S: Does it seem to you that there are more or less outlets for these alternative views than in the past? What I'm thinking of is the current controversy with Pacifica Radio. I saw a bulletin from Znet that Pacifica Radio may or may not be having this power struggle going on as to what kind of information they're going to be putting out. Do you have any insight into that situation?

D: I think it's so complex that it would take me hours to explain, and I'm not going to do it. It would just confuse your readers. Pacifica is beset by internal problems that would require months of explanation. I don't want to go into it.

S: Fine. Avoiding that topic specifically, do you see a growth of self-published zines?

D: I've seen growth. It's clear that there's been an explosion of zines, newsletters, and web sites. People are fed up with the corporate controlled media. It's like what Scoop Nisker used to say, "If you don't like the news, go out and make some of your own." People don't like the media. They don't like the news, and they're going out and doing their own. So there are a lot of so-called "pirate" radio broadcasters, micro radio, and zine publishers and the like. These are all democratic expressions. They're also expressions of frustration with the existing system, which as I said earlier gives you a range of opinion from A to B, on a good day. On a bad day, it's A to A. So that's very healthy, and that shows that the democratic instincts and impulses are alive in the populace, even though the educational system and the propaganda system have worked very hard to beat it out of them. You know, "Be a good consumer. Shop until you drop. Go to the mall. Get a car or an SUV. Think about objects. Think about your material life. You are what you own. There is no common good." This ideology is just reversing the classic union slogan of the early 1900s, which was "An injury to one is an injury to all." So that if my brother, if my comrade, my coworker is suffering, I feel that. It has an impact on me. Now that has been transformed into "An injury to one is an injury to one. You're on your own." It's this kind of savage indifferent capitalism.

S: It seems to be a divide and conquer strategy of the elite: If we can keep everyone distracted with just meeting their own needs, and never communicating about the system as a whole.

D: Right, and then give them a steady diet of diversion, in which sports plays a big part, as well as escapist entertainment and scandals. Monica Lewinsky. O.J. Simpson. Jon Benet Ramsey. Lorena Bobbitt. Tonya Harding/Nancy Kerrigan. Michael Jordan. Michael Jackson and on and on and on… It's an awesome propaganda system. Joseph Goebbels was considered an evil genius of propaganda. If he were alive today, he would be awestruck at the American system, which in a sense, seems to be not there.

S: It's invisible.

D: They were hands on. The Nazis were hands on. "You don't do this … to the death camp." There was no subtlety there. "Here's the truncheon. Do what I say, or you get your head split.

S: It's sort of a shift from overt censorship to covert censorship. We're not going to just beat you over the head, send you to the death camp, and ban and burn everything; we're going to just not present it at all, and get you to not even think about it at all.

D: And then there's the corporate media and ideological system, which hide behind the shibboleth of "We're just giving the people what they want. The people decide. No one forces them to watch the O.J. Simpson trial or Monica Lewinsky's oral sex scandal or Jon Benet Ramsey or what's happening with John Elway, will he retire or won't he retire? Can the Broncos go for a three-peat? We're just giving the public what they want. Well, that's a crock of crap. Because there's no evidence. The supply is creating the demand. The demand is not creating the supply. Here is the supply, and let's generate a demand. It's like how now people are totally into 3.2 [% alcohol] beer. They don't know, because they're not offered beer that has a much higher alcohol content. So they think "Oh, beer, 3.2, that's what you get. Coors light, that's beer." And everyone drinks it, not knowing that there are many other types of beer. So the supply creates demand.

S: One of the things that I would like to kind of wrap up with would be what can people do, perhaps approaching it within Boulder and C.U.? What are things you think people can do? And how about things on a larger scale?

D: Well in Boulder we're particularly blessed by having progressive organizations and institutions here. That's not the case in large parts of the United States. For example, there's a wonderful progressive bookstore here, Left Hand Books. You want to know what you can do? It's closed half the time because it's volunteer run and they can't find volunteers to staff the store. When I came to Boulder in 1978, the store had just opened. I spent a lot of time in there just volunteering. It was a very enriching experience for me. I got to read a lot of magazines and books. On the hill is the Rocky Mountain Peace and Justice Center, a remarkable institution. People can get involved, volunteer there, do interns. They can do the same at KGNU, one of the best community radio stations in the country. They can volunteer at Alternative Radio. I'm looking for people to help me all the time with transcribing, recording, office work, and a whole milieu of tasks. So there are four examples right there of what people can do. There's an organization run here by Jeff Milchin, called Epicenter. He's trying to fight and roll back corporate domination through organization of minds and organization in Boulder. They can get involved with that group. In Denver, there's a tremendous organization called Rocky Mountain Media Watch that very much needs volunteers and interns to get involved with them. There are lots of things to do. To say that there's nothing out there is, I think, avoiding the issue.

S: Yeah that's very important to me. What I'm trying to do with my contribution to this zine is to point out to people that it's not hopeless.

D: Well if you think it's hopeless, then you guarantee the outcome.

S: Exactly. And I see a lot of people buying into the "slacker/Generation X" stereotype that there's nothing we can do anyway, so why try? And I would like to help people see that there are plenty of things that you can do.

D: Well, I think Alternative Radio is a model. I started with no talent to speak of, no training, no resources, no capital—and I was able to build this. The program is now broadcast over one hundred stations in the United States or in Canada. Australia, South Africa, it's on short-wave to one hundred countries. This is not some achievement that others can not replicate, maybe in different ways. It can be done. There are openings here. I'm not saying the political culture is monolithic. There are openings, and you need to find those openings and drive wedges through them to make them wider, so that there will be one hundred "Alternative Radios." So one day Alternative Radio will not be alternative. It will be radio. There'll be nothing alternative about it. It will be what people hear.

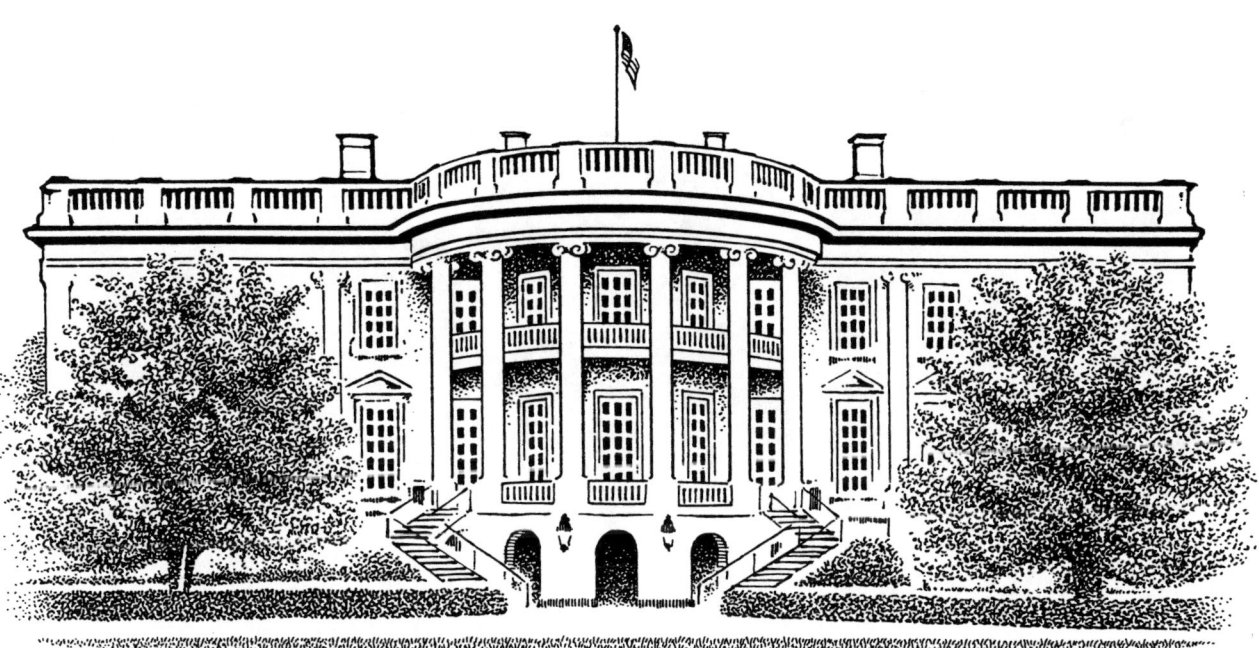

SERVICE/ADVOCACY EMPOWERMENT

"Where Stories Aren't Important: An Alternative Perspective on Library and Information Science Education"

Wayne A. Wiegand

My students have heard it so often they call it my "birdsong." At the beginning of a course I teach entitled "Information Agencies and Their Environments" required of all first semester University of Wisconsin–Madison School of Library and Information Studies students, I routinely run through a litany of statistics. There are more public libraries in the United States than McDonald's restaurants, I tell them; Americans make 3.5 billion visits to school, public and college libraries every year—three times more than visits to movies. School children visit their library media centers 1.7 billion times during the school year—two times more than visits to state and national parks. Generally, these statistics get their attention, but I don't quit there.

As many children participate in summer reading programs as play Little League baseball. College and university libraries loan 180 million items each year, the vast majority of which are books and periodicals. Two-thirds of Americans use a public library at least once per year, and of that number eighty percent (that's about 150 million people) go there to check out a book. And for decades now, among the books they check out, fiction has consistently accounted for 65–75% of the circulation in these ubiquitous civil institutions. These statistics, I tell students, amply demonstrate that the millions of Americans of both genders, all ages, ethnicities, races, creeds, classes, and sexual orientations who frequent the thousands of libraries billions of times every year are primarily coming to fulfill needs and interests satisfied largely by the act of reading, and what they read are largely the "stories" (e.g, biographies, mysteries, Civil War battles, Newbery-Caldecott winners, romances, and African-American diaspora narratives) that contain cultural information they value as important.

Several weeks later I hit them with a couple of lectures that capitalize on the growing literature on the act and social nature of reading (now over a generation old) that helps explain who reads the stories all types of American libraries disseminate, and why. I became interested in this literature twenty years ago as an American library historian; its richness convinced me in 1992 to join with Jim Danky to establish the Center for the History of Print Culture in Modern America as a joint program at the University of Wisconsin–Madison and the State Historical Society of Wisconsin, and to locate its university home in the School of Library and Information Studies.

I tell my students that the literature on the act and

Expanded version of "Librarians Ignore the Value of Stories," *Chronicle of Higher Education*, October 27, 2000, p. B20. Reprinted with permission.

social nature of reading divides into four broad categories: (1) literacy studies, which demonstrates that understanding the social and historical context in which literacy is practiced is essential to understanding why it is being promoted; (2) reader-response theory, which shows that in the reading process the reader is an active agent who exercises a great deal of creativity in making sense of texts; (3) an ethnography of reading, which acknowledges that reading is often a communal activity based in a social infrastructure grounded on shared interpretive frameworks and practiced in shared institutions; and (4) a social history of books and reading (or, post–Gutenberg, "print culture history"), which proves that the act of reading is and for centuries has been a multilayered, highly complex process. Print culture history is my personal favorite, and the one most relevant to my own research. Through its literature I can easily see how all cultures—the dominant and marginalized—have always used stories to validate their existences, make sense of their worlds, and pass on to future generations what they regard as their culture's collective wisdom.

For students, however, I like to add cultural studies to this mix, in large part because it broadens questions about the act of reading to also address how people "read" non-print cultural forms like videos and compact disks, both of which libraries also circulate. Cultural studies, I tell them, argues that people make their own culture out of the resources and commodities provided to them, and in interacting with these resources and commodities they freely "appropriate," "poach," even "construct" new meaning from them in order to meet their own unique group or individual information needs. Thus, by combining contemporary scholarship on literacy studies, reader-response theory, the ethnography of reading, and print culture history with cultural studies, I hope my students begin to see the broad outlines of the multiple answers to what I think is an essential question for anyone aspiring to positions in public, school, and academic libraries: Who "reads" the stories thousands of libraries provide billions of times to millions of their patrons, and why?

At the same time, however, I tell them that the literature on the social nature and act of reading which would help explain who reads these stories, and why, is almost totally ignored in LIS programs across the country. I never have to work very hard to prove the statement. Four months ago, for example, I downloaded the catalogs of the five top LIS programs listed in the latest *U.S. News and World Report* survey: Illinois, North Carolina, Syracuse, Michigan, and Pittsburgh. As I looked through the curricular offerings of these leading schools for references to the words "read" or "reading," or to the phrases "act of reading" or "social nature of reading," I found almost none. Michigan makes reference in several courses to "readers" or "readings," but only as required assignments for particular courses. Similarly, Syracuse talks about "key readings" in one course. North Carolina fails even to use words like "read," "reading," or "act of reading" in any of its curricular offerings. Only in an "Advanced Problems in Librarianship" course does Illinois say it provides "directed and supervised investigation of selection problems in library resources, reference service, research libraries, reading, public libraries, or school libraries." And Pitt has a History of Books, Printing and Publishing course that covers "manuscript origins, the nature and development of the printing process, the reading public, the book trade, binding, and book illustration."

As a library historian, I think I understand how this oversight evolved. Michel Foucault argues that centuries ago the "new order" we now call "modernity" separated the way people experienced daily life into "work" and "leisure." Business and government (and the sciences that served their interests) assigned a very high value to the former, a very low value to the latter. Except for the stories the state regarded as so essential to the social order they had to be taught in institutions like schools, the communication of stories—no matter their cultural form—became categorized as "leisure," and thus trivialized by the dominant culture. On the other hand, information that served the interests of business and government became privileged. One of the earliest manifestations of this distinction in American library history occurred in 1732, when Benjamin Franklin sent out the Library Company of Philadelphia's first order. It included dictionaries, grammars, and an atlas, and books on science and agriculture "suited to the tastes and purses of young tradesmen." Almost entirely "useful knowledge" here, very few stories—and none of the religious kind that dominated the world around them.

Three events in 20th century American library history reinforced or deeply influenced these value distinctions between useful knowledge and stories. First, with the help of a substantial grant from the Carnegie Corporation, the University of Chicago opened a Graduate Library School in 1928 to offer the profession's first Ph.D. program, which promised to concentrate on research. At the time, Chicago led the nation in efforts to make the social sciences more "scientific." The nomothetic positivism practiced at GLS effectively established the parameters of a professional discourse and quickly became the model LIS research has emulated ever since. And although in the first decade of its existence GLS faculty (and especially Douglas Waples) focused much of their research on the "scientific" investigation of reading, their scope betrayed a cultural bias. They ignored fiction (the stories most library patrons wanted) and instead concentrated on (and thus favored) the kinds of nonfiction information (i.e., useful knowledge) more likely to be asked at the library's reference desk.

Second, in 1939 the American Library Association adopted its first version of the Library Bill of Rights, which not only made ALA (at least rhetorically) a champion of intellectual freedom, it also made questions of what patrons read, and why, irrelevant to the profession's interests beyond supply and demand. From henceforth patrons were looked upon more as consumers whose transactions with the library ought to be kept confidential. Curiosity about—and investigation into—who reads the stories libraries circulate, and why, came to seem like an invasion of privacy, or a breech of professional ethics.

Third, at mid-century the Carnegie Corporation funded a "Public Library Inquiry" to examine its purpose. Led by Robert D. Leigh of Chicago's Political Science Department, project investigators (including Bernard Berelson, Oliver Garceau and Alice Bryan) concluded that American public libraries ought to minimize their practice of supplying the popular reading desired by nearly three-quarters of their users and instead concentrate on a small but more influential combination of "serious" readers, community leaders, and students of adult education who use public libraries to obtain useful knowledge. Like the research agenda at Chicago's GLS, however, PLI's research scope was culturally biased. Because it favored useful knowledge over stories, PLI overlooked entire patron groups whose needs and interests at the time were satisfied by the act of reading, including children who accounted for nearly half the American public library's user population nationwide.

As a result of these developments, by 1975 LIS education had become convinced (along with most of the rest of the library profession) that access to "useful" information—and especially the kind librarians thought people needed to become informed citizens and intelligent consumers—constituted librarianship's most important professional responsibility. At conferences and in its research literature, discussions about the stories most patrons wanted were either marginalized or ignored. Little wonder, then, that in the 1980s, when middle class patrons began using computers to obtain the kinds of information Franklin, Waples, and Leigh considered most valuable and librarians thought they were trained to supply, a substantial fraction of LIS education leaders (and especially those with business, computer science, engineering, and science backgrounds whose training taught them to privilege information that business and government appreciated most) began moving their curricula towards a definition of information that was largely driven by emerging technologies. By the year 2000, LIS education had evolved a distinct professional discourse. If a computer couldn't handle it, many LIS educators seemed to argue, then it wasn't information. And any LIS educational program wanting to be considered "on the cutting edge" didn't even have to add the words "of technology." It went without saying.

This discourse proved so powerful that LIS educators took no notice of another cutting edge body of emerging research, this one taking place mostly in the humanities. While LIS education was shifting its definition of "information" to one driven almost entirely by technology, increasing numbers of humanities scholars began shifting their focus from "culture as text" to "culture as agency" and "culture as practice." This new focus addressed questions of how people use the multiple cultural forms available to them to validate their existences and make sense of their worlds. It also studied the cultural information being passed from author/creator to reader/listener/viewer. It was out of this shift that the literature on the act of and social nature of reading itself emerged. And like its parent body of research, it concentrated not on "culture as text," but on "culture as agency" and "culture as practice."

By analyzing what LIS education does with the literature on the act of reading, the controlling nature of its current discursive formations becomes readily apparent. Foundations texts assigned LIS students in core courses include little or no coverage of literature on reading. With faculty advice and financial aid, LIS doctoral programs mostly recruit and encourage students to investigate information topics connected to newer technologies with traditional social science methodologies. Vacancy notices for new LIS faculty positions almost always emphasize teaching skills and research expertise in information technologies, and never mention a need to develop an understanding of the information millions in America's multicultural society find in the stories libraries collect and circulate. And in some "schools of information," story-centered courses and teaching positions—like children's librarianship—have been eliminated entirely. Even attempts at oppositional thinking can't seem to venture "outside the box." For example, not one of the nine letters to the editor CHE published in its May 12 issue that sought to debunk and/or clarify an April 7 article entitled "In Revamped Library Schools, Information Trumps Books" cited the library's primary role as a reading institution. Instead, what united all correspondents was agreement that "libraries are more than just books."

The blindered thinking effected by professional discourse in which the definition of information is driven by technology was made even more obvious when some LIS educators who received a Kellogg Foundation grant to redefine the LIS curriculum met in Washington, D.C. in 1996. Before them they had a Benton Foundation report of a focus group of suburban public library users who, in response to a number of questions, nonetheless collectively identified as their top two public library services: (1) "providing reading hours and other programs for children;" and (2) "purchasing new books and other printed materials." While any well-informed students of the scholarship on reading would immediately sense that focus group members are here bearing witness to the value they place on the culturally informing potential of stories that reading releases, the Benton Foundation seemed unable to tease out this possibility. As a result, Kellogg grantees seemed unable to fathom a potentially broader significance of these priorities as they contemplated a curriculum to fill the future needs of the profession. Another example drawn from the same focus group activity speaks to another failing. In oral remarks, one focus group participant criticized libraries for not stocking enough popular titles. "If you want to get the book that everybody is reading right now, it is just not in," s/he complained. Although scholars of the act of reading—and especially the social nature of the act of reading—would immediately recognize this as a plea for increased access to a community-based information-sharing activity, such a possibility seems never to have occurred to focus group organizers or Kellogg grantees, who otherwise liked what the Benton Report said about the library's need to upgrade technology.

But this kind of blindered thinking about reading is not unique to LIS discourse. With very rare exceptions, English, history and education departments have also failed to look at libraries as significant cultural, literary, intellectual, social or even educational institutions. Scholars in American, cultural, and area studies have been equally remiss. For example, in "Reading Groups Are Bridging Academic and Popular Culture," an article CHE published in its December 19, 1997, issue, author Mary Cregan notes that Americans spend more time reading than surfing the Internet or watching movies. She quotes a Census Bureau study of mass-media use recently published in the *New York Times*. "While people have been devoting less time to reading newspapers and magazines over the last decade, they have actually increased the time they spend on books" to average over 100 hours per year. She then summarizes the proliferation of reading groups across the country as a manifestation of this increased activity, and argues that the groups have potential to serve as a bridge between academic and popular culture. "People are turning back to books," she concludes, "refusing to give up the opportunity for meditative insight, for meaning, for the connection and community that reading—and discussing what one reads with friends—can bring." In the article Cregan never mentions the role that professionals in American public, school, and academic libraries (who in my opinion are better placed institutionally to function as the bridge) already play in this phenomenon.

Please let no one conclude from reading this essay that I am anti-technology. Not at all. Professional librarians—and the programs that educate them—absolutely have to tap the potential of information technologies in service to their patrons. But the contrast between the statistics cited in the first two paragraphs and the near total absence of attention to reading in LIS programs at universities across the country provides ample evidence of the kind of cultural and intellectual blinders powerful academic discourses can unknowingly effect. I would argue that rather than restricting the definition of information for LIS programs to what the technology provides, we should greatly expand our focus to be more inclusive and less culturally biased by looking at the act of reading that the library facilitates, whether it comes off the printed page, the video monitor, or the computer screen. Only then can we begin to explore entire information cultures and not just those fractions affected by technologies. And expanding our focus in this way would allow us to correct the major oversights committed by the GLS and PLI that I see repeated in contemporary LIS education by encouraging us to take as seriously as the millions of its readers do the stories that thousands of libraries circulate to them billions of times every year as patrons.

In the next year schools of "information" and "information and library science" will be graduating nearly 5,000 students from ALA-accredited programs into positions in public, school, and academic libraries, where reading stories that contain multicultural information continues to constitute the library's major source of activity. Although a literature now exists to enable these students to acquire some knowledge of who reads these stories and why, the vast majority won't have a clue. Worse yet, they will have been schooled to think that an intellectual curiosity about what millions of their patrons read, and why, is not only beyond the scope of their practice as an information professional, but actually none of their professional business. What a shame.

Against National Poetry Month As Such

Charles Bernstein

And they say
If I would just sing lighter songs
Better for me would it be,
But not is this truthful;
For sense remote
Adduces worth and gives it
Even if ignorant reading impairs it;
But it's my creed
That these songs yield
No value at the commencing
Only later, when one earns it.
—translated from Giraut de
   Bornelh (12th century)

April is the cruelest month for poetry.

As part of the spring ritual of National Poetry Month, poets are symbolically dragged into the public square in order to be humiliated with the claim that their product has not achieved sufficient market penetration and needs to be revived by the Artificial Resuscitation Foundation (ARF) lest the art form collapse from its own incompetence, irrelevance, and as a result of the general disinterest among the broad masses of the American People.

The motto of ARF's National Poetry Month is: "Poetry's not so bad, really."

National Poetry Month is sponsored by the Academy of American Poets, an organization that uses its mainstream status to exclude from its promotional activities much of the formally innovative and "otherstream" poetries that form the inchoate heart of the art of poetry. The Academy's activities on behalf of National Poetry Month tend to focus on the most conventional of contemporary poetry; perhaps a more accurate name for the project might be National Mainstream Poetry Month. Then perhaps we could designate August as National Unpopular Poetry Month.

Through its "safe poetry" free verse distribution program, the American Academy of Poetry's major initiative for National Poetry Month is to give away millions of generic "poetry books" to random folks throughout the country. This program is intended to promote safe reading experiences and is based on ARF's founding principle that safe poetry is the best prophylactic against aesthetic experience.

Free poetry is never free, nor is free verse without patterns.

Oscar Wilde once wrote, "Only an auctioneer admires all schools of art." National Poetry month professes to an undifferentiated promotion for "all" poetry, as if supporting all poetry, any more than supporting all politics, you could support any.

National Poetry Month is about making poetry safe for readers by promoting examples of the art form at its most bland and its most morally "positive." The message is: *Poetry is good for you*. But, unfortunately, promoting poetry as if it were an "easy listening" station just reinforces the idea that poetry is culturally irrelevant and has done a disservice not only to poetry deemed too controversial or difficult to promote but also to the poetry it puts forward in this way. "Accessibility" has become a kind of Moral Imperative based on the condescending notion that readers are intellectually challenged, and mustn't be presented with anything but Safe Poetry. As if poetry will turn people off to poetry.

Poetry: Readers Wanted. The kind of poetry I want is not a happy art with uplifting messages and easy to understand emotions. I want a poetry that's bad for you.

First issued by the University of Chicago Press in conjunction with the publication of *My Way: Speeches and Poems*. © 1999 Charles Bernstein. Reprinted with permission of the author.

Certainly not the kind of poetry that Volkswagen would be comfortable about putting in every new car it sells, which, believe it or not, is a 1999 feature of the Academy's National Poetry Month program.

The most desirable aim of the Academy's National Poetry Month is to increase the sales of poetry books. But when I scan some of the principal corporate sponsors of the program of the past several years, I can't help noting (actually I can but I prefer not to) that some are among the major institutions that work actively against the wider distribution of poetry. The large chain bookstores are no friends to the small presses and independent bookstores that are the principal supporters of all types of American poetry: they have driven many independents out of business and made it more difficult for most small presses (the site of the vast majority of poetry publishing) to get their books into retail outlets, since by and large these presses are excluded from the large chains. I also note this year that *The New York Times* is a major sponsor of National Poetry Month; but if the *Times* would take seriously the task of reviewing poetry books and readings, it would be doing a far greater service to poetry than advertising its support for National Poetry Month. The whole thing strikes me as analogous to cigarette makers sponsoring a free emphysema clinic. Indeed, part of the purpose of the Academy's National Poetry Month appears to be to advertise National Poetry Month and its sponsors—thus, the Academy has taken out a series of newspapers ads that mention no poets and no poems but rather announce the existence of National Poetry Month with a prominent listing of its backers, who appear, in the end, to be sponsoring themselves.

The path taken by the Academy's National Poetry Month, and by such foundations as Lannan and the Lila Wallace—*Reader's Digest*, have been misguided because these organizations have decided to promote not poetry but the idea of poetry, and the idea of poetry too often has meant almost no poetry at all. Time and time again we hear the official spokespersons tell us they want to support projects that give speedy and efficient access to poetry and that the biggest obstacle to this access is, indeed, poetry, which may not provide the kind of easy reading required by such mandates.

The solution: find poetry that most closely resembles the fast and easy reading experiences of most Americans under the slogans—Away with Difficulty! Make Poetry Palatable for the People! I think particularly of the five-year plan launched under the waving banners of Disguise the Acid Taste of the Aesthetic with NutriSweet Coating, which emphasized producing poetry in short sound bites, with MTV-type images to accompany them, so the People will not even know they are getting poetry.

This is the genius of the new Literary Access programs: the more you dilute art, the more you appear to increase the access. But access to what? Not to anything that would give a reader or listener any strong sense that poetry matters, but rather access to a watered down version that lacks the cultural edge and the aesthetic sharpness of the best popular and mass culture. The only reason that poetry matters is that is has something different to offer, something slower on the uptake, maybe, but more intense for all that, and also something necessarily smaller in scale in terms of audience. Not better than mass culture but a crucial alternative to it.

The reinvention, the making of a poetry for our time, is the only thing that makes poetry matter. And that means, literally, making poetry *matter*, that is making poetry that intensifies the matter or materiality of language—acoustic, visual, syntactic, semantic. Poetry is very much alive when it finds ways of doing things in a media-saturated environment that only poetry can do, but very much dead when it just retreads the same old same old.

As an alternative to National Poetry Month, I propose that we have an International Anti-Poetry month. As part of the activities, all verse in public places will be covered over—from the Statue of Liberty to the friezes on many of our government buildings. Poetry readings will be removed from radio and TV (just as it is during the other eleven months of the year). Parents will be asked not to read Mother Goose and other rimes to their children but only … *fiction*. Religious institutions will have to forego reading verse passages from the liturgy and only prose translations of the Bible will recited, with hymns strictly banned. Ministers in the Black churches will be kindly requested to stop preaching. *Cats* will be closed for the month by order of the Anti-Poetry Commission. Poetry readings will be replaced by self-help lectures. Love letters will have to be written only in expository paragraphs. Baseball will have to start its spring training in May. No vocal music will be played on the radio or TV or sung in the concert halls. Children will have to stop playing all slapping and counting and singing games and stick to board games and football.

As part of the campaign, the major daily newspapers will run full page ads with this text:

Go ahead, don't read any poetry.

You won't be able to understand it anyway: the best stuff is all over your head.

And there aren't even any commercials to liven up the action.

Anyway, you'll end up with a headache trying to figure out what the poems are saying because they are saying NOTHING.

Who needs that.

Better go to the movies.

Library of Congress Service Erosion

Editors' Note: In the July 24, 2000 issue of BULLETIN BOARD; The Voice of the Library of Congress Professional Guild, AFSCME Local 2910, Maureen Moore writes about the situation in L.C. cataloging in her article, "A New Dichotomy, a New Nightmare". L.C. Cataloging Director, Beacher Wiggins, had recently announced a new dichotomy in who does what in cataloging. Under the new dichotomy technicians would be responsible for the entire bibliographic description and possibly straight-forward authority creation and catalogers would establish and assign the more complicated access points. Another radical change proposed was to make catalogers responsible for shelflisting, hitherto a technician duty. The Guild had objected and called for a meeting with Mr. Wiggins to discuss the issues. Ms. Moore further describes erosion of cataloging quality during the administration of the current Librarian of Congress as follows:

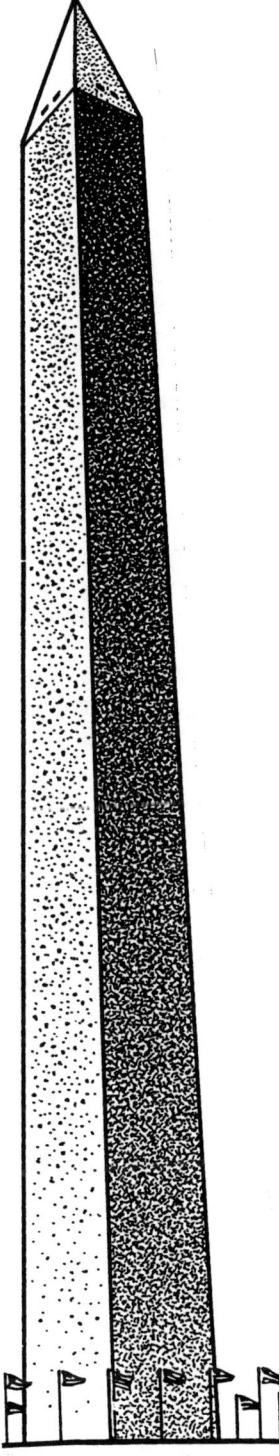

"The Director is certainly faced with difficult operational/management challenges. While the staffing level of his directorate continues to shrink, we have ever-increasing receipts and new demands for cataloging exploding online resources. Moreover, he is trying to carry out one of the Library's most important functions with little understanding, let alone support, of that function by his superiors.

"Although he proclaimed several times that the proposed changes of the new dichotomy were his idea and not his bosses', we all recognize the imprint of the Library's most senior officials. Their attitude toward our cataloging activities was neatly summarized in a 1989 memo to the Collection Services Transition Team by Ben Tucker, then chief of the Office for Descriptive Cataloging Policy and acting chief of the Shared Cataloging Division. "We are proud of the accomplishments of the Library in the field of cataloging: we have an excellent, world-wide reputation for cataloging, and we wish to guard that reputation. Yet some of the hearsay reported to us indicates that our work is regarded by some management officials as little different from processing insurance forms and that we, moreover, have mismanaged this essentially 'clerical' work."

"The most compelling proof of upper management's disdain for cataloging is the steep decline in Cataloging Directorate staff. In FY 1990 we had 727 FTE's; in FY 1999, 571. This drop in staffing might not seem remarkable if we did not remember that since arriving at LC the Librarian has proclaimed over and over again that the number one goal of his administration is to wipe out the Library's arrearages.

"Ironically, while Dr. Billington has repeatedly boasted during Congressional budget testimony about the work done by the Library's "knowledge navigators," he has led one attack after another on cataloging and catalogers since he arrived in September 1987. Dr. Billington's first cataloging target after his appointment as Librarian was subject headings. In December 1989 he instructed the then Director for Cataloging, Lucia Rather, to seriously consider giving up subject cataloging because those strings of words at the bottom of the catalog card were useless; Dr. Billington did not search by subject, but rather by author and title. Luckily, outsiders, including the *Washington Post*, learned of the attack on subject cataloging and there was a huge outcry at the prospect of losing this invaluable research tool. An inside study demonstrating the value of subject headings was done as well, and subject cataloging was saved.

"Not long after that tempest, Dr. Billington decided that the cataloging operation at the Library of Congress should be organized just like that of any other American library. The fact that we were the recognized leader in cataloging in this country, if not the world, and cataloged the largest collection in the world seemed to have no significance. The goal of this "whole book" reorganization was for one person to perform all cataloging duties, both descriptive and subject. (In 1941 the LC cataloging operation had been reorganized into separate descriptive and subject cataloging divisions precisely because Library management recognized the complexity of the work and the concomitant need to specialize in either descriptive or subject cataloging.)

"Catalogers strongly opposed the proposed whole book reorganization, as did many cataloging managers. In August 1990, 74 percent of the professional cataloging staff of the Descriptive, Shared, and Subject cataloging divisions signed a petition to Dr. Billington stating their objections and pleading with him to reconsider his decision. "Based on our years of experience as descriptive and subject catalogers, we expect a dramatic, permanent decline in cataloging quality, production, and hence staff morale . . . ." Our objections were ignored and the whole book cataloging reorganization of 450 staff members took place on June 14, 1992.

"The whole book cataloging reorganization was just the first major step in the process of erosion of the LC cataloging operation. Less than one year after this massive reorganization, Sarah Thomas, the new Director for Cataloging, proposed yet another major change: implementing "copy cataloging" by technicians throughout the Cataloging Directorate. Copy cataloging is a means of providing access to materials in LC by using cataloging records residing in external databases such as OCLC and RLIN. The Library of Congress began using cataloging supplied by outside libraries long ago (called "cooperative cataloging"). However, it was always edited so as to comply fully with Library of Congress standards.

"The modern history of copy cataloging at LC began in 1990. Staff in the Enhanced Cataloging Division looked for copy cataloging for "any item received at LC earlier than the current three years," in English and in foreign languages that they knew. It seems clear that the previous Director for Cataloging, Lucia Rather, had no intention of implementing copy cataloging extensively at LC. In the Travel Report she filed about a meeting of the New York Technical Services Librarians on May 10, 1990 she reported: "... The audience was generally friendly, but the issue around which most questions revolved was copy cataloging. This group was not at all enthusiastic, emphasizing the reliance of their libraries on authoritative LC cataloging. I empha-sized that LC would continue to provide original cataloging for the majority of its acquisitions and that 'copy cataloging' records would be labelled as such, but I'm not sure I convinced them. It is clear that many libraries are going to view copy cataloging, not as a method of expanding cataloging coverage, but. rather as a degradation of LC service. One gentleman with tongue in cheek (I hope) asked, 'Is there no level of cataloging below which LC will not stoop?'"

"Sarah Thomas could not be dissuaded from expanding the practice of copy cataloging at LC, and, in January of 1995 the Guild finally signed a mid-term bargaining agreement with management. This was the first "formal" attempt by management to "blur the edges" between the professional and paraprofessional job series; this was the first time that technicians were asked to regularly perform duties hitherto performed by professional staff.

"Technicians were given several weeks of in-house cataloging training and then told to, in effect, evaluate the quality of the cataloging performed by outside libraries. Incredibly, they were asked to decide when errors were "egregious" and "to insure that the name and subject headings present in imported records fit into the currently existing heading structure of the catalog." In effect, they were asked to become whole book catalogers for a GS-8 salary. Management called this "career enhancement." (I should mention that during the copy cataloging negotiations with the Guild, Beacher Wiggins and other members of the management team repeated to us numerous times that the reason LC was willing to use other libraries' cataloging without a regular review by LC's catalogers was because the outside cataloging was created by cataloging professionals.)

"The next significant attack on the cataloging process was "core level cataloging," introduced at LC as a six-month experiment in 1996 by the then Acting Director for Cataloging, Beacher Wiggins. Just seven months after the end of the "experiment," the Library announced adoption of the core level standard as LC's base level of cataloging in the Cataloging Directorate and the Serial Record Division; LC did not actually begin full-scale conversion to core cataloging until FY 1999."

In a nutshell, core level cataloging contains less data than "full level cataloging," but more than "minimal level cataloging." For books there are fewer notes, fewer subject headings, and fewer added entries. Many of the requirements stated by the *Anglo-American Cataloguing Rules* and accompanying LC documentation for notes and added entries should be ignored; many of the requirements of LC's *Subject Cataloging Manual* for subject headings should be ignored.

"What is not "simplified" in any way whatsoever is the rest of the bibliographic description, that area of the bibliographic record proposed to be turned over to the technicians in the new dichotomy. Obviously, until very recently, cataloging management deemed the 020, 245, 250, 260, and 300 fields so important that nothing about their formulation and construction was changed when the Library adopted core level cataloging.

"This brief, unhappy history of LC cataloging during the Billington years is not complete by any means. There simply is not enough time to fully describe the numerous schemes concocted by management, such as "speed cataloging," "collection level cataloging," "SWAT Teams," "production-only months," and my personal favorite, invitations to cataloging retirees to return to LC and catalog gratis.

"The fundamental source of the problem is the view that cataloging is not professional work and that almost anyone can do it. Do we ever hear about money-saving proposals for para-legals to defend the Library in its numerous legal battles, or for a library school student to take over as Chief of Staff? In 1993 Dr. Billington's appointee as Inspector General, John Rensbarger, demanded a report on why the Library of Congress needed to catalog at all! The terrible tragedy is that while James Billington has been Librarian of Congress, the Library of Congress has almost destroyed one of its crown jewels: a world-renowned cataloging operation. The value of that operation was eloquently described in the 1989 Collections Services Transition Plan:

"Catalog records produced by the Library's catalogers have long set the standard. Because the U.S. has no formal national bibliography, the Library's records serve that function and are, in consequence, a national resource. The Library does not and should not maintain its reputation for pre-eminent cataloging simply for cataloging's sake. To the contrary, it is the use made of these records that mandates their high quality. As is well known, in addition to providing access to the Library's collections, its records are used by thousands of other libraries in shared-cataloging networks. Commonly a library will repeatedly search a network for an LC record to copy. Libraries not only copy, but they and the scholars they serve use the Library's records for equally important purposes. The Library's records are used as guides to current practices in day-to-day cataloging; their heading and subject entries are used for creating authoritative bibliographies; and they are employed as exemplars in education and training settings. In most cases, the value of LC records is in exact proportion to their quality. Without that quality, their usefulness diminishes."

"Our proud legacy has been insignificant to LC's current management. Now we catalog in a library which has no money to spend on maintaining its professional cataloging staff, yet has millions for innumerable items that have absolutely nothing to do with librarianship: conferences on the brain, "Vision Training," Facilitative Leadership training, exhibits on Freud, Blondie, etc.

"Our current Librarian seems to believe that the primary function of this institution is to be an intellectual Disney World. Even the WASHINGTON POST (May 31, 1995 editorial "Being a Library") complained about this mindset of Dr. Billington's when he threatened in Congressional budget testimony to reduce reading room hours and cut back on exhibits, displays, and published items. "With all due respect, the latter three categories seem to us far riper for emergency cost-cutting than any of the more information-oriented and reader-oriented services the library was founded to offer . . . . There is a beautiful array of museums on and around the Mall, and the library adds to that array, but first and foremost it is a library."

"We have no money to replace retiring catalogers, but scores of non-bargaining unit positions have been funded for the Office of the Librarian, Development Office, Office of Communications, Office of the Inspector General, Office of Planning, Management, and Evaluation, and Office of Security - to name just a few. Moreover, with a workforce of 4000 we carry more than 200 Senior Level positions, each costing $101,566 - $130,200 per year. This represents about 5% of our total workforce, while in the Executive Branch, Senior Level, Executive Level, and Senior Executive Service positions take up only .83% of the total workforce (according to the Workforce Information Office of OPM).

"Despite many pronouncements to the contrary, cataloging at the Library of Congress is not a high priority for its top managers now and has not been for 13 years. Let us hope that their vision clears and that, in the end, they give the correct answer to the question posed to Lucia Rather in 1990: is there no level of cataloging below which the national library of the United States will not stoop?" ▫

TENDING TO THE CITY'S NEEDS, SERVING NEWCOMER IMMIGRANTS

The Value of Community Information

How are public libraries responding to the information needs of newcomers?

How can we improve the relationship of the public library to community organizations serving immigrants?

BY CHRYSS MYLOPOULOS

PHOTO BY CALUM TSANG

INTRODUCTION

The Toronto region has historically been a strong immigrant reception area. According to the 1996 census, the total immigrant population of the city of Toronto (persons not born in Canada) by country of origin was 47.6 percent, or 1,124,405 people. The North York, Scarborough, and Toronto regions included the largest concentration of people with immigrant origins. According to the Toronto *Social Development Atlas: Population Profile*, 29 percent of city residents speak a language other than English or French as their primary language at home. These are extremely relevant statistics for our services because they guide our decisions on the languages and the type of resources we are building for the immigrant community. The most interesting statistics for the purpose of this discussion are that in the city of Toronto between 1991 and 1996, 28 percent, or 315,460 people, were recent immigrants in great need of orientation, community information, and language training.[1]

A look at the countries of origin of these recent arrivals reveals that with few exceptions, such as immigrants from Jamaica, the United Kingdom, and Guyana, where English is spoken, recent immigrants come from countries where the knowledge and practice of English are not substantial.

For those new immigrants the process of becoming Canadian is not free of hardships. The immigrants are sustained through the initial period of adversity and adjustment by the belief that there are better things to come. It is during this period that information is needed, and it must be transmitted in a reliable and effective way.

The purpose of this article is to discuss the delivery of community information services as it has been developed in the libraries of the city of Toronto, offer suggestions for bringing organizations serving immigrants and public libraries closer, and create an understanding of the limitations of both organizations and of the complementary nature of their relationship. Diminishing public resources provide a good impetus for reviewing and possibly restructuring the delivery of services while at the same time contributing toward the formation of relationships among organizations serving immigrants and the public library.

For the public library, community information is recognized as an essential library-related need of the newcomers' community. While one of the objectives of multicultural library services is to meet this need, the ways by which we deliver this service have not been fully evaluated. For example, we have not looked at the total spectrum of immigrant service deliverers in the community, total resources across service boundaries, or cross training among service providers. Furthermore, we have not promoted the library's community information in a significant and effective way.

THE ACCOMPLISHMENTS OF THE PUBLIC LIBRARY IN THE AREA OF MULTICULTURAL SERVICES

The planning and gradual implementation of the library services that are offered to the Toronto multicultural community span a period of more than 20 years, when former municipalities adopted both the federal and provincial policy of multiculturalism and translated it into library services and programs. It is widely recognized and generally accepted that over the course of those years the public libraries in Toronto have become multicultural organizations and have addressed the diversity in their communities by becoming more diversified themselves. This diversification is manifested in their mission statements and in their goals and objectives, which address the needs and interests of their multicultural public. It is also manifested in the development of expertise in building multilingual collections; in the diverse cultural, linguistic, and racial staff profile; in the appropriate staff training that is provided; and in efforts toward removing linguistic, attitudinal, and other barriers to service delivery and information. This diversification highlights the multifaceted nature of serving a multicultural public.

For the past 20 years we have learned to use demographic and other statistical information to plan our service locations and to establish the level of the service and its scope. The former Metro Multicultural Services Committee and its work in this area attest to the degree of planning that has taken place for all these years. We have learned the complicated task of multilingual collection development in the planning, selection, and acquisition of multilingual materials from a variety of sources both in Canada and overseas. At present the public libraries of the city of Toronto are circulating collections in more than 30 languages. The unique aspects and challenges of multilingual materials acquisitions were long ago recognized and addressed and have resulted in more than 400,000 multilingual items on the shelves of the public libraries in Toronto.

We have also gained considerable experience in successfully providing bibliographic access to our materials by cataloguing and including our collections in our databases, and we have used the expertise of our multilingual library staff effectively in collection development and in public assistance. Contacts with community resource providers and participation in networks serving immigrants have long been part of the responsibilities of staff involved in the provision of services to the immigrant community. We have also developed considerable expertise in organizing cultural programs and exhibits and have for years aided in the acquisition of English as a second language by providing both resources and facilities.

Year after year our service objectives were reached through appropriate policies and procedures and through short- and long-term planning of how we can best address the needs of our ever-increasing diverse population. We believe that in doing so, not only have we facilitated some aspects of the settlement, adjustment, and integration process of the new immigrants, but we have also contributed and continue to contribute to their growth as individuals.

COMMUNITY INFORMATION AS A SOCIAL NEED

The public library is a community institution, and

any changes in the community give us an opportunity to reach new publics and offer relevant services. The public library is also a source of information, materials, and services for all groups in the community. In large urban settings with a diverse population, goals and objectives of public libraries state that part of the services they provide to new immigrants relate to their information needs coming from the fact that they have just moved into a new country and are learning a new language.

The general community we serve consists of a variety of special publics, each with equally special needs for information. Although community information is needed by all of us at some point in our lives, it is frequently the newcomer immigrant who needs it more and who is not only at a loss for how to access it but also needs help to understand it.

In terms of subject range, community information includes information on employment and training, housing, the immigration process, family matters, age-related problems, health and living with illnesses, education, language learning, a variety of instruction classes, legal rights, welfare benefits, disabilities assistance, services for children and seniors, pensions, individual rights, and race relations. Most of this information is published in ephemeral physical format—pamphlets, sheets, booklets, press cuttings, videos, and audiocassettes. A large amount of province-specific or country-specific materials relating to subjects such as law, government, education, business, welfare, and social services exist only in English or French. Information on matters of daily living, such as housing, health, and schools, is also available in English and possibly in only a few other languages. In general, we are dealing with information written in English, and we provide services to new immigrants who, by and large, do not speak English well enough to understand this information.

So far, we have managed to organize and house community information; however, this type of information requires more than cataloguing and classification. Often, it requires translation and interpretation—a dangerous area for us. Other times it requires translation from English into English. We have all had experiences with "official" information that is not comprehensible, especially to the learner of the language. The public libraries of Toronto, through their staff, speak "volumes of languages." According to a recent inside survey there are more than 35 languages spoken and understood by our staff, but not all these staff members are working with the public on a daily basis, and not all of them are trained in delivering and communicating this type of community information. Furthermore, not all of them are working at library locations where their linguistic expertise is used to its maximum.

The delivery of community information stumbles on two major blocks that need to be addressed: the language barrier and the complex nature of the information. Those two barriers are compounded by the fact that the community members who need this information are very often reluctant to approach a public place such as the library to satisfy this need. For many new immigrants the public library as a source of information is viewed with skepticism.

INFORMATION-SEEKING BEHAVIOR: HOW NEW IMMIGRANTS PERCEIVE PUBLIC LIBRARIES

It is important to try and understand information-seeking behaviors of multilingual communities. It would be naive to assume that all communities are the same and that members of the same community exhibit the same behavior when looking for information. The social, occupational, and economic environment within which one belongs and operates and his/her education and schooling influence the need and the approach to information.

Distinctions can easily be made between newcomers and settled immigrants regarding the degree to which individuals are self-reliant as a result of English proficiency and familiarity with the available channels of information. As the immigration policies and legislation change to encourage the immigration of those with substantial financial resources and/or professional expertise, more and more immigrants arrive with the necessary skills to approach and use the information resources of the library. It should be noted that there are newcomers who know a lot about the public library. They regard it as a link to their new environment and make extensive use of its information services and resources.

However, within settled immigrant groups there are individuals who despite the number of years they have resided in Canada have never felt comfortable approaching the public library for any kind of information or service. They lack the confidence to use the library. This may stem from low proficiency in English; lack of familiarity with the library and how it operates as an organization; a fear to use a public institution; social isolation related to age, disability, or gender roles; and the misconception that the library is a place associated with schools and formal education. According to DuMont, Buttlar, and Caynn, these are some of the many barriers to service and access that "culturally diverse groups have experienced in making optimum use, or even any use, of library facilities."[2]

In general, all immigrants, but mostly newcomers and

refugees, need information, but many times this information is not easily or fully accessible. According to a recent document prepared by the Scarborough Network of Immigrant Serving Organizations (SNISO) as a deputation to the Toronto task force on community access and equity, focus groups that covered eight separate communities and included 105 immigrants and refugees indicated that community information and information on services are provided by friends and relatives, community agencies, and ethno-specific media. Public libraries were never mentioned.[3] The same results were echoed in a similar study in the United States eight years ago. In a survey that was conducted of the Soledad (California) library, "friends, family, co-workers, churches" were reported as sources of information, "although these sources were inadequate to meet typical information, needs that relate to employment and jobs, medical and health concerns and how to fill out various standard forms."[4] Again the public library as a source of information was not mentioned.

The library literature indicates that a strong association has been found between knowledge of the functions of the library and library use. According to Chatman & Pendleton, we need to bridge any knowledge gap that may exist and engage ourselves in some basic research that could identify all constituencies within our community.[5] Fostering a greater awareness of the functions of the library might contribute to increased library use by the immigrant community.

It is equally essential that, together with increasing immigrants' awareness of the functions of the library, we introduce and promote the services we provide as relevant, reliable, and useful to the everyday needs of the people. According to Pendleton and Chatman, "it would make a significant contribution to everyday lives if it could be fully appreciated how libraries might make information more useful to 'small world living.' "[6] Newcomers live in their own "small world." We all live in our "small worlds." Promotion of information resources in a contextual way and the potential role that libraries can play in the everyday lives of people should be examined more closely.

IMMIGRANT SERVICE ORGANIZATIONS

Public libraries are not alone in the area of providing services to new immigrants. Ethno-specific organizations serving immigrants and other social agencies also address this need. Although the objectives are the same, with the overall aim of facilitating the settlement process of new immigrants, these organizations meet them using expertise and approaches that differ from those of the public library.

Immigrant settlement services identify three stages of the settlement process. The first is the orientation stage, with basic and immediate information needs that cover housing, initial language training, employment, documentation, education, and economic subsistence. The second stage includes information needs surrounding an immigrant's longer-term resettlement—more permanent employment, health care, permanent or long-term housing, language training, recreation, social networks, consumer and financial needs, and citizenship. The third stage centers on how one can get reliable and understandable information on a consistent basis. The third stage is universal across populations, nonimmigrant as well as immigrant.

Organizations serving immigrants and community-based settlement agencies assist newcomers in becoming part of the community through a range of services and programs. Community information, including all the areas described above, constitute the core of their services. People feel more comfortable receiving information in their language and from people who know the culture and can transmit information appropriately. The experience of dislocation and resettlement and the process of "translating oneself" into another language and culture are experiences with which many immigrants and refugees are familiar. Staff at agencies that serve immigrants generally share the same background and similar experiences with their clients; these staff members can connect and communicate more effectively with the newcomer.

According to the Ontario Council of Agencies Serving Immigrants (OCASI) "initiatives that enable newcomers to learn more about the new country in which they have chosen to build their lives have become a major vehicle in facilitating the settlement of the newcomers."[7]

Although the ethno-specific immigrant service organizations have the cultural sensitivity and the linguistic ability to provide a wide range of services, this overall ability is hindered by a limited infrastructure, especially with smaller organizations, and a lack of proper funding and support. In a recent meeting of SNISO, most of the participating agencies indicated that they did not have any computer equipment and that there was no interaction via electronic sources to other partners providing the same service. Some do not even have a fax machine, while others operate from inaccessible locations.

PERSPECTIVES ON THE DELIVERY OF COMMUNITY INFORMATION SERVICES

Our approach to delivering community information services deserves some reexamination. It is an area in which the library is in a position to make great contributions. We have developed the expertise, we have the knowledge, and we also have the resources to do so.

To achieve our goal of addressing the information needs of newcomers, we need to develop specific strategies in several areas. These are the organization of resources and user's advisory services, methods of publicity and promotion, ways to build up our resources by networking and information sharing, and increased collaboration in the delivery of services.

Organization of resources and user's advisory services

- Identify local immigrant needs and build up information files appropriately. Concentrations of newcomers from a specific geographic area may present unique information challenges. Ethnic origin, language, age, and other related characteristics of newcomer groups have an impact on the type of information we gather. For instance, in a library where the community accommodates transient newcomer refugee groups on a temporary basis, information on how they can register their children for school, explanation of the requirements imposed by the government or other limitations, and information on social assistance are of paramount importance.
- Locate, evaluate, reorganize, and repackage existing information resources. At present, information is published by a number of different government departments, each one assigning a different emphasis and presenting the information from a particular point of view. Information overload is taking place within the community information area, and assisting the newcomers to sort through the plethora of information is necessary. In addition, information is changing as new legislation or new guidelines or regulations come into effect, and updating of information is crucial.
- Display and shelve community information and resources as part of the ESL section. The ESL section can very well become an "ESL and orientation" section. At present, in most libraries community information is kept in Princeton files behind the reference/information desk. Generally the public cannot find it on their own; thus, accessibility to this information is limited. Newcomers are attracted to the ESL section because of language learning needs and other orientation matters, and they may expect to find community information in that section.

Publicity and promotion

- Focus publicity on community information for newcomers as an essential and unique part of multicultural services. Community information needs to be explained to newcomers in a way that they can easily understand. At present, community information is presented as part of the overall library services to the multicultural population. There has not been any emphasis on this type of service, and in fact we have stopped short of distinguishing and identifying it as a unique and greatly needed service.
- Communicate to the public what they can expect. A list of services is not enough to ensure understanding of the services. Specific examples of the contextual use of information resources can be a great incentive to use the library. The public has to understand why a particular service or program is useful and the question we have to ask ourselves is what is the best and most effective way of telling them. The "Welcome" brochure that lists services needs to be reexamined. As a communication vehicle it may belong to the past.
- Use ESL classes as a forum for publicizing library services and for identifying needs. There is no better place for the promotion of library services than the captive audience of a class of newly arrived ESL students. Frequent visits to these classes and invitations to ESL classes to tour our libraries are effective methods of building interest and creating awareness of our services. These visits also provide an opportunity to connect the newcomers with the appropriate ethno-specific agency and validate and reinforce the worthiness of these services.
- Communicate to the "information gate keepers"—the staff at the community and immigrant serving agencies—the services of the library. In many cases, it may be difficult to expend human resources in extensive community outreach. We all know the importance the immigrant services staff plays in the life of many newcomers. Often, all it takes is to establish a mutually beneficial rapport with staff at the community organizations and instill an understanding of the importance of the library in the life of the nation's new residents.
- Ensure that digital information services are responsive to the needs of diverse linguistic communities. As mentioned before, awareness of the services that

immigrants can expect to find in the public library and in the community is considered a factor in increasing the use of the library. The library home page is an effective way to publicize services and offer links to existing multilingual and immigrant resources in the community, information on collections, best-selling authors and titles, lists of new titles in languages other than English, and recommended titles by language selectors. These online resources, in the language of the immigrant, are some of the ways of truly integrating the multilingual resources and services with the rest of the library resources.

Resource networking /co-location of services: "one-stop shopping"

- Define the kind of information we need to share, discover the total resources in the community, and create a combined package of resources and services available to newcomers. It is time for the library to create information packages for the community. We have the expertise to identify, present, and disseminate information on community resources in a comprehensive and organized fashion. In fact, this may well be one of the roles we can play in the library environment of the new millennium.
- Collaborate with other organizations to access available funding. Changes in social priorities, available funding, and cost-reducing trends are definitely providing the motivation for initiating interagency collaborative efforts.
- Offer the facilities of the library to settlement agencies' staff to provide consultation, information, and referral in the immigrant's home language. This can be a new area of close collaboration and resource sharing. The model that is suggested here is the use of any suitable local library by visiting staff of ethno-specific organizations to provide consultation in the language of the newcomer, to use the community information available at the library, or to use the Internet service accessible through the library.
- Promote the availability of community rooms at the library and encourage their use by the local community organizations. In many cases the existence of these rooms is not known and the process of accessing them cumbersome and complicated. The library is an ideal place for community organizations, especially newly formed ones, to hold meetings, organize their activities, and develop their organization using resources and information available at the library.
- Use the library's technology to interact with government agencies not only to access information but also to send information. This may not be possible right now, but I believe that the time will soon come in Canada when registration for OHIP or social insurance numbers will be done electronically. The public library can be an easily accessible place for this.

Turning to the community-based agencies serving immigrants and looking at their services from the library's point of view, the following areas of resource networking, collaboration, and advocacy are essential.

Resource networking and collaboration

- Improve the ability to access resources from nontraditional partners such as libraries. It will be difficult to deny that many libraries have gathered community information resources that are not used as much and as frequently as they should be. If agencies can easily access this information without having to spend time gathering and organizing it, this will increase the time those organizations spend with their clients and it will also maximize the use of the library resources by the community.
- Provide networking opportunities where public institutions such as libraries can participate. Regular meetings of service deliverers from many different agencies to share information on the system as a whole can improve the networking among agencies and the library.
- Encourage more interagency collaboration and resource sharing. Sharing of office space by more than one ethno-specific agency, sharing of electronic resources and equipment, jointly applying for grants, and initiating joint projects can be some of the ways that this collaboration can take place.

Advocacy

- Increase public awareness of the needs of immigrants. This is an area in which many organizations are involved, with varying degrees of success. The public library can assist as a partner by cosponsoring events, by organizing background information for fact-finding delegations, and by facilitating community gatherings.

CONCLUSIONS

Service is a multifaceted competency for librarians. As new information needs emerge from demographic changes, new basic competencies and skills are also required of us. Knowledge of information resources and the ability to evaluate them and use them effectively are essential for librarians. The librarian's role is one of interpreting, filtering, and evaluating the sources of information. In this new library environment, service also includes the analysis and repackaging of material and human resources and the creation of value-added quality resources and services.

As librarians, we talk about service to the community as a prime value, yet the new immigrant population is sometimes turned away without a satisfactory resolution to their problems. Community information for newcomers needs to be promoted as a service that stands on its own. The public libraries have the necessary infrastructure and the material and human resources to achieve, together with other organizations, a better service for newcomers. The scarcity of written information in other languages and the language problem that newcomers face has been addressed by using the linguistic expertise of the staff whenever possible. But it can be addressed even more effectively by allowing the facilities of the library to be used by agencies serving immigrants. In this way we combine the information resources and expertise we have with the appropriate and much needed language and cultural interpretation by qualified staff of immigrant agencies to deliver the service in an effective way.

Libraries are also generally located in easily accessible places, as opposed to organizations serving immigrants, which make use of any affordable space available. Using well-publicized library locations at specific days and times for consultation, referrals, and other information has the potential of improving the delivery of this service. Immigrants need encouragement to come closer to the library. Agencies serving immigrants can bring them in by addressing their specific needs. At the same time, by using local library facilities, agencies can provide their services in ways that reduce physical/geographic barriers. Co-location of services and "one-stop shopping" should be looked at as possible models for the delivery of these services.

The complementary nature of the relationship between the public library and the community organization should be recognized and accepted by all who are involved in providing services to immigrants. Neither community organizations nor public libraries can afford to work alone in the area of immigrant services.

The planning of multicultural services is behind us in the sense that we know our community and what it requires of us. What we need to do now is to review and reengineer the delivery of this service. If public libraries are looking for ways to enhance their identity so that they can survive turbulent social and economic times, then building bridges with immigrant community services and using our expertise as information consultants should be fully utilized.

REFERENCES

1. Statistics Canada, 1996. Population census by country of origin.
2. Du Mont, Rosemary Ruhig, Buttlar, Lois, and Caynon, William. *Multiculturalism in libraries.* Westport, Conn.: Greenwood Press, 1994, p. 120.
3. Scarborough Network of Immigrant Serving Organizations (SNISO). *Immigrant and refugee communities in the Scarborough region: access and equity issues.* Fall 1998.
4. Pendleton, V. E. & Chatman, E. A. Small world lives: Implications for the public library. *Library Trends* (Spring 1998): 732-751.
5. Chatman, E. A. & Pendleton, V. E. Knowledge gap, information-seeking and the poor. *Reference Librarian* 49/50: 135-145.
6. Pendleton, V. E. & Chatman, E. A. Small world lives: Implications for the public library. *Library Trends* (Spring 1998): 732-751.
7. Ontario Council of Agencies Serving Immigrants. *OCASI Newsletter* 60 (August 1995).

Chryss Mylopoulos is the Multicultural Services Specialist for the Toronto Public Library.

"I defy any man to show me that there is pauperism in the United States."
—Andrew Carnegie

BERMAN'S BAG: MUST "THE POOR" ALWAYS BE AMONG US?

by Sanford Berman, U*L Contributing Editor

As a donor to St. Stephen's Shelter in Minneapolis, I lately got a letter from the shelter director, Ed Murphy. He wrote, in part:

"It used to be that if a person worked in America they'd be able to afford a place to live. For many who worked cleaning offices, washing dishes, or any of a number of essential jobs, home was a room at a downtown hotel or boarding house. Some lived most of their lives there, while others stayed long enough to save up for something better.

"But in the past few years, things have changed... Rapid downtown development destroyed hundreds of units of low-cost housing, leaving many workers with fewer options. Some people were able to double-up in apartments or find other housing. Others ended up in homeless shelters just to get off the streets and keep their jobs". A recent survey of homeless men at St. Stephen's shoed that 810 are working, most employed full time. Yet they live homeless because there are so few low-cost apartments and wages aren't high enough to afford the available housing.

"As a result, shelters fill quickly, leaving many on the streets . At St. Stephen's alone, 80 or more sober, homeless men each night try for one of our 40 beds. That means too many are left to sleep outside or on the floor in downtown refuges. What's worse, the vulnerable mentally ill who most need shelters are unable to get in and left to fend for themselves on the streets, seeing their lives spiral further downward."

Despite an undoubted economic

"boom" and much-vaunted "prosperity," one in five American children remains in poverty (42% of Black kids!), food shelf and shelter use rises, a third of the workforce makes *less* than livable wages, and some 45 million people have no health insurance. It's not widely reported, but many homeless people are murdered (29 last year), some also decapitated, and laws--for instance, against panhandling or loitering--frequently criminalize poor people just for being poor. So celebration of our collective "good times" seems a little premature.

By contrast, the very rich are becoming ever richer. Fortune 500 CEOs typically "earn" 400 times more than their lowest-paid employees, that pay gap being 5 times wider today than in 1990 and 10 times greater than in 1980. And the wealthiest fifth of the population receives more than half of the nation's income. In this context of persistent and growing inequality, class-based discrimination, and lack of such taken-for-granted basics as shelter, food, and health care, I propose as an analog to the well-established concept of "institutional racism" that we now start talking about "institutional classism." In libraries, we'd then be looking at policies, practices, and attitudes that either keep poor people out altogether or treat them as though they don't deserve equal, first-class service, and--in the realm of resources and bibliographic access--that banish or mute their voices and those of antipoverty allies.

To get specific: It may shock the innocent and idealistic among us to learn that fines for overdue materials are no longer collected to get the materials back or to promote responsibility among borrowers. They're levied to make money, to generate revenue. Indeed, if everyone returned materials on time, a library like Hennepin County in Minnesota would suddenly lose over $800,000 a year. What does that have to do with classism? Simply this: Fines demonstrably keep some low- and fixed-income people from using the library. When it's a question of putting milk on the table or paying an overdue fine (or paying for transportation to return materials on time), milk wins. As it should. But the result is often that folks then stay away from the library. Or keep their kids out. In short, fines are discriminatory. So are fees for core services like video borrowing. Three or more ALA policy statements unequivocally proscribe fees, yet libraries continue to assess them, in effect censoring certain resources and services for people without the ability to pay. (Bestseller and audiotape rental programs also exemplify services denied to persons strictly on an economic or classist basis. Jenna Freedman, incidentally, critically examined such programs in a recent U*N*A*B*A*S*H*E*D™ Librarian: "Express This--the Road To Ruin" no. 116 (2000), pages 28-31.)

Another form of institutional classism is the failure to provide catalog access to topics well represented in library collections but not yet sanctified by the Library of Congress, subjects like HOMELESS MENTALLY ILL PERSONS (explicitly mentioned by Ed Murphy), POOR PEOPLE--EMPOWERMENT, NONCLASSIST CHILDREN'S LITERATURE, LIVING WAGE LAWS (to complement the belatedly created LIVING WAGE MOVEMENT), FOOD SHELVES, STREET NEWSPAPERS (there are over 40 such tabloids--by, for, and about homeless people--in North America), and myriad "CLASSISM IN" forms, like CLASSISM IN EDUCATION and CLASSISM IN SOCIAL POLICY (which, as an example, perfectly fits such a work as Ruth Sidel's *Keeping women & children last: America's war on the poor* (Penguin Books, 1996).

The longstanding terms, PUBLIC WELFARE and PUBLIC WELFARE ADMINISTRATION, should be converted to the more readily findable WELFARE and WELFARE ADMINISTRATION. (Since not all catalogs furnish adequate cross-references, the most common and familiar version of a term ought always to be the primary form.)

And the Victorian-era descriptor, POOR, needs to be transformed into the more human, less objectified form: POOR PEOPLE. (Naturally, there's already a heading for RICH *PEOPLE*. In response to questions raised about the discrepancy between these two headings, an LC staffer explained: "'Poor' is an original subject heading, established in 1898, that followed a pattern, prevalent at the time, of referring to groups of people in this manner, similar to 'Blind' or 'Deaf.' 'Rich people,' however, was established in 1996 and follows the current pattern of including 'people' in the heading." So it seems that obsolete, dehumanizing terminology must be retained for the sake of historic preservation!)

Additionally, there needs to be more depth, breadth, and specificity in the cataloging of poverty and social policy titles. For examples of how LC typically under- or mis-catalogs such material and a comparison with Hennepin County treatments of the same works, have a look at my "Foreword" to Karen Venturella's *Poor people and library services* (McFarland, 1998), pages 7-13.

Still one more kind of institutional classism is the refusal to allow street papers to be distributed free in library foyers and entranceways. And there's the corollary failure to subscribe to, keep, and catalog local homeless and welfare rights periodicals, thus excluding the voices of the very people most affected by anti-panhandling laws, welfare repeal, and a host of other measures that further marginalize and oppress poor people, In the event there are few or no such local or regional publications, libraries should stock at least some representative titles from elsewhere, for instance:

> +*Catholic Agitator*. 632 N. Brittania St., Los Angeles, CA 90033. 8 nos. $1.00/year. ISSN 0045-5970. The feisty, fervent product of L.A.'s Catholic Worker movement. Heading a recent full-page review of *Word on the Street: Performing the Scriptures in the Urban Context*: "Reader beware! This book could be dangerous. It may compel you to practice Christian compassion on the streets of your city and get you in trouble… just like Jesus. You may depart from the comfortable confines of the safe seminary and quiet church to discover the reality that God dwells among the poor."'

> +*Long Haul: Speaking Out About Poverty*. End Legislated Poverty, No. 211, 456 West Broadway, Vancouver, BC, Canada V5Y 1R3, monthly. $30/year. Contains information on British Columbia policies and politics, an d how poor people and anti-poverty activists there agitate and mobilize to make life more dignified and fair for unemployed, homeless, and other low-income persons--together with Canada-wide and international reports, as well as spirited-volleys against wealthfare and poor-bashing. Done with style, verve, and solid data, the whole paper's an inspiring example of powerless, downtrodden folks getting it together and fighting back. Also--like *Survival News* and *Welfare Mothers Voice*--it's an effective antidote to cynicism and despair.

> +*Survival News*. Survivors, Inc., 95 Standard St., Mattapan, MA 02126. quarterly. individuals: $10/year, organizations: $25, low/no income people: free. A jumbo tabloid, partly in Spanish, featuring much Massachusetts news and opinion, but also many articles of general interest (e.g., in the Summer 2000 issue: "YWCA's Nazi tendencies?," "Hunger in the US," "Female poor getting poorer," "Which

way welfare rights?," and "Taking back Mother's Day") plus abundant survival tips and resource-listings.

+*Welfare Mothers Voice: a paper By, For, and About Mothers in Poverty*. Welfare Warriors, 2711 W. Michigan, Milwaukee, WI 53208. quarterly. individuals: $15, organizations: $25, mothers in poverty: free at distribution sites/$4 by mail. A vital, spirited, outspoken panoply of letters, photos, cartoons, essays, and news with a Wisconsin accent but global reach, making important links between issues as apparently diverse as environmental protection, welfare rights, corporate crime, campaign finance reform, globalization, women's resistance, and the prison-industrial complex. Their mission: "We want to share our knowledge and strength with each other, to validate each other, and support each other until the poverty community is strong and unified with a VOICE in all systems that affect our lives. We are angry and bored with the lies and stereotypes about moms whose children receive government child support (TANF). We will no longer remain silent. We will unite and fight for the lives of all mothers and children in poverty. We demand dignity."

+*By What Authority*. Program on Corporations, Law & Democracy (POCLAD), P.O. Box 246, So. Yarmouth, MA 02664. 3 nos, $30/year (for newsletter & "contact kit"). "An unabashed assertion of the right of the sovereign people to govern themselves," POCLAD's organ contends that "a minority directing giant corporations privileged by illegitimate authority and backed by police, courts, and the military define the public good, deny people our human and constitutional rights, dictate to our communities, and govern the earth."

+*Dollars and Sense: What's Left in Economics*. Economic Affairs Bureau, 740 Cambridge St., Cambridge, MA. 02141. bimonthly. individuals: $22.95/year. institutions: $42. "Edited and produced by a collective of economists, journalists, and activists...committed to social justice and economic democracy," D&S "explains the workings of the US and international economies" in accessible prose "and provides left perspectives on current economic affairs." This is where to find understandable analyses of such issues and developments as drug policy, corporate welfare, Third World debt, the clean-elections movement, neoliberalism, multinationals' influence, labor militancy, privatization, and income inequality. A necessary complement to *Business Week*, *Time*, *Newsweek*, and *U.S. News and World Report*.

+*Kids Can Make A Difference Newsletter*, P.O. Box 54, Kittery Point, ME 03905. 3 nos. free (but $5/year contribution welcome). "A program of World Hunger Year (WHY)," its goal is to "help young people understand the root causes of hunger and poverty and inspire them to end hunger in their communities, country, and world." This is the sort of priceless nugget often found in such out-of-the mainstream sources, the first two paragraphs of Dan Zuckergood's "RESULTS Educators Network: Helping Teachers Empower Students" (Fall 2000, pages 1-2):

Before becoming a professor of education at Springfield College, I was a Jr. and Sr. High Social Studies teacher for twelve years. For the first few years, I taught about hunger as just another "world problem" that we all needed to solve. Like many other issues, it seemed like an issue "too big" and "too unsolvable" to do anything about.

This all changed after a local church hosted an "Ending Hunger Briefing," put on by the Hunger Project. The speaker asked whether the crash of a plane carrying 400 children would make the headlines the next day. He then asked if the crash of two planes carrying 400 children would make the headlines the next day. After going through a few more "plane crash" scenarios, he informed us that on every single day, 40,000 children were dying as a result of hunger and hunger related diseases. That was the equivalent of 100 planes carrying 400 children! And this was happening each day! And no newspaper was carrying that as a headline!

(For more on the "street newspaper" genre, including details for several outstanding titles, see Terry Messman's "Dissenting Voices of the Street" and Chris Dodge's "Street Newspapers Create Lively Alternative To Establishment Media," both in *Alternative Library Literature, 1998/1999* (McFarland, 2000), pages 239-245.)

Finally, if we're truly committed to helping, empowering, and liberating low income persons, rather than passively accepting the hoary shibboleth that "the poor must always be among us," we have to get political. ALA's

"Poor People's Policy" mandates exactly that.

Stunningly absent from major-party election rhetoric in 2000 was an explicit commitment to genuinely aid low-income persons by fighting to *eliminate* low incomes, to dismantle poverty itself, to really achieve a more equitable "playing field." No citizen, no politician, no librarian can truly be neutral or passive about this, for within a context of inequity and injustice, neutrality and passivity invariably favor wealth and privilege, ensuring the continuing misery and hopelessness of the "less fortunate."

There's no mystery about what to do. Practically every social critic and antipoverty activist comes up with nearly the same "laundry list" of needed initiatives and policies, among them:

+a much greater public investment in affordable housing (in Minnesota, 43% of renter households can't afford the $591 Fair Market Rent for a two-bedroom unit--and nowhere in the U.S. is the minimum wage adequate to afford a two-bedroom dwelling)

+universal health care or national health insurance (perhaps based on the excellent Canadian, Dutch, German, or Scandinavian models)

+a higher--or living--minimum wage, guaranteeing that no working person stays below the poverty line (almost half of male workers in Minnesota earn too little to adequately support a family of four, while over 72% of women workers make less than what's required to maintain a single-parent family of three.)

+provision of child care, educational benefits, and transportation subsidies to welfare consumers (the recent "welfare repeal" act actually forced many poor women *out* of college or vocational school, and in West Virginia, as merely one example, 80% of former welfare recipients annually make $10,000 or less, almost half of those trying to exist on incomes below $5,000)

+ample welfare payments for people who need them and a moratorium on heartless, family-destroying time limits and sanctions

The real "trouble" with poor or homeless people isn't mental illness or physical disability or drug use or personal irresponsibility. It's that they don't have enough money. Or a network to support them. Affluent people with mental illness, disabilities, addictions, or bad luck get taker care of. The big difference is bucks. And readily available services. Thus the full challenge isn't simply to furnish temporary band-aid programs or goods to poor people. It's also to treat them with the same dignity and respect as anyone else, and to remove such barriers of "institutional classism" as--for instance, in public libraries--fines, fees, and unreasonable residence requirements for securing a library card. And ultimately the challenge is to work like hell to consign poverty itself to the dustbin.

Americans intent on "doing the right thing" might well emulate our Canadian neighbors, particularly the 160,000 individuals and 1,100 groups in Quebec who lately proposed legislation based on these three principles:

* The elimination of poverty is a priority
* Increasing the income of the poorest fifth of the population takes precedence over increasing the income of the richest fifth
* People living in poverty and their organizations must be involved in the creation, implementation, and evaluation of all future government initiatives.

Why not insist that every candidate, lawmaker, and public servant, including library boards and directors, embrace these sensible precepts---and act accordingly?

Express This — The Road to Ruin

"Audio Express" and "Bestseller Express" in Los Angeles, California and Hennepin County, Minnesota, respectively are speeding public libraries into the private sector by charging patrons for books-on-tape and new adult fiction. The lead car, however, is driven by libraries renting videotapes. "At the moment … video rentals are a major source of income for many libraries, neck-in-neck with reserve charges and surpassed only by photocopying and overdue fines. [Wendy Smith, "Fee-Based Services: Are They Worth It?" *Library Journal* 15 June 1993, 40-43] What is more distressing is that the library directors giving the green light to this practice are doing it in the name of service. The reasons they give include expanding library usage, giving "customers" quicker access to books that fall victim to months-long waiting lists, and covering overhead costs in order to provide additional value to library users.

These ideas seem noble and also clever at first. The genius of the Audio Express program in L.A. is undeniable. It identifies a need among the city's long-suffering commuters to have something to do while they sit in traffic. Drivers are sent, by U.S. mail, audiotapes from an attractively (and presumably expensively) produced 150-page catalog. With the first order, participants need to fill out application forms for library cards if they don't already have them. This is a brilliant plan. The only thing I have against it is the *ten-dollar* per month charge per item. [If a title comes in two parts, it is charged as two separate items.] Surely the brains behind this remarkable scheme could have come up with some grant money to make it work for free.

Bestseller Express, on the other hand, replaces a service that already existed and was already free. Library users who can afford it are given the chance to rent the hot ticket items for three dollars per week, on a first come, first served basis, an arrangement that inevitably leads to a first class among library patrons. This, from one of the leading institutions in the country, as evidenced by its fifth place ranking nationwide. [Thomas J. Hennen, Jr., Go Ahead, Name Them: America's Best Public Libraries. *American Libraries* (January 1999): 74.] This, from a library known worldwide in library circles, particularly among catalogers, for its unparalleled fairness in socially responsible subject headings and access for all. It is a sad day when such a bastion of equality is leading the way to classism in the public domain.

Perhaps "leading the way" is not entirely accurate, since some public libraries have been using revenue generated from video rentals—as much as two dollars per day—to support their programs for over fifteen years. Most library directors take the high ground, charging only for "entertainment" videos, while keeping educational materials free. This distinction effectively upholds class differences by continuing to retain the arts as sole property of those who can afford them. Poor patrons can learn German, but God forbid they should seek pleasure from Wim Wenders' *Wings of Desire*.

Hazardous Road Conditions

The ice patches on this road to destruction are the issues of discrimination against patrons who are unable or unwilling to pay for services, the potential misuse of public funds, and the de facto censorship that is inherent in fee-based practices. American Library Association (ALA) policies are clear in their condemnation of fees-for-service. "The American Library Association opposes the charging of user fees for the provision of information by all libraries and information services that receive their major support from public funds. All information resources that are provided directly or indirectly by the library, regardless of technology, format, or methods of delivery, should be readily, equally and equitably accessible to all library users. [Council, American Library Association, "*Economic Barriers to Information Access: an Interpretation of the Library Bill of Rights*," (Chicago: ALA. 1993).]

William P. Davis addresses the discrimination aspect in his analysis of ALA policy at the ALA Intellectual Freedom Committee Hearing on Fees, Chicago, Illinois, January 12, 1991. [Three Statements, *Alternatives in Print 1990/1991*. (Phoenix, AZ: Oryx Press, 1992): 127-130. John Swan and Sanford Berman provided the other two statements. Statements originally made at the ALA Intellectual Freedom Committee Hearing on Fees, Chicago, Illinois, Jan. 12, 1991.]

> Fees in the public sector are almost universally recognized as discriminatory on the basis of economic status. ... What are fees other than a 'poll tax' for the use of public services? What fundamental difference exists between requiring a fee to vote and requiring a fee to receive equal service from a public institution? ... Fees discriminate disproportionately against America's minorities. Those citizens faced with the greatest burdens to overcome become those barred from access to the information needed to overcome those burdens. [William P. Davis, "*Three Statements on Fees,*" in Alternative Library Literature, 1990/1991, Sanford Berman and James Danky, eds. (Phoenix, AZ: Oryx Press, 1992): 127]

I would like to be sure to include children in Davis' burdened minority group. Developing minds should have as few barriers to information as possible. Whether children are reading Danielle Steel or Toni Morrison, they are reading, and should be encouraged in every way. The same goes for videos, even those deemed to be of lesser educational value. The hard part is getting the child into the library. Once we get them there we can try to impose our notions of which materials they should be using, if we choose to. One of our greatest assets in luring innocent children into our enriching agenda is the fact that our services are traditionally free. Trading this human asset for potential financial gain is inexcusable.

Controversy was generated by the implementation of the Bestseller Express program in Minnesota. "I don't think Benjamin Franklin had in mind an almost-free library when he came up with the concept more than 200 years ago. I am very skeptical," challenges Randy Johnson, chair of the Hennepin County Library (HCL) Board in a local newspaper article. [Mark Brunswick, "Bestsellers for Rent? Hennepin Libraries Consider Leasing Books," *Star Tribune*, 10 May 1998, sec. B, p. 1.] HCL Director Charles Brown, who was surprised that there were any questions about the legitimacy of the program, responds by explaining the system, its no more than $250,000 start-up cost and how he "...thought it was customer service at its best." [Ibid.] Dissenting HCL Cataloger Sanford Berman, writing to his County Commissioner as a private citizen, charges, "It constitutes an elite, discriminatory service based entirely on a person's ability to pay. ...such fee-based services directly contradict the American public library's role as an egalitarian, democratic institution; unquestionably alienate low-income citizens; and explicitly violate American Library Association standards." [Sanford Berman, Edina, Minnesota, to Mike Opat 18 June 1998. [letter to Board of Hennepin County Commissioners, 1st District Commissioner]] A supporter of a similar program in nearby Ramsey County offers these words of wisdom, "That's life isn't it?' she asked. 'Everything isn't going to be exactly fair for everybody." [Mark Brunswick, "Bestsellers for Rent? Hennepin Libraries Consider Leasing Books," *Star Tribune*, 10 May 1998, sec. B, p. 7.]

The issue of how a library funds these fee-based services is not only questionable from a moral standpoint, it places the library at risk for legal action. California, for instance, home of Audio Express, bans libraries from charging fees for circulating materials. [Cindy Miller, "Driving to Work with Leo Tolstoy," *Wilson Library Bulletin*, June 1992: 28.] The ethical view is well expressed by John Buschman in *Poor People and Library Services*, "The Reagan privatization of public information era was a harbinger of culture change in librarianship. Essentially, librarians were introduced to the notion that they were sitting on a form of 'wealth' we were not fully exploiting." [John Buschman, "*History and Theory of Information Poverty*," in Poor People and Library Services, Karen M. Venturella, ed. (Jefferson, North Carolina: McFarland, 1998): 22.] Setting the precedent of thinking of public libraries as potential profit-makers is extremely dangerous. It is essential for librarians, politicians, and taxpayers to know that the library is not beholden to any commercial enterprise, and will not compromise free services in favor of those that generate revenue. The very concept in public librarianship that service itself is *all that must be returned for its tax-base* must be protected. These concerns are not limited to post-Reagan American libraries. A library in Victoria, Australia cites these fears:

- "Charges levied on users of public libraries effectively represent a double charge to residents who have contributed to the library through rates and taxes.
- "User fees would change the nature of the public library.
- "Charging for public library services would alter the traditional relationship between users and the library.
- "Charges would distort the library's priorities in favour of those services which produce revenue.
- "In order to actively solicit paying customers, libraries are likely to extend their services beyond their own community, thus weakening their traditional base.
- "As there is a greater number of potential paying customers in the business community than amongst other sectors of the community, public library services are likely to become heavily oriented towards business and commerce, thus overriding the principles upon which they are based." [User Pays: the Victorian Response. *APLIS* 3, March 1990, 41]

The last issue is that of censorship. "Whether a library decides to charge fees to fund the video collection or to raise needed revenue for the library, the user's access is greatly impacted and restricted. The video collection is no longer accessible to all once an economic factor becomes a determinant. 'About 30 percent of the public libraries in the country ... practice censorship by levying restrictive fees for the use of video services.'" [Deborah L. Vroman *RQ*, 35: 38] Once again I bring children into the discussion. Children are traditionally the most likely victims of censorship, and when the basis for access is financial, their position as #1 censorship target remains uncompromised.

The Privatization of Roadside Assistance
Many librarians believe they are doing the right thing, by charging for one service, in order to provide another. It's a similar idea to a multiplex movie theater justifying having nine screens of *Dumb and Dumber*, so it can afford one screen of *Pi*. [*Pi* is an independent film about a computer genius that was released in 1998.] Of course, multiplexes are commercial ventures, and we should be grateful for any crumb they decide to throw us. Public libraries must be held much more accountable.

However noble an idea it is to use fees paid presumably, by the "haves" to improve service for the "have nots," one simply can't escape the two-tiered system it creates. And sometimes the goal is not so noble; it is merely to make things easier for the "customer" who can afford it. BCPL takes a slightly different approach. They don't charge a rental fee, but instead a reserve fee. In director Charles Robinson's words this practice assists patrons whom "have more money than time. We will get something for you in due course, but if you want special treatment, you have to pay for it." [Wendy Smith, "Fee-Based Services: Are They Worth it?" *Library Journal* 118, (15 June 1993)] In order not to penalize non-fee-paying customers, Robinson suggests, "It should be like having a duplicate collection; the fees pay for the extra books you buy." [Ibid.] Two separate collections—sounds like a case of "separate but equal" to me.

Accident Report
In times of financial stress, it is no wonder that creative librarians are coming up with get-rich-quick schemes to fund library service, but we must prioritize our needs. If putting new books in patrons' hands hot off the presses—or at least before they fall off the bestseller list—is the most important job in your institution, then so be it. Order John Grisham by the carton, Barnes and Noble style and cancel your subscription to the *National Review*. But remember, if the patron has time to read the book, s/he has time to

wait to check it out. You can't be all things to all people. Once you accept the charging of fees, it is easy to lose track of the first priority of a public library—serving the public. This happened at the Prince George's County Memorial Library in Hyattsville, Maryland. When they "saw video circulation decline dramatically after it doubled borrowing charges from $1 to $2 per day, the response was essentially a shrug of the shoulders. 'Our usage did drop,' said Associate Director, Mickey Freeney, 'but we need the revenue.'" [Ibid.]

I am deeply committed to library service, and laud librarians for arriving at imaginative ways to provide and fund it, but once again quoting John Buschman in *Poor People and Library Service*, "…there is no such thing as a 'value-added' library service which justifies a fee."
[John Buschman, "*History and Theory of Information Poverty*," in Poor People and Library Services, Karen M. Venturella, ed. (Jefferson, North Carolina: McFarland): 23-4.

Berman Sanford, Edina, Minnesota, to Mike Opat, 18 June 1998. Letter to Board of Hennepin County Commissioners, 1st District Commissioner.

Brunswick, Mark. Bestsellers for Rent? Hennepin Libraries Consider Leasing Books. [Minneapolis] *Star Tribune*, 10 May 1998: B 1, 7.

Buschman, John. History and Theory of Information Poverty. Chapter of *Poor People and Library Services*. Jefferson, North Carolina: McFarland, 1998: 22.

Council, American Library Association, *Economic Barriers to Information Access: an Interpretation of the Library Bill of Rights*. Chicago: ALA. 1993.

Davis, William P. Three Statements on Fees. In *Alternative Library Literature, 1990/1991*. Phoenix, AZ: Oryx Press, 1992: 127-130.

Hennen, Jr., Thomas J. Go Ahead, Name Them: America's Best Public Libraries. *American Libraries* (January 1999): 72-76.

Miller, Cindy. Driving to Work with Leo Tolstoy. *Wilson Library Bulletin* (June 1992): 28-29.

Smith, Wendy. Fee-Based Services: Are They Worth it? *Library Journal* 118 (June 1993): 40-43

User Pays: the Victorian Response. *APLIS* 3 (March 1990): 41

Vroman, Deborah L. To See or Not to See: a Study of Video Collection Censorship in American Public Libraries. *RQ* 35 (fall 1995): 37-42.

Jenna Freedman, U*L Contributing Editor; this article originally was submitted for a Collection Development course assignment at the University of South Florida School of Library and Information Science.

James Chaffee's Fight
against the Bond Issue for the San Francisco Public Library
"A blank check for special interests"

San Francisco, California
November 11, 2000

Sanford Berman
Edina, Minnesota

Dear Sandy,

I want to keep you apprised of what we have been doing.

I am sure that you have heard that we lost our shirt. The proposition passed with flying colors at 74.5%. The percentage will drop one or two tenths more because late absentee ballots have been running for us. We were never able to get any major media to carry the story that the premise of seismic and disability problems was a fraud, and I think that was the key.

I have some more evidence of our activities enclosed. Also, the fact that the campaign consultants for the library are known political slime Barnes Mosher and Whitehurst, a.k.a. BMW, will have some repercussions. I consider my Library Manifesto #1 to be of some interest. Too bad I didn't do any more.

Very truly yours,

James Chaffee

Reprinted with permission from *Librarians at Liberty* (1716 SW Williston Road, Gainesville, FL 32608), v. 8, nos. 1/2 (December 2000), pp. 1, 3-7.

(Leaflet)

Stop the Privatization—
"No" on A

Endorsed by
  SF Tenants Union
  Gray Panthers
  Progressive Left
  Peace & Freedom Party

Do you care about your branch library? Don't let them to your Branch what they did to the New Main.

They call it a "public-private partnership," but it is nothing more than the exploitation of a public asset by corporate interests.
  Cathy Bremer, librarian and union activist, says, "Passage of the Library Bond measure—Prop. A on the SF ballot—will mean that the privatization of an essential public resource, the free public library, is complete. REMEMBER THE MAIN and the way privatization and corporatization destroyed hundreds of thousands of books (our past). That is why as a union activist, I urge you to join me in demanding that the public library remain public and freely accessible to all. Vote No on A for better libraries and better library service."
  They are using scare tactics to further the privatization. That is why Progressives, including Matt Gonzales, Lucrecia Bermudez, and many others are saying, "Now is the time to stop the corporations and Take Back Our Libraries."

No on the Library Bonds— No on A

SAVE OUR LIBRARIES
P.O. BOX 190306, S.F. CA 94119
FOR INFORMATION
PHONE (415) 705-0908

Save our Libraries– "No" on A Library Manifesto #1

Have you been in the New Main Library in Civic Center and tried to find a book? If you have, then you know that almost visceral sensation for the contempt that the architects and builders must have had for you and the enterprise you are undertaking. That sensation is not an illusion. An expensive study was done that shows that it takes four and a half times as long to find something in the New Main as in comparable libraries.
  The real function of the New Main was revealed when the private corporation-funded philanthropic organization, the Library Foundation, was set up in the party space rental business in the library. The promise of hundred of thousands in income for the city was introduced with great fanfare. There was no announcement at all when after several years it was a miserable failure and the City lost money.
  Still many major corporations held parties in the library, including the Chamber of Commerce, Young and Ribicam, *SF Chronicle*, Charles Schwab, American Bar Association, and Genetech. How many parties do you go to in the New Main Library?
  It is well known that the Library Foundation that operates as a corporate front is run by Pacific Bell, Bank of America, Chevron and a coalition of other major corporate interests. They call it a "public-private partnership," but it is nothing more than the exploitation of a public asset for its value as a public relations screen and to turn their network of influence peddling into the cash flow streams that become the source for those pools of so-called "soft-money."

How did they do it with the New Main?
They started with the Library Bond of 1988. As soon as the voters signed that $109.5 million blank check it became a feeding frenzy of graft as bond salesmen, contractors and architects fed at the public trough, augmented by the selling of naming opportunities, corporate influence, and tapping the social/philanthropic party circuit.
  That effort finally wound down and left a New Main Library that is unworkable and a $28 million bill in fix-up charges. So now they want to start over with Library Bond 2000 that will do the same things and bring you New Branch Libraries just like the New Main. It is $105.9 million this time.

What is most interesting is that they are not even pretending that it will be any different. The business-oriented, corporate-dominated Library Foundation is pouring over $600,000 dollars into the Yes on A campaign, and hired election mercenaries Barnes, Mosher, & Whitehurst. That same foundation has already made sure that they pay for the planning and have hired a notorious privatization advocate, selected and paid for by them, who will be in charge of planning.

What sort of privatization are they planning? They have tipped their hand about that too. They have openly announced that their goal is "very self-service libraries." Sometimes modernization is valid and sometimes it is just an excuse to provide less service. And it is all based on lies anyway. There are only three branches with real seismic dangers and only two branches with real disabled access problems. Proposition A is nothing but deception to support a fraud.

(Leaflet)
Save our Libraries – "No" on A

Proposition A, under the premise of helping our libraries, is an unnecessary and wasteful tax increase. This Bond is $105.9 million. This Bond will cost a homeowner with a $500,000 home up to $65.31 each year for the next twenty years (based on SF Controller's figures).

The Claim
- In 1988, they promised they "would also upgrade *all* city-owned neighborhood branches for earthquake safety, handicapped access, or other needed physical improvements."

- In 1994, we voted for "Increasing library hours throughout the system and acquiring books and materials."

- Now, they claim that "most branches are not wheel-chair accessible."

- Now, they claim that "most branches will collapse in a major earthquake."

- Now, they claim a $105.9 million bond issue is needed.

The Reality
- Only 5 branches were renovated.

- The Library's budget has grown to $49 million while the book budget fell and not a single hour was added to the system-wide total in the last five years.

- City studies show that except for restrooms, there are only two branches that are not wheelchair accessible.

- City studies show only three branches are at risk of collapse in a major quake.

- There are unused Earthquake bond funds. Statewide bond funds and even 1988 bond funds that are adequate to handle the immediate needs without the delays inherent in this mammoth project.

The same groups that designed and built the problem-plagued New Main Library now want to do the same thing to the branches. This means Bond funds without accountability.

This Bond will bring San Francisco within .25% of the debt ceiling, with many serious needs of the city still not addressed.

They cannot claim that they care about your branch, because this year staff in the New Main was increased by 24 positions and the branches lost 10.5 positions.

This is being rushed through before our new District-elected supervisors are seated because it is a blank check for special interests. The special interests have not been accountable for our money before, and they should not be trusted now.

This Bond measure will be used for a "service center" for overflow New Main offices, for Brooks Hall storage, and for new branches that will have to be run by stretching the operating budget for your branch even thinner.

No on the Library Bonds — No on A
SAVE OUR LIBRARIES
P.O.BOX 190306, S.F. CA 94119
FOR INFORMATION PHONE (415) 705-0908
SAVEOURLIBRARIES.COM

San Francisco Public Library
**Facts About the Branch Library Improvement Program
August 2000**

What:

The Branch Library Improvement Program is a general bond that would rehabilitate nineteen branch library buildings, including upgrades for earthquake safety and disability access, interior renovations, and some facility expansions. In addition, four new branch libraries would be built to replace current rented facilities, as well as a new branch library in the Mission Bay neighborhood. The bond would provide for a system-wide support center to house book ordering and processing, branch delivery services, and other system-wide services, and enable the Library to make tenant improvements to Brooks Hall to create a City Archive.

When:

This measure will appear on the November 2000 ballot. If approved, the time line for implementation, including planning, will begin in 2001. Construction on individual library buildings will be phased over the next nine years, beginning in 2003 and ending in 2009.

Cost:

The bond amount is $105,865,000, which includes renovation and construction, site acquisition, relocation costs, financing, and other program costs.

Why:

Most of the branch libraries are vulnerable to partial or total collapse in the even of a major earthquake. Neighborhood residents, including children and families, seniors, small business owners, students, teens, job seekers, and others heavily use these facilities. Fifty percent of the branch libraries were constructed over 50 years ago and are in need of improved infrastructure to meet modern technological needs and to allow access to up-to-date information. Most of the branches are not fully accessible to people with disabilities.

Other Funding:

The Library will be applying for funding to support branch renovations through Proposition 14, a state-wide $350 million bond for library construction approved by voters in March 2000. The process for receiving this funding will be competitive and each project must provide a 35% match.

The Friends & Foundation of the San Francisco Public Library have committed to developing a capital campaign to raise funds for furniture and equipment for all the branches. The bond program provides only for capital improvements ("bricks and mortar").

Press Release: October 24, 2000
Immediate Press Inquiries, Contact:
James Chafee 584-8999

SAVE OUR LIBRARIES —
NO ON PROP. A
P.O. BOX 190306, S.F. CA 94119
[415] 705-0908
SAVEOURLIBRARIES.COM

Diverse Interests Favor Keeping Library Public led by SF Tenant's Union

Save Our Libraries, the No on Proposition A campaign, has announces a growing slate of endorsers that includes key neighborhood groups, supervisorial candidates and community leaders.

The San Francisco Tenant's Union leads a list of endorsers that includes Democrats, Republicans, Greens and independents and other

Continued on the next page

SAVE OUR LIBRARIES

FOR THE NEXT GENERATION

P.O. Box 190306
SAN FRANCISCO, CA 64166
[415] 705-0908
SAVEOURLIBRARIES.COM

October 26, 2000

San Francisco Supervisorial Candidates

Re: San Francisco Public Library, No on A

Dear Candidate:

The Campaign to this Point

As we approach the final stages of the campaign against Proposition A and near election day, we should acknowledge there are some things about the early campaign that we misjudged.

Early on, quite frankly, we felt there were some issues that would stand on their own. We felt that district candidates would seize on the neglect of branch libraries and the betrayal of 1994's Proposition E, the Library Preservation Fund. The fact that the neighborhood libraries are not getting their fair share in favor of the library administration and the New Main under incumbent supervisors is something for which that those supervisors should now be held accountable. This is district elections after all: cheating the neighborhoods out of library service ought to be an issue. While we have been gratified both by the endorsements and support from the independent candidates across the City, no one made a sharp challenge on this issue.

Similarly, no one took up the issue of a rich and corporate-influenced "Friends & Foundation" that on the one hand hires Barnes, Mosher & Whitehurst to run its Prop. A campaign and at the same time has its vice chair appointed to a position designated by state law for the "underserved." There must be candidates out there concerned about minority representation and diversity, but no one challenged this open abuse.

Press release —*continued from the previous page*

who have come together from wide variety of political perspectives to reject Proposition A, the Branch Library Bonds. Whether the primary issue is the health of the public library or the health of the city, many groups and individuals who have examined the facts are now persuaded that the proposal for an $105.9 million bond issues, is either ill-conceived and unnecessary, or harmful to the values of a neighborhood library.

Supervisorial candidates that have endorsed No on Prop. A include:
  Rose Tsai (Dist. 1)
  Vu Duc Vuong (Dist.4)
  Jay Bagi, Matt Gonzales (Dist. 5)
  Gilbert Criswell, Garrett Jenkins, Marc Solomon (Dist. 6)
  Lucrecia Bermudez (Dist 9)
  John Huber, Carlos Petroni (Dist.11)

Candidates in other races include, Maria Dolores Rinaldi (Board of Education), and Erin Brown, Chris Finn, Abel Mouton (Community College Dist.), Terrence Faulkner (State Senate, 3rd Dist.), and Adam Sparks (Congress)

Community groups that have endorsed No on A include groups of widely differing perspectives, including: Peace & Freedom Party, Gray Panthers, Alliance for a Better District 6, Progressive Left, Immigrant Right Movement, Good Government Committee, and 57% of the Republican Central Committee (60% needed for official endorsement).

Distinguished individuals who have lent their names to the No on A effort included legendary retired librarian Sandy Berman, and historian and author Grey Brechin.

Peter Warfield in summarizing these endorsements said, "Some oppose higher taxes, others oppose regressive taxation, and still others see bonds as the most expensive way to pay for city improvements. We have spoken to many others who have voted for library bonds in the past but are concerned that bonds at this time may actually harm the branches, give undue influence to the private Friends and Foundation, and bypass the representation of district-elected supervisors."

Whether the concern is for City priorities as the City nears the charter-mandated bond ceiling, the waste of civic resources, the misrepresentation of the proponents of the increasing privatization of the library in recent years, a diverse coalition is coming forward to reject Proposition A and urge a "No" vote from their fellow citizens.

One of our goals in opposing this bond was a chance to educate people about library issues in this City and highlight the deception and betrayal that has characterized the public-private partnership in the library.

It is in the context of that betrayal that we turn our attention to the two key issues of this campaign. First, there is the deception contained in these library bonds that is analogous to the deception of the 1988 Library Bonds. Second, there is the privatization that was the cause of so much harm to the New Main Library.

Intentional Deception of the Voters

To illustrate the deceptive character that is at the heart of the Prop. A bonds we have enclosed original documents rather than simply describe the situation, because the clear evidence is itself so dramatic.

The official argument contained in the Voter Information Pamphlet signed by Mayor Brown and each of the eleven supervisors states, "extensive studies by both city and independent engineers have determined that most of our branch libraries are unsafe and vulnerable to collapse in a major earthquake." Similarly, a sheet entitled "Facts about the Branch Library Improvement Program" (enclosed) distributed in each library by the library administration states, "Most of the branch libraries are vulnerable to partial or total collapse in the even of a major earthquake."

In fact, the "Branch Library Improvement Program" prepared by San Francisco's Bureau of Architecture states that branch libraries rated "partial/total collapse" are only three: Marina, Noe Valley, and Richmond. The relevant pages are enclosed. This is nothing but a scare tactic.

The "Facts" sheet referred to above states, "Most of the branches are not fully accessible to people with disabilities." This falsehood appears in various forms throughout the Voter Information Pamphlet. Just one example is Congresswoman Nancy Pelosi, who states in a paid argument that "Many of our branches are not in **full compliance with the Americans with Disabilities Act** and are therefore nor fully accessible to all. Nine branches are currently **not accessible for either one of both of their floors. . . .**" (Emphasis in original). We have attached a sworn declaration by then Acting City Librarian Susan Hildreth on January 11, 2000 sworn under penalty of perjury. In response to a lawsuit involving disabled access, Ms. Hildreth swears (lines 23-25), "[Only] two of the SFPL's 26 branch libraries, the Golden Gate Valley Branch and the Noe Valley Branch, have problems with disability access which are not limited to those buildings' restrooms." We have also enclosed the penalty-of-perjury page. If voters want to approve $106 million to fix restrooms that us up to them, but they should be told the truth.

I am sure there are those who consider these "white lies." But nothing good can come from these lies. Nothing ever has. Certainly no one has been close to the campaign of abuse and contempt for democracy that built the New Main Library could ever think that. Nothing they could do would be worth the social cost of these lies. The lies must be stopped.

Ratification of Privatization is the Core Issue

The core of this campaign is the referendum on the privatization of the Public Library. The supporters of Yes on A will claim that they care about neighborhoods and children. But if Proposition A passes, they will be claiming that the voters have ratified the direction they are taking the library, which is to ever increasing privatization, commercialism and what Susan Hildreth, as head of the library administration, admitted in an unguarded moment was "very self-service branches."

The Post-Occupancy Evaluation produced by city funds at a cost of $240,000 stated that the goals of the planner were not "congruent" with those who operate the building. This was reference to the fact that the planners were the private foundation or those controlled by the private foundation. Did anyone learn from that? No. The present incumbent Board of Supervisors has accepted a gift from the private foundation "Friends & Foundation" to pay for the planning. And the foundation hired their own consultant to be in charge of the planning–notorious privatization advocate Dallas Shaffer. We had frankly expected that this would be concealed until after the election, but they don't want for brazenness.

It is clear that a vote for Proposition A is a vote for privatization. Everyone who is against deception, waste, bad management, and privatization should vote against Proposition A: It should be unanimous.

Very truly yours,
James Chaffee

Free Money, Just Sign Here/ Or the Bill Gates Road Show Comes to SF
by James Chaffee

Free Money, Free Drugs, Free Lunch. If it is too good to be true, it probably isn't (true). The Post Office has a public education campaign to attempt to warn people against the dangers of fraud. People for the most part seem to know better: it is community governments (like San Francisco's) that need the education.

Bill Gates is offering free money and San Francisco was a willing taker. All San Francisco had to do was agree to put in Windows Internet terminals in each of 14 branch libraries. There were conditions, of course. The terminals must be used "exclusively for unmediated public access and for Internet connectivity." "Unmediated" is a term of art within the Gates Grant which means that there can be no differentiation as to the type of use. If someone wanted to use the card catalog, check an educational database, or check other catalogs for information that would lead to an interlibrary loan, they would have no more or no less priority than someone who wanted to check his e-mail, play a game, log into a chat room, or even find a porn site. This is a delicate issue, because libraries themselves are also "unmediated" and do not discriminate on type of use, but still the library builds a collection that it regards as "serious" in terms of what is important to collect and also conserve for the local community and for history, no matter how it is used. That is why librarians are professionals. The Internet has no such guiding principles.

The Gates Grant also requires that the terminals be Internet accessible. The Grant is for 101 terminals distributed 6 per branch and 17 at the New Main (in a "training lab" requiring designated space in an already overcrowded building). This Grant requires that San Francisco wire the branches for the high speed connectivity that makes for optimum use. The first two of the Gates branches that received this wiring were paid for with a supplemental appropriation that cost $291,678. North Beach branch got electrical renovations totaling $94,312. Richmond branch got electrical renovations totaling $197,366. (In addition, this was Prop. E money legally mandated for a priority of books and hours. But don't get us started.) Each of the branches received computers valued by the Gates Grant at $15,150.00. It does not take a rocket scientist to do the math. At the same rate San Francisco will spend over 2 million to upgrade 14 branches and the total Gates Grant is $227,250 (not including $35,650 for the "training lab").

Once Bill Gates puts up his $15,150 per branch, his part is over. But under the contract for the Grant, San Francisco keeps paying and paying. We have agreed to not only "operate and supply" those Windows Internet terminals using public funds, but also "to assure adequate public funding for the proper maintenance and eventual replacement" of the terminals, presumably forever. There are requirements to train the staff and the public, including sending staff to Seattle.

Once Bill Gates puts up his $35,650 for the "training lab" in the New Main, his part is over. But under the contract for the Grant, San Francisco agrees to designate space for that purpose in an already crowded building that has no room for books or for crucial staff offices. That training lab must be open for public access when it is not being used for training, which means that it requires staff monitoring at some expense. What is the value of this space in a New Main that cost San Francisco millions to build, will cost millions to fix, not to mention the millions to fix Brooks Hall and the infamous "support center" for overflow space proposed by the Prop. A bonds?

Now that we have gone through the statistics, what does it mean? San Francisco never went through a cost-benefit analysis to decide how many Windows Internet terminals it wanted. Many of those branches will only have room for "Gates" terminals. San Francisco never decided where "Internet connectivity" fit into its educational goals. All we know is that it was "free money." And it seemed like a "lot" of free money. But how much was it really in the context of the $48.8 million the public spent this year and the millions it has spent every year for the past 125 years–SFPL founded 1875–to create a library of books and reading? The public might have decided that it wanted to keep it that way . . . , but there was free money.

And how good a deal is this for Bill Gates? For an amount of money that is too small of him to notice he has converted a public institution into a showroom and training center for his personal get-rich-quick scheme. But will libraries and librarians be the same for us after their new role as Windows help desks swallows them up?

SAVE OUR LIBRARIES
P.O. BOX 190306, S.F. CA 94119
FOR INFORMATION PHONE [415] 705-0908

CYBERSPACE/ VIRTUAL LIBRARIES

Digital Libraries for All

Donny Smith

Introduction

Non-governmental organizations (NGOs) such as ATD Fourth World are leading providers of information access to the poorest people in the world. Fourth World has supplemented its street libraries with computers and Internet access. Despite many useful new technologies, there is no world-wide digital library movement that takes into account the needs of the poor.

Yet there are many exciting digital projects going on in the world. For instance, activist-scholar Giti Thadani spent two months in 1999 travelling through India documenting lesbian and gay histories on digital video. She is recording examples of lesbian iconography before they are covered up, mutilated, or removed from temples, and before important sites are flooded by dams (*Thadani, 1999*; Thadani, in *Smith, 1997a*). This erasure of lesbian past has a direct connection to the physical and economic well-being of Indian women. A patriarchal mythology is constantly being constructed which traps lesbians in compulsory, often violent, heterosexuality (*Thadani, 1996*, pp. 101–123) and traps all women in economic bondage to men (Nasim, in *Smith, 1997b*).

During her years of research, Thadani has worked with several NGOs in India, taking part in workshops with rural women activists on the materials she has uncovered (*Thadani, 1996*, pp. viii, 1). When asked what she expected the women to get from the workshops, she replied, "Another consciousness. How this affects the other world is difficult to say. In some case I've seen very positive changes; in others, hard to say, as the social realities are so diametrically opposite and one would need to have sustained collective projects to carry on the integration of what I am doing" (Thadani, in *Smith, 1997a*). Ideally, Thadani could maintain communication with activists over time through email, and the activists could access Thadani's extensive archives through the World Wide Web. However, even if the activists had electricity and a computer, in India poor phone lines prevent Internet access in many places (*Cheung, 2001, January 4*). As in other economically poor areas, information access of all kinds is difficult.

Street Libraries

Various groups have made small steps. For example, in rural India, some authorities have set up libraries to "educate people in local history, village traditions, methods of cultivation, public health, and the message of the freedom movement against British colonialism" (Kalpana Dasgupta, in *Kagan, 1999*). In some of the poorest neighborhoods of Manila, in a program sponsored by ATD Fourth World and UNESCO, students from the National University of the Philippines have set up libraries in the streets, "where both children and parents have access to knowledge without the routine of their daily lives being disrupted" (*UNESCO, n.d.*). Near the city dump in Tegucigalpa, Honduras, ATD Fourth World volunteers have set up street libraries that encourage children to go to school (*Jacot, 1999*).

The street library or sidewalk library, as practiced by the group ATD Fourth World, was inspired by Joseph Wresinski, a Catholic priest from a very poor family. He founded the Fourth World Movement in 1956, in a camp for homeless people in France. Living with families stuck deep in poverty, he "saw knowledge as the key, and sharing knowledge as an essential action against poverty." In 1968, he urged rioting students in Paris to put their ideas into action and "share their knowledge with children in

---

Revised version of an article that first appeared at http://www.geocities.com/smithi653/final.html dodgend, May 31, 2001.

the streets of the shanty towns" (*Tardieu, 1999*, pp. 291–295). The basic philosophy of the street library is *connection*, not just connecting the users with what's "out there" but with their own feelings and ideas and with each other, and further connecting the outside world back to them. A homeless man told Bruno Tardieu that "ignorance is a big suffering in two ways. First of all, it's not knowing what's going on in the world.... [And second,] Ignorance is to be ignored—that's even worse—ignored by the world" (*Bamberger & Tardieu, 1996*). Street libraries attempt to bring value back to their users—attention, respect, a means of communication, basic human dignity. The goal is not just to reintegrate the users with the money economy, but with the economy of culture and spirit.

Street libraries are very simple—some blankets or maybe plastic sheeting laid down on a sidewalk or on the ground; maybe chairs, a folding table, or some boxes; and books, usually just a few picture and easy-reader books; some paper, pencils, crayons, and scissors. Young children come and street librarians read to them and gradually draw them into learning. Eventually older siblings and parents become interested as well. "The street library is non threatening, it is a very flexible structure meant to be visible, open and fully in the hands by the community" (*Tardieu & others, n.d.*).

Digital Street Libraries

In the early 1980s, Wresinski began asking Fourth World workers with computing knowledge to introduce computers into the street libraries (*ATD Fourth World UK Ltd., n.d.*). Tardieu (*1999*) describes his experiences bringing a computer to poor neighborhoods in New York City. One of the first things he observed was that the PC truly is a *personal* computer; meant for one user only, it excludes anyone else who might be near (pp. 299–300). What they wanted was a CC, a *community* computer. What they came up with was specially written software called Tapori Databank, which the children could use to make an encyclopedia of their accumulated knowledge. A child could type a text about a specific topic or have others do the typing, then print out the text and add it to the encyclopedia. The children could also search the database by keyword to see what other children had written. By the end of the summer they had the *Tapori Encyclopedia*, a printed book and an electronic database of their writings. The neighborhood's excitement over the encyclopedia drew adults to this "digital street library."

Even for 1985, their technology was not up-to-date. They had a $150 Commodore computer with a black-and-white television for a monitor, cassette tapes instead of a disk drive, and a plotter instead of a dot-matrix printer, all powered by extension cords running to the street from neighbors' windows (pp. 289, 299–301). The chosen technology reduced everyone's fear of breaking the equipment, allowed users to participate in machine maintenance, and importantly, slowed everyone down. Since one of the goals of street libraries is to pay attention to *people*, the slow process of saving to cassettes and printing with a plotter actually allowed more time for personal interaction and provided a more concrete understanding of the technology. As one activist later pointed out, "while you may not have had the latest technology, you had appropriate technology" (Jud Dolphin, in *Bamberger & Tardieu, 1996*).

Introducing computers into the street library was an important step. ATD Fourth World considered computers as a new type of tool or even a language, one that could be used to exclude poor people once again or to connect them to the world. "We shall condemn generations of children and teenagers from deprived backgrounds if we leave them out of the next language, one that shall create bonds between people" (Wresinski, in *ATD Fourth World UK Ltd., n.d.*). Fourth World's surveys revealed great interest and excitement, but very little knowledge about what computers really were and what they could do. Children and adults alike saw computers as something magical, but also as sure avenues to economic success (*Tardieu, 1999*).

The main obstacle now to bringing computers into other street libraries will be the current limitations of personal computers. A street computer would need to be portable and cheap, simple enough to be maintained by untrained users, lean enough to rely on solar power, batteries, or unreliable electrical lines, and robust enough to withstand dust, moisture, and rough treatment for several years, hundreds or thousands of miles from technical support.

Networked Street Libraries

Street libraries were networked fairly early. In 1986, Bruno Tardieu and Vincent Fanelli were considering how to use a modem in the street libraries where they worked. Starting in 1988, Fourth World volunteers worldwide were brought into an email network. Denis Cretinon set up an experimental website linking street libraries all over the world (*Tardieu, 1999*, pp. 307, 309).

Certainly the technology exists to network street libraries. In Chile, infobuses with computers drive to isolated areas to provide Internet access (*Acceso Universal, n.d.*). The Enersol organization is providing solar-powered computers with solar-powered cellular Internet connections to students in rural Dominican Republic and urban Massachusetts. The plan is to connect the various groups of students in an environmental education program (*Enersol Associates, n.d.*). The Malaysian education ministry and a computing company are providing about 4000 e-books supported by wireless local area networks, mostly to schools in rural Malaysia. The e-books are readable with a sub-notebook, described as "a cross between a notebook and a personal digital assistant" (*Manecksha, 2001*). NGOs in Uganda have been running computers on solar-powered batteries and have linked to the Internet by radio as well as by phone (IDSNET, 1997). Creative combinations of cellular, wireless, or satellite telecommunications with solar power could overcome many infrastructure problems.

Even so, street libraries do not necessarily need to be connected to the Internet to be networked. Tardieu describes a situation in 1987 in which a family involved in a street library suddenly left the neighborhood and lost all ties with their friends. When he tracked them down, the first thing they asked was that he bring them the street library computer. When he did, they immediately looked up all their friends' writings (*Tardieu, 1999*, pp. 305–306). Street libraries without Internet access might rely on CDs or diskettes sent by courier or mail back and forth between computers. In Uganda again, small airplanes carry email printouts to NGOs in remote areas (IDSNET, 1997).

Truly Public Libraries

If the Internet is to be a democratic resource, access for *all* is necessary, and it must be multifaceted access, so that users "can be active makers and builders of knowledge, instead of the passive consumers they become as the target of other people's goods and information" (Bamberger, in *Bamberger & Tardieu, 1996*). Some of the answers are simple: volunteers with a few books, a blanket, and a computer. Others are more difficult. If rural and poor areas of the world are ever to have telephone and Internet access, the wealthier nations will probably have to provide funding. And more than money, volunteers and community leaders are needed to organize and teach people and to put pressure on national and local authorities.

One benefit the wealthier nations would get from supporting digital library projects is that poorer countries' libraries may provide a model for the survival of the rich countries' public libraries. People in the United States are spending less time in public spaces, interacting face-to-face with fewer people, neglecting their democratic institutions, and allowing their communities to dissolve; public libraries might not survive (*Schement, 1997*).

Poorer nations such as India may be "an unlikely place to support a viable Internet model," yet India has some of the world's leading software companies and engineers (*Cheung, 2001, January 4*). Even though India's Internet users are mostly young middle-class males, where popular cybercafes have been combined with the ideals of the street library, access to information and knowledge has exploded (*Cheung, 2001, January 10*; *FT Asia Intelligence Wire, 2001*; *Lobo, 2000*). In contrast, access for most in the United States has already exploded, leaving many public libraries struggling; and without public libraries, information access for those who lack it seems less and less likely. Many librarians are pushing to make their libraries active community centers, with meetings, special events, and of course Internet access. "If patrons think 'library equals community,' will they ever again think that 'library equals book' ten years down the road?" (John Guscott, in *St. Lifer, 2001*, p. 62).

Tardieu (*1999*) describes a library where people crowd together, learn, teach, and produce and exchange ideas—a truly democratic forum. There are many examples of library-like places that come close to this ideal:

- Anarchist and punk infoshops operate as community centers and bookshops, mostly in the United States and western Europe, often providing the only real alternative to inadequate public libraries (*Dodge, n.d.*).
- Community technology centers provide training and access to computers to people in low-income U.S. communities (*Office of Vocational & Adult Education, n.d.*).
- SisterNet Resource Centers in hair salons link African American women to information tailored to their needs and to the Internet (*Bishop, Bazzell, Mehra, & Smith, 2001*).
- Infoplazas, government-sponsored private cybercafes in rural and urban Panama, provide educational programs and Internet access (*SENACYT, n.d.*).
- The village radio station in Kothmale, Sri Lanka developed a "radio browsing" show on which listeners asked questions in person, by phone, or by mail; then announcers searched for answers on the Internet on the air. Soon the station developed into a community computing center (*Arnaldo, n.d.*).
- Private Internet kiosks provide low-cost access to distance education and the Internet in isolated parts of Indonesia (*Rusdiah, 2001*).
- Multipurpose community telecenters link rural villages in the Philippines to each other and to the national network and provide local language translation software (*PCHRD, 1999*).

- Cyber kiosks in Bangladesh expand on a program in which women take out microloans to buy cell phones and provide phone service to their villages (*Grameen Bank, n.d.*).

All of these efforts are fragile, however. If its website is an indication, SisterNet is having difficulty taking off (http://www.sisternet.org; no DNS entry, August 12, 2001). Funding dries up, leaders move away, old conflicts come to the surface. Various outside forces would prefer more bureaucratized or brick-and-mortar or corporatized institutions. Government officials resist: "You got to be crazy to think of giving cell phones to illiterate poor women in the villages who never saw a conventional telephone in their lives; she would not know how to dial a number; anyway who is she going to call?" (*Grameen Bank, n.d.*). All these projects require constant nurture to survive, but they are important. As Chris Dodge says about infoshops, they operate "as though human beings can make a difference through thoughtful analysis, hard work, and commitment" (*n.d.*).

Money

The economic barriers are huge, but surmountable. Garcia & Gorenflo (*1999*) point to rural telephone cooperatives in the United States in the early twentieth century as a model. Despite lack of corporate or government interest, groups of mostly poor farmers got together to purchase equipment, set up poles, and string wires. With small initial investments, collective work, and yearly subscriptions, they were able to provide phone service for their own communities. When the Great Depression threatened to bankrupt cooperatives, the federal government did provide support; however, it kept the cooperatives' structure as a model, especially when it established the highly successful Rural Electrification Administration. In some areas of the U.S., rural cooperatives are again forming to support Internet access, as they are in Latin America and Asia.

An important source of income for many poor communities is money sent home by those who have left to find work elsewhere. Scott Robinson (2000) proposes setting up microbanks in the home communities. If these banks could perform secure digital transfers of funds, transfer and exchange fees could be cut significantly, freeing capital for investment in the community. In addition, the microbanks' electronic infrastructure could support local telecenters, distance education programs, and even e-commerce. As an example of the sums involved, Robinson cites estimates that every year Mexicans in the United States send $8 billion to Mexico, losing an average of 20% for transaction fees. If fees could be reduced to 5%, losses would drop from $1.6 billion to $400 million annually.

Conclusion

What part do digital libraries play in this future? They'll be just one tool among many for education and communication. In some cases, digital libraries will be superfluous, in others essential. The key is that they should be available to all, part of a universal toolkit of knowledge. Some communities can afford a full range of tools now, some cannot. But the real lack is not technology—"the scarce resource here is not a machine" (Joe Ferreira, in Bamberger & Tardieu, 1996)—it is people who are able and willing to work on these problems. As Amatul Hannan puts it, "too much wealth and not enough compassion" (in Bamberger & Tardieu, 1996).

Kathleen de la Peña McCook (2001) and Bruno Tardieu (1999) argue in different ways that poverty is not just a lack of money, that poverty cuts people off from connection with others around them, from participation in their culture and their government—that in fact poverty works against democracy. Digital libraries can have a small role to play in easing the participation of poor people. As McCook asks, "What better service can librarians provide to poor people than to develop support for them at the beginning of a journey to full participation in democracy?" (p. 39).

Almost 20 years ago, K.J. Mchombu argued that librarians might have to expand their training and knowledge to be "closer to sociology and the economics of underdevelopment than to traditional librarianship" (1982, p. 243). He urged administrators to avoid the temptation of grand buildings and concentrate funds on "Small, cheap units, located close to where people actually live" (p. 250). What he wanted was not a library system as it was known then, but what he called an *Information Infrastructure* (p. 245), a flexible, inexpensive network of information centers and technicians, responding to locally identified needs—not providing library service on a model learned at a library school in a wealthy country.

To work, digital libraries for the poorer people of the world will have to be part of the coordinated efforts of traditional libraries, educational institutions, government agencies, NGOs, computing companies, and the people themselves. Today, however, there seems to be no coordination, and as Robinson (2000) points out, "no measurable impacts are yet to be observed in this hit or miss strategy." NGOs providing Internet access often concentrate solely on economic development; without the involvement of librarians, they may overlook the many other benefits of access. Corporations that donate hardware and software rarely make long-term commitments of support and have little interest in the truly free access that is libraries' ideal. Government agencies have their own political agendas in providing access and often fear community networks and organizations, since they are "a powerful counter-weight to authoritarian governments" (*Garcia & Gorenflo, 1999*).

On the other hand, library organizations have not been very active in providing services. I have found much discussion of outreach, class issues, and poverty in the library literature, but when I look at who is actually doing the work of bringing books and computers to the poorest people, it is economic development specialists. The only group I have found that has a long-standing and practical commitment to traditional and digital library service for all is ATD Fourth World. Libraries and librarians must become more active, offer their particular talents in information management, and provide the necessary leadership for a world-wide digital library movement. After all, access for all is the highest ideal of librarianship. "Is not the conception of equality of human beings and democracy itself endangered if some cannot participate in the public conversations that shape our social, political, economical, spiritual, cultural and intellectual lives?" (*Tardieu & others, n.d.*).

References

Acceso Universal. (n.d.). *Infobus.* Retrieved August 12, 2001, from World Wide Web: http://www.telecentro.cl/modelos/infobus.htm

Arnaldo, Choy. (n.d.). *Kothmale—a Sri Lankan cybervillage.* Kothmale Community Radio. Retrieved August 12, 2001, from World Wide Web: http://www.kothmale.net/kcrwebsite/english/analdostory.htm

ATD Fourth World UK Ltd. (n.d.). *Information superhighways for everyone.* Retrieved May 21, 2001, from World Wide Web: http://www.atd.demon.co.uk/org/infoways.htm

Bamberger, Jeanne, & Tardieu, Bruno. (1996, April 17). *Youth, education, and technology.* Session summary, Colloquium on Advanced Information Technology, Low-income Communities, and the City. Department of Urban Studies and Planning, Massachusetts Institute of Technology. Retrieved May 21, 2001, from World Wide Web: http://web.mit.edu/sap/www/colloquium96/summaries/bamberger_tardieu.html

Bishop, Anne Peterson; Bazzell, Imani; Mehra, Bharat; & Smith, Cynthia. (2001, April). Afya: social and digital technologies that reach across the digital divide. *First Monday*, 6 (4). Retrieved May 11, 2001, from World Wide Web: http://firstmonday.org/issues/issue6_4/bishop/.

Cheung, Eddie. (2001, January 4). Profiling Indian Internet users: part 1. *eAsia newsletter.* Retrieved May 1, 2001, from World Wide Web: http://www.emarketer.com/analysis/easia/20010104_india1.html.

Cheung, Eddie. (2001, January 10). Profiling Indian Internet users: part 2. *eAsia newsletter.* Retrieved May 1, 2001, from World Wide Web: http://www.emarketer.com/analysis/easia/20010110_india2.html.

Dodge, Chris. (n.d.). *Street libraries: infoshops and alternative reading rooms.* Retrieved May 21, 2001, from World Wide Web: http://www.geocities.com/SoHo/Cafe/7423/infoshop.html.

Enersol Associates. (n.d.). *Environmental education: sharing the tools, spreading the message.* Retrieved May 28, 2001, from World Wide Web: http://www.enersol.org/act-iee.html.

FT Asia Intelligence Wire. (2001, May 18). India: the digital divide. *The Hindu.* Retrieved May 28, 2001, from LEXIS-NEXIS Academic Universe online database: http://www.lexis-nexis.com/.

Garcia, D. Linda, & Gorenflo, Neal R. (1999, April). The *first mile of connectivity: rural networking cooperatives: lessons for international development and aid strategies. SD dimensions.* Food and Agricultural Organization of the United Nations (FAO). Retrieved May 29, 2001, from World Wide Web: http://www.fao.org/sd/CDdirect/CDre0033.htm.

Grameen Bank. (n.d.). *Bangladesh: bridging the digital divide.* Microcredit Summit Campaign. Retrieved May 29, 2001, from World Wide Web: http://www.microcreditsummit.org/press/grameen.htm.

IDSNET. (1997, August 26). (Two reports from Uganda.) International Development Studies Network. Retrieved August 3, 2001, from World Wide Web: http://www.idsnet.org/Papers/Technology/AruaEmail.html.

Jacot, Martine. (1999, March). ATD's streetwise librarians. *UNESCO courier.* Retrieved May 21, 2001, from World Wide Web: http://www.unesco.org/courier/1999_03/uk/dossier/intro42.htm.

Kagan, Alfred, ed. (1999, August). *The growing gap between the information rich and the information poor, both within and between countries.* Social Responsibilities Discussion Group paper, International Federation of Library Associations and Institutions. Retrieved May 2, 2001, from World Wide Web: http://www.ifla.org/VII/dg/srdg/srdg7.htm. (Reprinted in Sanford Berman and James P. Danky, eds., *Alternative library literature, 1998/1999: a biennial anthology,* pp. 293–300. Jefferson NC: McFarland & Co.)

Lobo, Avina. (2000, November 6). Taking IT to the villages. *ZDNet India.* Retrieved May 31, 2001, from World Wide Web: http://www.zdnetindia.com/weblife/features/stories/2033.html.

Manecksha, Ferina. (2001, May 14). Rural schools for e-book pilot project. *New Straits times—computimes.* Retrieved May 28, 2001, from LEXIS-NEXIS Academic Universe online database: http://www.lexis-nexis.com/.

McCook, Kathleen de la Peña. (2001). Poverty, democracy and public libraries. In Nancy Kranich, ed., *Libraries & democracy: the cornerstones of liberty,* pp. 28–46. Chicago: American Library Association.

Mchombu, K.J. (1982). On the librarianship of poverty. *Libri,* 32 (3), pp. 241–250.

Office of Vocational & Adult Education. (n.d.). *CTC questions and answers.* United States Department of Education. Retrieved May 28, 2001, from World Wide Web: http://www.ed.gov/o‡ces/OVAE/CTC/ctcqa.html.

PCHRD. (1999). *Multipurpose community telecenter.* Philippine Council for Health Research and Development. Retrieved

May 29, 2001, from World Wide Web: http://www.barangay-mct.org/.

Robinson, Scott S. (2000, November). Rethinking telecentres in the Second World: knowledge demands, remittance flows, and microbanks. *SD dimensions*. Food and Agricultural Organization of the United Nations (FAO). Retrieved August 5, 2001, from World Wide Web: http://www.fao.org/sd/CDdirect/CDre0055g.htm.

Rusdiah, Rudy. (2001, January 25). *The technical challenge from prespective of Indonesian SME—the Internet Kiosk Association—AWARI*. International Seminar on Integrating New and Traditional Information and Communication Technologies for Community Development, Kothmale, Mawatura, Sri Lanka. Retrieved May 29, 2001, from World Wide Web: http://communities.msn.com/BridgingtheDigitalDivide&naventryid=115.

St. Lifer, Evan. (2001, April 1). What public libraries must do to survive. *Library journal*, 126 (6), pp. 60–62.

Schement, Jorge Reina. (1997). Preface: of libraries and communities. In *Local places, global connections: libraries in the digital age*. Benton Foundation. Retrieved May 28, 2001, from World Wide Web: http://www.benton.org/Library/Libraries/preface.html.

SENACYT. (n.d.). *Infoplazas*. Secretaría Nacional de Ciencia, Tecnología e Innovación, República de Panamá. Retrieved May 29, 2001, from World Wide Web: http://www.senacyt.gob.pa/infoplazas/.

Smith, Donny. (1997a). Wholeness is possible, perhaps, only with very hard work: an e-mail interview with the author of *Sakhiyani: lesbian desire in ancient and modern India*. (Interview with Giti Thadani.) *Dwan*, 21, unpaged. (Also available from World Wide Web: http://www.geocities.com/dwanzine/dwan21.html#wholeness.)

Smith, Donny. (1997b). At least the *possibility* of lesbianism: a quick email interview with a queer scholar. (Interview with Nasim.) *Dwan*, 22, unpaged.

Tardieu, Bruno. (1999). Computer as community memory: how people in very poor neighborhoods made a computer their own. In Donald A. Schön, Bish Sanyal, William J. Mitchell, eds., *High technology and low-income communities: prospects for the positive use of advanced information technology*, pp. 287–313. Cambridge: MIT Press.

Tardieu, Bruno, & others. (n.d.). Including the excluded poor in democracy: constructing dialogue between all parents and school system. *CIAO working papers*. Columbia International Affairs Online. Retrieved May 21, 2001, from World Wide Web: http://www.columbia.edu/dlc/ciao/wps/tab01/.

Thadani, Giti. (1996). *Sakhiyani: lesbian desire in ancient and modern India*. London: Cassell.

Thadani, Giti. (1999). Letters to editor. *Dwan*, 26, unpaged.

UNESCO. (n.d.). Street libraries in Manila. *Worldwide action in education*. Retrieved May 21, 2001, from World Wide Web: http://www.unesco.org/education/educprog/brochure/011.html#03.

Donny Smith is a grad student at Drexel University and electronic reserves coordinator at Swarthmore College.

Blind-Sided By Amazon.Com

Barry Hoffman

I am the publisher of Gauntlet Press, a specialty press that publishes signed limited editions of classic titles (Ray Bradbury's *Something Wicked This Way Come*, Richard Matheson's *Somewhere In Time* to name just two) and the works of contemporary authors (F. Paul Wilson, Poppy Z. Brite, Peter Straub). We publish six signed limiteds per year and sell our books to individuals through our website and mailing list, specialty dealers and on Amazon.com. That was, until last week. In the past several months prior to a new title's publication I would go to the Publisher's page on Amazon.com and fill out a form to list our title as a Special Order. I would also forward a .jpg of the cover art. Once the book was listed (within a week) I could provide additional information (publisher's comments, reviews, interviews and author's comments). I decided the discount. Amazon.com paid for shipping. Orders came directly to me and I would ship the very next day. Aside from exposing the book to the world (we've received emails from Poland, Israel, Japan and Australia regarding books purchased on Amazon.com) a major benefit was getting paid up-front. With the purchase order was Amazon.com's credit card. No paperwork. No waiting thirty, sixty or ninety days for payment. It seemed almost too good to be true.

It was.

When I went to register a forthcoming title last week I wasn't able to list the title. Instead (and with no notice whatsoever) Amazon.com changed their policy. To be listed your title had to be carried by Ingram or Baker and Taylor (two of the largest distributors in the country). Or, you could opt for Amazon.com's Advantage Program.

So, what's the problem? Ingram, Baker & Taylor, as well as the Amazon.com Advantage Program takes a 55% cut (plus the publisher pays for shipping) on all titles. Ingram and Baker & Taylor have a return policy (they can return any book for any reason. Baker & Taylor can do so for six months, Ingram for as long as the title is in print). Ingram pays in 90 days, Baker & Taylor in 60 days.

The ramifications of this change in policy can be enormous not just for a specialty press like Gauntlet. Almost all small presses (whether their focus is on poetry, literary fiction the mass market won't touch, publishing new authors who have little name recognition or controversial material) will suffer and have to decide how to deal with this new dynamic.

The small/specialty press loses an incredible amount of money as a result of this policy change. When we could list as a Special Order the publisher determined the discount, whether it be zero, 10%, 20% or 30%. You looked at your costs and determined what discount to provide. Now, you automatically have to allocate 55% for the distributor. Take a book that sells for $40. With the discount you take in $18 per book. *Not* $18 in profit, mind you. There's the cost of printing (which can be steep for small print runs), shipping charges required by Ingram and Baker & Taylor, cover and interior art, advertising and ... oh, yes, the author's royalty. If a publisher clears $5 profit per book, they're lucky. Yes, those of us in the specialty press do so more for the love of books than money. But, we do have rent to pay and food to put on the table. With this new policy we're almost giving books away. Some publishers will be squeezed out with the reader the ultimate victim.

How does this change the way I evaluate a project? Well, I can't take a chance on an unknown author, nor many mid-list authors we've published in the past. And you can forget about anthologies unless a big name is attached. They are more expensive to produce (in a signed limited format).

How does this change book publishing in general? The mid-list author has already been squeezed out of the mass market. Many reinvigorated their careers through

---

Reprinted with permission from *Library Juice* (http://libr.org/Juice), v. 4, no. 19 (May 23, 2001).

the small or specialty press. The late-Richard Laymon was extremely prolific, but until the specialty press began publishing signed limited editions of his novels he was virtually unknown in this country. As a result of both critical and commercial success with his specialty press titles he had finally landed a mass market paperback contract. The specialty press will be reluctant to take on such projects if their profit-margin is cut to almost nothing. New, unknown authors will be hurt even more. They don't yet have a fan base. Price a book at $20 and *before* expenses you have to give the distributor $12. The publisher could well lose money on such titles.

But what about Amazon.com's Advantage Program, some will ask? With the Advantage Program Amazon.com basically acts as a distributor, like Ingram and Baker & Taylor. Check their guidelines. They take a 55% non-negotiable cut. They say the advantage is you can list publisher's comments, author's comments, reviews and interviews. But, when the Special Order option was available I could do that *without* paying 55%. Amazon.com will scan and display cover art. I scanned and forwarded Amazon.com cover art and it cost me nothing as a Special Order title. Look at the fine print and you see that a book *won't* be displayed until it's actually published under the Advantage Program. As a Special Order I was able to list a book six months prior to publication. Even Ingram and Baker & Taylor provide better service in this regard. They encourage you to list a book prior to publication. They list the book and then post it on Amazon.com. So, the publisher is stabbing himself in the foot by going with the Advantage Program. If a book generates pre-publication buzz (via galley proofs, reviews, advertising) numerous orders can be pending prior to the book's publication. One of the books we published received orders for over 100 copies from Amazon.com the day it saw publication as it had been listed for months on Amazon.com as a Special Order title and orders had already been taken. Being paid immediately allowed us to pay a good portion of our printing bill. With the Advantage Program you must wait *until* the book is physically available before it is listed. The Advantage Program doesn't pay for shipping. Again, the publisher must absorb this cost along with the 55% discount. And the publisher gets paid once a month through the Advantage Program. Better than the others distributors, but not as good as with a Special Order title.

So, what can and should be done? In the best of all worlds, there would be a great outcry from libraries and the specialty press, buttressed by organizations that provide services for this segment of the book community. The adverse publicity will force Amazon.com to rethink their decision and Special Orders will be reinstated.

There's also the compromise. When I spoke with a representative at Amazon.com I was told the reason for the change was the bottom line. Amazon.com wants to generate profits. I can sympathize. I want to generate profits for Gauntlet Press. Why not agree to allow listing of Special Order titles at a 20–30% discount? I could live with that. Amazon.com would profit, as well.

Although many people condemn Amazon.com for a variety of reasons, the company's relations with alternative and small press publishers until now have been very positive. They opened the world to books offered by small and specialty press publishers. They prepaid. There was no need to generate time-consuming paperwork. Now they've become just another distributor out to make a buck. Without immediate action the impact on specialty and small presses, as well as mid-list and unknown authors may well be devastating. And that is the bottom line.

Barry Hoffman is the publisher of Gauntlet Press (www.gauntletpress.com), editor/publisher of *Gauntlet* magazine, the only mass market publication focusing on censorship and is the author of four published novels, *Hungry Eyes*, *Eyes of Prey*, *Born Bad* and *Judas Eyes*. Gauntlet Press won the 1999 HWA award for Best Small Press. Hoffman was a nominee this year for the PEN/Newman's Own First Amendment Award for censorship of his novel *Born Bad*.

REPORT FOR PUNISHMENT
723 6150

17. On Electronic Civil Disobedience

by Stefan Wray

Paper presented to the 1998 Socialist Scholars Conference
Panel on Electronic Civil Disobedience
March 20, 21, and 22
New York, NY

I heartily accept the motto, -- "That government is best which governs least;" and I should like to see it acted up to more rapidly and systematically. Carried out it finally amounts to this, which I also believe, -- "That government is best which governs not at all;"
                         - Civil Disobedience, Henry David

Thoreau.

Civil disobedience has been part of the American political experience since the inception of this country. But today, as we enter the next century, we are faced with the possibilities and realities of different, hybrid, electronic forms of civil disobedience. A fusion of computer technology with the more traditional forms of American civil disobedience has created new electronic and digital varieties of CD that take place in cyberspace, on the Net, or in the matrix.

The term electronic civil disobedience is borrowed from a book by that same name. The Critical Art Ensemble's (1996) Electronic Civil Disobedience provides us with a useful benchmark or launch pad from where we can travel back to the historical practice of civil disobedience in the United States and travel forward to the imagined practice of civil disobedience in the near future. One thing is certain, we have only begun to realize the full potential of how computers will change political activism. Another thing is also clear; electronic civil disobedience will be part of this trajectory.

One hundred and fifty years ago, in 1848, the same year that the Communist Manifesto was published in Europe, Henry David Thoreau delivered a lecture titled "Resistance to Civil Government," which was later published as an essay called "Civil Disobedience." Thoreau's essay on civil disobedience emerged from his own personal refusal to pay a poll tax as an expression of his opposition to the United States' war against Mexico. (Thoreau 1968) Since Thoreau's time the tactics of civil disobedience have become woven into the fabric of dissent in this country, as individuals at the grassroots have continually attempted to participate in civil society.

Thirty years ago, in 1968, evolving out of the experience of activists in the Civil Rights movement, civil disobedience became an important and widespread tactic used by the opposition to yet another imperialist war, the United States' war against Vietnam. In 1971, as historian Howard Zinn describes, "twenty thousand people came to Washington to commit civil disobedience, trying to tie up Washington traffic to express their revulsion against the killing still going on in Vietnam. Fourteen thousand of them were arrested, the largest mass arrest in American history." (Zinn 1995, 477)

Throughout the 1970s and 1980s, the tactics of civil disobedience and direct action were taken up by a number of social movements. The anti-nuclear movement began to engage in mass civil disobedience starting in the mid 1970s - with large arrests at the Seabrook Nuclear Power Plant in New Hampshire - and continued using this tactic through to the end of the 1980s - with mass arrests at the Nuclear Test Site near Las Vegas, Nevada.

In the 1980s, the radical wing of the environmental movement, represented by groups like Earth First!, reinterpreted notions of civil disobedience in order to apply these tactics to rural and isolated settings where old growth forests were being devastated. Thoreau's ideas were brought to life again by authors like Edward Abbey, who paid him homage in an essay called Down The River with Henry Thoreau. (Abbey 1981)

Other radical groups, like ACT-UP, made sure that civil disobedience maintained an urban presence. Using shock tactics, such as forcing ones way onto the set of a live national news broadcast, ACT-UP activists pushed civil disobedience more in the direction of in-your-face politics as a way to emphasize the urgency of the AIDS crisis.

In an odd twist of irony, by the late 1980s and more so in the early 1990s, even groups on the right began to adopt tactics of trespass and blockade. The so-called "pro-life" movement started to physically block abortion clinics.

At the beginning of the 1990s, the Gulf War - or more appropriately the U.S. war against Iraq - was yet another moment in which opposition was expressed in acts of individual, small group, and mass civil disobedience. In the fall of 1990, a small group of 14 anti-Gulf War activists, mostly students from U.C. Berkeley and San Francisco State, occupied and held for several hours an Army Recruiting Center in San Francisco before being arrested. Also that fall, an adhoc coalition opposed to the war, called the Bay Area Direct Action Network, began to strategize about different ways to block building entranceways and highways. When the United States started to drop its "smart bombs" on Baghdad tens of thousands of people poured into the streets of San Francisco.

One notable action at this time was the occupation and blockage of the Bay Bridge that connects San Francisco to Oakland and Berkeley. Following a physical blockade that delayed the opening of the U.S. Federal Building in San Francisco, thousands of protesters started to march downtown toward the financial district. At the last minute, these protesters turned, took another route, and easily pushed pass the dozen or so Highway Patrol attempting to protect the bridge. This throng of people made it nearly all the way to Treasure Island, the mid-way point on the bridge, before being met with a massive show of force by the Oakland Police Department. While unreported by the mainstream media, similar acts of blocking government buildings and major highways occurred all up and down the west coast.

So, over the course of the last 150 years, since the publication of Thoreau's Civil Disobedience, we have seen the tactics of individual, group, and mass civil disobedience applied to varying degrees by a quite a number of social movements in the United States. In the second half of the twentieth century, civil disobedience has been practiced in every decade. Sometimes it has been successful. Other times it has failed. Given that the objective realities of U.S. society are not likely to alter radically any time soon, we can safely assume that radical social movements, in one form or another, will continue to adopt the strategies and tactics of civil disobedience into the 21st century.

But, in the next century, most of us will witness, and some of us will perhaps directly experience, a striking difference in the form and manner of civil disobedience. Unlike in Thoreau's time, when the telegraph had barely gotten off the ground, and even unlike during the tumultuous 1960s, when the Vietnam War was televised - but when computers were still monster-sized machines off limits to most people - we, today, live in the age of the personal computer. We live in a computer-based information age.

As hackers become politicized and as activists become computerized, we are going to see an increase in the number of cyber-activists who engage in what will become more widely known as Electronic Civil Disobedience. The same principals of traditional civil disobedience, like trespass and blockage, will still be applied, but more and more these acts will take place in electronic or digital form. The primary site for Electronic Civil Disobedience will be in cyberspace.

In the next century, for example, we on the left will witness or be part of an increasing number of virtual sit-ins in which government and corporate web sites are blocked, preventing so-called legitimate usage. Just as the Vietnam War and the Gulf War brought thousands into the streets to disrupt the flow of normal business and governance - acting upon the physical infrastructure - future interventionist wars will be protested by the clogging or actual rupture of fiber optic cables and ISDN lines - acting upon the electronic and communications infrastructure. Just as massive non-violent civil disobedience has been used to shutdown or suspend governmental or corporate operations, massive non-violent email assaults will shutdown government or corporate computer servers. Given the expected continued rapid growth and development of computer technology, and given the increasing knowledge, sophistication, and expertise of a growing body of cyber-activists, there is no telling exactly how electronic civil disobedience will play itself out in the future. But we can be certain that electronic civil disobedience will undoubtedly become an important element in the emergence of new radical social movements in the years ahead.

There are already examples now in existence of the theory and the practice of electronic civil disobedience, as well as evidence of government and corporate awareness of the potential threat posed by sophisticated cyber-activism.

To gain some understanding of emerging theory on Electronic Civil Disobedience it is probably best to first look at several short pieces by the Critical Art Ensemble. In 1994 the Critical Art Ensemble produced a work called The Electronic Disturbance and in 1996 they produced a sequel called, not surprisingly, Electronic Civil Disobedience. Both works argue that capitalism has become increasingly nomadic, mobile, liquid, dispersed, and electronic. Moreover, they argue that resistance needs to take on these very same attributes. Instead of physically blocking a building entranceway, or occupying a CEO's office, Critical Art Ensemble argues that we need to think about how we can blockade and trespass in digital and electronic forms.

Not only do these works by the Critical Art Ensemble begin to establish a language with which we can develop ideas about and continue to practice electronic civil disobedience, they also make a case that practicing electronic civil disobedience has become imperative because increasingly traditional forms of CD have become less and less effective. They argue that the streets have become the location of dead capital and that to seriously confront capital in its current mobile electronic form, then resistance must take place in the same location where capital now exists in greatest concentrations, namely in cyberspace. While the second part of the Critical Art Ensemble's argument makes sense, the statement that the streets are completely useless needs to be qualified. For example, we can not discount the role that street protest played in the collapse of the Soviet Union and the fall of the Berlin Wall in 1989. This adds credence to the notion that rather than pure electronic civil disobedience, we are likely to see a proliferation of hybridized actions that involve a multiplicity of tactics, combining actions on the street and actions in cyberspace.

The intellectual roots of the Critical Art Ensemble's work, especially in relation to their nomadic conceptions of capital and resistance, can be first traced to Hakim Bey's (1991) T. A. Z. The Temporary Autonomous Zone, Ontological Anarchy, Poetic Terrorism, who in turn borrows ideas about nomadology from Gilles Deleuze's and Felix Guattari's (1987) A Thousand Plateaus. Bey's temporary - and nomadic - autonomous zones, existing in cyberspace, become the launch pads from where electronic civil disobedience is activated. The influence of A Thousand Plateaus, especially the chapter called "Treatise on Nomadology and the War Machine," can be seen running throughout the Critical Art Ensemble's work. All of these works just mentioned should be required reading for the serious student and practitioner of electronic civil disobedience.

Besides examining hypothetical ideas in these theoretical works, we can actually see that incipient electronic civil disobedience has started to be practiced. One site for discovering such practice is within the global pro-Zapatista movement that has come into being since the January 1, 1994 Zapatista uprising in Chiapas, Mexico. Since just days after the emergence of the EZLN onto the global political scene, computers, and more specifically, computer-based communication over the Internet, primarily and originally in the form of email, have become key and central to the existence of this global Zapatista inspired movement against neoliberalism and for humanity. With each passing year, since 1994, the level of computer sophistication has increased. What began as mere transmission of EZLN communiques and other information via email became also a network of hypertext linked web sites. In borrowing another term from Deleuze and Guattari's A Thousand Plateaus - in addition to nomadic - the movement of information through these various cyber-nets of resistance has been said to have occurred rhizomatically, moving horizontally, non-linearly, and underground.

Rhizome is word that comes from botany and is used to describe certain types of tubers, that as a system of roots expands horizontally and underground. The adjective rhizomatic have been used in a political context as a way to describe the distribution, spread, and dispersion of information on the Net about the Zapatistas. Rather than operating through a central command structure in which information filters down from the top in a vertical and linear manner - the model of radio and television broadcasting - information about the Zapatistas on the Net has been said to be moving from node to node, horizontally and non-linearly. This is relevant in that the method of announcing and distributing information about electronic civil disobedience actions has occurred in this rhizomatic fashion.

For example, arising out of this increased cyber-activism around the Zapatistas, and following the recent Acteal Massacre that took place in Chiapas just this past December, a group calling themselves the Anonymous Digital Coalition, which we believe originated in Italy, began to post messages onto the Net calling for cyber attacks against five Mexico City based financial institution's web sites. The intent of their plan, which was promulgated far and wide via this rhizomatic system of distribution, was for thousands of people around the world to simultaneously load these web sites on to their Internet browsers. The idea was that repeated reloading of the web sites on to numerous people's browsers would in effect block those web sites from so called legitimate use. The only evidence available to me that this action worked is an email message I received from someone who said that they made repeated attempts to access these sites during the aforementioned time, but could not do so.

Another example is even more recent. Last month, when it looked as if the United States was going to launch another bombing campaign against Iraq, a national news story appeared describing how the Pentagon had allegedly noticed an increase in the number of hacking attempts into Department of Defense computers. Whether these cyber assaults are real or a figment of the Pentagon's imagination is irrelevant. The point is that this level of cyber-activism directed against a government institution is yet another potential scenario that we will in the future either be witnesses to or participants in.

As is to be expected, the roots of future government crackdowns against electronic civil disobedience already exist in the present. Since as early as 1993 there were warnings coming from RAND of impending netwar (Arquilla and Ronfeldt 1993). Soon thereafter, the U.S. military establishment began to worry about netwar or its more universal term, information warfare. In 1996, The Nation published an article describing a report produced by the Pentagon's office on Special Operations Forces in which they make recommendations to counter or contain possible netwar or information warfare.

But as attempts to prevent people from engaging in traditional civil disobedience have failed before or have at least not been universally successful, we can expect that whatever net the government creates in attempts to capture future cyber-activists will be strewn with holes and ways of evasion will be possible. One possible technical solution that will enable cyber-activists to flood government or corporate email servers - potentially to the point of these servers crashing - is the off-shore spam engine, a web-site form-based means of directing multiple email messages to targeted email addresses, anonymously.

To conclude. While it may be partially true, as the Critical Art Ensemble claims, that participation in street actions has become increasingly meaningless and futile and that future resistance must become primarily nomadic, electronic, and cyberspacial, it is doubtful that physical street actions, involving real people on the ground, will end any time soon. What is more likely is that we will see electronic civil disobedience continue to be phased in as a component of or as a complement to traditional civil disobedience. In the near future, we can expect to see hybrid civil disobedience actions that will involve people taking part in electronic civil disobedience from behind their computer screens while simultaneously people are engaging in more traditional forms of civil disobedience out in the streets.

As we consider the trajectory of resistance in the United States and as we envision the possibilities of resistance increasingly taking place in cyberspace, it is important to remember that civil disobedience has been an important part of the history of political growth and change in this country. Thoreau's contribution, by example and by word, influenced generations that followed. But today, we stand at a new crossroads, one in which these older forms of resistance and protest are being transformed. While it is useful to consider the path that civil disobedience has taken up until now, we also need to be aware that our political terrain is changing dramatically. In the 21st century, electronic civil disobedience will occur.

- End -

(Stefan Wray is a doctoral student in the Dept. of Culture and Communication at NYU. His dissertation research focuses on international grassroots political communication on the Internet. He received an M.A. in Journalism from the University of Texas at Austin. His masters thesis, "The Drug War and Information Warfare in Mexico" is available at http://www.nyu.edu/projects/wray/ You can send email to him at: sjw210@is8.nyu.edu)

The Ethics of Hacktivism

Abby Goodrum *and* Mark Manion

Introduction

In a civil society, it is the responsibility of all ethical individuals to take a stand against oppression, inequality, and injustice. Civil disobedience is a technique of resistance and protest whose purpose is to achieve social or political change by drawing attention to problems and influencing public opinion. Civil disobedience requires that individuals be willing to peacefully break laws that are unjust and be willing to suffer the legal consequences of their actions. It does not condone violent or destructive acts against its enemies, focusing instead on nonviolent means to expose wrongs, raise awareness, and prohibit the execution of unethical acts by individuals, organizations, companies, or governments. Breaking specific laws that are unjust constitutes direct acts of civil disobedience. Symbolic acts of civil disobedience are accomplished by drawing attention to a problem indirectly. Sit-ins and other forms of blockade and trespass are symbolic acts of civil disobedience. While the underlying principles of civil disobedience have not changed much over the course of the past 150 years, the tactics of civil disobedience have been continually influenced by available technologies.

Abby Goodrum, College of Information Science & Technology, Drexel Univrsity, 3141 Chestnut Street, Philadelphia, PA 19104-2875.
Mark Manion, Department of Humanities and Communications, Drexel University, 3141 Chestnut Street, Philadelphia, PA 19104-2875.

Electronic Activism & Civil Disobedience

The Internet has created a brave, new world of digital activism by providing forums for organizing, communicating, publishing, and taking action. The use of the computer as a tool of civil disobedience has been termed Electronic Civil Disobedience (ECD). Electronic civil disobedience comes in many forms, and ranges from conservative acts such as sending email and publishing web sites, to breaking into computer systems. A distinction must be made between the use of computers to *support* ECD, and the use of computers as an *act* of ECD. If a US citizen wishes to speak out against the government's actions in Kosovo, it is legal to publish a web site or host mailing lists or chat rooms for this purpose. This activity does not constitute an act of civil disobedience; electronic or otherwise. Running a program such as FloodNet that posts the reload command to a web site hundreds of times a minute is also not against the law but it may constitute an act of ECD since the intended aim of such programs is to create an electronic disturbance akin to a sit-in or blockade. The effect of hundreds of persons reloading a targeted page on the web thousands of times effectively blocks entrance by outsiders and may even shut down the server. In 1998, pro-Zapatista activists took this action against Mexican Government web sites (Cleaver, 1998). This is easily seen as a symbolic act of ECD. The purpose of most ECD is to disrupt the flow of information into and out of institutional computer systems. The point is not to destroy information or systems, but to block access temporarily. This results in virtual sit-ins and virtual blockades. Since institutions today are no longer localized in physical structures but exist in the decentralized zones of cyberspace, electronic blockades can cause financial stress that physical blockades cannot. These activities in large part are not undertaken anonymously and seldom result in reprimands let alone arrests. Taken to an extreme, ECD has been interpreted to mean breaking into a computer system for the purpose of altering information and/or leaving political messages. In contrast to other forms of ECD, these acts of hacktivism are almost exclusively anonymous and have been prosecuted as felonies.

Hacktivist groups such as the Electronic Disturbance Theater, the Cult of the Dead Cow, and the Hong Kong Blondes, have used electronic civil disobedience to help advance the Zapatista rebellion in Mexico, protest nuclear testing at India's Bhabba Atomic Research Centre, attack Indonesian Government websites over the occupation of East Timor, as well as protest anti-democratic crackdowns in China. In addition, hacktivism has been used to inveigh against the corporate domination of telecommunications and mass media, the rapid expansion of dataveillance, and the hegemonic intrusion of the "consumer culture" into the private lives of average citizens.

Hacktivism has the potential to play an active and constructive role in the overcoming of political injustice, to educate, inform and be a genuine agent of positive political and social change. However, there is the fear that cyber-activism could transform into more radical and violent forms of cyber-terrorism (Arquilla and Ronfeldt, 1993). How governments and societies react to this new form of social activism has not been sufficiently addressed in the computer ethics literature. Researchers concerned with ethical issues in computing, policy makers, and computer professionals must come to terms with the complex set of issues surrounding the potential power of hacktivism.

The Relationship Between Hacktivism and Civil Disobedience

Nothing has fired debate about ECD so completely as the issue of hacktivism. In order to justify hacktivism's direct action praxis and to legitimate its theoretical foundations, two things must be demonstrated. First, it must be shown that hacktivism is *not* the work of teenagers with advanced technical expertise and a thirst and curiosity for infiltrating large computer networks for mere intellectual challenge or sophomoric bravado. In addition, the justification of hacktivism entails demonstrating that its practitioners are not cyber terrorists—breaking into systems for profit or vandalism. Hacktivism must be shown to be politically, i.e., ethically motivated. Second, politicized hacking must be shown to be a form of civil disobedience. The central question of whether hacking can reasonably be defined as an act of civil disobedience revolves around five basic tenets that have generally defined civil disobedience:

- No intentional damage done to persons or property
- Non-violent
- Not for personal profit
- Ethical motivation
- Willingness to accept personal responsibility for outcome of actions

May the same points be taken as evidence of hacking as an act of ECD? In order for hacking to qualify as an act of civil disobedience hackers must be clearly motivated by ethical concerns, be non-violent, and be ready to accept the repercussions of their actions. Examined in this light, the hack by Eugene Kashpureff clearly constitutes an act of ECD. Kashpureff usurped traffic from InterNIC to protest domain name policy. He did this non-anonymously and went to jail as a result. Similarly, members of the Electronic Disturbance Theater use their own names and emphasize disrupting Internet traffic rather than altering sites or crashing servers. Further evidence of an ethical motivation underlying hacktivism can be found in an examination of the style and messages left behind at hacked sites.

On October 12, 1998, the website of Mexican president Ernesto Zedillo was attacked. From all accounts, the Zedillo attack was not the work of bored teens. It was a political act, according to the Electronic Disturbance Theater, to "demonstrate continued resistance to centuries of colonization, genocide, and racism in the western hemisphere and throughout the world" (Wray, 1998). In August of the same year, the hacktivist group X-Ploit hacked the website of Mexico's finance ministry, defacing it by replacing the contents with the revolutionary hero Emiliano Zapata, in sympathy with the Zapatista rebellion in the Chiapas region of southern Mexico (Cleaver, 1998). These acts are protests that are drawing attention to what is perceived to be grave social injustices. One thing is clear: they are motivated by a socio-economic system that perpetuates discrimination, racism, and economic inequality — not the mere thrill and challenge of breaking into networks for fun.

In June of 1998, the hacktivist group MilwOrm hacked India's Bhabba Atomic Research Centre to protest against recent nuclear tests. In July of that year, MilwOrm and the group Astray Lumberjacks orchestrated an unprecedented mass hack of more than 300 sites around the world, replacing web pages with anti-nuclear statements and images of mushroom clouds. Not surprisingly, the published slogan of MilwOrm is "Putting the power back in the hands of the people" (Glave, 1998a). This appears to be more motivated by belief in the force of participatory democracy than mere vandalism or cyber-terrorism.

Several Indonesian government web sites were hacked to protest the targeting of Chinese and Indonesian citizens for torture, rape, and looting during the anti-Suharto riot in May of 1998. On August 1, the Portuguese hacktivist group Kaotik Team hacked 45 Indonesian government websites, altering pages to include calling for full autonomy for East Timor and the cessation of the harsh military crackdown on dissidents (Hesseldahl, 1998). Again, fighting for social justice and human rights is motivated by ethics, not anarchy. Many other hacktivist activities can be cited to demonstrate the ethical motivation behind this new form of political activism. These messages demonstrate a striking change from hacker attacks of the past. Prior hacks have had little, if any, socio-political content, and bear a closer resemblance to "tagging" and other forms of boasting graffiti. There has been a certain juvenile style to messages left by hackers in the past, but the hacks discussed above represent a new breed of hacker — one motivated by the advancement of ethical concerns. Hence, one can conclude that our thesis — that hacktivism is ethically motivated and constitutes an act of civil disobedience — can be clearly established.

The Law and Civil Disobedience

Historically, our legal system evolved in order to protect narrow economic interests, rather than administer to broader social concerns. Civil disobedience, therefore, is treated as a philosophical or political action, not a legal right, and is subject to penalty. How much penalty? Demonstrators or civil disobedients are commonly charged with disorderly conduct, trespass, or resisting arrest. Occasionally, protestors are charged with more serious crimes, which can include assault, rioting, and racketeering. If property damage occurs, protesters may be charged with criminal mischief, which is defined as "intentionally interfering with the lawful use, enjoyment or operation of property" (Herngren, 1993).

So, if civil disobedience compels us to accept the penalties for our actions, and if the law does not recognize civil disobedience as a legal right to break the law, one would expect sentences to be quite harsh. In fact, courts have considerable discretion in deciding how high a fine or how long a jail sentence to impose on those convicted of acts of civil disobedience. In most cases the courts have not pursued criminal sanctions against civil dissidents, and in so doing have informally established that penalties for civil disobedience should be lessened due to the ethical motivation supporting the action.

In contrast to older forms of civil disobedience such as trespass and blockade, hacking has not yet been recognized as a political activity having ethical motivations. Consequently, the penalties for breaking into computers can be extreme (Jaconi, 1999). For example, the hack of China's "Human Rights" website by the Hong Kong Blondes, attacks on Indian Government websites regarding policy in Kashmir, and on India's nuclear weapons research center websites to protest nuclear testing are all subject to felony prosecution if the perpetrators are apprehended. It is important to remember that in many countries any form of protest against the government is a capital offense. Seen in this light, the predominantly anonymous nature of hacktivism can perhaps be understood.

Penalties for hacktivism are meted out with the same degree of force as for hacking in general, regardless of the motivation for the hack or the political content of messages left at hacked sites. In fact, since many acts of hacktivism have been perpetuated against government websites, hacktivism is increasingly being equated with acts of information warfare and cyber-terrorism (Kovacich, 1997, Furnell & Warren, 1999). Under U.S. law, terrorism is defined as an act of violence for the purpose of intimidating or coercing a government or civilian population. Hacktivism clearly does not fall into this category, since it is fundamentally non-violent. Nevertheless, in August of 1998, the Center for Intrusion Control was established by a coalition of various government agencies to respond to these "cyber-warfare threats" (Glave, 1998b). Similarly, organizations such as RAND and the NSA have categorically ignored the existence of hacktivism as an act of civil disobedience and repeatedly refer to all acts of hacking as info-war or info-terrorism in an attempt to push for stronger penalties for hacking regardless of ethical motivations (Bowers, 1998; Gompert, 1998).

Power, Property, and Computerization

One rationalization for the vilification of hacktivism is the need for the power elite to rewrite property law in order to contain the effects of the new information technologies (Halbert, 1997). As a result of the newly evolving intellectual property laws, information and knowledge can now be held as capital. Since new information technology supports easy reproduction of information, the existence of these laws effectively curtails the widest possible spread of this new form of wealth. Unlike material objects, information can be shared widely without running out. Therefore, the intellectual-property laws help create a distribution of wealth that is unnecessarily limited.

Moreover, financial and banking institutions have gone digital, converting money itself into pure information. Traditional, sedentary forms of power and tangible capital are being replaced by capital constituted in electronic form that is fluid, mobile, and dispersed (Critical Art Ensemble, 1994). The result is the concentration of wealth in the hands of those most skilled at the appropriate manipulation of symbols. Hence any resistance to this power must take this fluidity, mobility, and dispersion into consideration; effective resistance must mirror these attributes.

The changing nature of authoritative and repressive power has necessitated qualitative changes in resistance to this power. Power/Capital, having constituted itself in a new electronic form in cyberspace, requires that opposition movements have to invent new strategies and tactics that counter this new nomadic power of capital. This entails that certain old ways of trespass and blockade — such as street demonstrations are being modified through hacktivism to meet the new conditions (Critical Art Ensemble, 1996).

The commercial control of computers and information technology will deepen class divisions nationally and internationally, as people divide into those who can afford the technology, services, and content — the information rich — and those who cannot — the information poor. The promise of freedom from work, participatory democracy, and global community, once hailed as the hallmarks of the computer revolution are nowhere to be found. The only entities that seem to benefit from the computer revolution are large transnational business corporations.

Technophilic Optimism v. Technophobic Pessimism

Every technology releases opposing possibilities towards emancipation or domination, and information technology is no different. This conflict is often couched as a distinction between two worldviews: technophilic optimism and technophobic pessimism. For technophiles, technology is the ultimate liberator of human freedom: freedom from the vicissitudes of nature and freedom from political oppression. Computer technology is seen as the utopian promise of total human emancipation and freedom. For technophobes, on the other hand, advanced technology may lead to an Orwellian nightmare of totalitarian domination and control or the dystopian nightmare of complete repression of free thought and behavior control. The Internet has been subordinated to the predatory interests of the techno-elite, who merely pay lip service to the growth of electronic communities and teledemocracy. These interests are devoted to shutting down the anarchy of the Net in favor of virtualized commercial exchange. The power elite must destroy the public cyber-sphere for its own survival. That is why the charges against hacktivism are so high.

Participatory Democracy and Participatory Technology

Computerization fosters great individual empowerment. One example is the hacktivist claim that a single individual can be as powerful as an entire government agency in effecting change. This requires that every person be a participant, creator, and producer rather than just a consumer of information. Active participation in information democracy leads to the creation of a more informed citizenry, and the reinvention of institutional functions and services (Friedland, 1996).

Hacktivism can affect changes in the democratic process through "disintermediation," or the elimination of control over communication by traditional intermediaries. These institutions have historically monopolized access to the flow of information and knowledge to the rest of society. The marriage of hacktivism to participatory democracy leads to (1) the empowerment of individuals — participatory democracy, (2) the breakdown of barriers — participatory pluralism, and (3) disintermediation of channels of communication — direct democracy.

Proposals

The following four proposals are presented in defense of an ethic of hacktivism.

1. Hacktivism, in its advocacy of civil disobedience, demonstrates the necessary relationship between ethics and politics. Computerized activism and electronic civil disobedience offer the potential for civic input into the political

process that is at once empowering and challenging. The role of civil disobedience is to act as an ethical check and outlet against governmental and corporate wrongdoing.

2. Establishing the validity of grass-roots activism reinforces the potential of computerization for civic empowerment. Resistance to the oppressive and unjust use of information technology, based on sound ethical principles and rooted in some sense of moral revolution, is not only possible, but also necessary. The multiplicity of tactics and forms of resistances of hacktivism attests to this.

3. The debate over control of intellectual property demands that we address issues of social justice such as wealth distribution and equality of opportunity. Politically, the resistance to domination must force not only the question of privacy and property, but it must also place the critique of the technological society itself at the center of pubic consciousness and debate. Hacktivists must put the issue of techo-control on the political agenda, laying out as clearly as possible the costs and consequences of computerized technologies. They must force awareness of the principle beneficiaries of the new technology and try to make public all the undemocratic ways they make the technological choices that affect us all. This will demonstrate the necessity for direct citizen participation in technology policy making.

4. Information technologies must not be conceptualized as mere neutral tools that can be used for good or evil; they must be understood as exhibiting an internal logic, a logic that bears the purposes and the values of the economic system that spawns them. Hacktivism, with its focus on pluralism, relativism, and pubic control of information and technology, reinforces and legitimates a "social constructivist" reading of (future) technological progress.

Conclusion

The power elite, often synergistically intertwined with the design and operation of information technologies, will always come to the aid and defense of technologies of control, making revolt difficult and reform hard. Intellectual Property laws attest to this, as do the excessively stringent laws against hacking. Nevertheless, if we say that we support civil disobedience and the power of people to organize themselves collectively for non-violent change, then we must support the computerization of these efforts as well. This means bringing penalties for hacking as an act of civil disobedience in line with penalties for traditional mechanisms for trespass and blockade.

Philosophically, resistance to political repression and oppression must be embedded in a well-articulated theory, one that is morally informed, and widely shared. Movements acting out of rage and outrage often dissipate. They need to be durable and sustain a commitment lasting through adversities of repression. This leads to the necessity of creating a form of technocultural activism and practice that can bring to reality the ideals of human emancipation. Activism today is no longer a case of putting bodies on the line; it requires and involves putting minds and virtual bodies on-line. This is the promise of combining the political consciousness of the activist with the technical expertise of the hacker — the promise of hacktivism.

References

Arquilla, J. and Ronfeldt, D. (1993). Cyberwar is coming. *Comparative Strategy, 12, 2,* 141–165.

Bowers, S. (1998, August). Information warfare: The computer revolution is altering how future wars will be conducted. *Armed Forces Journal International,* 38–39.

Cleaver, H. (1998). The Zapatistas and the electronic fabric of struggle. (accessed 5/18/99). http://www.eco.utexas.edu/faculty/Cleaver/zaps.htm

Critical Art Ensemble. (1996). *Electronic civil disobedience and other unpopular ideas.* Brooklyn, NY: Autonomedia.

Critical Art Ensemble. (1994). *The Electronic Disturbance.* Brooklyn, NY: Autonomedia.

Friedland, L. (1996). Electronic democracy and the new citizenship. *Media, Culture & Society, 18,* 185–212.

Furnell, S. & Warren, M. (1999). Computer hacking and cyberterrorism: The real threats in the new millennium. *Computers & Security, 18,* 28–34.

Glave, J. (1998a). Crackers: we stole nuke data. *Wired News* <http://wired.com>

Glave, J. (1998b). Hacker raises stakes in DOD attacks. *Wired News* <http://wired.com>

Gompert, D. (1998, Autumn). National security in the information age. *Naval War College Review, 51,* 4, sequence 364, 22–41.

Halbert, D. (1997). Discourses of danger and the computer hacker. *The Information Society, 13,* 361–374.

Harmon, A. (1998, October 31). Hacktivists of all persuasions take their struggle to the web. *New York Times,* 1.

Herngren, P. (1993). *Path of resistance: The practice of civil disobedience.* Philadelphia: New Society Publishers.

Hesseldahl, A. (1998). Hacking for human rights? *Wired News* <http://wired.com>

Jaconi, J. (1999). Federal Cybercrime Law, Section 1030 "Computer Fraud & Abuse Act. (accessed 6/17/99). <http://www.antionline.com>

Kovacich, G. (1997). Information warfare and the information systems security professional. *Computers & Security, 16,* 14–24.

Wray, S. (1998). Electronic civil disobedience and the world wide web of hacktivism: A mapping of extraparliamentarian direct action net politics. (accessed 2-22-99). http://www.nyu.edu/projets/wray/wwwhack.html

Local Cyber-Activism in the Age of Globalization: Lessons and Perspectives for Organizers

Martin Eder

The newspaper headline was a grabber, "Battle of Seattle Blazed by High-tech Tools: Hints of new-era Protests." Yes, I can say that my participation in Seattle was due in part to the extraordinary Internet communications, that organizers used to spread the word, exchange documents, make decisions, promote events and speak to the press. But as one of the leaders of a cyber-activist project, I want to both sing the praises of the new technology and sound the warning, that technology means little without traditional organizing on a personal and collective level.

Technology and the Internet are exceptionally powerful organizing tools. Yet we must remember that these are just the newest tools of our trade—not the panacea to replace grassroots organizing. Perhaps there have been social-justice activists who were convinced that the emerging technology of the printing press, newspapers, photography, radio, the telephone, video cameras, fax machines or the home computer would revolutionize and democratize information sharing. We must realize that technology will more likely be used to indoctrinate, monopolize and maintain the existing power structure than change it. Having said that I can not help, but express my enthusiasm for cyber-activism and its potential.

Activist San Diego: Cyber-activism with a Handshake

A bit more than a year ago ActivistSanDiego.org (thanks in part to a grant from RESIST) was born as a local communications and networking project to keep the left-progressive community informed about each others activities. Many wonderful websites serve national causes, national campaigns and national networking. Activist San Diego is one of the organizations at the forefront of creating *local* models of cyber activism as part of a comprehensive strategy to invigorate grassroots mobilization and communications. ASD arose out of the perceived need to have a common and centralized place to get and distribute information. While planning emergency response mobilizations to oppose the bombing of Iraq, local activists wondered how to let each other know where and when to meet if and when the atrocities began. A local web page, updated daily, best met the need. The beauty of the web and the Internet is that you can transfer massive amounts of vital information to huge numbers of people at virtually not cost. Synchronous and asynchronous conversations can occur to keep everyone in a group informed and involved. As the Zapatistas showed, it is possible to reach across the world creating solidarity to combat corporate globalization.

If we want to build the left-progressive movement it must ultimately be done at the local level where indi-

---

Expanded version of "Local Cyber-Activism Takes Off," *Resist* (259 Elm Street, Somerville, MA 02144), v. 9, no. 1 (August 2000), pp. 6–7. Reprinted with permission.

viduals and groups can organize face to face and join in collective action. The www.ActivistSanDiego.org web site was eventually built to serve a comprehensive set of *local* functions:

- A centralized activist calendar merged from Peace, Cultural, GLBT and Environmental calendars. While ASD administers it, anyone can post onto it.
- Web pages for Action Alerts, Events, General Info and Volunteers.
- An easy and automated "build-your-own-page" to post Alerts, events, announcements, etc.
- An Activist Directory listing organizations, contact info, meeting times, etc. (very much a work in progress)
- Listing of resources for activists and links to national and international groups and causes.
- A network of activist-partner organizations.
- And most recently a cyber-media center has been initiated.

Without continual and effective outreach few activist websites will develop a sizable audience. After handing out thousands of pieces of printed literature at rallies and events we got a flurry of visits to the site, but these diminished quickly without follow-up. We learned two primary lessons. First, cyber-activists must regularly contact their constituency to give them reason to visit the site. Our method is to send out an Activist e-Zine every week with dozens of Internet hot links back to our information-rich web site. Rather than filling up people's email boxes with full descriptions of many events, we send subscribers what is essentially a list of events, campaigns and causes that are described in greater detail on the site. ASD's e-Zine reaches about 1400 local activists every week and has begun to increase participation in local events.

Second, we have relearned learned the age-old lessons of grassroots organizing—nothing substitutes for personal contact and follow up. We created ASD as a cyber community center until we can get into a physical space. Those of us in the social justice movement are really hungry for a genuinely supportive community. Organizer and member must meet, share and socialize together. The Internet can be glitzy, but when push comes to shove the Web is not huggable.

The Downsides of Cyber-Activism: The Digital Divide

ASD in no longer just a cyber-activist project. Again cyber-activism is an aspect of grassroots communications and mobilization, not a substitute for it. ASD feels accomplished sending out 7500 emails to self-identified activists, but have we genuinely made a difference? Email is the most impersonal of all human communications and the easiest to ignore. Even most skeptical progressives will not throw away an unopened envelope, but we do not think twice about trashing email. Combining email with letters and phone calls on priority campaigns produces results. We have potluck dinner meetings with our members. We get commitment when we talk to people. Less than on in a hundred will respond to an email plea for monetary support, one in three will help us when asked by phone.

The primary challenge of cyber-activists relates to the digital divide. Crossing the color line has traditionally been the most important task facing the US left. It is even more crucial among cyber-activists. Technical elitism spells death. We must be ever cognizant that our fundamental mission is to empower the disenfranchised—immigrants, working classes, communities of color, the disabled, youth and the elderly—the very constituencies which have the slowest computers or no access to emerging technologies. ASD works to meet that challenge by seeking activist board and advisory board members from diverse communities to build connections to those sectors. We are also seeking funding to network the leading organizations and individuals. We also believe that concentrating our efforts among youth will help bridge the divide. It will be the computer-savvy youth alongside community organizers, who will bring these tools into new sectors.

The potential of the Internet as an organizing tool is unbelievable. ASD has tested the waters of streaming video and producing Internet radio. Eventually all of us will have tools, which can catapult us into radio and TV broadcasting without having to buy a transmitter. We could potentially deliver specially created news programs to activists. We could build universities without laying a brick. We will be able to have live meetings with video and audio with solidarity groups anywhere in the world. But for every democratic potential there will be the stronger pull of monopolization of the technology from government or corporations. Our ultimate power still lies in collective action and organization. New technologies will always be tools, just tools.

The vision of Activist San Diego is to create a collaborative software package with others, software which would allow activists in any city to set up a site and not have to worry about the technology. It would take a huge chunk of change, but it is possible. We dream of ActivistBatonRouge.org, ActivistAlbuquerque.org and ActivistYourHomeTown. Technological problems are eating up our organizing time, but they have also launched us into a leading role in our city. Eventually we think we could be communicating with 5–10% of the region's population, some 200,000 progressives.

"All politics is local" but the context must be global. Our task is to make the emerging technologies serve the people.

Martin Eder is the Director of ActivistSanDiego.org He is an educator, former union organizer and student organizer.

A Model of Cyber Volunteerism

Martin Eder

San Diego is the sixth largest city in the US and strategic in the sense that is at the busiest crossroad on the globe between the 1st and 3rd world. Activist San Diego is an organization whose mission is to fertilize the grassroots efforts of 100 other non-profit organizations through communications networking, training and information sharing.

One of our projects is the www.ActivistSanDeigo.org web site, which serves as the primary community calendar, and activist directory for the region. We believe that we are these nations' leading example of Cyber activism at a LOCAL LEVEL and we want to create a model that can be used by other organizations throughout the country.

During the coming year ASD will concentrate on bridging the digital divide by reaching out to youth of color to draw them into community service. As technology catapults some ahead it can leave others behind. ASD believes that the youth will be the best vehicle to bring new technologies and communications into distressed communities. In the year 2000 we will work to educate and mobilize youth to participate in volunteerism and to work for social justice.

The Purpose and Work of Activist San Diego

"Activist San Diego is a regional social justice network. ASD has set out to create America's leading example of cyber-networking to build a community of social activism and volunteerism at the local level. ASD provides an interactive Community Calendar, Action Alerts, free build-your-own-web-page, and weekly E-Zine. Activist San Diego links people who want to make a difference to local organizations. ASD promotes events and campaigns, which encourage civic involvement. With a rapidly growing network of more than 1000 community subscribers, Activist San Diego has set out to change the local landscape through grassroots participation."

Please contact us if you are interested in supporting this pilot project.

Sincerely,
Martin Eder
Activist San Diego Director
619-226-3336

Look What Activist San Diego Has Done in Two Years!

With your help think what we could do next year?

Cyber Activism:
- Set up one of the nation's leading cyber-activist project tied to LOCAL grassroots activism.
- Become progressive–San Diego's best source of organizing information.
- Advertised over 680 different political, cultural, ethnic, training events.
- Sent out over 78,000 e-newsletters, action alerts and informational emails to local subscribers.

Grassroots Activism:
- Spearheaded protest against the senseless shooting of an unarmed homeless man.
- Supported and mobilized to support Justice for Janitors and immigrant hotel workers.
- Co-sponsored GreenPeace's visit to SD against GMOs & "Franken Foods."
- Initiated the Coalition for Affordable Public Power—for green alternatives, exposing fraud.

Globalization:
- **Seattle** ~ had numerous members on the streets of this historic anti–WTO event.
- **Washington DC** ~ helped mobilize & network SD anti–IMF participants.
- **Los Angeles** ~ helped train and mobilize against corporate control of political parties.
- **Tijuana** ~ Helped build a bi-national festival anti-globalization in TJ and April 21st FTAA.

Partnerships:
- Formed partnerships with many of San Diego's leading activist organizations in the areas of labor, environment, peace, immigrant, police brutality, youth, racial & gender equality.
- Became a core member of the Youth Organizing Network for racial justice.
- Supported UCAN and others protesting rip-off utility rate hikes.
- Supported the Environmental Health Coalition & Peace Resource Center to stop environmental racism and homeporting of more nuclear carriers on the bay.
- Supported the Youth Organizing Network to protest the criminalization of more youth of color.
- Building Activist offices at the World Beat Center to help unite progressive culture & activism.

Training:
- Co-sponsored two multi-day Action Camps in preparation for major public mobilizations.
- Helped bring puppets, banners and color to numerous demonstrations.
- Committed to enhancing communications & organizing strength of local groups.
- Helped bring in more activist participation into our local social justice movement.

Media Recognition:
- Been featured in the local newspaper, the Reader and in the Nation magazine.
- Had our members interviewed on local TV on homeless, women's and utility issues.

~ You are Activist San Diego ~

Won't you *send a pledge today* so that we could double this list next year?

Send donations to: Activist San Diego, 4581 Alhambra St. San Diego, CA 92107 ~ (619)226-1116

Index

AACR (Anglo-American Cataloging Rules) 14, 100, 161
ABA (American Booksellers Association) meetings 39
Abbey, Edward 201
Abbreviations (cataloging) 14
Abolitionist periodicals 122
Abortion media coverage 70
Academic library collection development 47
Academic Press ownership 107
Accion International 115
ACLU CIPA-overturn suit 76
AcqWeb's directory of publishers and vendors (web site) 126
ACT-UP 201
Acteal Massacre (Chiapas, Mexico) 204
Activist e-Zine (ASD) 212, 214
Activist San Diego 211–15
ADA compliance (SFPL) 186
Adams, Henry 65
Adams, John 65
Adams, Nene 31
Adams, Noah 144
Adbusters 116–17
ADM (Archer-Daniels-Midland) 145
Administration, (libraries) 14–15; *see also* Collegial library administration; Hawaii State Public Library System management; Library budgets; Library funding; Library governance; San Francisco Public Library management
Adorno, Theodor 44
Adult comic selection 13, 52
Advance Publications 112
Advantage Program (Amazon.com) 197–98
Advertising 116; *see also* Cable television advertising; Radio advertising; Textbook advertising
Advertising/children relationship 72, 101
Advertising/editorial relationship (journalism) 66
Advertising industry 96
Advertising (textbooks) 100
Affordable housing 169, 175
Africa World Press 60, 120
African-American newspapers (Brooklyn, New York) 115
African-American women's information networks 193
African-American workers (Coca-Cola Company) 16, 52
AFSCME Local 2626 ii, 159

AFSCME Local 2864 ii
AFSCME Local 2910 ii, 49–50, 159
Against Civilization (Zerzan) 120
"Against National Poetry Month as Such" (Bernstein) 157–58
Agnes Inglis Papers (Labadie Collection) 130
Agriculture Department racism 116
Agriculture reporters (Iowa) 68
AIDS activists 201
AIP 36–40
AIP Task Force (ALA/SRRT) 37–40, 108, 112, 114
AK Distribution (web site) 126
AK Press 59, 62, 147
AL (American Libraries) 35, 49, 51–52, 177
AL Online 53–54
ALA 135, 155
ALA/alternative press partnerships 47
ALA Annual Conference (1970) 37
ALA Annual Conference (2001) ii
ALA "Banned Books Week" 52
ALA CIPA-overturn suit 75–76
ALA Code of Ethics 51
ALA Committee on Professional Ethics 51
ALA Congress on Professional Education (1999) 114
ALA Council 50–51, 178
ALA exhibits policy 38
ALA Gay, Lesbian, Bisexual and Transgendered Round Table 132
ALA Notable Books Council 113–14
ALA Poor People's Policy 174–75
ALA Professional Ethics Committee 51
ALA Publishing 38–40; *see also American Libraries; Booklist*
ALA/SRRT 46–47
ALA/SRRT Papers (University of Illinois Archives, Urbana-Champaign) 41
ALA/SRRT Task Force on Alternatives in Print 37–40, 108, 112, 114
ALA/SRRT Task Force on Gay Liberation 134–35
ALA tax status 47
ALA voting information pamphlet (2000) 102
Albany Public Library (New York State) management 15

Albarella, Joan 30
Albert, Michael 106
Albert Victor, Prince 137
Alcock, Taralee 41
Alewitz, Mike 1
Alexander, Jeb 138
Alien and Sedition Acts 65
ALISE (Association for Library and Information Science Education) 114
All-news cable channels 122
All That Glitters (Nera) 31
All Things Considered (Radio program) 144
Allegheny County Library System (Maryland) 14
Allison, Dorothy 29
"Almost Banned Books, 1998 and 1999" (Lee) 58–63
Alternative Acquisitions Project (Temple University Library) 120
Alternative grey literature 119–21
Alternative Knowledge: How Radical Ideas Are Communicated in Society (MCTC course) 128
Alternative Library Literature 36, 49–52, 63, 174, 178, 195
Alternative library press 35–42
Alternative Literature: A Practical Guide for Librarians (Atton) 36
Alternative Materials in Libraries (Danky, Shore) 36, 121
Alternative media 13, 105, 119–21, 143–49; *see also* Alternative press
Alternative media censorship 77–81
Alternative Media: Open Sources on What's Real (Tsang) 119–21
Alternative press 36–37, 109, 112–18, 122–23; *see also* Alternative library press; Feminist publishers; Small presses; Street newspapers; Underground press
Alternative press/American Library Association partnerships 47
Alternative press awards 126–127
Alternative Press Center 47, 63, 105, 114, 119; *see also Alternative Press Index*
Alternative press costs 97
Alternative press displays 38–39, 111
Alternative press funding 116
Alternative Press Index 38, 47, 105, 116, 119
Alternative Press/library relation-

ship 35–40, 47, 52, 58–63, 97–98, 109–14, 120, 128
Alternative Press Review 106
Alternative press review media 40, 106, 126–27
Alternative Publishers of Books in North America (Anderson) 36, 40, 98, 105–06, 114, 125
Alternative Radio (program) 143–49
Alternative Tentacles (record label) 147
"Alternatives" 93–149
Alternatives in Print 36–40
Alternatives in Print Task Force (ALA/SRRT) 37–40, 108, 112, 114
Althusser, Louis 44
Amana (press) 120
Amazon.com 31, 197–98
American Academy of Poetry 157–58
American Association of Publishers 110
American Bar Association library parties (San Francisco) 182
American Booksellers Association meetings 39
American Civil Liberties Union CIPA-overturn suit 76
American Directory of Writer's Guidelines (1999) 125
American Federation of State, County, and Municipal Employees Local 2626 ii, 159
American Federation of State, County, and Municipal Employees Local 2864 ii
American Federation of State, County, and Municipal Employees Local 2910 ii, 49–50, 159
American foreign policy 2, 69–70, 120, 122
American Heritage Dictionary 95
American Libraries 35, 49, 51–52, 177
American Libraries Online 53–54
American Library Association 135, 155
American Library Association/alternative press partnerships 47
American Library Association Annual Conference (1970) 37
American Library Association Annual Conference (2001) ii
American Library Association "Banned Books Week" 52
American Library Association CIPA-overturn suit 75–76

217

American Library Association Conference on Professional Education 114
American Library Association Council 50–51, 178
American Library Association Ethics Committee 51
American Library Association exhibits policy 38
American Library Association Gay, Lesbian, Bisexual and Transgendered Round Table 132
American Library Association Notable Books Council 113–14
American Library Association Poor People's Policy 174–75
American Library Association Professional Ethics Committee 51
American Library Association publishing 38–40; *see also American Libraries; Booklist*
American Library Association Social Responsibilities Round Table 46–47
American Library Association Social Responsibilities Round Table Papers (University of Illinois Archives, Urbana-Champaign) 41
American Library Association Social Responsibilities Round Table Task Force on Alternatives in Print 37–39, 108, 112, 114
American Library Association Social Responsibilities Round Table Task Force on Gay Liberation 134–35
American Library Association tax status 47
American Library Association voting information pamphlet (2000) 102
American National Biography (1999) 136
American Pie (film) 87, 91
American Political Science Association 102–03
American propaganda 69, 80, 143–45, 148
Americans with Disabilities Act compliance (SFPL) 186
Anarchist distributors 126
Anarchist librarians 9–12, 23
Anarchist Librarians web 23, 40
Anarchist materials selection 98, 112, 120
Anarchist publishers 129
Anarchist punk periodicals 116
Anarchists' media coverage 119–20
Anarchy 119–20
Anderson, Byron 98, 107, 112–14, 124–27
Anderson Valley Advertiser 50
Anglo-American Cataloging Rules 14, 100
Annotations 105, 123
Anonymous Digital Coalition 204
Anthology publishing 197
Anthony, Susan B. 122
Anti-abortion movement 201
Anti-Americanism 2

Anti-billboard campaigns 72
Anti-CIPA suits 75–76
Anticlericalism (Catalonia) 11–12
Anti-corporate globalization movement 211; *see also* IMF/World Bank protests (2000); WTO protests (1999)
Anti-humanism 44
Anti-loitering laws 170
Antinuclear movement 200, 207–08
Anti-panhandling laws 170, 172
Anti-poverty action 175–76
Anti-slavery periodicals 122
Antitrust regulations 71–72, 109, 118
Anti-violence films 85
Anti-war movement 200–02
APBNA (Anderson) 36, 40, 105–06, 125
APC (Alternative Press Center) 47, 63, 105; *see also API*
Apex Press 59
API (Alternative Press Index) 38, 47, 105, 116, 119
Appropriate technology 13, 192
Approval plans 47, 109, 113
APSA (American Political Science Association) 102–03
Arabs 2
Archer-Daniels-Midland 145
Archives; *see* Gay archives; Lesbian archives; Radical archives
Areopagitica (Milton) 45
Aristide, Jean-Bertrand 120
Aristocracy 45
ARL (Association of Research Libraries) 97
ARL holdings 110
Armenian-Americans 147
Armenian Genocide 146–47
Aronson, Theo 137
Art (libraries) 5
Arte Publico Press 60, 63
Arts and Humanities Citation Index 98
ASD (Activist San Diego) 211–15
Assertive women 21–23
Association for Library and Information Science Education 114
Association of Research Libraries 97
Association of Research Libraries holdings 110
Association publishing 125
Astray Lumberjacks 208
ATD Fourth World 191–92, 195
Atkinson, Hugh 38
Atlanta Journal and Constitution 102, 104
Atlases 8
Atrocity media coverage 109
Audio Express program (LAPL) 177–80
Audiotape rental programs 170–71, 177–80
Authority 10, 15
Autonomedia (press) 120
Autonomy (librarians) 45–46

Bad Libraries (Reid) 14–15
Badboy (Masquerade Books' imprint) 31
Baffler 117
Bagdikian, Ben H. 95
Baghdad, Ryan 77–81
Baker & Taylor 109, 197–98
Baker & Taylor Hawaii outsourcing contract 15
Baker, Stannard 122
Balaguer Library (Vilanova i la Geltru, Catalonia) 9, 12
Baltimore County Public Library reserve charges 179
Bangladesh cyber kiosks 194
Bank of America/SFPL Foundation relationship 182
Banned Books Week 52
BARC (Bay Area Reference Center) 36–37
Barnes and Noble 108, 111, 179
Barnes decision (Supreme Court) 88
Barnes, Mosher and Whitehurst 181, 183, 185
Barr, Bob 146
Barsamian, David 143–49
Bawer, Bruce 136
Bay Area Direct Action Network 201
Bay Area Reference Center (San Francisco Public Library) 36–37
BCPL (Baltimore County Public Library) reserve charges 179
Beatty, Warren 71
Bechdel, Alison 29
"Becoming a Gay, Lesbian, Bisexual or Transgender Collector" (Steven J. Schochet Center for GLBT Studies) 141–142
Bella Books 29–30
Bentley, Rosalind 27
Benton Foundation report (1996) 155–56
Bereano, Nancy 29
Berelson, Bernard 155
Berkeley Barb 35
Berman, Sanford 1–2, 14, 39–41, 49–57, 98–100, 107, 169–76, 178, 181, 185
"Berman's Bag: Must 'The Poor' Always Be Among Us?" 169–76
"Berman's Bag: The Top Censored Library Stories of 1998/2000" 49–53
Bermudez, Lucrecia 182, 185
Berninghausen, David 46–47
Bernstein, Charles 157–58
Berry, John 14–15
Bertelsmann (media conglomerate) 47–48, 95, 112
"Best books" concept 45, 113
Bestseller Express program (HCL) 176–80
Bestseller rental programs 170–71, 177–80
Bestsellers 112–13, 147
Betrayal of Science and Reason 58
Betty Lou (film character) 22, 24
Bey, Hakim 203
Bhabba Atomic Research Centre (India) protests 207–08
Biafra, Jello 147
Biased filmmaking 71
Biased library press 49–53
Biased library research 154–55

Biased media 65–72, 77, 106, 148; *see also* Biased press; Biased review media
Biased periodical indexes 40
Biased press 65–72, 77; *see also* Biased library press; Biased media
Biased reading research 154–55
Biased review media 37, 40, 47
Biased subject headings 39–40, 100
Biblio-Stalinism (Hennepin County Library) 53–57
Bickner, Carrie 73–76
"Big lie" technique (propaganda) 146
Billington, James 16–17, 49, 159–61
Biography selection 1
BIP 38, 113, 124–25
Birdsell, David 75
Bishop, Elizabeth 136
Bitch 21–24
Black book 61
Black Farmer's Association 116
Black Librarians Association 135
Black newspapers (Brooklyn, New York) 115
Black women's information networks 193
Black workers (Coca-Cola Company) 16, 52
"Blind-sided by Amazon.Com" (Hoffman) 197–98
Blind Spot censorship 78–79
Blockage (civil disobedience) 201–03, 206–10
"Blockbuster" rental programs 170–71, 177–80
"Blockbuster" selection 52
Blockbuster Video censorship 84
Blocked sites (censorware) 74
Blogs 23
Bloss, Marjorie 110
Blu 116
BMW (Barnes, Mosher and Whitehurst) 181, 183, 185
Boadecia's Books (San Francisco Bay Area) 29
Body modification web sites 23
Boeing stockholders 70
Bold coast love (Braund) 29
Bomb making 11
Bomb threats 80
Boojamra, Lee 30
Book banning (Hennepin County Library) 53
Book costs 97
Book distributors 109, 124, 126, 197–98
Book industry ownership 70, 95–96
Book Industry Study Group 124
Book review bias 37, 40, 47, 113
Book sales 5
Book selection 1–2, 13, 97–98, 109–10, 113; *see also* Academic library collection development; Approval plans; Challenges (libraries); Fiction selection; GLBT materials selection; Labor materials selection; Library Bill of Rights; Multicultural materials selection;

Poetry selection; Poverty materials selection; Reference book selection; Review media bias; Third World materials selection; Weeding (libraries)
Book thefts (Hennepin County Library) 53–57
Book weeding 15, 50
Booklegger magazine 36
Booklist 40
Books in Print 38, 113, 124–25
Books-on-tape rental programs 177–80
Booksense (web site) 126
Bookstore chains 29, 31, 108, 115, 158
Bookwire (web site) 126
Borneh, Giraut de 157
Borrowing fees 8
Bostwick, Arthur 45
Bowers, Sharon 31
Bowker, R.R. (press) 124–25, 127
Bowker's Annual Library and Book Trade 113
Boys Don't Cry (film) 26
Bradbury, Ray 197
Bragg, Laura 138
Brainy women 21–23
Branch libraries (SFPL) 182–87
Branding (marketing) 71
Braund, Diana Tremain 29
Brechin, Gray 51, 185
Bremer, Catherine M. ii, 182
Brite, Poppy Z. 197
Broadcasting industry librarians 21–22
Broken Pencil 126
Brooklyn College Library 38
Brooklyn newspapers 115
Brown, Charles 53, 55–56, 178
Browsing 49
Bruderhof Community 116
Brunswick, Mark 178
Bryan, Alice 155
Bryson, Kathleen 31
Buchanan, Pat 143
Budgets 8, 73, 183
Bugs Bunny 71
"Bulldog press" concept 65
Bulletin Board (LC Professional Guild) 49–50, 159
Bulletin of the Atomic Scientists 122
"Bulwarks of democracy" concept 2; *see also* Democracy/library relationship
Bulworth (film) 71
Burdett, Mark 77–81
Burtis, Judy ii
Buschman, John 178–80
Bush, Vannevar 24
Business/library partnerships 101
Business news 66
Business reporters 66
Buttafuoco, Joey 68
Buttons 1
Buy Nothing Day 116
By What Authority 173

Cable news channels 122
Cable television advertising 72
Cable television industry ownership 70
Caldicott, Helen 143
Calhoun, Jackie 29

CALL 36
California state librarian 37
Calm Before the Storm (Herring) 29
Campaign finance reform 45
Campbell, Angela 83
Candidate information 102–04
Capitalism 11, 44, 68–69, 202
Capitalism/democracy relationship 68
CARA (MPAA Classification and Rating Administration) 82–83
Carmichael, James V., Jr. 132–40
Carnegie Corporation 154–55
Carroll, Lewis 146
Carter, Jimmy 103
Cartoon selection 1
Carver, George Washington 136
Castro, Fidel 115
Catalan librarians 9–12
Catalog censorship (Hennepin County Library) 53–57
Cataloging 14, 98–100; *see also* Classification; Hennepin County Library cataloging; Library of Congress cataloging
Cataloging fiction 14
Cataloging poverty materials 171
Cataloging Special Materials (Berman) 54
Catalonian history 12
Catalunya 9
Catalyst 5–6
Catholic Agitator 172
Catholic Church/film censorship relationship 83
Catholic education 10
Catholic sacraments 5
Catholic University of America library school 39
Cats 21
CD (civil disobedience) 200–10
CD rating schemes 89
CD selection 1
Celebrity news 109
Censored Hollywood (Miller) 84
Censorship 15, 40, 45–47; *see also* Alternative media censorship; Economic censorship; Filtering (Internet); Film censorship; Library press censorship; Prior censorship; School censorship; Self-censorship; Video censorship
"Censorship and Discourse" (Harris) 43–48
"Censorship/Intellectual Freedom" 33–92
Censorware 73–74
Center for Intrusion Control 208
Center for Media Education 59
Center for the History of Print Culture in Modern America 153
Chaffee, James 51, 181–87
Chain bookstores 29, 31, 108, 115, 157
Challenges (libraries) 52
Chamber of Commerce (San Francisco) library parties 182
Channel One 101
Chaos (periodical) 10
Charles Schwab library parties (San Francisco) 182
Chavez, Cesar 1

Chevron/SFPL Foundation relationship 182
Chicago Tribune 66
Chicken Soup series 124
Child library users 5, 7–8
Child poverty 170, 174
Children/advertising relationship 72, 101
Children Are Dying 58–59
Children/pornography relationship 73–74
Children's book selection 1
Children's fines 14
Children's Internet Protection Act 73–76
Children's library services 5–8, 22, 156, 178; *see also* Children's book selection; Children's fines; Story hours
Children's marketing 101
Children's periodicals 116
Chilean infobuses 192
Chinese government web site hacking 207–08
Choice 37, 40
Chomsky, Noam 62, 98, 106, 120, 143–47
Chronicle of Higher Education 153–56
Churchill Livingstone ownership 107
CIA 120
CIA/drug trade relationship 67–68
Cinco Puntos Press 60
CIPA (Children's Internet Protection Act) 73–76
Circulation 8; *see also* Fiction circulation (libraries); Overdue charges
Citizen activists (libraries) 51, 181–87
Citizen activists (media) 72
City Pages (Minneapolis) 53
Civic Media Center and Library (Gainesville, Florida) 95, 104, 106
Civics textbooks 12
Civil disobedience 200–10
Civil liberties 1–2; *see also* Free Press; Free speech; Intellectual freedom
Civil Rights Movement 200
Clamor 77–81
Claremont (press) 120
Clark, Mike 84
Class struggle 11
Classical music radio programs 147
Classification 23, 49, 98
Classification and Rating Administration (MPAA) 82–83
Classist laws 170
Classist libraries 46, 73–76, 170–74, 177–80
Classist military policy 70
"Classless society" concept 70
Cleis Press 59, 63, 120
Clerks (libraries) 22–23
Cleveland Street Scandal 137
Cleyre, Voltairine de 13
Clinton Administration press coverage 67
Clinton, Bill 70, 73, 117

Clinton impeachment hearings 146
Clouds of War (Rivers) 31
CNN 102, 116
CNN Gulf War coverage 69
CNN ownership 70
CNT (Confederacion Nacional del Trabajo) 9, 11
Coca-Cola Company/Library of Congress partnership 16–17, 52
Cockburn, Alexander 120
Code of Ethics (ALA) 51
Cohn, Roy 135
COINTELPRO 78–80
Colbert, Claudette 137
Colbourne, Ruth 31
Cold War 80, 119–20
Collection building 129–31
Collection development 1–2, 13, 97–98, 109–10, 113 *see also* Academic library collection development; Approval plans; Challenges (libraries); Fiction selection; GLBT materials selection; Labor materials selection; Library Bill of Rights; Multicultural materials selection; Poetry selection; Poverty materials selection; Reference book selection; Review media bias; Third World materials selection; Video selection; Weeding (libraries); Zine selection
Collection Development Policies and Procedures (Futas) 113
"Collection level cataloging" (LC) 161
College and Research Libraries 110
College education 10; *see also* Library education
College library collection development 47
Collegial library administration 128
Collier's 122
Collins, Stephen Foster 136
Colonization 208
Color lines 118
Comic book rating schemes 89
Comic book selection 13, 52
Commercial newspapers 65–66
Commercialization (culture) 65, 105–06, 146
Commercialization (film industry) 71
Commercialization (libraries) 16–17, 51–52, 101, 186; *see also* Business/library partnerships; Pro-business library bias
Commercialization (publishing) 13; *see also* Commercial newspapers
Commercialization (schools) 100–01
Common Courage Press 59–60, 63
Common Good (Barsamian/Chomsky) 143, 147
Common Sense (Paine) 122
Communicator (LAPL Librarians' Guild) 50, 53, 159–61
Communism 68
Communists 12, 79
Community computers 192
Community/democracy relationship 68–69

Community information services (Toronto, Ontario) 163–68
Community organizing 211–213
Community technology centers 193
Community telecenters (Philippines) 193
Compact disc rating schemes 89
Compact disc selection 1
Complete Film Dictionary (Konigsberg) 83
Completely Queer 136
Computer revolution effects 209, 211
Computers (libraries) 22, 74–75, 187; *see also* Street library computers
Conable, Gordon 43
Confederacion Nacional del Trabajo (Spain) 9, 11
Confident women 21–23
Conglomerate media 45, 47, 65–72, 77, 95–96, 112, 117
Congress on Professional Education (1999) 114
Connecting Children to the Future 58–59
Connor-Dominguez, Billie ii
Consensus decision-making (libraries) 128
Conservative gays 135–36
Conservative news media 66
Conservative think tanks 79
Consortium Book Sales & Distribution (web site) 126
Consumerism (propaganda) 146, 147
Consumerism (Publishing) 13
"Continuing a Legacy" (Herrada) 129–31
Continuity (films) 88–89
Control (library objective) 45
Copy cataloging (LC) 160
Core collections 110
"Core level" cataloging (LC) 160–61
Cornell University Library James Mariposa Human Sexuality Archives 134
Corporate librarians 21–22
Corporate media and the Threat to Democracy (McChesney) 64
Corporate power 45, 117, 146, 173
Corporate radio sponsors 145
Corporate rights 43
Corporate welfare 174
Corporate welfare media coverage 70
Corporatization (libraries) 16–17, 51–52, 182; *see also* Privatization (libraries)
Corson, Suzanne 29–31
Cortez, Carlos 1
Council (ALA) 50–51, 178
Counterculture 119; *see also* Alternative media
Counterpoise 35–48, 52, 58–63, 95–114, 119–20, 124–25
County reporters (Iowa) 68
Cradle Will Rock (film) 1
Cranky Notions (column) 129
Creason, Glen ii
Creedence Clearwater Revival 70
Cregan, Mary 156

Cretinon, Denis 192
Crime stories (journalism) 66
CRISES Press 40, 42, 95, 107, 125–26
Critical Art Ensemble 200, 202–03, 205
Crockett, Ethel 37
Cromwell, David 106
Cromwell, Oliver 45
Cross-border links directories 58–59, 61–62
Cross Fire: A Journey Through Gender Mayhem (Intermedia Arts project) 27
Crumb (film) 86
Cruzan, Carla 25–26
Cuba media coverage 120
Cult of the Dead Cow 207
Cultural commercialization 65, 105–06, 146
"Cultural critique" methods 44
"Cultural hegemony" concept 47
Cultural studies 154
"Culture as agency" research 155
Culture industry 44
Culture wars 44
Curious Wine (Forrest) 30
Curiosity 13, 22
Current awareness—Library literature 37
Curtis, Austin W., Jr. 136
Cyber activism 199–216; *see also* Internet radicalization
Cyber kiosks (Bangladesh) 194
Cyber Patrol (Censorware) 74
Cyber terrorism 207–08
"Cyber Volunteerism Model" (Eder) 214
Cyber warfare 204–05; 208
Cybercafes (Panama) 193
"Cyberspace/Virtual Libraries" 189–215

D'Adamo, Charles 105, 116–17, 120
Daft, Doug 17
Dallas decision (Supreme Court) 83
Dana, Jonathan M. 85–86
Danky, James P. 1–2, 153
Daring to Find our Names (Carmichael) 134
Database tampering (Hennepin County Library) 53–57
Daughters of the Great Star (Rivers) 31
Davidson, Kenneth H. 85
Davis, Angela 143
Davis, Debra 25–28
Davis, William P. 178
DC Metropolitan Police micro-radio raids 79
DDC (Dewey Decimal Classification) 23, 98
"Dear Library People" (Berman/Danky) 1–2
Death Understood (McNab) 30
De Bornelh, Giraut 157
Debs, Eugene V. 1
De Cleyre, Voltairine 13
De la Pena McCook, Kathleen 194
Deleuze, Gilles 203
Demand (collection development criterion) 113

Democracy *see* Information democracy; Media democracy; Participatory democracy
"Democracy as a Contact Sport" (Mokhiber/Weissman) 16–17
Democracy/capitalism relationship 68
Democracy/community relationship 68–69
Democracy/computer revolution relationship 209
Democracy/equality relationship 68–69
Democracy/information relationship 68, 122, 143–44, 209
Democracy/library relationship 2, 46, 48, 193
Democracy/poverty relationship 194
Democratic Leadership Council 16
Democratic media 104–05, 118, 148
Democratic Party campaign spending (2000) 96
Demublican National Convention (2000) protests 80, 215
De Palma, Brian 91–92
Department of Defense hacking 204
Department of Justice Antitrust Division 97
De-politicization 146
Deprofessionalization (LC) 159–61
Deregulation (radio) 118
Des Moines Register 68
Desert Moon 116
Desert of the Heart (Rule) 30
DeSirey, Jan ii, 54
Desk Set (film) 21–22, 24
Deskilling (LC) 159–61
Developing Library and Information Centers (Evans) 113
Dewey Decimal Classification 23, 98
Dewey, Melvil 23, 45
Diary collecting 142
Differently gendered (term) 27
Digital activism 199–216
Digital civil disobedience 199–210
Digital divide 75, 209, 212, 214
Digital fund transfers 194
"Digital Libraries for All" (Smith) 191–96
Digital video 191
Direct action 200; *see also* Civil disobedience
"Director's cut" films 92
Directory of Poetry Publishers (Dustbooks) 125
Directory of Small Press/Magazine Editors & Publishers (Dustbooks) 125
Directory of the American Left 38
Discarding library materials 15, 50
Discounts 197–98
"Discourse and Censorship" (Harris) 43–48
Discourse theory 44, 46
Disintermediation (communication) 209
Dismissals 15, 68
Disney Company (media conglomerate) 70–71
Displays 2, 22, 163; *see also* Library posters; Small press displays
Dissidents 145; *see also* Repression
Dissmeyer, Clark 50
Distributors (books) 109, 124, 126, 197–98
District of Columbia Metropolitan Police micro-radio raids 79
DLC (Democratic Leadership Council) 16
DOD hacking 204
Dodge, Chris 13, 54, 174, 194–95; *see also Street Librarian* (web site)
Dogmatism 12
Dollars & Sense 115–16, 173–74
Domain name policy protests 207
Donations (archives) 141–42
Donations (libraries) 16–17, 52, 130–31
Douglass, Frederick 122
Douglass monthly 122
Dow Jones press coverage 67
"Down By Law" (Bickner) 73–76
Down There Press 52, 59, 62
Drafting women 25
Dressed to Kill (film) 90–91
Drug trade/CIA relationship 67–68
Drug use (films) 91
Duke University Library gay archives 134
Dumb and Dumber (Film) 179
"Dumbed-down" films 88, 90–91
Dunne, Nann 30
Dustbooks 125, 127
Dykes to Watch Out For (Bechdel) 29

E-books 193
E Magazine 116–17
E-rate discounts 48, 73, 75
E-text Archives (web site) 121
E-zines 212, 214
Earth First! 200
Earth Resources Research 120
Earthquake risks (SFPL) 183–84, 186
East Timor protests 207–08
East Village other 35
Ebert, Roger 88
ECD (electronic civil disobedience) 199–210
Eckstein, Denis iv
Economic Barriers to Information Access (ALA) 178
Economic censorship 45, 179; *see also* Editorial/advertising relationship (journalism); Library fees; Library fines; Market censorship; Media conglomerates
Economic Policy Institute web site 117
Eder, Martin 211–14
Edited films 88, 90–91
Editorial/advertising relationship (journalism) 66
Edward VII 137
Edwards, Bob 144, 147
Edwards, David 106
EEOC complaints 26, 52
Ehlers, Lesa ii
Ehrenreich, Barbara 64, 143
Eland, Tom 128

El Cid 12
Elections (2000) 102–04, 175
Electronic books 193
Electronic civil disobedience 199–210
Electronic Disturbance Theater 207–08
Electronic fund transfers 194
Elements of Refusal (Zerzan) 120
Elites 44, 69, 110, 146, 148, 209–10; *see also* Aristocracy; Corporate power
Elitist libraries 45–46; *see also* Classist libraries
Elway, John 148
Email 212, 215
Email assaults 202, 205
Email collecting 142
Email (NYPL) 74
Email printouts (Uganda) 193
Email server crashes 205
Emancipation Proclamation 122
EMERAC *(computer)* 22, 24
Emergency Librarian 35–36
Employment discrimination (Coca-Cola Company) 16, 52
Enersol solar-powered computers 192–93
English-as-a-second-language sections (libraries) 166
Enlightenment 44–45, 47
Environmental reporters 66
Epicenter (Boulder, Colorado) 148
Equal Employment Opportunity Commission complaints 26, 52
Equal Rights Amendment 25
Equality/democracy relationship 68–69
ERA (Equal Rights Amendment) 25
Erotic fiction 31
Erotica selection 13, 52, 58, 61, 98, 112
Erotica (word) 87
ESL sections (libraries) 166
Ethics Committee (ALA) 51
"Ethics of Hacktivism" (Goodrum/Manion) 206–10
Eubanks, Jackie 38–42
Evans, G. Edward 113
Everything You Always Wanted to Know about Sandy Berman…(Dodge/DeSirey) 54
Everything You Always Wanted to Know about the Movie Rating System (MPAA) 82, 91
EVO (New York City) 35
Executions (Texas) 115
Exhibits 2, 22, 163; *see also* American Library Association exhibits policy; Small press displays
Exodus: Diary of a Spanish Refugee (Mistral) 9
"Express This—The Road to Ruin" (Freedman) 171, 177–80
EXTRA! 117
Exxon 145
Eyes Wide Shut (film) 91–92

Factor Press 52
Factsheet five 119
FAI (Federacion Anarquista Iberica) 9
FAIR 117

Fairchild, Lucy 5–6
Family Research Council 74
Fanelli, Vincent 192
Farber, Stephen 87
Fasanella, Ralph 1
Fatal Attraction (film) 90
FBI micro-radio raids 79
FCC 75, 77, 88
FCC micro-radio raids 79
Federacion Anarquista Iberica 9
Federacion Iberica de Juventudes Libertarias 9
Federal Communications Commission 75, 77, 88
Federal Communications Commission micro-radio raids 79
Federal Communications Law Journal 93
Federalists 65
Fees (libraries) 8, 170–71, 176–80; *see also* Overdue charges
Feinberg, Elizabeth 56
Feinberg, Leslie 29
Feinberg, Renee 108
Felipe, Leon 9, 12
Female-to-male transexuals 26
Feminist bookstores 31
Feminist Collections 36
Feminist publishers 29–31
Feminist Studies 122
Ferreira, Joe 194
Feudalism 45
Fiber optic cable clogging 202
Fiction cataloging 14
Fiction circulation (libraries) 153
Fiction publishing 197–98
Fiction reading 153–56
Fiction selection 52
Fifth Estate 35, 119
Film censorship 82–92
Film industry bias 71
Film industry ownership 70–71
Film programs 2, 8
Film ratings 82–92
Film selection 1, 87
Film sex 85, 87, 90–91
Film theater censorship 84, 87
Film violence 85, 87, 89–91
Filtering (Internet) 14, 73–76
Finch, Peter 134
Fines (libraries) 14, 170, 176–77
Firebrand Books 29, 59–60, 62–63
Firecracker Alternative Book Awards 126
Firings 15, 68
First Amendment 65, 76, 82–84, 87–88, 90, 144; *see also* Free Press; Free Speech
First Resort (Little) 31
Fishman, Israel 134, 139
Flight From Reason (Berninghausen) 47
Flights from the Iron Moon 58–59
Flint Sit-Down Strike (1937) press coverage 66
FloodNet (software) 207
Flyer collecting 142
Food shelf use 170
FOOD SHELVES (proposed subject heading) 171
Forbes 146
Forced resignations 14, 55, 57
Ford, Gerald 103
Ford, Henry 136

Foreign policy (United States) 2, 69–70, 120, 122
ForeWord Magazine 126–27
Forrest, Katherine V. 30
"Fortunate Son" (song) 70
Fortune 146
Fortune ownership 70
Foster, Jeanette Howard 134, 138
Foucault, Michel 43–44, 154
Foundation (SFPL) 51, 182–86
Fourth World Movement 191
Franklin, Benjamin 154, 178
Franklin, Robert 53
"Free Money, Just Sign Here" (Chaffee) 187
Free press 45, 65–72; *see also* First Amendment
"Free Press for Sale" (McChesney/Jensen) 64–72
"Free Press for Sale" (McChesney/Jensen) 64–72
Free the Media (McChesney/Nichols) 64
Free Trade Area of the Americas protests (2001) 77, 81
Freedland, Jonathan 106
Freedman, Jenna 171, 177–80
Freedom Press 120
Freedom To Read Statement (ALA) 46, 110
Freeney, Mickey 180
Freethought libraries 12
Freethought materials selection 52
Friends of the Library groups 8
Frier, Alice 30
Fry, Stephen 134
FTAA protests (2001) 77, 81
FTR Statement (ALA) 46
Full-frontal 58–59
Fulton, Len 113, 125
Funding (alternative press) 116
Funding (libraries) 8, 15, 73, 97, 177; *see also* Budgets; Fundraisers; Gifts (Libraries); Library fees; Library fines; San Francisco Public Library bond issue (2000)
Fundraisers 22; *see also* Book sales
Futas, Elizabeth 113
Future of History (Barsamian/Zinn) 143
Future Primitive (Zerzan) 120

G (film rating) 83, 85, 88, 90
Gabrielle (TV series character) 30
Gag orders (Hawaii State Public Library System) 15
Gag orders (Seattle IMC) 81
Gainesville Sun 102
Gannett Company (media conglomerate) 68
Garceau, Oliver 155
Garfias, Pedro 10
Gates, Bill 68, 187
Gates Grants 187
Gauntlet Press 197–98
Gay Almanac 136
Gay and Lesbian Biography 136
Gay and Lesbian Library Service (Gough/Greenblatt) 134
Gay and Lesbian Studies 133–34

Gay archives 133–35, 138
Gay biographies 133–34, 136–37
Gay collecting 141–42
Gay conservatives 135–36
Gay diaries 138, 142
Gay film actors 136–37
Gay history 132–42
Gay history (India) 191
Gay, Lesbian, Bisexual and Transgendered Round Table (American Library Association) 132
Gay letters 132–33, 138, 142
Gay Liberation Task Force (ALA/SRRT) 134–35
Gay librarians 138
Gay literature 133–34; *see also* Gay biographies; Gay diaries; Gay letters
Gay materials selection 134
Gay rights media coverage 70
Gay spirituality 137–38
Gebner-Hart Archives 134
Geller, Evelyn 45–46
Gender Education Center (Maple Grove, MN) 25–26
General Workers Union (Spain) 11
Genetech library parties (San Francisco) 182
Genocide 208
Gerhard, Kristin 47, 52, 110
Germinal (film) 1
Gifts (archives) 141–42
Gifts (libraries) 16–17, 52, 130–31
Gilda Stories (Gomez) 29
Gillon, Margaret 31
Gingrich, Newt 103, 146
Ginsberg decision (Supreme Court) 83
Girl Press 63
Gittings, Barbara 134, 139
"Give people what they want" concept (journalism) 68, 148
Gladney, Rose 135
Glazer, Fred 14–15
GLBT archives 133–35, 138, 141–42
GLBT biographies 133–34, 136–37
GLBT collecting 141–42
GLBT conservatives 135–36
GLBT diaries 138, 142
GLBT film actors 136–37
GLBT history 132–42
GLBT history (India) 191
GLBT letters 132–33, 138, 142
GLBT librarians 25–28, 134, 138
GLBT literature 133–34; *see also* GLBT biographies; GLBT diaries; GLBT letters
GLBT materials selection 134
GLBT rights media coverage 70
GLBT spirituality 137–38
GLBTF (ALA/SRRT) 134–35
GLBTRT (American Library Association) 132
Global community/computer revolution relationship 209
Global Exchange web site 117
Global Media (McChesney/Herman) 64
Goebbels, Joseph 69, 148
Goin, Sandy 42
Goldwater, Barry 103

Gomez, Jewelle 29
Gonzales, Matt 182
Good, Melissa 30
Good Vibrations Guides 61–63
Goodrum, Abby 206–10
Gordon, Jill 47
Gordon, William 139
Gore, Al 70
Gough, Cal 134
Governance (libraries) 8; *see also* Library administration; Library trustees
Graduate (film) 7
Graham, Gary 115
Grant, Cary 137
Grant, Gary 116
Graphic novel selection 52
Grassroots organizing 211–13
Gray, Richard A. 39–40, 42
Great Waldo Pepper (film) 87
Greater Victoria Public Library (British Columbia) 15
Greaves, David 115–16
Green Party 103, 118
Greenblatt, Ellen 134
Greenpeace 215
Greenville County (South Carolina) Public Library collection development policy 113
Grey literature 119–21
Grier, Barbara 29
Grimes, Andrea V. ii
Grimes, William 84
Grisham, John 179
Grove Atlantic 112
Guattari, Felix 203
GUI interfaces 74
Gulf War 1–2, 80
Gulf War media coverage 69
Gulf War resistance 201–02
Gun in Betty Lou's Handbag (film) 21–22, 24
Guscott, John 193
Gutenberg Bible (NYPL) 74

Hacktivism 202–10
Hadleigh, Boze 137
Hadra Books 31
Haines, Billy 136–37
Haiti media coverage 120
Haiti Progress 115
Haitian newspapers (New York City) 115
Halfhill, Robert 53
Halpern, Sue 7–8
Hannan, Amatul 194
Harcourt General 97, 107
Harmon, Charles 51, 114
HarperCollins 109
HarperCollins ownership 95
Harrington Park Press 60
Harris, Daniel 136
Harris, Michael 44–45
Harris, Steven R. 43–48
Hass, Paul iv
Hatch, Mary (film character) 21
Hawaii State Public Library System management 15
HCL Bestseller Express program 177–80
HCL Board 53, 56–57
HCL catalog 54
HCL cataloging 55, 98; *see also* HCL subject headings

HCL cataloging bulletin 53–54, 98–99
HCL fee revenue 170
HCL Librarians Union ii
HCL repression 14, 53–57
HCL subject headings 99–100, 177
Health Communications 124
Health insurance availability 170, 175
Height-shelving (LC) 49–50
Heins, Marjorie 83–84
Hennen, Thomas J., Jr. 177
Hennepin County Librarians Union ii
Hennepin County Library Bestseller Express program 177–80
Hennepin County Library Board 53, 56–57
Hennepin County Library cataloging 55, 98; *see also* Hennepin County Library subject headings
Hennepin County Library cataloging bulletin 53–54, 98–99
Hennepin County Library fee revenue 170
Hennepin County Library repression 14, 53–57
Hennepin County Library subject headings 99–100, 177
Henry and June (film) 90
Hepburn, Katharine 21
H.E.R.E. Local 2 ii
Herman, Edward S. 64, 104, 120
Hermes, Kris 80
Herrada, Julie 129–31
Herring, Peggy 29
High school librarians 25–28
High school restroom access 25–26
Higher education 10; *see also* Library education
Hildreth, Susan 186
Hill, George Roy 87
Hill, Gerri 30
Hill, Joe 1
Hill, Linda 30
Hillsborough High School (Florida) commercialization 101
Hip-hop periodicals 116
Hitchcock, Lorena 135
Hitler, Adolf 147
Hoffert, Barbara 108
Hoffman, Barry 197–98
Hollywood Gays (Hadleigh) 137
Hollywood (procensorship term) 89
Holmes, Oliver Wendell 47
Holtzbrink (media conglomerate) 112
Home video censorship 84, 88
HOMELESS MENTALLY ILL PERSONS (proposed subject heading) 171
Homeless people 169–70
Homeless shelter use 169–70
Homophobic libraries 133–35
Honduran street libraries 191
Hong Kong Blondes 207–08
Hope, Constance 26
Horkheimer, Max 44
Hotel Employees and Restaurant Employees Local 2 ii

Hours 8, 183
How It Works (MPAA website) 87, 90
Howe, Barb 96
Hugo, Victor 10
Human Rights Act (Minnesota) 25–26
Human rights materials selection 98, 112
Humanism 11, 44, 47
Humanist 82–92
Hunger 174; *see also* Food shelf use
Hupp, Stephen L. 110
H.W. Wilson Company 40; *see also Wilson Library Bulletin*
H.W. Wilson Library Periodical Award winners 37
Hymson, Craig 78

I Am My Lover 58–59
Ideology 44–45, 47, 144–45, 148
IFIDA (International Film Importers and Distributors of America) 88
Image of librarians 21–24
IMCs 77–81
IMF/World Bank protests (2000) 78–80, 116, 215
Immigrant library services 162–68
In These Times 116
Income inequality 170, 174
Independent booksellers 31, 115, 158
Independent films 83
Independent Media Centers 77–81
Independent Press Association 114, 122–23
Independent presses 36–37, 109, 112–14, 124–27; *see also* Alternative press; Feminist publishers; Small presses
Independent Publisher Online (web site) 127
"Independent Publishing Matters" (Schulman) 122–23
Independent (San Francisco) 51
India 147
Indian government web site hacking 208
Indonesian government web site hacking 207–08
Indy media centers 77–81
Inequality 170, 174, 208
Infobuses (Chile) 192
Infomercials 109
Infoplazas (Panama) 193
Information (definition) 155–56
Information democracy 209; *see also* Media democracy
Information/democracy relationship 68, 122, 143–44, 209
Information for Social Change 36
"Information infrastructure" concept 194
Information literacy courses (MCTC) 128
Information superhighway 110
Information technology control 209–10, 212
Information warfare 204–05, 208
Infoshops 106, 193–94
Infotainment 148; *see also* Infomercials

Info-terrorism 208
Inglis, Agnes 129–30
Ingram (distributor) 109, 197–98
"Inside" censorship 1, 13–15, 46, 52–63; *see also* Library fees; Library fines
Institutional classism 170, 176
Intellectual freedom 1, 15, 43–44, 46, 48, 57, 75–76, 110, 114, 125, 155; *see also* Censorship; Challenges (libraries); Free press; Free speech; Library Bill of Rights; Repression (libraries); Right to know
Intellectual Freedom and Social Responsibility (Samek) 41
Intellectual Freedom Manual (ALA/OIF) 42–43, 110
Intellectual freedom/social responsibility relationship 35–42, 46–47
"Intellectual Freedom Within the Profession" (Samek) 35–42
Intellectual property laws 209–10
Intellectual women 21–23
Intellectuals (definition) 106
Intelligent women 21–23
Interlibrary loans 8
Intermedia Arts (Minneapolis, MN) 27
International Action Center 59
International Anti-Poetry Month (proposed) 158
International Directory of Little Magazines and Small Presses 113, 125
International Film Importers and Distributors of America 88
International Journal on Grey Literature 119–21
International Monetary Fund/World Bank protests (2000) 78–80, 116, 215
International Standard Book Number 124, 126
Internet 106, 122
Internet access 8, 73–76, 187, 191–93; *see also* Internet filtering
Internet commercialization 101
Internet connectivity (SFPL) 187
Internet filtering 14, 73–76
Internet radicalization 119–21; *see also* Cyber activism
InterNIC traffic disruption 207
Interview radio programs 143–49
IPA (Independent Press Association) 114, 122–23
Iraq bombing 204, 211
ISBN (International Standard Book Number) 124, 126
ISDN line clogging 202
Islam 2
It's a Wonderful Life (film) 21

Jack the Ripper murders 137
"James Chaffee's Fight Against the Bond Issue for the San Francisco Public Library" 181–86
James, Henry 134
James Hormel Collection (San Francisco Public Library) 134
James Mariposa Human Sexuality Archives (Cornell University Library) 134

223

Jansen, Sue Curry 44–45
Jean-Nickolaus Tretter Collection (University of Minnesota Library) 142
Jeb and Dash (Alexander) 138
Jefferson, Thomas 16, 65
Jeffrey Pollack's Congressional Campaign (website)
Jensen, Carl 49
Jensen, Derrick 64–72
Jewish Labor Bund 1
Job discrimination (Coca-Cola Company) 16, 52
John Birch Society 79
Johnsburg Library (New York State) 7–8
Johnson, Randy 178
Jones, Mother 1
Jones, Paula 109
Jordan, Michael 71
Journal costs 97
Journal index bias 40, 120
Journal of Information Ethics 51, 53, 206–10
Journalism 45, 67; *see also* Advertising/editorial relationship (journalism); "Give people what they want" concept (journalism); Media bias; Official sources (journalism); Press freedom; Press history; Press ownership
Journalistic neutrality 66; *see also* Media bias
Journalistic objectivity 66, 117; *see also* Media bias
Joy of Cataloging (Berman) 54
Junk food promotion 16–17, 52
Justice House Publishing 30–31
Juvenile fines 14

Kallmaker, Karin 30
Kaotik Team 208
Kashpureff, Eugene 207
Katz, Jonathan 133
Kazen, Brenda 30
Keeping Women and Children Last (Sidel) 171
Kellogg Foundation 155–56
Kester, Norman 134
Keynes, John Maynard 139
KFAI (Minneapolis community radio station) 26
KGNU-FM (Boulder community radio station) 143–44, 148
Kick, Russ 61–62
Kids Can Make a Difference Newsletter 174
Killer Elite (film) 87
Kimball, Richard 103
King, Karen 30
Kinko's closings (Washington, DC) 78–79
Kirkus Reviews 37
Kitchen Table: Women of Color Press 29
Kmart video censorship 84
Knopf ownership 95
Konigsberg, Ira 83
Kosovo media coverage 67, 69, 109
Kothmale (Sri Lanka) radio station 193
Kranich, Nancy 52, 108–11
Krauschaar, Andy iv

Kreuter, Katherine 30
Kronos Quartet 147
Kubrick, Stanley 91–92
Kuda, Marie 134
KUT (Austin radio station) 145

Labadie Collection (University of Michigan) 129–31
Labadie, Joseph A. 129
Labor Heritage Foundation 1
Labor materials selection 1, 52, 98, 112
Labor movement/nonprofit media relationship 118
Labor news 66–67
Labor notes 118
Labor reporters 66
Labor unions (libraries) ii, 15
LaDuke, Winona 143
Landers, Jay 89
Language/power relationship 96
Lannan Foundation 158
Lansky, Ellen 25–28
LAPL Audio Express program 177–80
LAPL Librarians' Guild ii
La Rocque, Rod 137
Larsen, Laurie ii
Latin American Bureau 120
Latin American Perspectives 122
Latinisms (cataloging) 14
Laugh Lines Press 29
Lavender Magazine 25–28
Lawrence Hill Books 120
Lawrence, T. E. 139
Laymon, Richard 198
LBR (Library Bill of Rights) 2, 37–38, 40–41, 43–44, 46–47, 50–51, 55, 110, 155, 178
LCC (Library of Congress Classification) 98
LC cataloging 49, 100, 109, 159–61; *see also* LC subject headings
LC commercialization 16–17, 52
LC height-shelving 49–50
LC Professional Guild ii, 49–50
LC registry 124
LC staffing 161
LC subject headings 14, 39–40, 98–100, 171
LC Subject Headings Weekly Lists 99
LC Communicator (LAPL Librarians' Guild) 50, 53, 159–61
Learning 13
Learning Center (Library Marketing Network) 101
Lee, Earl 52, 58–63
Lee, Spike 91
Left Bank Books 120
Left Bank Books Collective (web site) 126
Left Hand Books (Boulder, Colorado) 148
Legal classism 170
Le Gallienne, Eva 137
Lehman, James O. 40
Leigh, Robert D. 155
LeNoir, Cathy 30
Leroy C. Merritt Humanitarian Fund 15
Lesbian archives 133–135, 138
Lesbian biographies 133–34, 136–38

Lesbian collecting 141–42
Lesbian diaries 142
Lesbian erotica 31
Lesbian fiction 29–31
Lesbian film actors 137
Lesbian Herstory Archives 134
Lesbian history 132–42
Lesbian history (India) 191
Lesbian letters 142
Lesbian librarians 25–28, 134, 138
Lesbian literature 133–34; *see also* Lesbian biographies; Lesbian diaries; Lesbian erotica; Lesbian fiction; Lesbian letters
Lesbian materials selection 134
Lesbian publishers 29–31
Lesbian rights media coverage 70
Lesbian spirituality 137–38
Lesbians in Print 31
Lesbigay biographies 133–34, 136–37
Lesbigay conservatives 135–36
Lesbigay diaries 138, 142
Lesbigay film actors 136–37
Lesbigay history 132–42
Lesbigay history (India) 191
Lesbigay letters 132–33, 138, 142
Lesbigay librarians 25–28, 134, 138
Lesbigay literature 133–34; *see also* Lesbigay biographies; Lesbigay diaries; Lesbigay letters
Lesbigay materials selection 134
Lesbigay rights media coverage 70
Lesbigay spirituality 137–38
Lesbigay Studies 133–34
Let's Go: The Budget Guide to New York City 74
Levine, Leonard 85
Levins Morales, Ricardo 1
Lewinsky, Monica 109, 148
Lewis, Alison 9–12
Lewis, Jack 79
Lexis-Nexis database (University of Florida Libraries) 102, 104
LHF (Labor Heritage Foundation) 1
Liberated Librarian's Newsletter 36
Liberating Minds (Kester) 134
Librarian Avengers (website) 23
Librarian.net 40
Librarian of Congress 16, 49, 159–61
Librarian web sites 23, 40
Librarians; *see* Corporate librarians; GLBT librarians; High school librarians; Image of librarians; Librarian of Congress; Public librarians; Reference librarians; State librarians; Women librarians
"Librarians and the Ideology of Freedom" (Harris) 43–48
Librarians at Liberty 36, 40, 51–57, 95, 181–87
Librarians' cats 21
Librarians' Caucus (SEIU Local 790) ii
Librarians for Social Change 35–36
Librarians' Guild (LAPL) ii, 159
Librarians' image 21–24
Librarians in films 21–24
Librarians' sexuality 21
Librarianship degrees 24, 96

Libraries *see* Public libraries; Rationalist libraries; Rural libraries; Street libraries
"Libraries: An American Value" (ALA) 47
Libraries and Culture 132–40
Libraries as "bulwarks of democracy" 2
"Libraries As Media" (Willett) 95–107
Library activists 51, 181–87
Library/alternative press relationship 35–40; 47, 52, 58–63, 97–98, 109–14, 120, 128
Library administration 14–15; *see also* Collegial library administration; Hawaii State Public Library System management; Library budgets; Library funding; Library governance; San Francisco Public Library management
Library and information science education 38, 44, 113–14, 153–56; *see also* Library science degrees
Library Bill of Rights 2, 37–38, 40–41, 43–44, 46–47, 50–51, 55, 110, 155, 178
Library bond issue consultants (SFPL) 181
Library book sales 5
Library budgets 8, 73, 183
Library buildings 5–8, 15
Library/business partnerships 101
Library card residence requirements 176
Library cards 5, 7–8, 177
Library classism 46, 73–76, 170–74, 177–80
Library clerks 22–23
Library commercialization 16–17, 51–52, 101, 186
Library Company of Philadelphia 154
Library computers 22, 74–75, 187; *see also* Street library computers
Library corporatization 16–17, 51–52, 182; *see also* Library commercialization; Library privatization
Library degrees 24, 96
Library/democracy relationship 2, 46, 48, 193
Library displays 2, 22, 163; *see also* Library posters
Library donations 16–17
Library education 38, 44, 113–14, 153–56; *see also* Library science degrees
Library elitism 45–46; *see also* Library classism
Library fees 8, 170–71, 176–80; *see also* Library fines
Library fines 14, 170, 176–77
Library for Social Reconstruction (Mexico City) 10, 12
Library Foundation (San Francisco) 51, 182–86
Library funding 8, 15, 73, 97, 177; *see also* Library budgets; Library fees; Library fines; Library fundraisers; Library gifts; San

Francisco Public Library bond issue (2000)
Library fundraisers 22; *see also* Book sales
Library gifts 16–17
Library governance 8; *see also* Library administration; Library trustees
Library homophobia 133–35
Library Hotline 53
Library hours 8, 183
Library Internet access 8, 73–76, 187, 191–93; *see also* Internet filtering
Library Journal 35–36, 39, 46, 49, 51–52, 97, 108, 177
Library Journal Digital 53–54
Library Journal reviews 40
Library Juice (web site) 40, 52–53, 122–23, 197–205
Library Literature 40
Library management 14–15; *see also* Collegial library administration; Hawaii State Public Library System management; Library budgets; Library funding; Library governance; San Francisco Public Library management
Library Marketing Network 101
Library neutrality 1, 36–38, 52
Library of Congress cataloging 49, 100, 109, 159–61; *see also* Library of Congress subject headings
Library of Congress Classification 98
Library of Congress commercialization 16–17, 52
Library of Congress height-shelving 49–50
Library of Congress Professional Guild ii, 49–50, 159
Library of Congress registry 124
"Library of Congress Service Erosion" (Moore) 159–61
Library of Congress staffing 161
Library of Congress subject headings 14, 39–40, 98–100, 171
Library paraprofessionals 22–24
Library posters 23
Library press 35–42
Library press bias 49–53
Library press censorship 37
Library privatization 182–87
Library programs 2, 8, 163; *see also* Story hours
Library research 47
Library research bias 154–55
Library science degrees 24, 96
Library Services in Technology Act grants 73, 75
Library/small press relationship 35–40, 47, 52, 58–63, 97–98, 109–14
Library support staff 22–23
Library surveys 155–56
Library Trends 43
Library trustees 8, 46
Library unionists ii, 1
Library unions ii, 15
Library use 153, 165
Library users' rights 13
Library/vendor relations 47

"Library Viewing" (Fairchild) 5–6
Library volunteer workers 7–8
Library watchdogs 51, 181–87
"Life of Reilly" (*Sports Illustrated* column) 27
Lila Wallace-Reader's Digest Foundation 158
Lincoln, Abraham 65, 122
Lion King (film) 71
Lipstick Librarian (web site) 23
LIS education 38, 44, 113–14, 153–56; *see also* Library science degrees
List Apart 73–76
Literacy studies 154
Literary Market Place (Bowker) 125
Little Engine That Could (NYPL 1st edition) 74
Little, Nanci 31
Litwin, Rory 52
Living wage 170, 175
Living Z (Peattie) 36
LJ 35–36, 39, 46, 49, 51–52, 108, 177
LJ Digital 53–54
LJ reviews 40
LMN (Library Marketing Network) 101
LMP 125
Local 2 (H.E.R.E.) ii
Local 790 (SEIU) Librarians' Caucus ii
Local 2626 (AFSCME) ii, 159
Local 2864 (AFSCME) ii
Local 2910 (AFSCME) ii, 49–50, 159
"Local Cyber-Activism in the Age of Globalization" (Eder) 211–13
Locke, John 45
Lockheed Martin stockholders 70
Loitering laws 170
Long Haul 172
Long, Scott 143–49
Loompanics Unlimited 59
Los Angeles Demublican National Convention (2000) protests 80
Los Angeles Free Press 35
Los Angeles Public Library Audio Express program 177–80
Los Angeles Public Library Librarians' Guild ii
Louganis, Greg 136
Love of books 22; *see also* Reading
Low-power radio repression 77–79
Lowell, Amy 136
LSTA grants 73, 75
Lucifer Rising (Bowers) 31

M.A.P. (Minnesota Alliance of Peacemakers) 1–2
MCAC/HCL relations 56–57
MCTC Alternative Press Collection 128
MGM archives 136
MLA/HCL relations 56–57
MLIS degree 24, 96
MLS degree 24, 96
MPAA ratings 82–92
MPPDA 82–83
MP3 119
MSRRT Newsletter 119
MTV ownership 71

McBride, Donna 29
McCain, John 73
McCarthyism 46
McChesney, Robert 45, 47, 64–72, 117–18
McClure's 122
McCook, Kathleen de la Pena 194
McCormick, Colonel 66
McGovern, George 103
McGraw-Hill textbook commercialization 100
MacInnes, Kate 41
McKenney, Mary 39
McNab, Claire 30
McNaughton, James 85
Madwoman Press 29, 31
Magazine costs 97
Magazine index bias 40, 120
Mainstream library press 35
Mainstream library press bias 49–53
Majority opinions 47
Makeovers 22
Maldon Institute 79
Male-to-female transsexuals 25–28
Management fads 159–61
Management (libraries) 14–15; *see also* Collegial library administration; Hawaii State Public Library System management; Library budgets; Library funding; Library governance; San Francisco Public Library management
Managerial prerogatives 51
Mandel, Donna ii
Manila street libraries 191
Manion, Mark 206–10
Manley, Will 15
Mann, Thomas ii, 49
Mann, William J. 136–37
Manufacturing Consent (film) 144
MAP (Minnesota Alliance of Peacemakers) 1–2
Mapplethorpe, Robert 139
Marcuse, Herbert 44–45, 117
Marian (musical character) 21
Marinko, Rita 47, 52, 110
Market censorship 109–10
Marketing to children 101
"Marketplace of ideas" concept 47
Marram (press) 120
Marriott Hotel boycott (San Francisco) ii
Marshall, Joan 38, 42
Marshall, Thurgood 88
Marxism 44
Masquerade Books 31
Mass media activism 72
Mass media bias 65–72, 77, 106, 148
Mass media conglomerates 45, 70–72, 77, 108–09, 112, 117
Mass media democracy 104–05, 118
Mass media ownership 45, 65; *see also* Book industry ownership; Cable television industry ownership; Film industry ownership; Mass media conglomerates; Music industry ownership; Press ownership
Materials selection 1–2, 13, 97–98,
109–10, 113; *see also* Academic library collection development; Approval plans; Challenges (libraries); Fiction selection; GLBT materials selection; Labor materials selection; Library Bill of Rights; Multicultural materials selection; Poverty materials selection; Reference book selection; Review media bias; Third World materials selection; Video selection; Weeding (libraries); Zine selection
Mathematics: Applications and Connections 100
Matheson, Richard 197
Maxwell, Elsa 137
Mayer, Louis B. 137
Mchombu, K. J. 194
Media activism 72
Media bias 65–72, 77, 106, 148
Media conglomerates 45, 47, 65–72, 77, 95–96, 108–09, 112, 117
Media democracy 104–05, 118, 148
Media Monopoly (Bagdikian) 95
Media ownership 45, 65; *see also* Book industry ownership; cable television industry ownership; Film industry ownership; Media conglomerates; Music industry ownership; Press ownership
Media Ownership Project 47
Media (word) 95–96
Megastores 29, 31, 108, 115, 158
Meikeljohn, Alexander 87
Mellon, Thomas 70
Memex (database) 24
"Memory hole" 53–54
Merritt Humanitarian Fund 15
Messman, Terry 174
Mestre, Ricardo 9–12
Mexican librarians 9–12
Miami Herald 102, 104
Microbanks 194
Microloans (Bangladesh) 194
Micro-presses 124
Micro-radio repression 77–79
Middle East 2
Mid-list authors 197–98
Milchin, Jeff 148
Military classism 70
Military spending media coverage 69–70
Mill, John Stuart 45, 47
Millennium Fever (Wood) 31
Miller, Cindy 178
Miller, Frank 84
Miller, Marilyn 139
Miller, Penelope Ann 22
Miller vs. California decisions (Supreme Court) 90
Milton, John 45
MilwOrm 208
Minerva Editions 9
Minimum wage 175; *see also* Living wage
"Minneapolis Community & Technical College Alternative Press Collection" (Eland) 128
Minnesota Alliance of Peacemakers 1–2
Minnesota Coalition Against

Censorship/HCL relations 56–57
Minnesota Family Council 26
Minnesota Human Rights Department complaints 25–26
Minnesota Library Association/HCL relations 56–57
Minority students (Minneapolis Community & Technical College) 128
Les Miserables (Hugo) 10
Mistral, Sylvia 9
Mobil Corporation 145
Mobilization Radio repression 78–79
"Model of Cyber Volunteerism" (Eder) 214
Modified Librarian (web site) 23
Mokhiber, Russell 16–17, 52
Mommsen, Pete 116
Monoculture 109
Monthly Review 64, 122
Monthly Review Press 120
Moon, Eric 40, 42
Moore, Maureen 159–61
Moore, Michael 1
More you Watch, the Less You Know (Schechter) 69
Morley, Robert 134
Morning edition (radio program) 144
Morris, Sandra 30
Moses 65
"Mothball outing" 135–36
Mother Jones 7–8, 116
Motion Picture Association of America ratings 82–92
Motion Picture Producers and Distributors of America 82–83
Movie censorship 82–92
Movie industry bias 71
Movie industry ownership 70–71
Movie industry (procensorship term) 89
Movie programs 2, 8
Movie Rating Game (Farber) 87
Movie ratings 82–92
Movie selection 1, 87
Movie sex 85, 87, 90–91
Movie theater censorship 84, 87
Movie violence 85, 87, 89–91
Moyers, Bill 64
Ms. 116
Muckrakers 122
Multicultural library services 163–68
Multicultural materials selection 2, 163
MultiCultural Review 162–68
Mu'min, Ridgely 116
Murdoch, Rupert 65, 95, 109
Murphy, Ed 169, 171
Music industry ownership 70
Music Man (musical) 21
Music selection 1, 13
"Must the Poor Always Be Among Us?" (Berman) 169–76
Mylopoulos, Chris 162–68

Nader, Ralph 64, 101, 103, 118, 143
Naiad Press 29–30
Nash, Sheila ii
Nation 116, 204, 215

National Association of Theatre Owners 84, 88
National health insurance 175
National Labor Confederation (Spain) 9, 11
National Lawyer's Guild (Seattle) 78
National Poetry Month 157–58
National Review 179
National Security Agency 208
National Telecommunications and Information Administration 75
National Women's Studies Association meetings 39
Nationalism and Culture (Rocker) 10
NATO (National Association of Theatre Owners) 84, 88
NATO bombing (Former Yugoslavia) 106
Nazi propaganda 69, 146
Nazimova, Alla 137
NCIPA (Neighborhood Internet Protection Act) 73–76
NC-17 (film rating) 82–84, 86–88, 90–91
Necessary Illusions: A Critical Introduction to the Information Age (MCTC course) 128
Neighborhood Internet Protection Act 73–76
Nera, Franca 31
Netwar 204–05, 208
Neutrality (journalism) 66; see also Media bias
Neutrality (libraries) 1, 36–38, 52, 175
New Directions for Women 116
New Line Cinema ownership 70
New Main Library (SFPL) 182–83, 185–87
New Pages 36
New Pages Online—Alternatives in Print & Media (web site) 126
New Press 60–61, 109
New Society Publishers 60, 63, 120
"New Waves in Lesbian Publishing" (Corson) 29–31
New York Public Library gay archives 134
New York Public Library Rose Main Reading Room 74–75
New York Times 84, 102, 117, 156, 158
New York Times bias 67, 104
New York Times Reviews 40, 158
New York Times strike coverage 67
New York Times WTO protest coverage 120
NewBreed Librarian 13, 23
Newhouse (media conglomerate) 112
News cable channels 122
News Corporation 70, 95
News media bias 65–72, 77, 106, 148
News media conservatism 66
News media racism 72
News media violence 72, 109
Newspaper collecting 142
Newspaper history 65, 68
Newspaper ownership 65, 68, 70–71, 117; see also Media conglomerates

Newsweek 102, 104, 174
Nichols, John 64
Nickelodeon (cable TV channel) ownership 71
Nietzsche, Friedrich 44
Nilsen, Solveig ii
9/11 attacks 1–2
Nisker, Scoop 148
NLG (Seattle) 78
No-protest zone (Seattle WTO demonstrations) 78
Nomous, Otto 77–81
Nong Toom 2
Non-sexist children's periodicals 116
Nonviolence materials 2
Noonan, John 138
Norris, David 139
Norton, W.W. (press) 112, 124
Notable Black American Women (Smith) 138
Notable Books Council (ALA Reference and User Services Association) 113–14
NSA (National Security Agency) 208
Nuclear test protests (India) 207–08
NWSA (National Women's Studies Association) meetings 39
NYPL gay archives 134
NYPL Rose Main Reading Room 74–75

Obedience 144–46
Obesity causes 16–17
Objectivity (journalism) 66; see also Media bias
Obscenity laws 46, 90
OCAS (Ontario Council of Agencies Serving Immigrants) 165
OCLC 14, 98
OCLC holdings 58–63, 120
OCLC Newsletter 55
Odd Girls Press 31
Off Our Backs 122
Off Season (Calhoun) 29
Off-shore spam engine 205
Official sources (journalism) 66, 68
O'Hara, Craig 61–62
Ohio library holdings 110
Ohio State University Press 38
O.J. Simpson Trial media coverage 68, 148
Olsen, Erica 23
Omicrom Inforium—Small Press Connection (web site) 126
"On Electronic Civil Disobedience" (Wray) 199–205
On Equal Terms (Marshall) 36
One-newspaper towns 66
One-person presses 124
O'Neill, Thomas 53
Online booksellers 31, 197–98
Online catalog censorship (Hennepin County Library) 53–57
Online resource guides 2; see also Weblogs
Onscreen violence (film term) 89
Ontario Council of Agencies Serving Immigrants 165

Opat, Mike 178
Open-access computers (New York City) 75
Open forums 2
Open Source Solutions 120
Oracle 35
Orbis Books 60, 120
Oregon anarchists' media coverage 119–20
Oreo cookies (mathematics textbooks) 100
Organization publishing 125
Orthodox library press 35
Orthodox library press bias 49–53
Orwell, George 53–54, 144, 209
"Other 90 Percent" (Anderson) 112–14
Our Time Press 115
Out in All Directions (1995) 136
OutFront Minnesota 27
Outing (gays, lesbians) 135–36
Outposts (Kick) 61
Outsourcing (Hawaii State Public Library System) 15
Overdue charges 14, 170, 176–77
Overweight causes 16–17
Owensby, Earl 86
Owner-editors (newspapers) 65

Pacific Bell/SFPL Foundation relationship 182
Pacifica Radio 147–48
Paine, Thomas 64, 122
Palma, Brian De 91–92
Pamphlets 163; see also Political pamphlets
Panamanian infoplazas 193
Panel discussions 2, 27
Panhandling laws 170, 172
Paper (East Lansing, MI) 35
Papier Mache Press 29, 63
Paramount Pictures 71
Paraprofessional copy cataloging 160
Paraprofessionals (libraries) 22–24
Parenti, Michael 143
Parent's Guide to the TV Ratings and V-chip (V-Chip Education Project) 88
Participatory democracy 208–09
Party Girl (film) 21–24
Paterson-Reed, Robin 30
Pathfinders 2
Patriarchy (India) 191
Patriotism 46, 70
PBS 102, 144
PCA (Production Code Administration) 83
Peace studies materials selection 98, 112
Pearl Jam 147
Pearson (media conglomerate) 112
Pearson (media conglomerate) acquisitions 108
Peattie, Noel 41; see also *Sipapu*
Peckinpah, Sam 87, 91
Peeping laws 26
Peer-based library administration 128
Peiro, Juan 9
Pelosi, Nancy 186
Pena McCook, Kathleen de la 194
Penchansky, Mimi 38
Penis thrusting (films) 87

Pentagon hacking 204
Pentagon-World Trade Center attacks (September 11, 2001) 1–2
People *ownership* 70
"People/work" 3–17
Periodical costs 97
Periodical index bias 40, 120
Perlstein, Jeff 77–81
Perot, Ross 143
Perrault, Anna 47, 110
Perrine, Becky 77–81
Perron, Nancy LeReau 56
Persian Gulf War 1–2, 80
Persian Gulf War media coverage 69
Persian Gulf War resistance 201–02
"Person of the year—Debra Davis" (Lansky) 25–28
PG (film rating) 83, 85, 88, 90–91
PG-13 (film rating) 88, 91
Philadelphia Republican National Convention Protests (2000) 79–80
Philippine community telecenters 193
Philipsburg (Montana) 104
Phillips, Peter 109
Philosophy of Punk (O'Hara) 61–62
Photocopying charges 177
Pi (film) 179
Picket line chants ii
PLG (Progressive Librarians Guild) 40; *see also Progressive Librarian*
Plumb, Abigail Leah 21–24
Pluralism 45, 47
Pluto Press 60, 63
POCLAD (Program on Corporations, Law & Democracy) 173
Poetry promotion 157–58
Poetry publishers 125
Poetry selection 52, 98, 113
Police micro-radio raids 79
Police riots (Los Angeles) 80
Political advertising reform 72
Political component (films) 87
Political hacking 202–10
Political newspapers 65
Political pamphlets 122, 130
Political Science departments (universities) 145
Pollock, Jeffrey 74, 76
POOR (LC subject heading) 171
Poor People and Library Services (Venturella) 36, 63, 171, 178, 180
Poor people's library services 169–76; *see also* Street libraries
Poor People's Policy (ALA) 174–75
Pornography/children relationship 73–74
Posey, Parker 22–23
Postcard collecting 142
Poster selection 1
Posters 23, 130
Postman, Neal 109
Post-structuralism 43–44, 47
Poverty/democracy relationship 194
Poverty materials cataloging 171

Poverty materials selection 98, 112, 172–74
Power/language relationship 96
Prague IMF/World Bank protests (2000) 80
PR Watch 64
Pravda 67
Prejudices and Antipathies (Berman) 36, 39–40, 54
Presidential campaign spending (2000) 96
Presidential elections (2000) 102–04
Press bias 65–72; *see also* Library press bias; Media bias
Press freedom 45, 65–72; *see also* First Amendment
Press history 65, 68
Press neutrality 66; *see also* Press bias
Press ownership 65, 68, 70–71, 117; *see also* Media conglomerates
Pressure Point 14–15
Price, David 15
Prince Eddy and the Homosexual Underworld (Aronson) 137
Prince George's County Library video rental program 180
Princess Di publications 113
Print culture history 154
Print-on-demand publishing 30
Prior censorship 37, 40, 79
Pritchard, Tom 26
Privacy 75
Private/public partnerships 16–17
Privatization 51
Privatization (libraries) 182–87
Pro-business library bias 179, 182–83; *see also* Business/library partnerships; Commercialization (libraries)
Pro-business press bias 66–67, 70
Procensorship groups 88–89
Production Code Administration (film industry) 83
"Production only" months (LC) 161
Profane Existence 116
Professional autonomy (librarians) 45–46
Professional Ethics Committee (ALA) 51
Professional Guild (LC) ii, 49, 159
Profit motive (media) 65, 68; *see also* Profit motive (publishing)
Profit motive (publishing) 98, 108–09, 113
Program collecting 142
Program On Corporations, Law & Democracy 173
Programs (libraries) 2, 8, 163; *see also* Story hours
Progressive 116–17
Progressive Librarian 9–12, 36, 40, 121
Progressive Librarians Guild 40; *see also Progressive Librarian*
Project Censored 49, 109, 111, 117
Project on Media Ownership 47
Project Vote Smart 102–04
Proletariat 11, 45; *see also* Class struggle
Pro-life movement 201

Prometheus Books 60, 63
Promotion 44
Propaganda; *see* American propaganda; Nazi propaganda; Soviet propaganda
Propaganda systems 69, 80
Property law 209
Proposition A (SFPL bond issue) 181–86
Protection (library objective) 46
Psychotropedia (Kick) 61–62
Public bandwidth giveaways 48, 72, 118
Public broadcasting movement 72, 144
Public forums 2
Public librarians 22–23
Public libraries 5–8, 10, 12–15, 153, 193
Public library censorship 54–57, 73–76
Public Library Inquiry (Carnegie Corporation) 155
Public library restrooms 25
Public policy component (films) 87
Public/private partnerships 16–17, 182; *see also* Business/library partnerships
Public radio 147
Public relations industry 96
Publisher's Catalogues (web site) 126
Publisher's Directory (Gale Research) 125–26
Publisher's International ISBN Directory (Bowker) 126
Publishers (Mexico) 9–12
Publishers Weekly 124, 127
Publishers Weekly reviews 37, 40
Publishing commercialism 13, 109
Publishing industry 108–09, 112–14; *see also* Book distributors; Small presses
PubList (web site) 126
Punctuation (Cataloging) 14
Punk anarchist periodicals 116
Punk music selection 13
Puritanism 45
"Pursuing Small, Independent Book Publishers" (Anderson) 124–27
Puschak, Russell 7–8
PW 124, 127
PW reviews 37, 40

Quebec anti-poverty initiative 176
Quebec City FTAA protests (2001) 77, 81
Queer archives 133–35, 138, 141–42
Queer biographies 133–34, 136–37
Queer collecting 141–42
Queer conservatives 135–36
Queer diaries 138, 142
Queer film actors 136–37
Queer history 132–42
Queer letters 132–33, 138, 142
Queer librarians 25–28, 134, 138
Queer literature 133–34; *see also* Queer biographies; Queer diaries; Queer letters
Queer materials selection 134
Queer rights media coverage 70

Queer spirituality 137–38
Queer Studies 133–34
"Question of Balance" (Kranich) 108–11
Questioning technology (1991) 120

R (film rating) 83–88, 90–91
R2K Legal Collective 80
Racism 2, 16–17, 208
Racist news media 72
Radical America 116
Radical archives 129–31
Radical environmentalism 200–01
Radical radio programs 143–49
Radical Research Center 38–39, 41
Radical web sites 119–21
Radio advertising 118
Radio deregulation 118
Radio interview programs 143–49
Radio talk shows 122
Radnitz, Robert B. 85
Ragge, Ken 61–62
Rain Taxi Review of Books 127
Rainey, Ma 137
Ramparts 117
Ramsey, JonBenet 68, 148
RAND Corporation 204, 208
Random House 109
Random House ownership 95, 112
Rather, Lucia 159–60
Ratings (film) 82–92
Rationalist libraries 11
Reader-response theory 154
Reading 8, 10–12, 24; *see also* Fiction reading; Literacy studies; Love of books
Reading ethnography 154
Reading preferences 153–56
Reading research bias 154–55
Reagan Administration information policy 178–79
Reagan, Ronald 37
Real AA (Ragge) 61–62
"Real Thing" (Mokhiber/Weissman) 16–17
RealAudio (web site) 119
Reality 96
Red-baiting 46, 79
Reed Elsevier 97, 107–08
Rees, John H. 79
Reference and User Services Association Notable Books Council 113–14
Reference book selection 58–59, 61, 125–27
Reference librarians 21–22
Register (Des Moines) 68
Reid, Carol 14–15
Reilly, Rick 27
Rejano, Juan 12
Religion 11
Religious Right (WorldCat entries) 137–38
R.E.M. 147
Renaissance Alliance Publishers 30–31
Rensbarger, John 161
Repression 209; *see also* Red-baiting
Repression (libraries) 14–15
Reprimands 55
Republican National Convention protests (2000) 79–80

Republican Party campaign spending (2000) 96
Research library acquisitions 97–98
Research paper collecting 142
Reserve charges (libraries) 177, 179
Resist 115–18, 211–13
"Resistance to Civil Government" (Thoreau) 200
Resource Center Press 58–60
Resource guides 2
Rest of *Us (Book Industry Study Group)* 124
Retention policy (SFPL) 50
Rethinking Schools 63
Review media bias 37, 40, 47, 113
Review of Radical Political Economy 117
Revolting Librarians (West/Katz) 36
Revolution 122
"Ricardo Mestre (1906-1997)" 9–12
Rich Media, Poor Democracy (McChesney) 64, 118
RICH PEOPLE (LC subject heading) 171
Riera, Jose 9–12
Right to know 109–10
Right-wing think tanks 79
Riley, Melissa ii
Rising Tide Press 30
Rivers, Diana 31
Roach, Steve 81
Robbins, Louise 44–46
Roberts, Crystal 74
Roberts, Gene 117
Robinson, Charles 179
Robinson, Scott 194
Rocambole 10
Rocker, Rudolph 10
Rocky Mountain Media Watch (Denver, Colorado) 148–49
Rocky Mountain Peace and Justice Center (Boulder, Colorado) 148
Roger and Me (film) 1
Rollins, Sonny 147
Roosevelt, Eleanor 135
Rosebud (Masquerade Books' imprint) 31
Roth, Chris 82–92
R.R. Bowker (press) 124–25
RRC (Radical Research Center) 38–39
Rugrats (film) 71
Rule, Jane 30
Rural libraries 7–8
Rural telephone cooperatives 194
RUSA Notable Books Council 113–14
Ruskin, Gary 16
Rustin, Jane 14

"Safe poetry" 157
Said, Edward 44, 143
St. Stephen's Shelter (Minneapolis, Minnesota) 169
Salt Lake City Main Library 5
Samek, Toni 35–42, 47, 52
San Francisco Chronicle library parties 182
San Francisco Marriott Hotel boycott (2001) ii
San Francisco/Oakland Librarians' Caucus (SEIU Local 790) ii

San Francisco Public Library Bay Area Reference Center 36–37
San Francisco Public Library bond issue (2000) 51, 181–186
San Francisco Public Library Foundation 51, 182, 86
San Francisco Public Library Gates grant 187
San Francisco Public Library James Hormel Collection 134
San Francisco Public Library management 15, 51, 182–87
San Francisco Public Library New Main Library 182–83, 185–87
San Francisco Public Library retention policy 50
San Francisco Public Library shelving policy 50
San Francisco Tenants' Union 182, 184
San Jose Mercury News 68
Sandoval, Enrique 10
Sandstone (film) 86
Sanford Berman Papers (University of Illinois Archives, Urbana-Champaign) 41
"Sanitized" films 88, 90–91
Sankofa, Shaka 115
Sanra, Nancy 30
Sapphire (Virgin Publishing imprint) 31
Sassoon, Siegfried 137
Satellite television censorship 80
Saturday Review 40
Savage, Eleanor 27
Save Our Libraries—No On Prop A. (San Francisco) 51, 182–85
Scarborough Network of Immigrant Serving Organizations 165
Scarecrow Press 40
Scarface (film) 85, 91
Schechter, Danny 69
Schelshorn, Christine iv
Scher, Abby 115–18
Scherler, Sasha 22
Schiffrin, Andre 109
Schiller, Herbert 44, 105–06
Schmidt, Karen A. 114
Schniderman, Saul ii
Schochet Center for GLBT Studies (University of Minnesota) 141–42
School censorship 73–76
School commercialization 100–01
Schulman, Beth 105, 122–23
Schuman, Patricia 37, 47, 114
Science-technology-medicine (STM) journal costs 97
Scott, Randolph 137
Screw (NYPL holdings) 74
Seal Press 60, 63
Seale, Bobby 143
Sears, James T. 134
Seattle National Lawyers' Guild 78
Seattle WTO protests (1999) 77–78, 119–20, 211, 215
See Sharp Press 62
SEIU Local 790 Librarians' Caucus ii
Self-censorship 1, 13, 46, 52–53, 58–63
Self-confident women 21–23

"Self-service library" concept 183, 186
Sensational stories (journalism) 68
Sensual women 21–22
September 11 attacks 1–2
Septimus, Jacob 90
Serebnick, Judith 47
"Serious reader" concept 155
"Service/Advocacy/Empowermen" 151–87
Service Employees International Union Local 790 Librarians' Caucus ii
Seven Stories Press 60–61, 63–64, 69
Sex (film term) 87
Sex in films 85, 87, 90–91
Sex-related content (film term) 87
Sex scandal media coverage 109, 148
Sex Side of Life 58, 61
Sex, Sin, and Blasphemy (Heins) 83–84
Sexuality materials selection 13, 52, 58, 61
SFPL Bay Area Reference Center 36–37
SFPL bond issue (2000) 51, 181–86
SFPL Foundation 51, 182–86
SFPL Gates grant 187
SFPL James Hormel Collection 134
SFPL management 15, 51, 182–87
SFPL New Main Library 182–83, 185–87
SFPL retention policy 50
SFPL shelving policy 50
SGBIP (Bowker) 125
Shady Ladies (press) 31
Shaffer, Dallas 186
Shakur, Asaka 116
Sharing 13
Shelflisting (LC) 159
Shelter use 169–70
Shelving 23
Shelving policy (LC) 49–50
Shelving policy (SFPL) 50
Shields, Jimmy 137
S.I. Newhouse (media conglomerate) 112
Sidel, Ruth 171
Sidewalk libraries 191–95
Siegel, Robert 144
Silkwood (film) 1
Silva, Linda Kay 30–31
Simon and Schuster 109
Simon and Schuster ownership 95, 108
Simon, Herbert 24
Simpson Trial media coverage 68
Simulated sex (film term) 87
Simulated violence (film term) 89
Single-newspaper towns 66
Sipapu 36, 42
SisterNet Resource Centers 193–94
Sixties' press coverage 117
60 Minutes (TV program) 119–21
Skeels, Troy 78
Sklar, Holly 143
Skyscraper Magazine 143–49
Small press awards 126–27

Small Press Center (web site) 126
Small press displays 38–39
Small Press Distribution 47, 114, 126
Small press/library relationship 35–40, 47, 52, 58–63, 97–98, 109–14
Small press marketing 158, 197–98
Small Press Month 126
Small Press Review 127
Small press review media 40, 126–27
Small presses 36–37, 109, 112–14, 124–27; *see also* Alternative press; Feminist publishers
Smart Voting Starts @ Your Library (ALA) 102
Smart women 21–23
"Smarty Girl: Three Librarians on Film" (Plumb) 21–24
Smith, Bessie 136
Smith, Betty 21
Smith, Donny 191–96
Smith, Jessie Carney 138
Smith, Kelly 29
Smith, Lillian 135
Smith, Wendy 177, 179
Snelling, Paula 135
SNISO (Scarborough Network of Immigrant Serving Organizations) 165
So Far 58–59
Social Change and Information Systems 36
Social control (library objective) 45
Social justice 210, 214
Social justice materials selection 2
Social protest archives 129–31
Social Responsibilities Round Table (ALA) 46–47
Social Responsibilities Round Table (ALA) Papers (University of Illinois Archives, Urbana-Champaign) 41
Social Responsibilities Round Table (ALA) Task Force on Alternatives in Print 37–40, 108, 112, 114
Social Responsibilities Round Table (ALA) Task Force on Gay Liberation 134
Social responsibility/intellectual freedom relationship 35–42, 46–47
Social Studies (periodical) 10
Sojourner 29–31
Solar-powered computers 192–93
Soldier Blue (film) 85, 91
Solidaridad Obrera 9–10
Song selection 1
Songs of the Spanish Civil War (Garfias) 10
Sounder (film) 85
Sourcing (Journalism) 66, 68
Southwest High School (Minneapolis, MN) 25–28
Soviet press bias 67
Soviet propaganda 69
Space Jam (film) 71
"Speaking Volumes" (Halpern) 7–8
"Speed cataloging" (LC) 161

Spinifex Press 59
Spinsters Ink 31, 62–63
Sports Illustrated ownership 70
Sri Lankan village radio stations 193
SRRT (ALA Social Responsibilities Round Table) 46–47
SRRT Newsletter 37
SRRT Papers (University of Illinois Archives, Urbana-Champaign) 41
SRRT Task Force on Alternatives in Print 37–40, 108, 112, 114
SRRT Task Force on Gay Liberation 134
Standing orders 111
Stanley decision (Supreme Court) 88
Star Tribune (Minneapolis) 27, 178
State Historical Society of Wisconsin 41, 153
State librarians 14–15, 37
Stauber, John 64
Steele, Robert 120
Stein, Gertrude 134
Steinberg, Michelle 77–81
Steven J. Schochet Center for GLBT Studies (University of Minnesota) 141–42
Stevens, Arnold 7
Stevens, Delta "Storm" (fictional character) 30
Steward Update Newsletter 1
Stielow, Fred 45–46
STM journal costs 97
Stole, Ingr 64
Stone, Roy ii
Stone Butch Blues (Feinberg) 29
Storm Rising (Silva) 30
Story hours 8, 22
Straub, Peter 197
Street Librarian (web site) 40, 126
Street libraries 191–95
Street library computers 192–93
Street newspaper selection 13, 174
Street newspapers 171–72, 174
Street protests 203, 205, 209
Strike press coverage 66–67
Students of color (Minneapolis) Community & Technical College) 128
Subject Cataloging (Berman) 54
Subject cataloging policy (LC) 159–60
Subject Guide to Books in Print (Bowker) 125
Subject heading bias 39–40, 100, 134
Subject headings 14, 38, 134; *see also* Hennepin County Library subject headings; Library of Congress subject headings
Sullivan, Andrew 135–36
Summer was a Fast Train Without Terminals 58–59
Sumner, Richard (film character) 22
Sunne in Gold (Adams) 31
Sun 64–72
Sunday Times WTO protest coverage 120
Superstores 29, 31, 108, 115, 158
Support staff (libraries) 22–23
Supreme Court decisions 83, 88, 90

SurfControl (censorware firm) 74
Survival News 172–73
"Survival of the fittest" concept 47
Swan, John 178
SWAT teams (LC) 161
Symonds, John Addington 136
Synergy 36–40
Szymanski, Therese 29

Talking book rental programs 176–80
Tampa Technical High School commercialization 101
"Taking the (Bad) News With the Good" (Scher) 115–18
Talk radio shows 122
Tape rental programs 170–71, 177–80
Tape selection 1
Tapori Databank (software) 192
Tarbell, Ida 122
Tardieu, Bruno 192–94, 196
"Targets of Repression" 77–81
Task Force on Alternatives in Print (ALA/SRRT) 37–40
Task Force on Gay Liberation (ALA/SRRT) 134–35
Teacher Librarian 36
Teaching 10, 13
Technician copy cataloging (LC) 160
Technology policy 210
Technophilia 209
Technophilic library education 155
Technophobia 209
Teen Voices 116
Teena, Brandon 26
Teenage library users 10
Tegucigalpa (Honduras) street libraries 191
Telecommunications Act 45, 108
Television commercial donations 16–17
Television news 69
Television news reform 72
Television rating schemes 88
Temple University Library Alternative Acquisitions Project 120
Temporary Autonomous Zone (Bey) 203
"Tending To the City's Needs" (Mylopoulos) 162–68
Tennant, Emma 138
Tennant, Stephen 137–38
Tenure 44
Terra Iliure 9
Terrorism 2; *see also* Cyber terrorism
Terrorism (definition) 208
Testimonies 10
Texas executions 115
Texas politicians 146
Textbook advertising 100
Textbook bias 12
Thadani, Giti 191
"'They Sure Got to Prove It on Me'" (Carmichael) 132–40
Third Woman Press 29
Third World debt 174
Third World materials selection 98, 112
Third World media coverage 120
Third World street libraries 191–96

This Bridge Called My Back 29
Thistlethwaite, Polly J. 134
Thomas, Bill 7–8
Thomas, Deborah 117
Thomas, Sarah 99, 160
Thomas, Timothy 81
Thomison, Dennis 45
Thomson acquisitions 108
Thoreau, Henry David 199–201, 205
Thousand Plateaus (Deleuze/Guattari) 203
"Three Decades of Film Censorship" (Roth) 82–92
Ticket stub collecting 142
Time 104, 174
Time ownership 70
Time Warner (media conglomerate) 70–71
To Live and Die in L.A. (film) 87
Tobin, Debra 30
Tolerance 45
Tolstoy, Leo 10, 12
Toom, Nong 27
"Top Censored Library Stories of 1998/2000" (Berman) 49–53
Topless dancing (keyword filtering term) 74
Toronto (Ontario) Public Library immigrant services 162–68
Tory's Tuesday (Silva) 31
Tower Records 147
Town of Johnsburg Library (New York State) 7–8
Tracy, Spencer 22
Transgender librarians 25–28
Translation selection 112
Transvestite (term) 27
Trash (Allison) 29
Traven, B. 10
Treasure of Sierra Madre (Traven) 10
Treasured Past (Hill) 30
Tree Grows in Brooklyn (Smith) 21
Tremain Braund, Diana 29
Trespass (civil disobedience) 201–03, 206, 208–10
Tretter Collection (University of Minnesota Library) 142
Tropical Storm (Good) 30
Trow, George 117
True Colours (King/Dunne) 30–31
Trustees (libraries) 8, 46, 56–57
Tsang, Daniel C. 52, 119–21
Tucker, Ben 159
Ture, Kwame 143
Turner, Ted 136
TV commercial donations 16–17
TV news 69
TV news reform 72
TV rating schemes 88
Two-dimensional violence (film term) 89

U2 147
UAW (United Auto Workers) 66
UCS (Union Communication Services) 1
Ugandan street libraries 193
UGT (Union General de Trabajadores) 11
UMW Pittston Strike press coverage 67
Unabashed Librarian 36, 49–53, 169–80

Uncivilized Books 120
Underground press 35, 37, 117, 130
Understanding the Business of Library Acquisitions (Schmidt) 114
UNESCO 191
Unforgettable (Kallmaker) 30
Union Communication Services 1
Union Distribuidora de Ediciones 10
Union General de Trabajadores (Spain) 11
Union materials selection 1, 52
Unions (libraries) ii, 15
Unisex restrooms 25
United Auto Workers 66
United Mine Workers Pittston Strike press coverage 67
United States Department of Agriculture racism 116
United States foreign policy 2, 69–70, 120, 122
Universal health care 175
Universal rating systems 89
Universal Service Fund for Schools and Libraries (e-rate discounts) 48, 73, 75
University education 10; *see also* Library education
University library collection development 47
University of California-Irvine Libraries Political Literature Collection 119
University of Chicago library school 38, 154–55
University of Colorado 145
University of Florida Libraries Lexis-Nexis database 102, 104
University of Illinois Archives (Urbana-Champaign) 41
University of Michigan Library Labadie Collection 129–31
University of Minnesota Library Jean-Nickolaus Tretter Collection 142
University of Minnesota Steven J. Schochet Center for GLBT Studies 141–42
University of Texas-Austin radio station 145
University of Wisconsin-Madison School of Library and Information Studies 153
University presses 109, 126
Unrated films 83–84, 87–88, 90
Uplift (library objective) 45
U.S. foreign policy 2, 69–70, 120, 122
U.S. News and World Report 102, 104, 154, 174
USDA racism 116
"Useful information" concept 155

V-chip 88
Vaid, Urvashi 143
Valenti, Jack 83, 87, 90
"Value-added" library services 180
Vendor/library relations 47
Vendors (books) 109, 124, 126, 197–98
Venturella, Karen 36, 63, 171, 179–80
Viacom (media conglomerate) 70–71, 95–96, 108, 112

Vidal, Gore 137
Video Censorship 84, 88
Video rental programs 170, 177, 179–80
Video selection 1, 87
Videogame rating schemes 89
Videos 7
Vietnam War 15, 120
Vietnam War media coverage 70, 117, 202
Vietnam War resistance 200, 202
Vilanova Library (Catalonia) 10, 12
Villa, Moreno 12
Village radio stations (Sri Lanka) 193
Village telephone service (Bangladesh) 194
Violence against homeless people 170, 215
Violence-related content (film term) 89
Violent films 85, 87, 89–91
Violent news media 72, 109
Virgin Publishing 31
Virtual blockades 207
Virtual sit-ins 207
Voice of Youth Advocates 36
Volunteer library workers 7–8
Von Holtzbrink (media conglomerate) 112
Von Scherler, Sasha 22
Vote Smart Project 102–04
Voter turnouts 146
Voter's Research Hotline 102
VOYA 36
Vroman, Deborah 179

Waddell, Lynn 100
Waging War on Dissent (Seattle NLG) 78
Wal-Mart video censorship 84
Wall Street Journal 145
Wall Street Journal WTO protest coverage 121
Wallace, Amy 91
Walt Disney Company (media conglomerate) 70–71
Waples, Douglas 154
Warfield, Peter 51, 185
Warner Brothers censorship 83
Warner Brothers ownership 70
Warner Home Video releasing policy 84
Washington, D.C. IMF/World Bank protests (2000) 78–79
Washington Post 104, 159, 161
Watchdogs (libraries) 51, 181–87
Watson, Bunny (film character) 21–22
Waxman, Sharon 89
W.B. Saunders ownership 107
Wealth distribution 170, 210; *see also* Income inequality
Web site blocking 204
Webb, Gary 68
Weber, Edward 130
Weblogs 23
Webster, Duane 97
Webster's Third New International Dictionary 95
Weeding (libraries) 15, 50
Weekly Planet (Tampa, Florida) 100
Weintraub, Joanne 86
Weissman, Robert 16–17, 52
Welch, Janet 8
Welfare benefits 175–76
Welfare Mothers Voice 173
Welfare rights materials selection 172–73
Wenders, Wim 177
West, Celeste 36–37, 41
West, Cornel 143
West Virginia public libraries 15
"What makes librarianship exciting to you?" (Dodge) 13
Wheelchair-accessible libraries 183–84, 186
When Evil Changes Face (Szymanski) 29
When I Am an Old Woman, I Shall Wear Purple 29
"Where Have All the 'Berman Books' Gone?" 54–57
"'Where Stories Aren't Important'" (Wiegand) 153–56
White, Mary 2
Whitehead, Fred 50
Whitman, Walt 134
"Whole book" cataloging (LC) 160
Wholesalers (books) 109, 124, 126, 197–98
Who's Afraid of Virginia Woolf? (film) 83
WHY (World Hunger Year) 174
Wiegand, Wayne 43–45, 153–56
Wiggins, Beecher 159–60
Wilde, Oscar 134–36, 139, 157
Willett, Charles 52, 95–107, 120, 128
Wilson Company 40; *see also Wilson Library Bulletin*
Wilson, F. Paul 197
Wilson Library Bulletin 35
Wilson Library Bulletin reviews 40
Window-peeping laws 26
Windows Internet terminals (SFPL) 187
Wings of Desire (video) 177
Wisconsin State Historical Society 41, 153
WLB 35
WLB reviews 40
WLW Journal 36
Wolfe, Milton 110
Wolff, Leslie R. 101
Woman's Prerogative (bookstore) 29
"Women" 19–31
Women combat troops 24
Women draftees 25
Women intellectuals 21–23
Women in libraries 36
Women librarians 21–28
Women Library Workers 36
Women wheelchair users 31
Women's assertiveness 21–23
Women's bookstores 29, 31
Women's braininess 21–23
Women's intelligence 21–23
Women's microloans (Bangladesh) 194
Women's Presses Library Project 114, 126
Women's restroom use 25–26
Women's self-confidence 21–23
Women's sensuality 21–22
Women's smartness 21–23
Wood, Julia 31
Woodworth, Fred 50
WordViews 119
Working class libraries (Catalonia) 11
Working class materials selection 1
Working class students (Minneapolis Community & Technical College) 128
Working poor people 169–70
Workplace speech 14–15, 50–51
World Bank/IMF protests (2000) 78–80, 116, 215
World Hunger Year 174
World Trade Center-Pentagon attacks (September 11, 2001) 1–2
World Trade Organization protests (1999) 77–78, 119–20, 211, 215
WorldCat (database) 120, 134, 137
Worth Noting (Berman) 54
Wray, Stefan 199–205
Wresinski, Joseph 191–92
Wright, Donald E. 40
Writer's Voices (NYPL e-journal) 75
WTC-Pentagon attacks (September 11, 2001) 1–2
WTC protests (1999) 77–78, 104, 119–20, 211, 215
W.W. Norton 112, 124

X (film rating) 83, 86, 90–91
X-Ploit 208
Xena: Warrior Princess (TV series) 30
Xenaverse websites 30
YAAN 36

Young Adult Alternative Newsletter 36
Young and Ribicam library parties (San Francisco) 182
Youth Organizing Network (San Diego) 215
Yugoslavia bombing 106

Z Magazine 104, 106, 147
Zaid, Gabriel 10
Zapatista cyber activism 119, 203–04, 207–08, 211
ZapMe! 101
Zed Books 120
Zedillo, Ernesto (web site) 208
Zeman, Milos 80
Zerzan, John 120
Zine Guide 119
Zine review media 126
Zine selection 13, 52
Zines 118, 128, 148; *see also* E-zines
Zinn, Howard 143, 200
Znet Daily Commentaries 106, 147
Zoia! Memoirs of Zoia Horn 36
Zuckergood, Dan 174